# PROPERTY AND SOCIAL RESILIENCE IN TIMES OF CONFLICT

# Law, Property and Society

Series Editor:
Robin Paul Malloy

The Law, Property and Society series examines property in terms of its ability to foster democratic forms of governance, and to advance social justice. The series explores the legal infrastructure of property in broad terms, encompassing concerns for real, personal, intangible, intellectual and cultural property, as well as looking at property related financial markets. The series is edited by Robin Paul Malloy, and book proposals are welcome from all interested authors.

**Robin Paul Malloy** is E.I. White Chair and Distinguished Professor of Law, and the Kauffman Professor of Entrepreneurship and Innovation at Syracuse University College of Law, USA. He is Director of the Center on Property, Citizenship, and Social Entrepreneurism. He is also Professor of Economics (by courtesy appointment) in the Maxwell School of Citizenship and Public Affairs, Syracuse University. Professor Malloy writes extensively on law and market theory and on real estate transactions and development. He has authored eight books (one now in its third edition and another in its second edition), and edited seven additional books. He has also written more than 30 scholarly articles, and contributed to 12 other books. His recent books include: *Law and Market Economy* (2000, in English and translated into Spanish and Chinese); *Law in a Market Context* (2004); and *Real Estate Transactions 3rd Edition* (with James C. Smith, 2007).

# Property and Social Resilience in Times of Conflict

## Land, Custom and Law in East Timor

By

DANIEL FITZPATRICK
*The Australian National University*

ANDREW MCWILLIAM
*The Australian National University*

SUSANA BARNES
*Monash University*

Routledge
Taylor & Francis Group
LONDON AND NEW YORK

First published 2012 by Ashgate Publishing

2 Park Square, Milton Park, Abingdon, Oxon OX14 4RN
711 Third Avenue, New York, NY 10017, USA

*Routledge is an imprint of the Taylor & Francis Group, an informa business*

First issued in paperback 2016



**British Library Cataloguing in Publication Data**
Fitzpatrick, Daniel.
Property and social resilience in times of conflict : land,
custom and law in East Timor. -- (Law, property and society)
1. Land tenure--Law and legislation--Timor-Leste.
2. Right of property--Timor-Leste. 3. Internally displaced
persons--Legal status, laws, etc.--Timor-Leste.
4. Customary law--Timor-Leste.
I. Title II. Series III. Fitzpatrick, Daniel.
IV. McWilliam, Andrew. V. Barnes, Susana.
346.5'9870432-dc23

**Library of Congress Cataloging-in-Publication Data**
Fitzpatrick, Daniel.
Property and social resilience in times of conflict : land, custom and law in East Timor / By Daniel Fitzpatrick, Andrew McWilliam and Susana Barnes Ashgate.
p. cm. -- (Law, property and society)
Includes bibliographical references and index.
ISBN 978-1-4094-5381-9 (hardback) 1. Land tenure--Law and legislation--Timor-Leste.
2. Customary law--Timor-Leste. I. McWilliam, Andrew.
II. Barnes, Susana. III. Title.
KNW5068.6.F58 2013
346.598704'32--dc23

2012026363

ISBN 978-1-4094-5381-9 (hbk)
ISBN 978-1-138-25702-3 (pbk)

# Contents

# List of Maps

# List of Tables

# Preface

The passage of a land law by the national Parliament of East Timor in February 2012 appeared to achieve, for the first time in the history of the young nation, a regulatory framework for state administration of land. More than a decade in development, the land law underwent a series of draft iterations and partial ratification of component elements. This extended time frame left the legal status of multiple land transactions, disputes and claims to entitlement uncertain since the departure of the Indonesian administration in November 1999. The hiatus reflects something of the complex history and politics of East Timor as it comes to terms with its legacy of overlapping titles from successive colonial regimes, extensive population displacement and coercive resettlement during Indonesian occupation, and the widespread existence of undocumented customary systems of land tenure and resource use.

The story of land law development in East Timor, however, is not yet over, as on 20 March 2012 the then President Jose Ramos Horta refused to assent to the law, and referred it back to Parliament with a list of proposed revisions. The Parliament will not have time to consider these revisions before parliamentary elections due in June 2012. Given the challenges of developing land law in East Timor, the monograph provides a timely discussion and analysis of the background, context and implications of legal options and proposals relating to customary land in East Timor. The monograph presents a sustained study into post-conflict indigenous land relations in East Timor and the challenges for effective regulation of customary land after armed conflicts. The research for this study has been carried out, for the most part, under the auspices of an Australian Research Council Discovery Grant (DP0556531) entitled Waiting for Law: Land, Custom and Legal Regulation in East Timor (2005–08). The project title reflected the much delayed legislative process for dealing with land issues in Timor and provided an opportunity to contribute research and policy perspectives on these matters.

Each of the authors has made distinctive contributions to the research from disciplinary perspectives that include the fields of law, anthropology and economics. The study combines an informed understanding of the law and economics of customary land regulation with detailed field-based ethnographic research into the significance and persistence of customary forms of land tenures following the long period of conflict and occupation. The study highlights the resilience of customary land systems in East Timor, and its implications for the post-conflict regulation of customary land. While the work is a combined interdisciplinary effort, there are individual contributions to the chapters that deserve acknowledgement. Daniel Fitzpatrick is the primary author of Chapters 1, 3, 4, 5, and 11. Andrew McWilliam is the primary author of Chapters 2 and 7. Susana Barnes is the primary author of Chapters 6, 8 and 9. All the authors contributed to Chapter 8.

East Timor has more than 16 distinctive spoken languages reflecting a complex settlement history that combines both Austronesian and non-Austronesian speaking communities. Over generations of residence, each language group has developed its own particular traditions, practices and cultural protocols, but at the same time there has also been extensive exchange and interaction between communities leading to what is now a widely recognizable and shared Austronesian cultural heritage (McWilliam 2007). This common heritage is expressed in a wide range of foundational concepts and practices expressed throughout East Timor including certain fundamental orientations towards customary land ownership and control, and the authority structures that inform its reproduction.

Our broadly based understanding of customary patterns of land tenure and land use in Timor Leste integrates complementary and comparative perspectives on land issues and the legacies of occupation by focusing primarily on a series of regional case studies. Each of the case studies highlights different aspects of the impact of past colonial settlement policies and the Indonesian occupation. They are also directed towards an appreciation of contemporary processes for restoring and asserting claims to land in the post-occupation period. In this respect the case studies seek to integrate the range of comparative features of Timorese society, upland and lowland areas, rural and peri-urban sites, geographical distribution of settlements and examples of displacements and endemic land disputes.

The majority of the ethnographic research has been undertaken in four selected regions of East Timor. They comprise Naueti-speaking communities of Darlari in Viqueque district near the southern coast; Fataluku-speaking communities in rural Lautem in the far east; Mambai settlements in the central western highlands of Ainaro including peri-urban settlements around the district capital of the same name; and Kemak- and Bunaq-speaking communities in highland Bobonaro in the far west. Much of this material is presented in the four central chapters of the present volume. The case studies serve as a rich source of comparative information on customary Timorese practices expressed in relation to land.

Field data from Viqueque, Ainaro and Bobonaro was generated by Susana Barnes over extended periods of fieldwork from 2004 to 2008. As a senior research associate with the project, her work combined observations and participatory engagement in the social and ritual life of selected communities in each of the three districts. Ethnographic enquiries and multiple open-ended conversations were held with customary ritual and political authorities as well as members of the principal 'house'-based origin groups of the constituent communities. The intent was to generate both specialist and more generalized knowledge of local land practices and contemporary debates around local land issues. Participation in cultural ceremonies and ritual exchanges in different sites provided opportunities for further enquiries and clarification around shared understandings of local ideas, values, expectations and obligations. The ability to engage directly with participants and protagonists over questions of land access and ownership histories provided rich insights into the dynamic and often contested nature of Timorese landed traditions.

Susana's work is complemented by ethnographic data on Fataluku displacement and customary land relationships gathered by Andrew McWilliam, who builds on his own sustained periods of fieldwork in the region. In addition to the ARC project funding, McWilliam has undertaken broader longitudinal studies of post-occupation and post-colonial processes of livelihood restoration and rebuilding among Fataluku from 2000 to 2010. The Fataluku case study presented here draws on land research and social histories of resident Fataluku communities with particular reference to the settlements of Tutuala, Com, Muapitine and the district capital Los Palos. Ethnographic enquiries encompassed a broad selection of local Fataluku householders and generated insights into Fataluku cultural principles and practices in relation to customary land tenures, including the historical processes that have so transformed settlement patterns and contemporary distribution over the last century. The research benefited from the opportunity to observe the establishment of the Nino Konis Santana National Park in Lautem during 2008. The creation of the national park brought into focus key questions around customary and state land issues for resident Fataluku communities, and the wider issues of comparative land management and resource entitlements.

In addition to the detailed ethnographic enquiries among customary communities, each of the authors undertook extensive interviews and discussions with local government representatives and officials of the National Land and Property Directorate over a number of years. This included a collaborative workshop convened with regional representatives of the National Directorate in 2006. The workshop reviewed patterns of land disputation and the progress of land dispute mediation processes across the country. Daniel Fitzpatrick has had a long involvement with the development of land law and policy in East Timor. In 2000 he worked as the land adviser for the United Nations Transitional Administration in East Timor (UNTAET). In 2004–05 he was a consultant for the USAID Land Law Project in East Timor. In 2010 he authored a World Bank policy options paper on implementing Chapter V of the draft land law, as a result of a request from East Timor's Minister of Justice. These advisory roles, and a long history of formal and informal consultations with land policy actors in East Timor, have informed a number of contributions to land policy debates in East Timor (for example Fitzpatrick 2002, Fitzpatrick et al. 2008, Fitzpatrick and Barnes 2010).

The monograph uses the expression 'East Timor' for consistency of description across the historical periods of Portuguese colonization (Portuguese Timor), Indonesian occupation (East Timor or Timor Timor) and independence (Timor Leste). 'Leste' means East in Portuguese. It also uses English translations of indigenous Timorese towns, except in cases where there is no appropriate English-language equivalent. The description of sensitive land disputes uses pseudonyms in those cases where the disputants have not given permission for use of their names. The monograph attempts to avoid overuse of technical law and economics terminology as it is aimed at a broad multidisciplinary audience, including policymakers in East Timor itself.

Over the long gestation period of the project, there have been a large number of colleagues that have provided insights, comments and criticisms on different aspects and components of the final work. In particular, the authors would like to thank Carol Rose, Hanoch Dagan, Nestor Davidson, Robert Ellickson, Ibere Lopez, Nigel Thompson, Frank Upham, Lisa Palmer, Deborah Cummins, Janet Gunter, Josh Trindade, Fidelis Magalhaes, Rod Nixon and participants at the 2011 Association for Law, Property and Society Conference in Washington DC, participants at a Regulatory Institutions Network (RegNet) seminar in October 2010 (Australian National University), and members of the World Bank Justice for the Poor Program in East Timor and Solomon Islands. A special debt of gratitude is owed to many East Timorese who participated in the research, in particular host families in Maliana, Ainaro, Uatolari and Lautem, as well as Staff of the National Directorate of Land and Property. The authors would also like to thank their rather patient family members: Susan, Madeleine and Lachlan, Sally, Georgie and Maddy, and Mark and Santiago.

Daniel Fitzpatrick, Andrew McWilliam and Susana Barnes.

## References

Fitzpatrick, D. 2002. *Land Claims in East Timor*. Canberra: Asia Pacific Press.

Fitzpatrick, D. and Barnes, S. 2010. The Relative Resilience of Property: First Possession and Order without Law in East Timor. *Law and Society Review*, 44(2), 205–38.

Fitzpatrick, D., McWilliam, A. and Barnes, S. 2008. Policy Notes on Customary Land in East Timor. *East Timor Law Journal*, 1–10.

McWilliam, A. 2007. Austronesians in Linguistic Disguise: Fataluku Cultural Fusion in East Timor. *Journal of Southeast Asian Studies*, 38(2), 355–75.

# Chapter 1
# Property Systems after Armed Conflicts: Custom, Possession and Dispossession

## Introduction

Contemporary peace-building efforts in countries such as Iraq, Afghanistan and Sudan involve weak states and influential tribal systems. State building requires strategies of accommodation or co-option relating to custom, including customary systems for the governance of land (Braithwaite et al. 2010: 103, 113–16, El Zain 1996: 523, 528, MacGinty 2010: 391, 404–5). Yet property systems in post-conflict states can fall into chronic instability as claims of possession and dispossession interact with emergent tensions over custom/state relations (Alden Wily 2009: 30, 36–8). Historical cycles of war and population displacement create endemic disputes over the possession of land, which entangle with long-standing customary conflicts, and then merge with post-conflict competition for authority over land (Alden Wily 2002: 61–2). In these circumstances, the formulation of new land law – including the relationship between law, the state and custom – may undermine attempts at peace-building by crystallizing tensions over possessory entitlements to land.

This book explores the relationship between custom, possession and land law in the conflict-affected circumstances of East Timor. East Timor is a new nation-state that lies northwest of Australia in the Lesser Sunda Islands at the eastern end of the Indonesian archipelago (see Map 1.1).

From 1974 to 1999, at least 102,800 and as many as 183,000 East Timorese died from conflict-related causes. These deaths represented between 15 per cent and 25 per cent of East Timor's then population, a mortality rate equivalent to the killing fields of Cambodia (CAVR 2005: 44). Most deaths took place during the period of Indonesian occupation from 1975 to 1999. Many resulted from forced relocations by the Indonesian military, an ill-fated attempt to separate civilians from the armed resistance that led to widespread food shortages and famine. Others were due to killings by the Indonesian military and its proxies, pro-Indonesian militia groups that went on a rampage of house burning and forced population displacement after the 1999 vote for independence. This forced displacement in 1999, which affected most of the then population of East Timor, repeated earlier episodes of involuntary population movements, particularly after the 1975 invasion and during the intense phase of military conflict in 1978–79 (CAVR 2005: 76, Fitzpatrick 2002: 5–6, 33–8, 115–19). According to the Truth and Reconciliation Commission established by the new state of East Timor (CAVR 2005: 73):

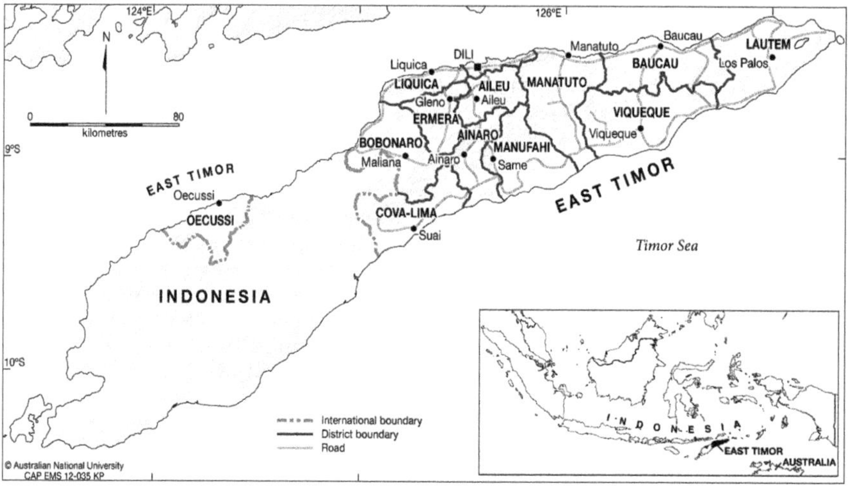


**Map 1.1 East Timor**
*Source*: ANU Cartography 2012

> The people of Timor Leste experienced repeated periods of displacement, often in massive numbers, between 1975 and 1999. Most individual East Timorese alive today have experienced at least one period of displacement. Many have experienced several …

Our study identifies resilient processes of reconstitution of property rights in customary systems after the mass deaths and displacements of Indonesian occupation. In districts of long-standing customary practice, Timorese attachments to land were re-established through mythologies of origin, which provide points of reference for social affiliation and precedence based on proximity to a source of common derivation. These mythologies of origin are reproduced through ceremonial enactment, the reconstruction of sacred houses and the recitation of ritual languages recalling the histories of the forebears. In war-torn circumstances, the traditional Timorese ordering principle of ancestral origin appears to have encouraged property claimants to nest their claims in customary structures rather than engage in disorderly racing for entitlements and authority relating to land. Even though origin principles are socially constructed, and often contested, they remain a powerful source of collective action as they provide a widely understood mechanism for avoiding costly and disruptive conflicts over land. This mechanism acts as a focal point for the cooperative reproduction of property rights, after periods of displacement, in circumstances where the alternative would be races for control over vacated land and housing.

While a finding of customary resilience is not new to postcolonial contexts, a novel aspect of our study lies in its structured explanation for resilience in circumstances of war and displacement. Our explanation draws on an analogy between Timorese notions of ancestral origin and legal principles of first possession. Rules of first possession provide the basis for ownership in many social and legal contexts (Rose 1985: 75, Sugden 1986: 87–97). Even in the absence of law, first possession norms may emerge as focal points to facilitate conflict avoidance and the development of cooperative forms of resource use. Because they guide initial patterns of behavior and predictions of future action, customs or norms of first possession are said to ameliorate the potential for conflict when claims to an unused or unoccupied resource are first made, or are subsequently contested by an influx of other prospective users (Sugden 1986: 70–71; 1989: 88–90, Zerbe and Anderson 2001: 119). The oft-cited example is that of the first car to enter a one-way bridge: all parties expect it to have the right of way as any other rule would be highly conducive to uncertainty and conflict (McDowell 2004: 774, Sudgen 1986: 70–71, 1989: 88–90). Another example is the development of first possession rules in the Californian goldfields, which contributed to conditions of order without law notwithstanding the potential for conflict inherent in the competitive nature of the gold rush itself (Umbeck 1981, McDowell 2002, 2004, Zerbe and Anderson 2001).

Timorese narratives of origin are analogous to principles of first possession as they provide a point of reference for calculating precedence and authority in relation to land. Yet Timorese principles of origin and first settlement are not so much matters of historical fact as mythical events that define the establishment of cosmological orders. As Chapter 2 describes, origin principles are embedded in complex local idioms of language, ceremony and identity. They comprise narratives that incorporate justifications for the displacement of earlier groups, while co-opting other points of legitimacy, such as Christian mythology or evidence of recognition by colonial authority. As a consequence, while origin principles may facilitate social order in circumstances of population movement, as social constructs they are also open to contested interpretations of social precedence, including the property significance of claims based on origin. Origin principles are resilient because of their potential to maintain social order and authority in a context of heightened fears of social disorder. At the same time they have also lost a degree of legitimacy and ordering capacity in areas where competing sources of property authority have intruded, including political arrangements established under various forms of colonial and neo-colonial rule. Our explanation for resilience in traditional Timorese property systems thus incorporates the possibility of disorder, where alternative sources of possessory legitimacy and property enforcement emerge to compete with norms of origin or ancestral first possession.

We identify the emergence of competing interpretations of property authority, and their relationship with cultural constructions of possession, in a number of districts of East Timor. In some areas the intrusion of colonial authority, and the opening of new land under colonial supervision, has moderated the influence of customary authority and left some claims based not on ancestral principles of first possession, but on histories of actual possessory acts involving clearing land and digging irrigation channels (Gunter 2007). In a number of cases, the entanglement of possessory claims with state-affiliated authority has contributed to chronic land conflicts, as periodic regime change revives disputes based on narratives of grievance and histories of past cultivation and occupation. These cases support our conclusion that the resilience of customary property arrangements in East Timor is relative and constrained, rather than absolute in nature, as the capacity of origin principles to maintain social order in the context of relocation and associated land tensions has been limited by the emergence of state-affiliated sources of public authority and the potential for contested interpretations of the implications of possession itself.

Recent regulatory recommendations for customary property systems focus on recognition and adaptation rather than replacement with statutory systems of registered land titles (see Fitzpatrick 2005). These recommendations are consistent with Elinor Ostrom's studies of successful community-based systems for resource management (for example, Ostrom 1990). Yet there is a basic difficulty in the provision of legal space for customary resilience, namely the socially embedded complexity of customary norms. Timorese principles of origin may be analogous to principles of first possession, in their capacity to maintain conditions of order without law, but they are not capable of translation into legal rules without substantial risks of incomplete, variable and contested interpretation. The literature on colonial and postcolonial land relations highlights the risks of reification and distortion of custom as it is translated into 'customary law' (for example, Chanock 1991, Colson 1971; Lavigne Delville 2000; Moore 1986). Somewhat perversely, the resilience of custom renders it resistant to translation into law. The act of regulating customary resilience, through law and the state, may lead to a loss of resilience because customary norms and rules are complex living constructs, embedded in social relations with land, and vulnerable to reified or distorted interpretation by state-affiliated authority.

### *The 2012 Draft Land Law of East Timor*

With the creation of the independent state of East Timor in 2002, the challenges of managing entitlement to land now include a scale of governance beyond the localized mechanisms of customary systems. After a long wait since independence, the National Parliament of East Timor approved a new law on land on 6 February 2012. However, the President of East Timor vetoed the law on 20 March 2012. The vetoed Parliamentary bill, which we call the 2012 draft land law, reflects an emergent state's desire to regulate resources at a national scale, based on 'territorializing' notions of default state title to land (see Blomley 2003; Vandergeest and Peluso 1995). The law defines land held under the 'private domain' of the state to include private land 'without an identifiable owner' (art. 6 (3)). This provision establishes a bright-line default: the burden of proving private title lies with the claimant. The law then sets out the primary basis for claiming private title. Ownership rights shall be awarded to claimants who 'hold Timorese citizenship and possess the property with the intention of ownership, continuously, publicly and notoriously'; and who 'initiated possession in a peaceful fashion before or on December 31 1998 (art. 19).[1] Possession is defined as the use of property for the purposes of habitation, cultivation, business, construction or any other activity requiring physical use of land. Evidence of possession includes acts of construction, planting, fencing and enclosures (art. 9).

The rule of possession is bright-line in nature (and far removed from customary understandings of possessory entitlements) as individuals may claim ownership based on acts of physical use and control alone. In terms, however, the rule is subject to an exception for 'mere occupants'. Article 10 (2) states that 'mere occupants' cannot obtain ownership on the basis of long-term possession. Article 10 (1) defines mere occupants to include people using land with no intention of ownership, such as lessees; and representatives and agents of the possessor, as well as anyone exercising possession on behalf of someone else. This approach is similar to the common law distinction between actual and legal possession, which allows owners to transfer physical control without losing legal entitlements to possess, or remedies based on entitlement to possess. While distinctions between actual and legal possession create interpretive complexity, relative to a simple rule of possession, they allow for efficient transfers of control to non-owners for temporary periods. In analogous terms there are benefits in East Timor, in terms of social order, to identifying and enforcing agreements between customary groups and persons relocated to customary lands during Portuguese colonization or the Indonesian military occupation. Making legal space for these types of agreement means that relocated households on customary lands could fall into the category of mere occupants – lessees or agents of the possessor – and not the category of legal possessor, which would be the customary group.

While agreements between customary landholders and relocated households are information-intense, our case studies suggest that they are often the best available institutional mechanisms for managing the legacies of forced relocation in East Timor, particularly in circumstances of state remoteness and weakness (see also Alden Wily 2007). And yet, in an excess of bright-line enthusiasm, the draft law forecloses the possibility of context-specific distinctions between mere occupants and legal possessors in areas of customary domain. Article 10 (3) states that:

> Possessors will be those who reside in, have erected buildings on, or have cultivated land … with ownership claimed by another party based on the belief of ancestral customary domain, even when rent is paid to that party.

1 The draft law also provides for restitution of ownership titles issued by the Portuguese and Indonesian administrations, and held by East Timorese citizens. However, there were relatively few ownership titles issued by the Portuguese and Indonesians, and the draft law grants priority to claims based on possession over claims based on limited term Portuguese or Indonesian titles, which were far greater in number: see Fitzpatrick (2002).

Article 10 (3) allows individuals the right to claim alienable ownership even when they pay rent or otherwise acknowledge the 'belief of ancestral customary domain' of another party. As our case studies illustrate, this category of property claimant includes large numbers of groups displaced to customary lands during Portuguese and Indonesian periods of control over East Timor. The intent of the draft law seems clear: as a matter of *in rem* entitlement individual possessors of customary land may claim ownership notwithstanding *in personam* obligations arising from contracts with customary landholders.[2]

The National Parliament of East Timor has made a choice to prefer a broad property audience, including potential investors in rural land, over the specialized audience of customary systems. As a result of the proposed rule of possession, future negotiations among competing resource claimants in rural districts would not involve a shared principle of origin, as a focal point for calculating cost/benefit strategies of cooperation or conflict, but competing norms of custom and possession that disable longstanding conditions for authoritative allocation of entitlements by establishing alternative bases for property legitimation (see Trebilcock and Veel 2008: 447). We conclude that the draft land law has the potential to undermine the resilience of customary systems because it seeks to substitute possession and state authority for contextualized local principles of origin, which in some areas continue to act as focal points for the avoidance of violent conflict over resources.

## The Path-Dependence of Property: Competitive Racing Rights after Armed Conflicts

Our study identifies a relationship between social order and institutional complexity – both in the resilience of customary systems affected by population movement, and in the stabilization of a new nation-state emerging from violent military occupation. The analysis includes the initial causes of institutional complexity in customary systems, and provides a potential explanation for the persistence of institutional complexity in post-conflict states or political orders. In particular, the analysis suggests that property systems with histories of weak state authority and resilient customary authority may have path-dependent legacies of institutional complexity that developed in response to exigencies associated with social ordering. In customary systems property rule complexity may take the form of rules on abandonment, hierarchies of entitlement within a group, and distinctions between entitlements based on actual possession and ancestral first possession. This form of rule complexity is interpretive in nature: for outsiders, in particular, it is more difficult to interpret these types of rules than a simple rule that entitlements flow from acts of possession alone. Alternatively, institutional complexity may

2 *In personam* rights are limited to specified parties to a contract or Court judgment, whereas *in rem* rights of property establish duties of non-interference in a broad class of potential violators.

arise from the inability of the state to enforce legal rules of property over customary objections, which can lead to a process of 'legal forum shopping', involving the affiliation of competing property claimants with competing sources of customary and legal authority (Bruce, 1998, Fitzpatrick, 1997: 184, Platteau, 1996: 41–6, Toulmin et al., 2002: 13; Toulmin and Quan, 2000: 219; Trebilcock and Veel 2008: 447–53). This type of complexity is functional in nature: it arises not from the interpretive content of rules, but from their application in a pluralist enforcement environment. East Timor provides an unusual opportunity to analyze the potential emergence of both forms of institutional complexity, in circumstances of custom without law, and in the development of land law in a new nation-state.

A central theme of this book is the potential for armed conflicts to create path-dependent trajectories in property systems, particularly as a result of institutional responses to risks of costly races for control over resources. For the purposes of our analysis we describe 'social order' in terms of avoiding violent conflicts over resources as a result of population movement, particularly in a context of armed conflict. Armed conflicts create conditions for conflicts over land (Alden Wily 2009: 30–2). Land becomes newly available to claim as landowners are killed and violence forces mass displacement of civilian populations. Untended land is open to possession by persons without access to housing or sources of livelihoods. At the same time, the supply of land and housing is put under increased pressure as damage and destruction reduce the housing stock, and those who are displaced congregate around areas of economic activity, water sources and arable land (Unruh 2001: 2–3; 2004: 12, 16, 20–1). Taking these circumstances together, armed conflict may increase the net value of land, and create incentives to race for property rights, including by occupying land claimed by a customary group (Alden Wily 2009: 36). While racing for rights occurs in all property systems, property systems affected by armed conflicts are more likely to experience land grabs and violent contests over property as a result of population displacement and the destruction of housing (Alden Wily 2009: 33–4).

Daniel Lewis (2004: 6–7) identifies costly contests over the possession of land left vacant by displaced persons in Kosovo, Iraq, Afghanistan, and Somalia. These contests overlay or exacerbate grievances arising from competing claims to land and resources prior to the armed conflict. Generally, they take place in conjunction with breakdowns in government functioning and order, which creates further opportunities for competitive racing and resort to violent means for asserting property claims. Jon Unruh (2004: 16) provides an example in relation to Rwanda:

> When 2.3 million refugees quickly re-entered Rwanda between 1994 and 1997, the land tenure system was not functioning well enough to handle the influx. The consequence was the resettlement occurred with often little influence by state agencies and included sometimes violent land grabbing and taking of abandoned land.

When resources are newly available to claim, the incentives to obtain resource control can lead to competitive forms of racing for rights of property (Anderson and Hill 2004: 13, Anderson and Hill 2002: 490). The phenomenon of competitive racing for property rights has been analyzed in a number of contexts, including homesteading settlements in the American West (Anderson and Hill 2002), applications for patents (Barzel 1968, Kitch 1977), rights to oil and gas (Libecap and Wiggins 1984), and mining claims in the Californian goldfields (McDowell 2004; Morriss 2005). These studies conclude that competitive racing for rights can be costly and wasteful, as resources are dissipated in the act of racing, or rights are obtained before the resource is ready for production. Racing incurs expenses that may be wasted should a claimant fail in the race. It may also dissipate resources through acts of defence or aggression against other claimants. Even if a claimant succeeds in a race for rights, there are risks that the resource will not be ready for productive exploitation, because the imperatives of racing create incentives for premature acquisition. In these circumstances, a claimant will seek to obtain property rights in order to stave off other claimants, rather than on the basis of the commercial viability of the resource itself (Lueck 1995, 203–4).

### *Customary Systems and Collective Responses to Racing for Rights*

Although the effects of war and displacement encourage disorderly racing for rights to land, they may also expose resilient principles of social organization. In the absence of effective state-imposed legal order, resource users will look for shared norms or focal points to avoid social disorder and structure co-operative forms of property arrangements (Ellickson 1991: 52–62). Customary systems tend to recover faster from the effects of war than the state, particularly in terms of retaining a collective capacity to manage the disruptive effects of displacement (Fitzpatrick and Barnes 2010). Customary land systems in postcolonial contexts have evolved and survived over long periods of time, in response to resource and environment-specific conditions. Their long-run survival, as mechanisms for resource governance, implies a capacity for social ordering where shared desires to avoid the social costs of resource conflict outweigh incentives to claim property rights through acts of violence, or acts conducive to violence (Platteau 2000: 182–3, 198–201; cf. Ellickson 1993: 1357–61).

Comparative studies illustrate the way in which small, stable and homogenous groups of individuals develop rules that respond to social costs, including the risk of costly racing for rights to resources (Krier 1992; Ostrom 1990; Rose 1986). Examples discussed by Anderson and Hill (2004: 6–7) include the cooperative property systems of American Indians, the mining districts of California and Nevada, and the cattlemen's associations of Montana. Other examples are cooperation among settlers at the Amazonian frontier (Alston, Libecap and Mueller 1999: 98–152), and nineteenth-century whaling communities in the United States and Great Britain (Ellickson 1989). In all these cases, the customary system not only provided collective sanctions for the enforcement of property claims , but granted rights to resources relatively early in the racing process, leading other potential claimants to forgo efforts to engage in racing, or to forgo their efforts before undue costs were incurred (Lueck 1995: 400; Rose 1985: 81).

Even though customary systems provide institutional responses to risks of costly racing for rights to resources, conditions of war and population displacement also undermine the capacity of customary systems to engage in collective action. In-migration and population movement undermine the prospects for collective action where they increase the numbers and heterogeneity of resource users. Even in the absence of in-migration, customary mechanisms for collective action may degrade due to conflict with another group, or as a result of antagonistic state law and encroachments by state institutions. The threat to cooperative capacity will be exacerbated as resource values rise, increasing the risk of incursion by outsiders and strengthening demand for more exclusionary property rights for insiders (Fitzpatrick 2006: 1033–38, Trebilcock 1984: 401–06). As resource values rise, members of a common property system have a greater incentive to defect in order to capture the gains of asserting increasingly exclusionary rights. Property claims based on individual acts of possession, in particular, provide a mechanism for group members to exit customary systems (Krier 2009: 150). Increases in land value create incentives for acts of possession that then create demand for individuated entitlements, which may not be supported or recognized by customary mechanisms. Contests over possession, arising from population displacement, may thus combine with rising resource values to exacerbate degradations in the collective capacity of customary systems.

Harold Demsetz's well-known theory of evolving property rights, under the influence of rising resource values, suggests a ready transition from collective rights under customary systems to private property rights enforced by the state (Demsetz 1967; see also Fitzpatrick 2006: 1003–7). Rising resource values increase the benefits of capturing resource rents through exclusionary property rights to the point that they outweigh the costs of establishing and enforcing a private property interest (Demsetz 1967: 350). The recognition of exclusionary rights of possession, at individual and household levels, rewards out of territorial entitlements from collective areas of control (Krier 2009: 150–58). Yet in a number of postcolonial circumstances – involving resilient customary systems and weak or illegitimate states – attempts at replacing context-specific customs with purportedly simple laws have served only to overlay formal institutions on informal arrangements, and allowed disputants the opportunity to manipulate competing property enforcement mechanisms through 'legal forum shopping' (see Fitzpatrick 2006: 1011–15, 1039–41). As Alston, Harris, and Mueller (2011) note, the result can be violent conflict where the state is unable or unwilling to enforce legal claims, and there is a degree of equivalence in the capacity for violence of competing property claimants. In cases of armed conflict, the risk of property conflicts merging with group violence is exacerbated when possessory claimants defect from customary systems, without the prospect of authoritative enforcement by the state, and other claimants seek state-based remedies for dispossession as a result of histories of displacement and regime change (Alden Wily 2009: 28; Pantuliano et al. 2007).

*Rules of Possession and Competitive Racing for Rights*

Game theorists argue that social order can emerge autonomously from spreading patterns of respect for possessory claims (Sugden 1989). Possessory norms develop as a result of mutually reinforcing expectations of respect for possession (Hayek 1979). In circumstances of competitive racing for rights, the iconic example of Hayekian 'spontaneous order' is rules of first possession developed by groups of miners in the Californian goldfields between 1848 and 1852. The 19th-century Californian gold rush involved large numbers of miners entering an area that had recently been annexed by the United States from Mexico (Clay and Wright 2005). There were no courts, police or jails, and only a small military force. (McDowell 2004: 771, Morriss 2005: 47). According to McDowell (2004: 77), the rule of first possession – represented by digging a hole and maintained by leaving tools in that hole – provided a basis for cooperative action, at least among American miners, in response to risks of costly racing for rights to resources. It provided a marker of who would win and who would lose in the event of competition for a claim (Morris 2005: 48). Because it signaled prior allocation of rights, the first possession rule generated patterns of rule compliance because of mutually reinforcing expectations of relative success as first possessors were more likely than prospective dispossessors to defend their claims with confidence and aggression (McDowell 2004: 773, Zerbe and Anderson 2001: 115).

The mining rule of first possession in California was generated by a customary system in the absence of law and legal order. Custom and a rule of possession combined to manage the risks of violence arising from competitive racing for rights to resources (at least among American miners: see Chapter 3). In California, at least, the relationship between possession and social order was not separated from a system for property interpretation and enforcement. Respect for possession cannot be a basis for social ordering without acts that are interpreted as possessory by other prospective users, or an interpretive mechanism to ascribe the character of possession to certain acts of resource use and control (Tay 1964: 497). Possession is a cultural text that 'reads' according to its interpretive community: there are substantial differences in the understanding of possession as between swidden cultivators or mobile transhumants, and settler farmers or even lawyer legislators (see Rose 1986). In fact, possessory rules or norms may have a range of effects on social ordering, not only because of the interpretive nature of possession, but because possessory claimants have a natural tendency to affiliate with sources of property enforcement authority (Lund 2002; Platteau 2000: 28 –82). In cases of armed conflict, some possessory claimants will affiliate with state rather than customary authority, leaving them vulnerable to regime change and forced displacement as a result of association with a discredited regime. Regime change and forced displacement can then create narratives of grievance that manifest in violent acts of re-possession where there are further changes in the political order (Lund 2009: 1–15).

Merrill and Smith (2007) argue that a property system is more likely to resolve the problem of social order through simple property principles because of the costs of communicating property information to a large audience. A simple rule that respects possession, or provides remedies for dispossession, facilitates shared expectations of cooperative behavior, which is essential for a property system to avoid high cost reliance on coercive enforcement (Merrill and Smith 2007:1858–59). In conflict-affected circumstances of population displacement, establishing the cooperative foundations of a property system may be challenged by tensions between rules favoring possession, and the provision of remedies for dispossession. Those in possession include secondary occupiers – people who occupied someone else's land (including customary land) in circumstances of displacement. Conversely, those seeking restitution of possession include competing claimants from different historical events of dispossession. There is reduced prospect of a broad property consensus based on respect for possession or remedies for dispossession, and increased potential for chronic property uncertainty as a result of unresolved conflicts between actual and prior possessors.

## International Legal Standards on Post-conflict Restitution of Land

International legal standards relating to armed conflicts now promote remedies for wrongful dispossession, through restitution of rights to 'housing, land and property', as a preferred policy response to population displacement. For example, the 1998 Guiding Principles on Internal Displacement ('the Deng Principles') require competent authorities to establish the conditions and means to allow internally displaced persons to return voluntarily and safely to their homes, or else to resettle voluntarily in another part of the country.[3] The 2005 United Nations Principles on Housing and Property Restitution for Refugees and Displaced Persons ('the Pinheiro Principles') provide that 'states shall demonstrably prioritize the right to restitution as the preferred remedy for displacement, and as an essential element of restorative justice', and that refugees and displaced persons have a right to restitution where they were 'arbitrarily or unlawfully' deprived of housing, land and/or property.[4]

The preamble to the Pinheiro Principles states that 'the right to housing, land and property restitution is essential to the resolution of conflict and to post-conflict

3 *Id.*, Principles 28, 29, 30. In 2005, the United Nations General Assembly ('UNGA') 'recognized' the Guiding Principles on Internal Displacement as 'an important international framework': see the *2005 World Summit Outcome*, GA Res 60/L.1, UN GAOR, 60th session (2005), paragraph 132.

4 United Nations Principles on Housing and Property Restitution for Refugees and Displaced Persons, U.N. doc. E/CN.4/Sub.2/2005/17 (2005), Principles 2.1, 2.2.

peace-building', and that 'the implementation of successful housing, land and property restitution programs, as a key element of restorative justice, contributes to effectively deterring future situations of displacement and building sustainable peace'. Yet the proposition that restitution of property rights to displaced persons is essential to peace-building is often asserted as a matter of a priori reasoning (for example, Paglione 2008, Pinheiro 2002), rather than a conclusion of causation derived from a representative sample of conflict studies. While cases such as Bosnia-Herzegovina and Kosovo involved 'one-off' acts of ethnic cleansing, where restitution sought to redress recent discriminatory practices, other conflicts such as Afghanistan and Rwanda involve much more complex histories of dispossession where the restitution of land to one category of claimant runs the risk of inflaming the grievances of other claimants. In more complex histories and circumstances of armed conflict, restitution may form part of contested territorial strategies, to extend the authority of an emergent regime or state, or to assert ethnic or tribal authority in a long-standing conflict over control of frontier land (see Alden Wily 2002).

### *The Politics of Custom and Law after Armed Conflicts*

In addition to providing incentives for physical races to occupy vacated land and housing, armed conflict creates opportunities for political competition to obtain rights or authority relating to land (Zartman 1995: 108). North Wallis and Weingast (2009: 59) argue that an elite coalition may stabilize the state, and manage the potential for group violence, by co-opting 'violence entrepreneurs' through inducements based on control over the mechanisms of the state, including the legal authority to grant privileged access to rights and resources. In the aftermath of violent conflict, flexible property rules may emerge as a tool to accommodate interest groups within a stabilizing elite, through readjustment of privileges in response to shifts in the balance of power (North Wallis and Weingast 2009: 77–8). Their depiction of flexible property rules includes *ex post* interpretive discretion to adjust property rights. A corollary – not explored by North, Wallis, and Weingast – is that members of the state-controlling elite have an incentive to adopt a bright-line default rule of state title to land, in order to extract rents from the grant of land concessions for economic development (Alden Wily 2009: 36–8). In either case, the political economy of stabilization after armed conflicts affects the design of rules relating to custom and the management of contested claims to possession of land (see Chapter 5).

In emergent states a politico-legal community must form around common points of epistemic reference in order to establish the broad cognitive basis for a cooperative property system (Braithwaite 2002: 50–1; see also Dworkin 1986: 211). Yet a challenge for new post-conflict states or political orders is that rules emerging from processes of elite-formation and state-stabilization may not lend themselves to the development of epistemic or social consensus on property rights in land. Chronic property uncertainty may develop in post-conflict environments as legislative configurations of interpretive rule complexity and simplicity respond to a stabilizing elite, and imperatives to avoid state-destabilization, without resolving legacies of population displacement and tensions over possessory claims to land. Societies with histories of violent conflict may develop private property rules characterized by complexity or flexibility, which may be sub-optimal in the long run because of their information costs relative to correspondingly simple rules. Yet these rules may be difficult to revise because they form part of the process of elite-formation that allowed initial formation of state order after episodes of armed group violence. As a result, while there will be incentives for emergent states or political orders to adopt simple property rules – to facilitate investment and the broad-based cooperation implicit in a property system – there will also be contingent historical events that help to explain the persistence of interpretive complexity in rules of private property.

## Outline of Chapters

In the next chapter we explore the basis for the resilience of customary property systems in East Timor, through an ethnographic discussion of the organizing principle of origin and its symbolic articulation in traditional Timorese clan houses. Principles of origin are reproduced through ceremonial enactments and repetitive linguistic formulations, and are embedded in the landscape of East Timor through sacred houses and symbolic representations of ancestral connections. They have acted as key sources of social resilience in historical circumstances of migration, forced displacement and inter-group warfare. Yet their capacity to absorb in-migration is not absolute or unconstrained. The effects of Portuguese mechanisms for village government, and the large-scale movement of peoples during Portuguese and Indonesian times, have degraded or suppressed traditional mechanisms for incorporating in-migrants into customary order. In a number of districts, the adaptive capacity of origin principles has been affected by the emergence of multiple sources of public authority, and the potential for competing interpretations of entitlements created by acts of land clearing and cultivation.

Chapter 3 explores structural explanations for the resilience of customary property systems in East Timor. In East Timor, local narratives of origin, reproduced through rituals and invocations of ancestral spirits, are well known to all newcomers and neighboring groups. They have the potential to generate patterns of compliance and anticipated compliance because newcomers and their neighbours know they can avoid costly forms of conflict and obtain access to land by incorporating themselves into origin group hierarchies through marriage alliances and ritualized relationships of gift exchange and reciprocity. In a game-theoretic sense, origin principles in East Timor have provided a focal point for the constitution of social order in circumstances of population mobility, and a mechanism for avoiding conflict over land by incorporating newcomers and neighbours into a broadly understood system of precedence for allocating and managing the use of land. We illustrate this focal point analysis by reference to game-theoretic explanations for the relationship between first possession principles and social order in the goldmines of nineteenth-century California. We also discuss Robert Ellickson's analysis of first possession principles among the nineteenth-century whaling communities of the United States and Great Britain (Ellickson 1989).

In Chapter 3 we argue that the development of interpretive complexity in customary rules of first possession, in close-knit community contexts, can correlate with concerns for social order in circumstances of in-migration and threats to socio-political stability. The argument leads to a key hypothesis of this book: that different complexity/simplicity trade-offs in the interpretive content of property rules apply in different circumstances of social ordering. The hypothesis provides a fresh perspective on Ellickson's well-known hypothesis (Ellickson 1989) that in close-knit community contexts more complex rules may emerge where the increased costs of their interpretation are outweighed by increased gains from trade. Examples from the customary societies of East Timor suggest that rule complexity may emerge where the increased costs of their interpretation are outweighed by reductions in property enforcement costs, at least in environments where there are risks of costly racing for rights to resources. Complex norms of ancestral first possession have evolved in East Timor as a response to fears of property conflict, in a context of population mobility, rather than as a direct response to potential gains from trade in agricultural products. While social order creates conditions for gains from trade, East Timor's complex systems of customary resource governance suggest a correlation between possessory rule complexity and reductions in property enforcement costs through maintenance of social order.

Chapter 4 considers whether a relationship between social order, and the interpretive complexity of possessory rules, applies when possessory rules move beyond a close-knit customary context. Henry Smith (2009) suggests an information cost trade-off in matters of custom and law: where complex customs are recognized by law, either the process of communicating property information is made more costly for remote third parties, or standardization is required to strip the custom of its informational complexity. The East Timor example suggests that standardizing customary rules of first possession may reduce information costs, but may also create conflict in frontier areas where the state is unable or unwilling to engage in coercive enforcement of legal claims over long-standing customary claims. The analysis builds on Lee Alston, Edwyna Harris and Bernardo Mueller's hypothesis (2009: 6, 2011: 5) that violent land conflicts may emerge at a frontier when a state is unable to enforce *de jure* property rights against competing *de facto* claims developed by frontier mechanisms for private ordering. In these conflict-affected circumstances, there is a potential trade-off between the greater information costs of recognising complex customary rules of first possession, and the capacity of complex customary rules to reduce the enforcement costs of property. This trade-off illustrates our argument that social ordering affects choices among configurations of interpretive complexity and simplicity in the formulation of rules relating to property.

Chapter 5 identifies incentives for social and political ordering, to avoid violent conflicts over scarce resources, as a key factor in the development of draft laws on land in East Timor. It draws on recent work by North, Wallis and Weingast (2009) on social order and state-formation in circumstances of violence. Their typology of social orders provides a basis for understanding initial choices of legal rule complexity and simplicity in the formation of social order. Chapter 5 argues that there is a relationship between post-conflict social order and the interpretive content of new property law. In particular, it suggests that the political economy of rule formulation in fragile states may result in bright-line rules of state title to public land and complex rules of property rights in private land. In relation to state land, the sovereign state assumptions of land law will suit elites engaged in races to extract private benefits from state control over resources. Default rules that the state holds title to unowned land, in particular, create opportunities for extraction of private benefits from the grant of rights to public land, including through licenses or concessions to commercial interests (Alden Wily 2009: 36–7). Conversely, high levels of interpretive discretion relating to private property not only allows flexible redistribution of rights to balance competing interest groups, but also creates rent-seeking opportunities through control over discretionary powers to allocate or adjudicate rights to land.

Chapters 6 to 9 set out our case studies from selected sites in East Timor. The case studies are based on extended ethnographic fieldwork undertaken from 2006 to 2009. The field sites illustrate a range of contemporary land issues, including resilient processes of reconstituting property relations, tensions created by localized processes of displacement and relocation, and emerging uncertainties associated with land markets, competing land claims and state-related sources of political or public authority. Our sites include a number of small rural settlements: Babulo in the district of Viqueque, Vero in the district of Lautem, and Saburai in the district of Maliana. We also provide an urban/peri-urban study from Ainaro township and its hinterland within Ainaro district. These sites illustrate the potential for different historical trajectories of property, in a context of population movement and increases in settlement density. While some cases highlight the resilience of customary property arrangements, as sources of social ordering, others illustrate the relationship between contested interpretations of possession and the emergence of chronic land conflicts. Our case studies thus provide a broad comparative basis to analyze the relationship between land, custom and social order in a conflict-affected context.

The Babulo study in Chapter 6 illustrates the reconstitution of origin group authority after the Indonesian occupation. We describe a ceremony to commemorate reconstruction of a sacred house destroyed during the Indonesian occupation, involving ritualized invocation of relations with the ancestors to reproduce the privileged status and authority of origin group elders. As with our study of Saburai in Maliana (Chapter 8), the Babulo study supports the hypothesis that customary principles of land authority, typified by narratives of origin and symbolized by sacred houses, have retained a substantial degree of relevance and resilience, and provided the basis for orderly restoration of property rights, notwithstanding the effects of Indonesian occupation. However, the Babulo study also illustrates a finding of constrained resilience, including indications that traditional mechanisms for incorporating in-migrants have been suppressed or degraded, in parallel with the emergence of state-affiliated village government structures. As a result, while in-marrying remains a resilient adaptive technique – with some relocated groups commencing marriage relations with origin groups – there remains a great deal of social tension over the long-term status and rights of relocated groups from both Portuguese and Indonesian times.

Chapter 7 provides a case study of the Fataluku language group in the district of Lautem. As with other ethno-linguistic groups in East Timor, the Fataluku interpret relationships of land through localized understandings of social and spiritual order. Conceptions of possession are interwoven with mythical narratives of ancestral origin, and complex histories of migration and attachment to land. There is no customary norm among the Fataluku that acts of possession *per se* give rise to property entitlements, because the implications of possession are calculated by reference to principles of origin and social precedence. Inevitably, Fataluku preferences, norms, languages, and cognitive understandings of property will shape the interpretation of a new legal rule of possession. Yet the interpretation of a new rule of possession in Lautem will also involve strategic negotiation of claims outside the epistemic world of the Fataluku, as a result of opportunities created by new law. In particular, Fataluku settlements displaced during the Indonesian military occupation have incentives to take advantage of a legal rule of possession by asserting entitlements to land over and above current customary arrangements. We illustrate this possibility through a social history of settlement movement in Lautem, including one small settlement (*aldeia*) named Vero in the village of Tutuala.

The Maliana study in Chapter 8 begins with an account of the mountain community of Saburai, which is in the borderlands with Indonesian West Timor. In Saburai the process of return after mass population displacement, as a result of the Indonesian military invasion, has been marked by a revitalization of cultural practices that provide social stability in times of change and uncertainty. Saburai offers an example of the resilience of customary communities in East Timor where sacred houses and the various markers of customary authority provide a widely accepted pathway for the orderly acquisition of rights to land through marriage-based alliances and the incorporation of newcomers. Chapter 8 then contrasts the Saburai study with contested claims to land in and around Maliana town and on the broad Nunura plain in Maliana district. The discussion explores the effects of different forms of colonial intervention on local claims to land, particularly in lowland areas 'opened' through Portuguese agricultural programmes. We consider the capacity of customary institutions to manage land conflict in upland and lowland settings, and illustrate the politicization of land claims and the complex genealogies of chronic land disputes in lowland areas.

The Ainaro study in Chapter 9 examines the way in which customary tenures have adapted and adjusted to historical processes of land differentiation and commodification within a predominantly peri-urban setting. It illustrates the subsidence of customary authority over land as a result of Portuguese policies, including the introduction of local government structures, and the destructive effects of Indonesian occupation. The study also illustrates various categories of competing land claimants in independent East Timor, including current occupiers and Portuguese and Indonesian titleholders, and the way in which these competing claims are complicated by emerging issues of individuation, commodification and titling of rights to land. The peri-urban example includes a greater role for the state, under its various guises in East Timor, as the infrastructure needs of urban development have led to land acquisition under legal powers of eminent domain. As in Lautem, but more prominently because of its urban context, increased demand for land has promoted individuation of property claims, while also promoting chronic uncertainty and conflict where overlapping claims have interacted with multiple reference points for property legitimacy and authority.

Chapter 10 further analyzes the relationship between social order and the possession of land by reference to chronic possessory conflicts in East Timor. The chapter illustrates cycles of dispossession, grievance and repossession in a weak state context with reference to a number of land disputes lodged for mediation with the Land and Property Directorate of the government of East Timor. In particular, we discuss histories of possession and dispossession on the Uato Lari coastal lands of Viqueque, the floodplains of Ainaro and the Nunura plains of Maliana. These complex land conflicts illustrate the limits of resilient local responses to population displacement, particularly in terms of traditional mechanisms for incorporating relocated groups into customary order through marriage and agreement. Not only is customary authority contested in areas first cleared under colonial supervision, but the transaction costs of complex land conflicts in these areas are too large for mediated agreement because of the large numbers and high stakes involved, especially given the circumstances of poverty and the importance of land to livelihoods. In these circumstances, there are arguments favouring a relatively simple rule of possession, in lowland areas 'opened' under colonial supervision, as it avoids the need for forced evictions by a weak state, and builds on the 'home-court' defensive advantage of current possessors. At the same time, a simple rule of possession – in the sense of respect for current possession – may cause violent counter-reactions by groups with grievances over historical events of dispossession, and contribute to chronic social disorder in countries with histories of weak state authority, periodic regime change and associated population displacement. Chapter 10 concludes that the appropriate choice of rule complexity or flexibility in post-conflict cases of contested possession, including rules of possession and remedies for dispossession, involves context-specific assessment of the respective capacity for violence of the claimants, relative to the capacity for violence of the state.

Chapter 11 maps the potential application of the draft land law to rural districts in East Timor. The chapter highlights a further aspect of rule complexity and simplicity in conflict-affected environments, namely the likelihood that all legal rules will take on interpretive complexity as they traverse a variety of administrative, communicative and cognitive frameworks (Luhmann 1985). In fragile post-conflict contexts, in particular, even rules with a low level of interpretive content may be interpreted and applied in an indeterminate fashion as a result of different epistemological understandings of law, and a process of competition for public authority relating to property claims. This analysis draws on recent literature that highlights two features of property in plural socio-political environments: its negotiability across contested landscapes of legitimacy and authority (for example, Berry 1993, 1997, Bourdieu 1990, de Sardan 1999, Lund 2002: 14, Moore 1986, 1998), and its communicative variation across diverse epistemic and cognitive sub-systems (Teubner 1993, 1998, Gillespie 2010: 245). The chapter concludes with a brief discussion of appropriate – or least worst – options for configurations of interpretive complexity and simplicity in rules governing land, custom and possession in the plural epistemic and enforcement setting of East Timor.

## Conclusion

Our discussion of customary principles of origin in East Timor has resonances of Malinowski's description of a 'charter myth' – namely a myth that: 'conveys, expresses and strengthens the fundamental fact of local unity and of the kinship unity of the group of people descendant from a common ancestress … . the story of origin literally contains the legal charter of the community' (Malinowski 1954:116). While our analysis has echoes of Malinowskian traditions of anthropology, which highlight structural or functional features of customary social systems, we also stress the constructed, contested and negotiable qualities of origin principles in East Timor, even as they play a focal point role in managing population displacement. Equally, while we apply collective action literature on institutions as 'rules', we understand institutions broadly as patterns of behaviour that are also subject to processes of contestation, negotiation and change. We adopt both structuralist and post-structuralist perspectives of anthropology in order to explore certain conflict-related phenomena: the resilience of customary systems after population displacement, the resistance of custom to translation into law, the relationship between social order and rules of possession, and the potential for chronic property uncertainty in post-conflict property systems.

Our analysis is not structuralist or functionalist in the manner of colonial studies of 'custom', which were co-opted and translated into 'customary law', as part of strategies to legitimize the colonial state (Benda Beckmann, von F. 1984; Colson 1971; Chanock 1991; Fitzpatrick, P. 1984). Enquiries into custom from a legal or state-strengthening perspective are asymmetrical: without notions of state or law there is no need for the normative category of 'custom' (Filer 2006). Moreover, once enquiries into custom are framed by reference to law or the state, the interpretation of custom takes on reflexive qualities as interpretive actors manipulate the content of custom through reference to categories and opportunities established by the state (McDougall 2005; Hviding 1993, 1998; Berry 2009). It is important to emphasize that we do not look for, or even recommend, 'customary law' as an instrument of state-building in East Timor. We seek structural explanations for the capacity of property systems to maintain social order in periods of rapid, and at times violent, social and demographic change. In doing so we highlight pathways for strategic choice-making across multiple processes for property legitimacy and adjudication (see Shipton 1994:348; Lund 2002: Berry 1997:1228; Moore 1998:33).

## References


Alden Wiley, L. 2002. *Land Rights in Crisis*. Kabul: Afghan Research and Evaluation Unit.

Alden Wily, L. 2007. *So Who Owns the Forest? An Investigation into Forest Ownership and Customary Land Tenure in Liberia*. Brussels: Sustainable Development Institute and FERN.

Alden Wily, L. 2009. Tackling Land Tenure in the Emergency to Development Transition in Post-conflict States: From Restitution to Reform, in S. Pantuliano (ed.), *Uncharted Territory. Land, Conflict and Humanitarian Action*. Warwickshire: Practical Action Publishing.

Alston, L., Libecap, G. and Mueller, B. 1999. *Titles, Conflict, and Land Use: The Development of Property Rights and Land Reform on the Brazilian Amazon Frontier*. Ann Arbor: University of Michigan Press.

Alston, L., Harris, E. and Mueller, B. 2011. Property Rights, Land Settlement and Land Conflict on Frontiers: Evidence from Australia, Brazil and the U.S., in K. Ayotte and H.E. Smith (eds), *Research Handbook on the Economics of Property Law*. UK: Edward Elgar.

Anderson, T. and Hill, P.J. 2004. *The Not So Wild, Wild West: Property Rights on the Frontier*. Stanford, California: Stanford Economics and Finance.

Benda-Beckmann, von F. 1979. *Property in Social Continuity: Continuity and Change in the Maintenance of Property Relationships Through Time in Minangkabau*. West Sumatra.

Benda-Beckmann, von F. 1984. Law Out of Context: A Comment on the Creation of Traditional Law. *Journal of African Law*, 28(1/2), 28–33.

Berry, S. 1993. *No Condition is Permanent: The Social Dynamics of Agrarian Change in Sub-Saharan Africa*. Wisconsin: University of Wisconsin Press.

Berry, S. 1997. Tomatoes, Land and Hearsay, Property and History in Asante in the Time of Structural Adjustment. *World Development*, 25(8), 1225–41.

Berry, S. 2002. The Everyday Politics of Rent-Seeking: Land Allocation on the Outskirts of Kumase, Ghana, in K. Juul and C. Lund (eds), *Negotiating Property in Africa*. Portsmouth: Heinemann, 107.

Berry, S. 2009. Property, Authority and Citizenship: Land Claims, Politics and the Dynamics of Social Division in West Africa. *Development and Change*, 40(1), 23–45.

Blomley, N. 2003. Law, Property and the Geography of Violence: The Frontier, the Survey, and the Grid. *Annals of the Association of American Geographers*, 93(1), 121.

Bourdieu, P. 1990. *The Logic of Practice* [trans. Richard Nice]. Cambridge: Polity.

Braithwaite, J., Dinnen, S., Allen, M., Braithwaite, V. and Charlesworth, H. 2010. *Pillars and Shadows: Statebuilding as peacebuilding in Solomon Islands*, 103.

Bruce, J.W. 1998. Learning from the Comparative Experience with Agrarian Reform, in J. Barry (ed.), *Proceedings of the International Conference on Land Tenure in the Developing World.* Cape Town: University of Cape Town.

Chanock, M. 1991. Paradigms, Policies and Property: A Review of the Customary Laws of Land Tenure, in K. Mann and R. Roberts (eds), *Law in Colonial Africa.* London: James Currey, 61–84.

Clay, K. and Wright, G. 2005. Order without Law? Property Rights during the Californian Gold Rush. *Explorations in Economic History*, 42: 155.

Colson, E. 1971. The Impact of the Colonial Period on the Definition of Land Rights, in V. Turner (ed.), *Colonialism in Africa.* Cambridge: Cambridge University Press.

Cousins, B. 2002. Legislating Negotiability: Tenure Reform in Post-Apartheid South Africa, in K. Juul and C. Lund (eds), *Negotiating Property in Africa.* Portsmouth: Heinemann.

Demsetz, H. 1967. Toward a Theory of Property Rights. *American Economic Review*, 57 (May), 347–359.

El Zain, M. 1996. Tribe and Religion in the Sudan. *Review of African Political Economy*, 23: 523, 528.

Filer, C. 2006. Custom, Law and Ideology in Papua New Guinea [PDF, 132KB]. *Asia Pacific Journal of Anthropology*, 7(1), 65–84.

Fitzpatrick, D. 1997. Disputes and Pluralism in Modern Indonesian Land Law. *Yale Journal of International Law*, 22, 171.

Fitzpatrick, D. 2005. Best Practice Options for the Legal Recognition of Customary Tenure. *Development and Change*, 36(3).

Fitzpatrick, P. 1984. Traditionalism and Traditional Law. *Journal of African Law*, 28(1/2), 20–7.

Gillespie, J. 2008. Towards a Discursive Analysis of Legal Transfers into Developing East Asia. *N.Y.U. J. Int'l Law & Pol.*, 40: 657.

Gunter, J. 2007. Communal Conflict in Viqueque and the 'Charged' History of '59, in J.J. Fox and A. McWilliam (eds), Traditional Justice in Timor. *The Asia Pacific Journal of Anthropology*, Special Issue, 8(1), 27–42.

Hayek, F.A. 1979. *Law, Legislation, and Liberty*. Chicago: University of Chicago Press.

Hviding, E. 1993. Indigenous Essentialism? 'Simplifying' Customary Land Ownership in New Georgia, Solomon Islands. *Bijdragen tot de taal – land – en volkenkunde*, 149(4), 802–824.

Krier, J.E. 1992. The Tragedy of the Commons, Part Two. *Harv. J. L. & Pub. Pol'y*, 15: 325.

Krier, J.E. 2009. Evolutionary Theory and the Origin of Property Rights. *Cornell L. Rev.*, 95: 139.

Lewis, D. 2004. Challenges to Sustainable Peace: Land Disputes Following Conflict. Paper presented at a Symposium on Land Administration in Post Conflict Areas jointly organized by the Federation of International Surveyors, the Kosovo Cadastral Agency and UN-HABITAT, Geneva, Switzerland, 29–30 April.

Lund, C. 2002. Negotiating Property Institutions: On the Symbiosis of Property and Authority in Africa, in K. Juul and C. Lund (eds), *Negotiating Property in Africa*. Portsmouth: Heinemann.

Lund, C. 2009. Access and Property: A Question of Power and Authority, in T. Sikor and C. Lund (eds), *The Politics of Possession: Property, Authority and Access to Natural Resources*. Oxford: Wiley-Blackwell.

MacGinty, R. 2010. Hybrid Peace: The Interaction Between Top-Down and Bottom-Up Peace. *Security Dialogue*, 41: 391, 404–405.

McDougall, D. 2005. The Unintended Consequences of Clarification: Development, Disrupting, and the Dynamics of Community in Ranongga, Solomon Islands. *Ethnohistory*, (52)1, 81.

McDowell, A. 2002. From Commons to Claims: Property Rights in the California Gold Rush. *Yale Journal of Law and Humanities*, (14)1.

McDowell, A. 2004. Real Property, Spontaneous Order, and Norms in the Gold Mines. *Law & Social Inquiry*, 29.

Moore, S.F. 1986. *Social Facts and Fabrications – 'Customary' Law on Kilimanjaro 1880–1980*. Cambridge: Cambridge University Press.

Moore, S.F. 1998. Changing African Land Tenure: Reflections on the Incapacities of the State. *European Journal of Development Research*, 10(2), 33.

Ostrom, E. 1990. *Governing the Commons: The Evolution of Institutions for Collective Action*. Cambridge: Cambridge University Press.

Paglione, G. 2008. Individual Property Restitution: From Deng to Pinheiro – and the Challenges Ahead. *International Journal of Refugee Law*, 20: 393.

Pinheiro, S. 2002. The Return of Refugees′ or Displaced Persons' Property. U.N. Economic and Social Council Working Paper.

Pantuliano, S., Buchanan-Smith, M. and Murphy, P. 2007. The Long Road Home: Opportunities and Obstacles to the Reintegration of IDPs and Refugees Returning to Southern Sudan and the Three Areas, Report of Phase I, ODI, London.

Platteau, J.P. 2000. *Institutions, Social Norms and Economic Development*. Oxford, New York: Routledge.

Rose, C. 1985. Possession as the Origin of Property. *University of Chicago Law Review*, 52: 73.

Rose, C. 1986. The Comedy of the Commons: Custom, Commerce, and Inherently Public Property. *U. Chi. L. Rev.*, 53: 711.

Sardan, de, O. 1999. A Moral Economy of Corruption in Africa? *Journal of Modern African Studies*, 37(1), 25–52.

Smith, H.E. 2009. Community and Property: Community and Custom in Property. *Theoretical Inquiries in Law*, 10: 5.

Sugden, R. 1986. *The Economics of Rights, Cooperation, and Welfare*. Oxford: Blackwell.

Sugden, R. 1989. Spontaneous Order. *Journal of Economic Perspectives*, 3(85), 88–90.

Tay, A. 1964. The Concept of Possession in the Common Law: Foundations for a New Approach. *Melb. Univ. Law Rev.*, 4: 476–97.

Teubner, G. 1998. Legal Irritants: Good Faith in British Law or How Unifying Law Ends Up in New Divergences. *Mod. Law. Rev.*, 61(15).

Trebilcock, M. 1984. Communal Property Rights: The Papua New Guinean Experience. *U. TORONTO L.J.*, 34: 377, 382–83.

Trebilcock, M. and Veel, P. 2008. Property Rights and Development: The Contingent Case for Formalization. *University of Pennsylvania Journal of International Law*, 30: 397.

Toulmin, C. and Quan, J. 2000. Harmonizing Formal Law and Customary Land Rights in French-Speaking West Africa, in P. Delville, C. Toulmin and J, Quan (eds), *Evolving Land Rights, Policy and Tenure in Africa*. International Institute for Environment and Development.

Toulmin, C., Delville, P. and Traore, S. 2002. Introduction, in C. Toulmin, P. Delville and S. Traore (eds), *The Dynamics of Resource Tenure in West Africa*, London: International Institute for Environment and Development 1.

Vandergeest, P. and Peluso, N.L. 1995. Territorialization and State Power in Thailand. *Theory and Society*, 24: 385–426.

# Chapter 2
# The Ethnography of Austronesian Origin Principles

## Introduction

In this chapter we seek to explore the range and character of Timorese social formations as they are expressed in relationships to land. We are interested in what features they share in common and how they differ, both in terms of the cultural values brought to bear on issues of land relations and the historical factors that have influenced their contemporary expression. The discussion is directed towards the development of an analytical model of customary land tenures in East Timor, and to consider the nature of their engagement with state mechanisms for land administration. In particular we examine the extent to which cultural authority and local legitimacy accorded customary land tenures is seen to persist across East Timor in the face of long term colonial state intervention and associated external shocks that have worked to subsume, deny or otherwise transform Timorese customary arrangements. The empirical evidence for our study derives from an evaluation of comparative cultural practices across a range of socio-political contexts in East Timor combined with a series of detailed case studies exploring the changing patterns of customary attachments to land and its resources. In the process, the Timorese capacity for what Sahlin's has called the 'inventiveness of culture', is shown to form a constituent part of the adaptive response to contingent history; a culturally specific 'structure of the conjuncture' where 'externalities become indigenized through their engagement with local configurations and different from what they were' but still very much integrated as recognizably adapted cultural forms (Sahlins 1999: 412). In developing an analytical model for customary land tenures in East Timor, the comparative lessons of Austronesian ethnology, particularly across the island context of eastern Indonesia, provide an interpretive lens.

There is a high degree of indigenous language diversity across the island of Timor with upwards of 26 distinct resident ethno-linguistic communities (Hull 1998). This language complexity is further compounded by the existence of a major linguistic division between a majority Austronesian grouping of languages, and a second non-Austronesian family of languages thought to have Papuan origins (see Map 2.1).

In this context language diversity may be taken as a proxy for cultural differences that extend to multiple expressions of customary land tenures. Each language area has its own system of equally rich and culturally specific land access practices and, in this sense, all are somewhat different with their own histories, customary protocols and emplaced cultural traditions. At the same time, however, because of generations of interaction and a substantially shared linguistic and Austronesian cultural heritage they also share a range of adaptive principles and practices in common (see Fox (ed.) 1980, Fox and Sather 1996, Bellwood 1995, Reuter 2007). Even non-Austronesian-speaking Timorese groupswith extensive histories of cultural association with Austronesian societies, utilize principles of origin and common derivation to structure social hierarchy and relations with land (McWilliam 2007).

The notion of origin reflects a pervasive and shared orientation in Austronesian societies for social affiliation founded on celebratory forms of common derivation (Bellwood et al. 1995).[1] This derivation is socially constructed and 'may be variously based on the acknowledgement of a common ancestor, a common cult, a common

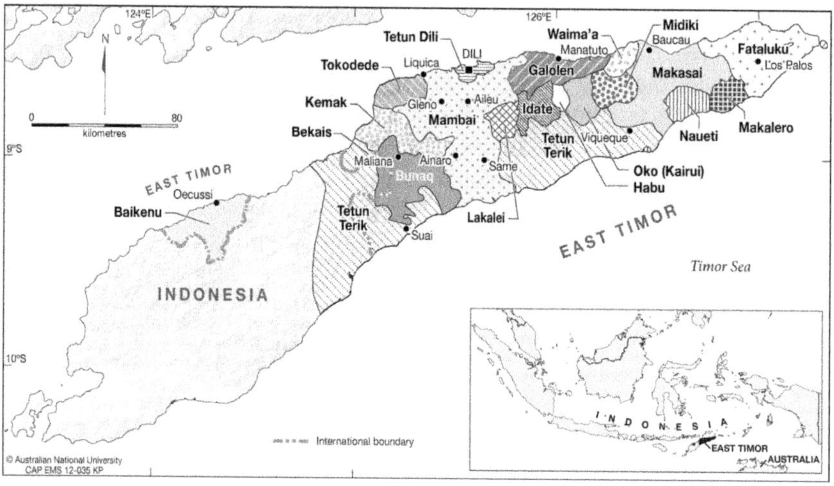


**Map 2.1 Language communities in Timor**
*Source*: ANU Cartography 2012

1 There are an estimated 1,200 spoken Austronesian languages in total of which all but 14 form part of the Malayo-Polynesian subgroup. P. Bellwood, J. Fox & D. Tryon (ANU E Press 1995). The spread of Austronesian-speaking populations out of southern China and Taiwan around 5,000BP have seen the language family disperse across the Pacific and island southeast Asia. The Austronesian language communities of Timor are associated with the Central-Malayo-Polynesian sub-grouping (although see Donahue and Denham (2009) for revised categorization).

name or set of names, a common place of derivation, and or a share in a common collection of sacred artifacts' (Fox 1996: 132). As Fox has argued, ideas of origin and related conceptions of ancestry can vary significantly between Austronesian-speaking populations, but typically the ideas by which they are expressed rely on combinations of common relational metaphors recursively applied. Paired notions such as 'trunk and tip', 'inside and outside', 'elder and younger', 'head and tail/foot', 'before and after', among others, provide the rhetorical categories for asserting and contesting relative proximity to ancestral origins (Fox and Sather 1996, McWilliam 2002, 2009). The analytical significance accorded the concept of 'origin' and origin groups have thus found significant comparative purchase in the ethnographies of Austronesian-speaking societies.

The focus on origins and the authority accorded to appeals to ancestral legitimacy extend to the cultural politics of identity, status and rank. Austronesian social formations reflect dynamic and contested arenas for assertions of political and temporal precedence, where persuasive claims of a relatively proximity to one's origins confer status and reputation. The language of precedence here is the political dimension of the discourse of origin and finds expression in contexts where relative pre-eminence is asserted or contested.

The interplay of particular metaphorical dual categories, 'symbolic operators' in Fox's terms (1989), may be deployed to assert priority or temporary precedence in particular local contexts. Recursive sequences of relational differences [for example, Elder–Younger/Elder–Younger] establish order of precedence and relational hierarchies of status difference. To be the source or point of origin of a particular ordered set of relationships is to be accorded seniority and status. The real issue is which origin point matters (McWilliam 2002: 20) and it is often on this point that such matters are contested and upon which status hierarchies are negotiated. The principles apply equally in terms of the internal social relations between sibling lines of ancestral houses, as they do between external social relationships of political alliance and subordination.

## Houses of Origin: Signaling and Symbolism

As with assertions of first possession (Rose 1985), the notion of origin requires communicative acts that have meaning to an interpretive audience. The central social and symbolic communication of origin principles takes place through the semantically rich concept of the Austronesian house, a concept based around variations on the cultural template of elevated four-posted platforms supporting stylized thatched roof structures and highly decorated timber beams, posts and cross-ties. These clan houses act as symbols and manifestations of emplaced concepts of origin and authority. Many studies have highlighted the enduring significance of traditional architectural forms and their configurations as storehouses of knowledge and cultural meanings, especially among largely nonliterate societies (for example, Fox 1993, Waterson 1990, McWilliam 2002). Houses are repositories of memory according to Fox (2003: 371) and the culturally prescriptive ordering of the elements of traditional house structures is expressed in their orientation, the articulation of structural elements, spatial demarcation and relational symbolic properties.

Austronesian 'houses of origin' are simultaneously physical constructions and social constructs, and numerous studies have highlighted the role of vernacular forms of indigenous house architecture as an important focus for the articulation of sociality and ritualized modes of social interaction (Fox 1993, McWilliam 2005, Schefold et al. 2003). Membership of one's 'house of origin', through birth or integration via marriage, confers a range of entitlements and obligations that are periodically expressed through forms of ritual celebration and house group solidarity. In this respect Austronesian 'houses' present defining structures for what Claude Levi Strauss called 'house societies', describing them as:

> a corporate body holding an estate made up of both material and immaterial wealth, which perpetuates itself through the transmission of its name, its goods and its titles down a real or imaginary line, considered legitimate as long as this continuity can express itself in the language of kinship or of affinity and, most often both. (1983: 174; see also Carsten and Hugh-Jones 1995)

In East Timor, as elsewhere in eastern Indonesia, the significance of these iconic clan houses, as symbols and emblems of the concept of a 'house of origin' (in Tetun: *uma lisan*, origin or traditional houses) is widely acknowledged in the comparative ethnographic record of social life in East Timor prior to Indonesian occupation in 1975. Anthropological studies undertaken during the 1960s and early 1970s, particularly by European and US-based researchers such as Hicks (1976), Clamagirand (1982), Lameiras Campagnolo (1975), Traube (1986), Forman (1980) and Lazarowitz (1980) and Metzner (1977) all provide a generalized ethnographic baseline for social and cultural practice in East Timor prior to the dislocations of Indonesian occupation. A consistent and comparative feature of these studies is the central importance of agnatic or clan 'houses' to social identity and emplaced affiliation.

Elizabeth Traube, for example, who worked extensively with Mambai communities in the central highlands of Ailieu during the early 1970s, made the following remarks:

> Mambai social life was shaped by multiple ideas of unity and division. Individuals belonged to male ordered units known as houses, *fada*, a term that designated both a group and its dwelling. The socially significant dwelling was not an everyday residence, but a named ancestral origin house where the group's sacred heirlooms were stored. House members or 'people of one house' were scattered for much of the year, living in what Mambai represented as the 'outer

> realm of space', but they reconvened at their origin house on ritual occasions to re-enact their mythical unity. (1995: 46)

The idea of a dispersed social collectivity that is affiliated to one or another 'sacred' house of ancestral origin, and that celebrates its unity and bound identity in ceremonial performance, appears to have been widely expressed throughout East Timor. Shephard Forman, who worked with Makassai groups in upland Baucau district, noted a similar set of practices:

> [...] although there is now (1974) a marked tendency toward residential dispersion in individuated garden homes, membership in and affinity with a named sacred lineage house (*ome bese*: big house) are clearly recognized both within and without the house and are often used to locate a person in the makassai social universe. (1980: 154)

In a similar fashion, Clamagirand identified the basic organizational unit of Ema (Kemak) society in Bobonaro as one centred on 'the core house, a unit whose membership is defined by groups of elder/younger brothers and which provides their name, status and networks of alliance' (1980: 135).

Each of these examples highlights one common mode of reckoning membership to focal houses, namely through ramifying paternal lines of origin from ancestral fathers to contemporary sons. But a contrasting and also frequently encountered cultural pattern of 'house' formation in East Timor is one where members are affiliated agnatically through their mothers and maternal origin ancestors. It is always one way or the other in Timor and the different patterns of affiliation have different implications for cultural and socio-economic practices across Timor. These issues are explored in more detail in later chapters. Here the point to be stressed is that, historically speaking, all East Timorese, whether rural cultivator, coastal fisher, commercial trader or urban bureaucrat, belong to agnatic groupings of one kind or another and owe allegiance to their ancestral house community.

Our depictions of 'house groups' in East Timor, including their distinctive and different ethno-linguistic and geographical identities, highlight the central significance of the house as a 'structure of common origin' where members are located and mapped on to a defined social field by virtue of their shared relationship to the founding ancestors of the group. They form part of what Fox has described as a 'fundamental epistemological orientation' providing for the articulation and celebration of connections that bind individuals and households within an historical and symbolic unity (1993: 160). These connections are manifest in multiple ceremonial practices and life-cycle rituals enacted in and through the 'sacred house' (*uma lulik*). They include house-specific cultural knowledge and entitlements expressed through narrative traditions of ancestral itineraries and the founding events of the house, its settlement history and the land to which it lays collective (communal) claim. They also find expression in the ownership of certain names, the rightful transmission of ancestral relics and the arcane knowledge of magical spells, hunting techniques, house-specific weaving designs and curing properties of medicinal treatments.

## Networks of Alliance

Whereas legal systems based on first possession tend to move smoothly from the fact of possession to attribution of ownership, Timorese concepts of origin have translated into social ordering without support or intervention by law. This is an important difference between social ordering principles of origin and legal principles of first possession. Over a long span of history, Timorese origin groups have attempted to maintain authority and precedence in the face of population growth, migration and war. In East Timor, the adaptive pathways for responding to demographic and political changes include the development and maintenance of marriage-based alliances among different groups.

All East Timorese origin groups are exogamous and therefore seek marriage partners with members of other house groups in order to reproduce their memberships. As the Makassai (Baucau) reported to Forman, 'Our house has been made but we must now marry out in order to prosper' (1980: 176). This process across Timor is constituted in complementary and asymmetric terms. Houses and households that 'bestow' women in marriage are conceived of as the progenitors, the life-givers, for their wife receiving affines. Through marriage and the subsequent 'gift' of children, they create the conditions for the continuity of their affine's house, their progeny. Typically this relationship is expressed in gendered terms between 'wife-givers' who are symbolically male (Tetun: *mane*) and their counterpart 'wife-takers' who are symbolically female (*feto*): hence the composite Tetun language pairing of marrying groups as *Umane-Fetosawa*; the unity of marriage expressed in complementary terms of difference. Timorese agnatic houses may be paternally or maternally ordered by principles of descent, giving rise to a diversity of marriage practices and post-marital living arrangements.

The structured asymmetry of marriage alliance creates lifelong and inter-generational exchanges of gifts and labour services between allied houses. Houses representing the interests of the husband are beholden and indebted to their wife-giving affines and are expected to provide appropriate levels of material support (especially livestock in the form of buffalo, cattle, horses and their monetary equivalent) and labour services when called upon to do so. Marriage is usually accompanied by extended periods of negotiation to settle on the terms of the bride-wealth exchange (*barlaki*) and the post-marriage living arrangements. To deny or neglect these social responsibilities carries social and spiritual (*lulik*) sanctions that may result in ostracism, misfortune or illness. Wife-giving houses reciprocate in different ways, but characteristically provide cloth, woven textiles (*tais*), pigs and life-cycle services to their sisters and daughters who have either married into other groups or accepted husbands (*mane foun*: new men) into their hamlets. The articulation and reproduction of relationships between 'houses of origin' are founded on these principles of exchange, which Shephard Forman has described for Makassai but the sentiment applies more generally, as 'the idiom of life, symbolically, ideologically and pragmatically' (1980: 153).

These conventions of marriage and alliance also highlight the understanding that, in East Timor, house groups and their constituent households operate as fundamental units of the domestic economy, where livelihoods were enmeshed in processes of production, consumption and exchange (see Gudeman and Riviera 1986, Vel 1994), and where interdependency and obligatory reciprocity create the conditions for historically emplaced and resilient communities. East Timorese 'houses of origin' and the marriage alliances that bind together house communities in negotiated and enduring relationships form the basis of residential settlements and the spatial networks that link affiliated groups across the landscape. Local politics, landed authority and claims to clan-based territorial jurisdictions also formed part of the cultural context and social practice of Timorese communities in the period immediately prior to the end of Portuguese colonialism and the intervention of Indonesian forces in 1975.

### *Adaptation to Growth and Mobility: Stranger Kings and Subsidiary Houses in Timor Leste*

Mobility and displacement have been constituent properties of Austronesian social forms over the long histories of their spatial expansion across southeast Asia and the Pacific. Migration, warfare, conquest, trade and alliance are part of the cultural make-up of mobile settler populations, and the Austronesians have proved to be highly adept and successful in these endeavours. In the process they have demonstrated a range of comparable strategies for securing access to land and of building political alliances and security. The role of marriage alliance and the mythic significance accorded the cultural motif of the 'stranger king' is an exemplary model of mobility. In this narrative type, typically there is 'an original transfer of power to an immigrant prince signified by the surrender, usually in marriage, of a native or autochthonous woman of rank' (Sahlins 1985: 87). Fox, in a variation on the same theme, has explored the complex recursive patterns expressed in the notion of 'installing the outsider inside'. The idea speaks to the historical processes of Austronesian displacement whereby influential or powerful outsiders become political leaders—holders of secular authority—through distinctive cultural processes of incorporation (Fox 1995). At a more mundane level, the narrative is also a leitmotif for the 'path' of marriage whereby strangers become friends and familiars and are accorded entitlements in the lands of their affines.

Not all migrants to origin group areas are incorporated as 'stranger kings' in Timorese customary hierarchy. Many obtain access to land through marriage alliances or ritualized agreements known as *juramento* (oaths), without taking up privileged positions in spiritual or political life. Historically, new arrivals to origin group domains have been granted land on which to settle and farm by the 'lord of the land' (*rai na'in*) by means of various 'traditional' contracts, including *juramento* or marriage, aimed at incorporating the migrants into local social and political structures. As discussed below, the *rai na'in* is most proximate to the mythical source of origin, and the embodiment of ritual authority relating to ancestral land. Typically, origin group lineages provide wives to in-migrants and thereby establish a 'wife-giver/wife-taker' relation between the respective houses. This process reproduces asymmetric patterns of origin and precedence, with latecomer lineages often referred to either as sisters and children, where their house has long-standing marriage relations, or as friends and acquaintances where they are more distantly related. As noted, wife-giver/wife-taker relationships provide the basis for enduring patterns of exchange and reciprocity between traditional groups, and have been cited as a prime resource of resilience and resistance to the Indonesian occupation (McWilliam 2005).

From the perspective of in-marrying men, the opportunities of marriage alliance offered access to their wife's group's land resources while still retaining entitlements to the lands of their own source house (*uma lisan*). While there may be much variation in particular cases, principally associated with the terms of agreement over bride-wealth, historically in Timor the process of settling lands has always been one where immigrant men marry the daughters of resident clans or house groups and, through the ensuing alliance, obtain rights in land in return for their labour and political support as co-residents. In this way Timorese social organization has been predicated on mobility and a cultural preparedness to relocate residence and adjust group relationships in the face of changing circumstances. Making place and making room for newcomers in culturally approved ways has been the long-term project of East Timorese societies, and their capacity to adjust to the exigencies and challenges of social life has contributed to their collective resilience. Needless to say, these cultural features remain significant in the contemporary context of conflict-caused mass population movements.

While no doubt it serves other social functions, including the custom of marrying 'out' among exogamous groups in order to forge political alliances, the institutional technique of 'bringing the outsider in' through marriage exchange may be viewed as an adaptive mechanism to reduce the costs of reaching land access agreements among different kinship-based groups. In any negotiations over access to land, there are difficult decisions involved in negotiating the amount, value and location of the land to be allocated. These issues may prevent agreement altogether, in which case conflict over land is a more likely result. Alternatively, inter-group agreement may be reached on basic questions of access, but key questions of heritability and authority are left uncertain or imprecise because prevailing circumstances do not necessarily require crystallized forms of contract or entitlement. In either case, the value of an established and broadly understood mechanism for reaching agreement is that it provides a facilitative template for decision making on central issues that require agreement. The marriage alliance mechanism also provides pathways for repeat multifaceted interactions, through enduring wife-give/wife-taker relationships of reciprocity and inter-marriage, and thereby reinforces conditions favourable to cooperative forms of collective action relating to resource governance.

We conclude that two key principles of traditional Timorese societies – the concept of origin and the technique of incorporating in-migrants – have acted as key sources of adaptive capacity and property ordering resilience in historical circumstances of migration, political change and inter-group warfare. In general terms, where a migratory group approaches land claimed by another, and that land claim is identifiable by the presence of venerated ancestral heirlooms, or symbolic structures including sacred houses, there is a greater likelihood of bargaining rather than conflict where there is an a priori acceptance of the principle of origin, and greater likelihood of agreement where there is a template for negotiation through marriage alliances. While concepts of origin and incorporation have not prevented inter-group warfare, particularly over boundaries to group land, they have acted over a long period of time in East Timor as institutional techniques to promote cooperation and avoid conflict among kin-based groups. It is true that first possession principles are socially constructed, and provide an adaptive response to in-migration and demographic changes. Nevertheless, they also appear to be resistant to ad hoc or opportunistic acts of appropriation, reinvention or reinterpretation of insider and outsider status, precisely because of their key role in ordering social relations in circumstances of population mobility.

Much of the recent literature on customary property relations in sub-Saharan Africa has highlighted underlying characteristics of negotiability and indeterminacy (for example, Berry 1993, 1997, Bourdieu 1990, de Sardan 1999, Lund 2002, Moore 1986, 1998). While notions of 'custom' remain prominent in postcolonial discourse, custom itself is prone to reinvention and indeterminacy as resource claimants manipulate customary references across multiple forums for property legitimation and authority (Berry 1993:104). Land-related issues of group identity and status can also be relatively porous and subject to opportunistic acts of manipulation and reinterpretation (Juul 2002). In East Timor, by way of contrast, origin principles have been relatively resistant to situational processes of reinvention, ambiguity and contestation, and have continued to provide clear delineations of group identity and status. We suggest that the resilience of custom in East Timor derives from the inherent ordering capacity of origin principles themselves (Fitzpatrick and Barnes 2010: 207). In other words, while there are qualities of negotiability and indeterminacy in the pluralist property arrangements of East Timor, the signaling and focal point functions of origin principles – symbolized by sacred houses (*uma lulik*) and reproduced through ritual and recursive linguistic techniques – have had a powerful influence on decisions by property claimants to engage in acts of post-displacement cooperation rather than conflict. We explore this explanation for successful collective action in conflict-affected East Timor further in Chapter 3.

## Origins, Precedence and Landed Authority

The cultural politics of origins, of being senior, earlier, older, greater or closer to the centre, combined with the significance of origin structures expressed in the material form of traditional Austronesian houses, provide a starting point for exploring the regional diversity of customary land management practices in East Timor. Ideas of origin extend to narrative inscriptions of attachment to particular places and landscapes. The spatial trajectory of the agnatic house through time creates emplaced social identities and sources of locally legitimate landed authority over defined jurisdictions, a status typically reinforced and articulated through ritual performance. Land is integral to life in Austronesian contexts and provides the strategic basis for economic subsistence as well as political authority for socio-territorial units (Reuter 2007). For the majority of Timorese farmer households, land relationships both within and between groups are informed and sustained through these patterns of social, symbolic and economic association. The extent to which they remain as relevant to contemporary interests as they have in the past is one of the empirical questions addressed in our study.

The intricate networks of affiliation and alliance within and between Timorese houses of origin represent the historical and continuing basis for the reproduction of Timorese society. As forms of historical narrative that serve to legitimate and confirm the relative standing and entitlements of variously allied houses, patterns of marriage alliance have also created distinctive forms of indigenous political leadership and differential social ranking between houses. The relative standing of house groups is typically founded in the mythic narratives of origin that derive from the earliest settlements of the political community and form the sometimes contested grounds upon which assertions of contemporary authority rest. As Bruner has observed, narratives are not only structures of meaning but structures of power (1986: 152), and in this respect the mythic 'discourse of origins' has served as a foundation for claims to authority in East Timor and inherited land within defined or customary jurisdictions. These intricate interactions between property rights and claims of original socio-political authority are central to understanding the avoidance, emergence and resolution or otherwise of land conflicts in war-torn East Timor.

According to the ethnographers of pre-1975 East Timor, all ethno-linguistic communities in East Timor recognized local forms of indigenous authority based on inherited entitlements to leadership (Fox 1980). Renard-Clamagirand concluded of Ema (Kemak) society in highland Bobonaro that: '[A]t the collective level, social organization is based on a hierarchy of houses built around the houses of chiefs' (1982: 293). Our case studies provide examples of Timor's hereditary authority structures as they relate to customary land. 'Lord of the land' (*rai na'in*) concepts, in particular, are strikingly prevalent in the Austronesian- and non-Austronesian-speaking societies of East Timor. The authority of the 'lord of the land' is typically vested in the senior lineages (or 'source houses') of the origin group. Their direct descent from mythical ancestor-settlers provides them with spiritual and ritual authority relating to land. This authority is sustained by their cultural knowledge of the history of founding ancestors, the establishment of sacred houses, and land allocations and alliances involving subsequent settler and neighbouring groups. Designated elders of the senior lineage often embody the authority of the lord of the land. These elders claim privileged information on the rituals, invocations and offerings required to mediate access to land and natural resources through relations with the guardian spirits of land and natural resources. Their proximity to the ancestors makes them privileged intermediaries between the 'light and open' world of the living, and the 'dark and hidden' world of the spirits. They have the authority to pronounce what is sacred or forbidden (*lulik*) and what is permitted, particularly but not exclusively in terms of resource use. Many of these ritual prohibitions – known in the Tetun lingua franca as *tara bandu* – have environmental significance as they concern use of water sources, old-growth forests and other areas requiring sustainable resource management.

There are diarchic distinctions between ritual and political authority in the customary structures of East Timor (McWilliam 2011, Fox 1995). While ritual and political authority can be shared, and at times contested, among founding houses that trace direct descent to a mythical ancestor, there are also distributions of political authority to powerful in-migrant or allied lineages that involve the mythology of the 'stranger king'. Stranger king myths speak to an 'original transfer of power to an immigrant prince signified by the surrender, usually in marriage, of a native or autochthonous woman of rank' (Sahlins 1985: 87). In other words the immigrant man marries into a senior house of origin via an autochthonous woman of rank. The lineage of the stranger king had obligations to 'defend the borders' of the customary domain, which over time included carriage of relations with external actors such as the colonial state. This process is clearly seen in historical examples of mestizo Portuguese (Topass or so-called Black Portuguese) figures in Timor during the eighteenth century, marrying into 'ruling households' of Timorese domains and becoming rulers themselves through the process. It may also involve 'trickster mythologies' where the 'rightful leadership' of a founding house is said to have been duped by the trickery of a usurping newcomer.

For centuries, indigenous authority in Timorese customary systems was influenced and shaped to varying degrees by the long and uneven engagement of Portuguese colonial interests. Initially the Portuguese referred to the various executive figures or chiefs that they encountered – commonly those with political authority in a customary domain – as 'kings' (*rei*) or 'rulers' (*regulo*), and to the territories perceived to be under their jurisdiction as 'kingdoms' or *reino*. The latter term has entered into and remains common in indigenous vernaculars. The term *rei* was later partially replaced with the Tetun title *liurai* – literally, 'he who crosses over the land'. But over many years the Portuguese, for their own political purposes, were active in supporting certain favoured *liurai* and opposing others. This in turn gave rise to a range of complex inter-generational political rivalries between local clan leaders over legitimacy and rightful sources of political authority. In some places there is considerable complexity and confusion at times over who is and who is not, the rightful *liurai*. As a general proposition, there tends not to be the same level of uncertainty when it comes to ritual leaders – the *rai na'in / lia na'in*– because their position is ascertainable by reference to long-standing narratives of origin, and for that reason are less amenable to co-option or transfer.

Across customary areas of East Timor, generational growth in group numbers or territory and political changes in house authority have also created a substantial degree of transition and specialization in land functions among the house-based lineages of an origin group. In the course of our fieldwork, a number of origin group elders claimed that in the past their ancestors held both ritual and jural power over the territory and people of their domain, but that at some stage in their history their forefathers began to 'retreat into darkness', and delegated specific tasks to members of other house-based groups. Ostensibly, the elders state that this retreat was a conscious decision to keep the secrets of their land from 'outsiders', in particular the colonial authorities (and the Catholic Church). However, they also acknowledge that the delegation of tasks to other groups was also a means of appeasing subsidiary houses and in-migrant groups that represented a potential threat to their authority. In the event, most rural districts of East Timor have highly nested structures of customary authority, where overall ritual authority is claimed by a senior 'lord of the land' lineage (*rai na'in*), while specific – and at times contestable – aspects of executive political authority, including issues of land access, allocation, use and succession, are devolved to constituent or allied lineages of the origin kin group. This devolution of land-related authority to constituent or influential allied lineages indicates the adaptive capacity of origin groups to respond to changed demographic or political circumstances, while also highlighting the increased complexity and contextualization of customary land arrangements as origin principles have moved through space and time.

To summarize the nested customary property arrangements of East Timor: there is a default conception of a common landed inheritance among customary groups, extending not only to areas of group control but to areas of ancestral activity, and manifesting in the overarching ritual authority of senior male lineage representatives of the group. Within each group, there are areas of common property authority structured around the constituent lineages of the group, which include lineage rights to allocate land through agreements with in-marrying allies. The landed authority of a lineage may default to the broader 'origin' group where there is a long-term loss of access and control. Finally, there are household rights of use, exclusion and inheritance – but not alienation – for areas of residence and cultivation (either permanent or swidden). While these household rights correlate with acts of possession and input of labor, their strength and scope turns on the status of the householder lineage within the group, including its relative proximity to the source of group origin. This nested property system has evolved and survived over a long period of time, in response to resource and environment-specific conditions at multiple levels of scale. The collectivity of the group provides economies of scale in terms of defence; the devolution of authority to lineages reflects attempts to maintain collective action notwithstanding generational increases in group numbers; and the control rights of households provide incentives for available forms of investment in housing and agriculture.

The different structures and scales of resource governance in East Timor create incentives for customary group members to attempt to enhance entitlements to land.[2] For example, households pursue entitlements through construction of concrete block housing, claims to land left fallow, and acts of inter-generational transfer. Lineage representatives make claims to precedence within the group through constructions of origin, the re-shaping of mythical narratives, or leadership of rituals. In the history of East Timor, there have been dynamic social ordering equilibria within groups where multiple scale incentives within a group to confirm entitlements through acts of violence, or acts conducive to violence, have been balanced by shared desires to avoid the social costs of resource conflict and shared experiences of the focal point principle of origin. A key argument of this work is that these social ordering equilibria are threatened by a legal rule of possession that provides incentives for individuals to claim the benefits of alienable ownership, without incurring the costs of ensuing degradations in local capacity to undertake collective action, particularly in terms of managing in-migration and conflict-caused population displacement.

The foregoing perspectives on social relations and land connection highlight a defining principle within East Timorese customary communities, namely, that attachments to land are deeply embedded within dynamic relationships of social obligation and reciprocity. Claims to resources are therefore simultaneously assertions and statements about particular kinds of emplaced social relationships. The idiom of reciprocity here encompasses both the living world of agnates and familial allies as well as the less immediate but no less significant realm of ancestors and the spirit world (*lulik*) that has traditionally been thought to animate and influence events in the natural environment (McWilliam 2007, Forbes 1989). The continuing efficacy of indigenous religious beliefs and practices, notwithstanding the prevalence and importance of Catholicism across East Timor, has been a conservative influence on the perpetuation of customary land relationships. Transgressions or acts of omission in relation to ancestral lands are widely thought to place the perpetrator and their immediate family under threat of sanction or

2 The literature identifies incentives for group members to appropriate benefits and shift burdens in both commons and semi-commons system (Smith 2000; Fennell 2007: 1448–52). In the commons, incentives for benefit appropriation may manifest in unsustainable rates of resource use – the 'tragedy of the commons' – in circumstances of resource scarcity and 'free-riding' on second party attempts to enforce rules of resource governance (Smith 2000: 132; 136–7). In a semi-commons, involving household rights to cultivation and group rights to grazing, incentives for benefit appropriation or burden sharing arise where holders of rights to farming land encourage grazing livestock to trample on the farm land of others, or deposit disproportionate amounts of manure on their land (Smith 2000: 138–44). These types of incentives do not have significant social cost implications in Lautem, where land is relatively abundant and grazing involves small numbers of pigs and chicken, at the household level, rather than group grazing of livestock herds.

retribution from ancestral or spirit agency. In our case studies, a key empirical question is whether this highly contextualized interaction between origin group structures and relations with land remains true notwithstanding the effects of military occupation and widespread population displacement (McWilliam 2008).

## The Constrained Resilience of Customary Property Relations in East Timor

While our case studies highlight the resilience of customary property relations, notwithstanding the effects of the Indonesian military occupation, we do not suggest that the adaptive capacity of ancestral origin principles in East Timor is absolute or unconstrained. All our fieldwork sites provide indications that traditional mechanisms for incorporating in-migrants have degraded or were suppressed in parallel with the emergence of state-affiliated village government structures. While in-marrying remains a resilient adaptive technique, with some relocated groups commencing marriage relations with origin groups, there remains a great deal of social tension over the long-term status and rights of relocated groups from both Portuguese and Indonesian times. This tension often has roots in Portuguese policies of agricultural settlement, and shifting political alliances during the Portuguese and Japanese periods. The trend has been exacerbated by the sheer scale of relocation under the Indonesian administration and the active processes of erasure that marginalized customary authorities. It is now influenced by the still developing state of East Timor, with some relocated groups in particular seeking alternative sources of property rights legitimacy and enforcement to those offered by customary principles of origin. These alternative sources of property legitimacy include claims based on actual possession rather than allocation pursuant to origin group authority. In the following section we provide an introduction to these issues of possessory claims, and their relationship with plural systems of public authority, by reference to the war-torn history of East Timor itself.

### *Village Government and Agricultural Settlement: The Effects of Portuguese Rule*

It is sometimes said that Portuguese rule on the island of Timor, following the appointment of the first colonial governor in 1701, did not encroach significantly on traditional forms of village life (Gunn 1999: 4). This may have been true, at least until the late 1800s, as, in common with many colonial regimes, the Portuguese administration was largely interested in trade and revenue. Its settlements were on the coast, and the hinterland served as a site for extraction of taxes and trade commodities. In any case, for much of the pre-twentieth-century colonial rule, the Portuguese capacity to assert and control internal political and economic affairs was chronically weak and allowed considerable leeway for local Timorese authorities to act independently (Pelissier 1996). In these circumstances, the Portuguese attempted a de facto system of indirect rule through indigenous authorities in the countryside (Gunn 1996: 192), which involved engagement as favoured allies or rebellious enemies at different times over the long period of colonial association.

In the late 1800s – again in common with most colonies – Portuguese economic policy shifted its focus from tax and trade to cash-crop agriculture and an export-oriented plantation sector. This change from basic trade to systematic exploitation required an extension of political control, particularly into the mountainous interior (Taylor 1999: 10–11). It was now necessary to obtain labour and land for a plantation sector, and to extract an agricultural surplus from East Timor's hitherto largely subsistence farmers. As a result, the Portuguese forcibly introduced coffee plantations into Ermera district, and demanded a head tax (*capitação*) for all Timorese males aged between 18 and 60. Coffee in the central highlands, along with coconut, sisal and timber plantations in favourable areas were also widely promoted with varying degrees of success. There was circularity to the Portuguese strategy that required East Timorese families to produce an agricultural surplus for sale in order to raise money to pay for its imposts.

In parallel with its new economic policies, the Portuguese administration renewed its military efforts to assert control over the chronically rebellious Timorese mountainous interior (see Pelissier 1996). Punitive expeditions into the hinterland by Portuguese troops, in combination with co-opted local militias (*moradore*s), created periodic havoc with destruction of settlements and the enslavement of war captives (Freycinet (1827) 1986). Conversely, as the Portuguese extended its military control across all districts, eventually including Lautem in the East, there was a marked reduction in endemic forms of retaliatory warfare among Timorese groups (Forbes 1884). As we shall discuss further in Chapter 7, with reference to Lautem, these processes of war and pacification contributed to long-term changes in Timorese settlement patterns, particularly in terms of movements from fortified hilltops to dispersed villages, and then to more concentrated settlements under overall Portuguese control.

From the early twentieth century, and gathering momentum after the Second World War, the Portuguese sought to restrict shifting cultivation and clear new areas, particularly in the fertile lowlands of the southern coast, for rice fields and other forms of intensive cultivation. These activities contributed to the gradual but sustained historical trend from shifting and scattered mobile populations to more closely settled and concentrated residential communities adjacent to roads. Much of this containment and resettlement was induced by the Portuguese, particularly following the reinstatement of the Portuguese colonial government after 1945, in order to facilitate taxation, security and agricultural development projects. At the same time, Portuguese administrative mechanisms began to overlay and at times suppress customary systems of land allocation and authority with new forms of administrative legibility, particularly under the policy of concentrating the population into larger, visible and more sedentary settlements. The concepts of hamlets (*povocão*) and villages (*suco*), in particular, were established under charter from the Portuguese administration and the appointed heads of these administrative units were then expected to ensure payment of the head tax (*finta*), and to organize labour for Portuguese agricultural development projects.

In lowland areas cleared under Portuguese supervision, especially in areas like Manatuto, Viqueque and Suai, the extent of origin group authority had not necessarily been tested to that point, as historically much of the lowlands was a mixture of open grasslands and lightly forested savanna, and used at most for hunting parties or traversing to access settlements further afield. In the event, access to cleared land was not necessarily determined by customary hierarchy or alliances with origin groups, but by village heads acting under authority from the Portuguese administration. In newly cultivated areas, a common symbol of property rights was a hoe or other agricultural instrument issued by the Portuguese. The Portuguese did not issue formal documents of title to those who had cleared land but there was a gradual acceptance among participants and members of the settler communities that the act of clearing and working the land bestowed nascent forms of transferable possessory rights that accrued to the cultivator and their rightful heirs. From the settlers' point of view the land did not form part of the ancestral body of communal land held collectively by members of the constituent lineage or clan.

While the intrusion of colonial structures of land authority and legitimacy was more marked in districts such as Manatuto, which had long been a faithful ally of the Portuguese colonial regime, and Ainaro, where there was a large Portuguese military post, even areas such as Lautem or Manufahi, with a history of armed resistance against the Portuguese, experienced sustained movements of settlement and associated increases in the land-related authority of village heads. The result was an emerging plurality of authority over land as village heads (*chefe do suco*) and other officials favoured by the Portuguese administration were appointed without reference in some cases to senior resident origin group lineages. Thus a new dynamic emerged in the governance of rural land in East Timor, namely the relationship between origin group elders and village administration heads. As we have seen, there were diarchic divisions in ritual and political authority among the customary groups of East Timor, and varying degrees of devolution of authority to constituent lineages. The introduction of village government structures created further potential for pluralist forms of local authority, which other studies of colonial systems have shown to be of great significance in the development of postcolonial property relations.

All colonial systems of indirect rule by definition were marked by a plurality of local authority, as designated chiefs or representatives were fixed with forms of administrative authority under the colonial state (Colson 1971). The operations of the Dutch East Indies Company and, after 1800, of the Dutch colonial government in Indonesia followed very similar patterns of conduct in their relations with the myriad island societies they encountered across the Indonesian archipelago (Fitzpatrick 1997). This authority was sometimes clothed in notions of custom or indigenous tradition, but was always a creature of colonial convenience and rarely a reflection of pre-colonial arrangements (Chanock 1991). Those favoured under colonial systems used their power to further their own interests, particularly through the allocation or transfer of rights to land. At the same time, other local actors drew on claims of customary legitimacy to reassert rights and authority relating to land in contexts of political change and anti-colonial activity (Berry 1993). As Lund (for example, 2002, 2008: 2–3) has argued, the result in many colonial and postcolonial systems has been a close relationship between property and authority, with claims based on possessory entitlements to land interacting with competition for political authority over land.

In East Timor, there is no doubt that the Portuguese used the grant of village government authority as another instrument of divide and rule, to dilute and complicate resistant forms of customary authority. This approach extended to the appointment of village officials from subsidiary lineages that may have been in political competition with a senior group. At times it extended to recognition of loyal customary elders, in preference to a 'disloyal' group that may have claimed customary precedence. Yet there were processes of accommodation and co-option as colonial influences were endogenized in local ordering arrangements. For example, in our fieldwork areas we identified village heads traditionally drawn from an in-migrant lineage, consistent with their designated authority as gatekeepers to the customary domain. In other cases, hamlet heads were the sons of elders in the senior origin group lineage. The elders confined themselves to the ritual and spiritual sphere, while the designated son engaged in administrative and political activity. In these last cases, the long-standing Timorese diarchic distinction between ritual and political authority adapted to the development of village government structures under the Portuguese. On the basis of our case studies, we suggest as a working hypothesis that there has been a greater degree of accommodation and co-option of village government structures into customary systems of origin and precedence than in a number of other colonial contexts, including for example those of Ghana (Lund 2008) and Indonesia (von Benda-Beckmann 1979, Warren 1993: 239–66).

While we highlight patterns of cooperation among village government officials and customary elders in our case studies, an important implication of colonial village government policy was that the designation of villages and hamlets as administrative structures, rarely corresponded to jurisdictions of particular origin groups. Rego, an East Timorese anthropologist and administrator during late Portuguese times, comments that many villages were classified as part of an acknowledged customary domain; others were independent of an acknowledged customary domain; while others again were classified as villages when they should have been classified as a customary domain (Rego 1968 as translated by Sherlock 1983: 3–4). Moreover, the definition of a village (*suco*) was based around a related group of people rather than on territoriality, a feature of colonial rule that may have been related to the imposition of the much resented head tax. An important result of this approach has been that those who were relocated in Portuguese and later during Indonesian times have usually retained affiliation with their source villages, notwithstanding lengthy periods of residence in another area. We conclude that the classificatory scheme of Portuguese village administration did not undermine the enduring attachments that

Timorese people retain with family and communities of origin, but rather worked to disrupt the capacity of origin groups to manage in-migration through traditional mechanisms of incorporation such as marriage alliance.

## Displacement, Resettlement and Repression: The Effects of Indonesian Rule

Gunn (1996: 236) estimates that the short period of the Japanese occupation of Timor during the Second World War led to the deaths of between 40,000 to 70,000 East Timorese out of a total pre-war population of around 450,000. A harsh system of food collection and corvée labour was implemented, as well as a low-level guerilla resistance campaign, leading inevitably to famine for a population heavily reliant on seasonal rain-fed agriculture for subsistence (Gunn 1999: 236; see also Dunn 1996). Severe as these consequences were, the disruptive impacts of the Japanese rule pale in relation to the effects of the Indonesian military occupation (1975 to 1999). Indonesian rule had a major impact on the capacity of Timorese communities to maintain customary relationships to land. The extent of the disruption varied across the island but the impacts were everywhere significant and continue to inform issues of land attachment and entitlement to the present day. Something of the scope and effects of the Indonesian intervention is outlined in the following discussion.

In 1975, after the Carnation Revolution and the fall of the dictator Salazar, Portugal abruptly withdrew from all its colonies. The new political administration in Portugal did not implement mechanisms for orderly decolonization. On 28 November 1975, in the ensuing political vacuum, a local political party – Fretilin (Frente Revolucionária de Timor Leste) – issued a declaration of independence for East Timor. In response, a rival party – UDT (Uniao Democratica Timorense) – issued a statement on behalf of a group describing itself the 'Anti-Communist Movement', and calling for intervention by the Indonesian government and integration of East Timor into Indonesia (Gusmão 2000: 17). On 7 December 1975 Indonesian armed forces invaded East Timor, leading to the displacement of over 300,000 East Timorese in the months after the invasion (Fitzpatrick 2002: 5). Some of the displaced fled the territory to become long-term political refugees and exiles.

During the initial phase of the military operation in 1975–76, Indonesian forces asserted control over most of the townships and main arterial road networks. But the Fretilin resistance, well-equipped with new European weaponry abandoned by the Portuguese military, provided a level of resistance that reportedly had not been expected by Indonesian military planners. By the end of 1976 approximately 80 per cent of East Timor still remained outside the control of Indonesian forces. In September 1977, the Indonesian military embarked on a new offensive, which included the destruction of food crops and forced resettlement of villagers into 'strategic camps' (Fitzpatrick 2002: 51). According to Indonesian military figures cited by Fitzpatrick (2002: 135), 372,921 people, as many as one-half of the population, were refugees in these temporary settlements by December 1978. Initially 150 camps, known as 'settlement areas' (*daerah pemukiman*), were established across the territory with an average camp population of 2,000 people. Budiardjo and Liem (1984: 81) cite the example of Baucau, where, of the estimated 74,000 resident population of the district, fully 61,000 people were forced to live in cramped conditions around the town of Baucau proper. They also cite a contemporary report of the situation, which noted that (1984: 76): '[V]illages (*povoção*) as we knew them before the Indonesian invasion simply don't exist anymore. All village life has stopped. Everyone has been brought together in the settlements around the *postos* (sub-district centres).'

In these early years of Indonesian occupation the camps were sites of great crowding, suffering and deprivation. Residents were forbidden from travelling outside the tightly controlled zones. Suspected collaborators were gaoled or eliminated. Agriculture was severely disrupted, and camp residents were forced to cultivate the rocky and often infertile soils in the immediate area. Under these conditions starvation and sickness became widespread (Budiardjo and Liem 1984: 30–31). In the event, and largely as a result of the Indonesian relocation programme, East Timor's Truth and Reconciliation Commission estimates that at least 84,200, and as many as 183,000, East Timorese died from conflict-related hunger and illness between 1974 and 1999, with most deaths likely to have resulted from the famine in the late 1970s and early 1980s (CAVR 2005: 44). As in the period of Japanese occupation, reliance on seasonal agriculture created vulnerability to famine as a result of lost access to arable land.

Relocations were organized or induced by the Indonesian military, at times in consultation with compliant local hamlet and village heads. Customary elders were often not consulted and, in a chaotic environment of military reprisals and conflict, had little or no opportunity to prevent relocated groups settling on their ancestral lands. In the independent East Timor, many of these groups have remained in their places of displacement because they have established homes and cultivated fields, with greater access to transport, schools and sources of cash-based employment. Some households have commenced processes of incorporation or affiliation with origin houses through marriage alliances and formalized agreements (*aforamento*). There are cases where the children of relocated groups have inherited residential and cultivated land without resistance from customary elders, particularly in areas where there are large amounts of available land. Nevertheless, in many areas there is considerable tension between origin houses and resettled groups, even though there may be a degree of inter-marriage, with some relocated groups now denied rights to inherit land, to cut trees for fuel, or to clear further land for housing or cultivation (Myat Thu 2008). We note a number of examples of these tensions in the following chapters.

Over time the complex military logistics of maintaining the relocation camps, combined with an evident weakening of armed resistance (Budiarjo and Liem 1984), led to a gradual lessening of Indonesian restrictions on settlement and population movements. Communities regarded as reliable and supportive of the new national regime were permitted to return to their former settlement areas, or to relocate to new areas adjacent to sealed roads and communication links. Other communities were encouraged to relocate from their mountain settlements and take up more permanent opportunities for irrigated rice cultivation on newly developed project sites and areas of transmigration. Still others remained under suspicion and tight security arrangements for many years, especially in regions known to harbour armed resistance fighters. For those communities there was continuing surveillance and restrictions on movement and congregation. The militarization of Timorese society continued throughout the Indonesian occupation and, while over time substantial Indonesia government investment in infrastructure and social services ameliorated some of the excesses of the regime, it was only with the eventual withdrawal of Indonesian forces in late 1999 that a reconsideration of settlement choices could be freely made.

### *Further Displacement and Return: The Events of 1999*

In 1999 the Indonesian government agreed, over the objections of its military command, to hold a popular referendum on independence for East Timor. At the time of the UN-organized vote in August 1999, Indonesian statistics estimated the population of East Timor to be almost 900,000. When a resounding majority of Timorese voted against continuing autonomy within the Indonesian state, they declared their collective desire for full independence. What followed was a planned and destructive withdrawal of Indonesian military forces from the territory, and a period of violence and turmoil instigated by military-backed militia groups, determined to exact a costly price for rejecting Indonesian sovereignty. Over 400,000 people were internally displaced within East Timor itself, and a further 300,000 fled or were forcibly transported across the border to West Timor as a direct result of the chaos that followed the referendum (Fitzpatrick 2002: 5–6). On 25 October 1999 the United Nations Security Council passed Resolution No 1272, establishing the United Nations Transitional Authority in East Timor (UNTAET). Article 1 vested all legislative and executive authority with respect to East Timor, including the administration of justice, in the hands of UNTAET. With the restoration of authority under UNTAET, conditions were established for settlements to choose whether to return or to stay in their locations.

It is difficult to estimate the numbers of households that have sought to re-establish former homeland settlements. Just as there is no comprehensive documentation of the extent and patterns of population displacement in East Timor brought about by Indonesian rule, there are similarly no reliable surveys on the degree to which Timorese have set about re-establishing old settlements and rebuilding their connections to ancestral lands (see McWilliam 2005). Some preliminary mapping of displaced communities has been undertaken in collaboration with staff of the National Directorate of Land and Property but a full accounting of the impact of Indonesian occupation on settlement patterns remains to be undertaken.

Examples, however, can be found in all districts of East Timor and our surveys indicate a number of characteristic displacement patterns. As a general comment it is evident that, in the immediate years following the Indonesian 1975 invasion, almost every East Timorese suffered some form of residential displacement and forced relocation. For many thousands of households, however (precise numbers are not available), these coercive relocations, albeit traumatic, were temporary in nature. Over the ensuing years many of these households were allowed to return to their homeland areas and re-establish their communities. In a similar fashion, another large group of households were either internally displaced within home villages (*suco*) or perhaps sub-districts (*posto*), or forced into linear settlements lining the main roads or in settlement areas close to the sub-district centres. Both these cases of displacement are of a different order to the more dramatic wholesale removals of settlements to entirely different districts or from highland areas to lowlands, either as punishment for supporting resistance or as part of the broader state objectives of bringing populations into closer proximity for surveillance and the provision of cost-effective services such as health clinics, schooling and effective administration. In short, coercive displacement in East Timor under different colonial regimes was never a unitary concept nor experienced as such. As a result the impact and effects on associated connections to land among cultural communities are also highly variable, and remain an empirical question for comparative study.

Among households who remain living in relocation settlements in the post-occupation era, many express ambivalence about their situation and hold out the prospects of return, but remain unable or unwilling to act on the decision. In some cases a generation or more of settlement along the main road, or within the confines of administrative centres, makes it difficult to relinquish established investments and government services for more distant homelands lacking most amenities. Patterns of dual settlement arrangements provide one partial solution where families spend seasonal periods of time in both areas, often returning to former settlement sites to cultivate garden lands and nurture tree crops in areas where their own customary land tenures are maintained while retaining access rights to land in their resettlement areas. Gravesites of ancestors and the still powerful sites of sacrificial veneration in homeland areas continue to connect people to ancestral traces of past sociality (Bovensiepen 2009). In these and other ways, the legacy of politically motivated displacement continues to inform settlement choices and residential patterns across Timor Leste. One of the effects is a much more pronounced orientation to translocality and more expansive residential choices among Timorese communities that marks a reversal of the historical processes of population concentration and movement restriction that has accompanied colonialism in its different guises (Myat Thu 2012).

One of the enduring aspects of Indonesian occupation however, is the widespread experience among East Timorese communities of coming to terms with displacement and its lingering effects. Histories of displacement, to adapt an observation by Sahlins (1985: vii), are felt differently by different groups according to their own meaningful cultural schemes. These variable effects are dependent on the circumstances of displacement itself, the degree of disruption, the distance from homelands and the conditions under which displaced people accommodate to their new circumstances. For heuristic purposes displacement may be thought of as a continuum; from local relocations of settlement – which may still allow for regular access to lands of customary entitlement – to long-distance dislocations of exile, diaspora and practical severance of access to homelands. Both situations work to disempower and constrain choice, and both situations damage the social fabric and devalue the habitus of emplaced sociality (Bourdieu 1990). Nevertheless the felt effects and the capacity to assert continuing entitlement to lands are ones of degree; the more radical the displacement the more difficult it may be to retain active demonstrations of connection and landed authority over ancestral lands. The issue of displacement, which by definition here is one driven via forms of state-backed coercion, rather than inducements or spontaneously motivated relocation, provides another illustrative theme informing the analytical perspectives in this study.

A further complication of coercive displacement policies has been the creation, often inadvertently, of conflicts over land entitlements and rights of access between relocated households and their host communities. Although communities were often resigned to accepting guest settlers when directed to do so by government authorities, their forbearance has not extended into the post-occupation era. One commonly expressed sentiment is that with the achievement of independence the 'newcomers' should now return to their original homelands and free up the rightfully owned land of the host community. For their part the relocated settlers counter that they were given no choice by Indonesian authorities, and, having made the best of the circumstances, are in no position to return to an area lacking housing and services. Some of the more entrenched and acrimonious disputes over land in East Timor are seen to have originated in government manipulations of local settlement protocols and agreements. This observation includes instances of Portuguese colonial policies to concentrate populations and promote economic development. Land conflicts of this nature are often deeply entrenched and almost impossible to resolve through local customary channels (see Gunter 2007). One of the objectives of the present study is to develop a better understanding of the pattern of land conflicts in East Timor, especially conflict arising from circumstances of coercive displacement.

## Conclusion

While claims of origin group authority are constructed and relative in nature, and are affected by colonial and neo-colonial policies of village resettlement in local government, the overarching social ordering emphasis on origin is embedded in the landscape of East Timor through artefacts and symbolic representations of ancestral connections. Across rural East Timor, there are sacred sites marked by rituals and material instantiations of ancestors known to have 'spoken' into the landscape, usually through acts of intermediation with local guardian spirits. Our case studies include such sites as coastal altar posts marking the first landing of ancestor-settlers, prohibited old-growth forests and water sources guarded by local spirits, abandoned hilltop villages that were sites of first settlement, and sacred houses that contain regalia and other symbols of origin group legitimacy. Typically, these sites provide places for periodic rituals and ceremonial invocation to ancestors while reproducing the privileged status and authority of origin group elders. In Chapter 6, for example, we discuss a ceremony in the village of Babulo, which reproduces origin group authority through commemoration of the reconstruction of a Darlari sacred house that was destroyed during the Indonesian occupation. The example supports our hypothesis that customary principles of land authority, typified by narratives of origin and symbolized by sacred houses, have retained a substantial degree of relevance and resilience notwithstanding the effects of Indonesian occupation. In other words, even though origin stories are inherited narratives and metaphors of legitimacy, they derive a high degree of resilience from their intertwined symbolic, spiritual and physical manifestations in the landscape of rural East Timor.

## Bibliography


Bellwood, P., Fox, J.J. and Tryson, D. 1995. *The Austronesians: Historical and Comparative Perspectives*. Canberra: Research School of Pacific and Asian Studies, The Australian National University.

Berry, S. 1993. *No Condition is Permanent: The Social Dynamics of Agrarian Change in Sub-Saharan Africa*. Wisconsin: University of Wisconsin Press.

Bovensiepen, J. 2009. Landscapes of Life and Death in the Central Highlands of East Timor, in C. Allerton (ed.), *Spiritual Landscapes in Southeast Asia: Changing Geographies of Potency and the Sacred*. Special Edition of the *Anthropological Forum*, 19(3), 323–338.

Bruner, E. 1986. Ethnography as Narrative, in V. Turner and E. Bruner (eds), *The Anthropology of Experience*. Urbana and Chicago: University of Illinois Press.

Budiardjo, C. and Soei Liong, L. 1984. *The War against East Timor*. United Kingdom: Zed Books.

Commission for Reception, Truth and Reconciliation in East Timor (CAVR) 2006. *Chega! The Report of the Commission for Reception, Truth and Reconciliation in East Timor*. Dili: Government of Timor Leste.

Carsten, J. and Hugh-Jones, S. 1995. *About the House: Levi-Strauss and Beyond*. Cambridge: Cambridge University Press.

Dunn, J. 1996. *Timor: A People Betrayed*. Sydney: ABC Books.

Fitzpatrick, D. 2002. *Land Claims in East Timor*. Australia: Asia Pacific Press.

Fitzpatrick, D. and Barnes, S. 2010. The Relative Resilience of Property: First Possession and Order without Law in East Timor. *Law and Society Review*, 44(2).

Forman, S. 1980. Descent, Alliance and Exchange Ideology among the Makassae of East Timor, in J. Fox (ed.), *The Flow of Life: Essays on Eastern Indonesia.* Cambridge, MA: Harvard University Press.

Forbes, H.O. 1884. On Some of the Tribes of the Island of Timor. *The Journal of the Anthropological Institute of Great Britain and Ireland*, 13.

Forbes, H.O. 1989. *A Naturalists Wanderings in the Eastern Archipelago.* Oxford and New York: Oxford University Press.

Fox, J.J. 1980. *The Flow of Life: Essays on Eastern Indonesia.* Cambridge: Harvard University Press.

Fox, J.J. 1989. Category and Complement: Binary Ideologies and the Organisation of Dualism in Eastern Indonesia, in D. Maybury Lewis and L. Almagor (eds), *The Attraction of opposites: Thought and Society in a Dualistic Mode*, pp 33–56. Ann Arbor: University of Michigan Press.

Fox, J.J. 1993. Comparative Perspectives on Austronesian Houses: An Introductory Essay, in J.J. Fox (ed.), *Inside Austronesian Houses: Perspectives on Domestic Designs for Living.* Canberra: Department of Anthropology, Comparative Austronesian Project, Research School of Pacific Studies, The Australian National University.

Fox, J.J. 1995. Installing the Outsider Inside: The Exploration of an Epistemic Austronesian Cultural Theme and its Social Significance [Revised draft]. Paper presented at the first Conference of the European Association of Southeast Asian Studies: Local Transformaitons and Common Heritage in Southeast Asia 29 June –1 July, Leiden University, The Netherlands.

Fox, J.J. 1996. The Transformation of Progenitor Lines of Origin: Patterns of Precedence in Eastern Indonesia, in J.J. Fox and C. Sather (eds), *Origins, Ancestry and Alliance: Explorations in Austronesian Ethnography.* Canberra: Research School of Pacific and Asian Studies, The Australian National University.

Fox, J.J. 2003. Perpetuating Ancestral Foundations: Some Transformation of Austronesian houses, in R. Schefold, G. Domenig and P. Nas (eds), *Indonesian Houses: Tradition and Transformation in Vernacular Architecture.* Leiden: KITLV Press.

Fox, J.J. and Sather, C. 1996. *Origins, Ancestry and Alliance: Explorations in Austronesian Ethnography.* Canberra: Research School of Pacific and Asian Studies, The Australian National University.

Freycinet, Louis, C.D. de, 1827. Voyage autour du monde, executé sur les corvettes S.M. l'Uranie et la Physicienne pendent les années, 1817, 1818, 1819, 1820, Historique du Voyage, Paris: Tome I.

Gudeman, S. and Riveira, A. 1986. *Conversations in Columbia: The Domestic Economy in Life and Text.* Cambridge, New York: Cambridge University Press.

Gunn, G. 1999. *Timor Loro Sae: 500 Years.*

Gunter, J. 2007. Communal Conflict in Viqueque and the 'Charged' History of '59. *The Asia Pacific Journal of Anthropology*, 8(1), 27–42.

Hicks, D. 1976. *Tetum Ghosts and Kin: Fieldwork in an Indonesian community*. Palo Alto, CA: Mayfield.

Hull, G. 1998. The Languages of Timor 1772–1997: A Literature Review, in *Studies in Languages and Cultures of East Timor*, vol. 1.

Lameiras-Campagnolo, M.O. 1975. L'habitation des Fatuluku de Lo′ rehe (Timor Portugais). Paris: The`se de doctorat de 3e`me cycle, Universite′ Rene′ Descartes, Sorbonne.

Lazarowitz, T.F. 1980. *The Makassai: Complementary Dualism in Timor*, Phd Thesis. Stonybrook: SUNY.

McWilliam, A.R. 2002. *Paths of Origin, Gates of Life: A Study of Place and Precedence in Southwest Timor*. Leiden: KITLV Press.

McWilliam, A.R. 2005. Houses of Resistance in East Timor: Structuring Sociality in the New Nation. *Anthropological Forum*, 15(1), 27–44.

McWilliam, A.R. 2007. Austronesians in Linguistic Disguise: Fataluku Cultural Fusion in East Timor. *Journal of Southeast Asian Studies*, 38(2), 355–375.

McWilliam, A.R. 2007b. Customary Claims and the Public Interest: On Fataluku resource entitlements, in D. Kingsbury and M. Leach Lautem (eds), *East Timor: Beyond Independence*. Melbourne: Monash Asia Institute Press.

McWilliam, A.R. 2008. Trunk and Tip in West Timor: Precedence in a Botanical Idiom, in M.P. Vischer (ed.), *Precedence: Processes of Social Differentiation in the Austronesian World*. Canberra: ANU E-Press, pp 111–132.

McWilliam, A.R. 2011. Fataluku Living Landscapes, in A. McWilliam and E.G. Traube (eds), *Land and Life in Timor-Leste: Ethnographic Essays*. Canberra ANU E-Press, pp 61–86.

Metzner, J. 1977. *Man and Environment in Eastern Timor: A Geo-ecological Analysis of the Baucau-Viqueque Area as a Possible Basis for Regional Planning*. Canberra: Australian National University.

Myat Thu, P. 2008. Land Forgotten: Effects of Indonesian Re-Settlement on Rural Livelihoods in East Timor, in D. Mearns (ed.), *Democratic Governance in Timor Leste: Reconciling the Local and the National*. Darwin: Charles Darwin University Press, pp 143–159.

Myat Thy, P. 2012. Negotiating Displacement: A study of Land and Livelihoods in Rural East Timor. Phd Thesis: Australian National University.

Pelissier, R. 1996. *Timor en Guerra: le crocodile et les Portugais (1847–1913)*. Paris.

Renard-Clamagirand, B. 1982. *Marobo: Une société ema de Timor*. Langues et Civilisation de L'Asie du Sud-Est et du Monde Insulindien 12. Paris: SELAF.

Reuter, T. 2007. Land and Territory in the Austronesian World, in T. Reuter (ed.), *Sharing the Earth: Dividing the Land: Land and Identity in the Austronesian World*. Canberra: ANU E-Press.

Sahlins, M. 1985. *Islands of History*. Chicago: University of Chicago Press.

Schefold, R., Dominig, G. and Nas, P. 2003. *Indonesian Houses: Tradition and Transformation in Vernacular Architecture*. Leiden: KITLV Press

Sherlock, K. 1983. *East Timor: Liurais and Chefes de Suco; Indigenous Authorities in 1952*, Darwin.

Strauss, L. 1983. *The Way of the Masks* (trans. S. Modelski). London: Jonathan Cape.

Taylor, J. 1999. *East Timor: The Price of Freedom (Politics in Contemporary Asia)*. Annandale: Pluto Press.

Traube, E. 1986. *Cosmology and Social Life: Ritual Exchange among the Mambai of East Timor*. Chicago: University of Chicago Press.

Vel, J. 1994. *The Uma-economy: Indigenous Economics and Development Work in Lawonda*. Sumba: Landbouwuniversiteit te Wageningen

Warren, C. 1993. Adat and Dinas: Balinese Communities in the Indonesian State.

Waterson, R. 1990. *The Living House: An Anthropology of Architecture in Southeast Asia*. Singapore: Oxford University Press.

# Chapter 3
# The Structures of Resilience: Rule Complexity and Customary Land Systems

## Introduction

In Chapter 1 we highlighted the Timorese capacity for what Sahlins (1999: 412) has called the 'inventiveness of culture': the adaptive capacity to respond to contingent history through a culturally specific 'structure of the conjuncture', where 'externalities become indigenised through their engagement with local configurations'. In the history of East Timor, external perturbations such as migration and demographic change have triggered endogenizing events that serve to adapt and reconstruct the original exogenous influence according to organizational principles of origin. The adaptive capacity provides a Timor-specific explanation for institutional resilience in the face of war and population movement. This chapter situates our finding of endogenizing resilience in the institutional literature on collective action. While much of the literature on collective action concerns efficient responses to resource management problems, including preventing the so-called 'tragedy of the commons', we highlight the relationship between collective action and social ordering in a close-knit community context. We suggest that collective action, in the form of resilient responses to environmental stress, can develop not only to ensure resource use efficiency but as a direct response to fears of costly races for rights. In subsequent chapters we will argue that this relationship between social ordering and collective action has important implications for the development of legal frameworks relating to customary property systems in post-conflict contexts.

East Timor is an unusual case as there has been a lengthy absence of law and legal institutions relating to private land ownership, and relatively little involvement in the governance of rural land by actors at the national and international levels. Our case studies provide an opportunity to test notions of order without law, which assert that groups of resource users can act collectively in relation to resource governance without reference to a state or formal law (Ellickson 1991, McDowell 2004, Morriss 2005). Most economic studies on order without law are substantive explorations of the preconditions and nature of successful private ordering systems. From eighteenth-century whaling communities, to the lobster gangs of Maine, to the cattle ranchers of Shasta County, California, the strength of self-organized resource systems has been explained by reference to conditions of member homogeneity, regular interaction, and information availability (Fitzpatrick 2006: 1030). In Robert

Ellickson's well-known formulation, close-knit communities generally prefer their own norms to the rules of formal law because they tend to be collectively cost-minimizing and welfare-maximizing (1991: 167, 283). Ellickson (1989: 84) further argues that more complex norms or rules emerge in close-knit community contexts where the increased costs of their interpretation are outweighed by increased gains from trade.

The origin groups of East Timor have characteristics that fit institutional criteria for collective action in the absence of law (Ellickson 1994: 192–204, 1993: 1336–44). They are kin-based structures with a high degree of member homogeneity, repeat interaction and access to information on resource use activity (Forman 1980: 154, McWilliam 2007: 165, Traube 1986, Fitzpatrick and Barnes 2010). All our case studies highlight incentives for member cooperation based on a sophisticated system of sanctions including shaming, fines and – most powerfully – fear of sickness arising from lack of respect for ancestral spirits and the spirits of the land. Yet these characteristics do not of themselves provide an explanation for the long-standing capacity of East Timor's customary systems to endogenize exogenous effects, particularly in dynamic circumstances relating to the incorporation of in-migrants into customary order. In-migration by group outsiders threatens the homogeneity, stability and internal sanctions that underpin group cooperation. In this chapter we adopt game-theoretic explanations for collective action in dynamic circumstances of in-migration, in order to suggest that origin principles have acted as resilient sources of social ordering in East Timor because they provide a visible signal of relations with land, which are interpreted by in-migrant property claimants as focal points to avoid costly conflict and secure access to resources. This argument is illustrated with reference to the nineteenth-century gold mining associations of California, which adopted rules of first possession to balance the claims of first-comers and latecomers.

Game theorists argue that rules of first possession were important to circumstances of order without law in the Californian goldfields as they provided bright-line signals of likely success in the event of competition for a mining claim (Zerbe and Anderson 2001: 133–34). However, the Californian first possession rules had complex interpretive elements because they allowed the possibility of abandonment based on failure to meet work requirements. This chapter argues that rule complexity developed in the Californian goldfields as a direct response to fears of costly racing for rights rather than concerns for efficient resource extraction. While increased access to unworked claims improved private returns from extraction, there were no net gains from accelerated extraction because gold is a finite resource, exploitable just as efficiently under freehold private property arrangements (Clay and Wright 2005: 177). The argument is significant because it suggests that interpretively complex customary rules of resource allocation may develop in response to concerns for social order and the maintenance of collective action within a self-organized group of resource users.

Our hypothesis that complex possessory rules may correlate with concerns for social order, arising from exogenous effects such as in-migration, provides a fresh perspective on Ellickson's hypothesis (1989) that more complex community rules may emerge where the increased costs of their interpretation are outweighed by increased gains from trade. Examples from East Timor suggest that rule complexity may have a broader canvas than gains from trade, and include reproduction of public authority in environments where there are risks of costly racing for control over resources. In East Timor complex norms of ancestral first possession have evolved in response to fears of social conflict, in a context of in-migration, rather than as a direct response to potential gains from trade in agricultural products. While complex rules that promote social order also allow rewards for resource use efforts, the East Timor case supports our hypothesis that insecure socio-political environments may produce different simplicity/complexity trade-offs in rule formation than stable environments. For example, the customary groups of East Timor could have developed a simple rule of possession that would have granted rights to in-migrants engaged in clearing and cultivation. Yet interpretively complex principles of origin emerged to reproduce social authority in a historical context of in-migration and tribal warfare.

The relationship between social ordering and complex customary rules, in a conflict-affected context, helps to explain both the resilience of custom and its resistance to translation into law. As we discuss in the next chapter, the draft 2012 land law of East Timor applies standardized legal constructs of possession and community property to context-specific customary relationships with land. It assumes a ready transition from complex rules of custom to standardized rules of law. Yet, in relatively weak state circumstances, the transition from custom to law is likely to be incomplete and contested, even when there are efficiency gains from resort to law. The resistance of custom to legal translation arises from its contextualized, information-rich complexity, which includes resilient environment-specific processes to reproduce social authority and cosmological order. In East Timor information-rich customary rules of origin will retain relevance, notwithstanding standardized legal rules of possession and community property, because long-standing origin principles provide an ongoing basis for avoiding costly conflict over land, and the state lacks the capacity to apply legal rules in a coercive manner. As in other postcolonial environments with resilient customary systems and weak states, any attempt by the East Timorese state to replace non-state systems with unitary state law is likely only to create a poly-normative system of official law, semi-legal practice, and unsanctioned informality (Fitzpatrick 2006). This is a functional form of institutional complexity, as set out in Chapter 1. The likelihood of incomplete and contested transitions from custom to law further highlights the challenges for legal regulation arising from our finding of customary resilience, as it undermines economic accounts of efficient transition from collective property to private property, under pressure from increased competition from land. Our analysis suggests that this optimistic story, first suggested by Harold Demsetz (1965), fails fully to take into account the relationship between social ordering and the development of property rules.

Notwithstanding our explanations for the resilience of custom, and its resistance to legal translation, there are a number of mechanisms that lead to the degradation of customary forms of collective action, including the development of markets in the land and the emergence of state-based forms of authority. In Chapter 2 we identified these types of degradation in the authority of Timorese customary systems, which created constraints on their resilient capacity to absorb in-migration. The extent to which a customary property system will lose its capacity to maintain a local system of order will depend on questions of resilience, including the capacity to engage in collective action in the face of in-migration, dealings with outsiders, and encroachment by state authority (Platteau 2000: 94–6). Even resilient collective action mechanisms in relation to land can fail when competing land claimants affiliate with competing forms of property authority and legitimacy. The result can be a worst-case scenario: the partial disintegration of a viable local ordering system without the provision of effective substitutes by the state. In East Timor, this prospect raises a number of regulatory challenges. On the one hand, the fact of customary resilience suggests the need for laws that provide regulatory space for successful community-based forms of collective action. This type of regulatory approach is consistent with the analysis of Ostrom (1990). On the other hand, degradations in customary resilience as land markets develop and group members defect from systems of customary order suggest a need for laws that accommodate transitions to state-based forms of legal order, even though – as we suggest – the transition from custom to law may be incomplete or contested. This type of regulatory approach is consistent with the analysis of Demsetz (1965).

## Collective Action and Social Resilience in Close-knit Community Contexts

Elinor Ostrom (2005: 258–9) has formulated criteria for community resilience to environmental disturbances that reflect her Nobel Prize-winning work on common property management. Ostrom's criteria for community resilience include legal space and support for community rule-making. In particular, the legal system should identify the community unit and its scope of jurisdiction, support its rule-enforcement and conflict-resolution mechanisms, and define its interaction with the broader regulatory system (Ostrom 2005: 259). Writing in the emerging field of social-ecological resilience, Neil Adger similarly applies institutional theories of collective action to community adaptation contexts (Adger 1999; Paavola and Adger 2006). He adopts Ostrom-like criteria for assessing the prospects of successful community-level resilience, including factors such as the size of the group undertaking the collective action, the boundaries of the resource in question, the homogeneity of the decision-making group, and the distribution of the benefits of management (Ostrom 2005: 26–7, 257–8, Adger et al. 2005: 12–13).

Both Ostrom and Adger apply the heuristic concept of resilience, first developed in ecological literature, to collective action in circumstances of environmental stress. The concept of system resilience derives from ecological studies of ecosystems and their responses to external disturbances (Holling 1973). The resilience heuristic recognizes that there is no single steady state equilibrium in a complex system, and that exogenous shocks may lead to transitions in system equilibria that correlate with the capacity for resilience. In the ecological literature, resilience has two primary aspects: an absorptive element, which means system capacity to absorb shock and retain essential structures and processes and a reconstitutive capacity which includes recovery of structures and processes after damage (Adger et al. 2005: 1036). Absorptive capacity includes the amount of disturbance an ecosystem can withstand without sudden transition – a 'phase shift' – to an alternative state (Adger et al. 2003). Social resilience includes the ability of groups or communities to self-organize in the face of social, political, or environmental stresses and disturbances (Adger 2000).

In property system terms, resilience may be defined as the ability to absorb exogenous disturbances while maintaining the capacity to deliver basic property rights outcomes, including security of tenure and sustainable management of resources. Economic analysis discusses property systems in terms of internalizing 'externalities' (Demsetz 1967: 350). Externalities are the social costs that individual actions impose on others. Two primary types of externalities relating to land are the positive externality of resource rents (that is monetary or non-monetary returns from a resource); and the negative externality of wasteful competition and resource consumption in an open access environment. Property system functions include the internalization of each of these externalities. First, a property holder will have the right to capture the benefits of her use of a resource, which provides an incentive to invest in the resource (Trebilcock and Veel 2008, 404–5). Second, a property holder will have a right to exclude others, which provides an incentive to prevent wasteful resource consumption and competition. (Demsetz 1967: 347–48; Merrill 2002: S332). In cases of armed conflict, this latter property system function includes managing the costs of competitive racing for control over resources, through effective allocation and enforcement of rights to property.

Ostrom's criteria for resilience include an emphasis on rules, formal and informal, that is a characteristic of economic approaches to collective action (Ostrom 1990: 52). In the literature on collective action, the notion of informal rules can encompass social norms or principles of organization, including norms or principles that are contested and negotiated (North 1990: 36). 'Rules', as broadly defined, constrain self-interested acts by individuals and facilitate socially beneficial forms of collective action (North 1990: 1–3). For example, in a context of competition for property rights, individuals may race to possess land or natural resources based on self-interested calculations that the net benefits of possession outweigh the costs of racing, even though there are net social detriments from competitive racing, and greater mutual benefits from acts of cooperation among potential racers. The social cost of competitive racing includes dissipation of resources in the act of racing, or in the exploitation of a resource before it is ready for production (Lueck 1995). In relation to East Timor, the resilience of customary property systems provides an example of collective action after armed conflict to mitigate the potential for costly racing for control over resources, including strategic acts of violence in the process of racing. The collective action takes the form of shared efforts to avoid conflictual racing to possess land left vacant by displaced persons, through the reconstitution of rights to land around long-standing 'rules' of ancestral origin. While the fact of displacement created incentives to occupy vacated lands, which could have led to conflicts over acts of possession, members of customary groups in East Timor acted collectively to restore rights to land in accordance with pre-displacement principles of customary order (Fitzpatrick and Barnes 2010).

Collective action theory identifies the potential for small groups to overcome free-riding that would otherwise prevent acts of cooperation. Free-riding incentives arise when the benefits of cooperation are open to all members of the group irrespective of whether they take part in cooperative efforts (North 1990: 13). Free riding can prevent cooperation when group members delay incurring the costs of cooperation in the hope that other group members will bear those costs (Olson 1965: 1–2, Ostrom 1990: 6). All else being equal, smaller groups are more likely to reach agreements to prevent free riding, if only because there are fewer people involved in the act of reaching agreement. Moreover, the more stable and homogenous a small group the more likely there will be agreement on the mechanisms of group cooperation (Taylor 1997). Repeat interactions associated with group stability and homogeneity increase the prospects for cooperation because opportunism or free riding in previous agreements increases the light of exclusion from future agreements (Axelrod 1984; North 1990: 13). Repeat behaviour tends to create self-perpetuating norms of behaviour and expectations, which may then be passed down inter-generationally in the form of group 'culture' (North 1995: 20, Ostrom 1990: 35, 43). All these criteria – group size, homogeneity and stability – not only reduce the costs of reaching cooperative agreements, they also tend to increase the availability of information to monitor agreements, which is important to provide disincentives to shirking and opportunistic acts of free riding by group members.

Much of the literature on collective action and natural resource management identifies circumstances of group stability, homogeneity and repeat interactions as conducive to prevention of a 'tragedy of the commons' (Krier 2009: 148–9). A tragedy of the commons arises when insufficient incentives exist for resource conservation, because no user bears all the costs and consequences of her resource use. No resource user has the capacity to prevent access by other users, which leads to escalating exploitation of the resource as each user appropriates more in anticipation of increased appropriations by other users (Posner 1993, Eggertsson 2003: 77–79). While Garrett Hardin (1968) identified this 'tragedy' as a product of common access to a resource, there may be incentives for sustainable resource appropriations even though more than one party may access the resource. Ostrom's insight (1990: 15–18) was to identify community-generated rules for resource appropriations as an alternative either to state regulation of resource appropriations, or to private property controls on access by other users. In identifying successful examples of sustainable community-based forms of collective action, to overcome free-riding incentives to over-exploit a resource, Ostrom built on criteria for small group collective action identified by Mancur Olson and others. In particular, Ostrom (1990: 58–101) identified common features of successful community-based resource management systems, across a number of resource and country contexts, which included legal support for small, stable and homogenous groups to develop, monitor and enforce their own rules of resource use.

While some economists argue for the individuation of property rights, as an instrument of economic development (see De Soto 2004), collective action in close-knit settings can also encompass collective rights to land, where rights of exclusion and governance are vested in a group of resource users (Platteau 1990: 182–3). Collective land-holding aspects of customary property systems may provide efficient (and resilient) responses to environmental circumstances because of the nature of the resource and its exploitation techniques, or the need to insure against climatic risks (Eggertsson 2002: 84–5, Ellickson 1993: 1332–44, Smith 2002: S468–71). For example, shifting cultivation, nomadic herding, and wet-rice farming are production techniques suited to communal control of a particular area and the development of rules for resource use by community members (Baland and Platteau 1998: 645–6, Bailey 1992: 183, Smith 2000: 131). Under these production techniques, no further parcelization of areas or allocation of exclusionary rights is necessary because the production technique requires a high degree of cooperative activity, or entails some shifting of areas for resource exploitation, or is optimal under circumstances of large parcelization alone. In all these situations, economies of scale exist in exploiting the resource through collective governance mechanisms rather than parcelized rights of exclusion vested in individual resource users (Deininger 2003: 29). As in East Timor, collective control over areas of rural land – with rights of access and use for collective members – provides a low-cost governance mechanism for mobile swidden cultivation techniques, and insures against micro-climate risks by allowing multiple plots for a diversified supply of food, notwithstanding the increased governance, monitoring and coordination costs of collective action.

## Collective Action, In-migration and Complex Rules of First Possession

Criteria such as small numbers, homogeneity and repeat interactions do not necessarily explain dynamic forms of institutional efficiency, including collective action in the face of in-migration and conflict-caused displacement (see Platteau 1990: 16). In-migration and population movement undermine the prospects for collective action because they increase numbers, heterogeneity and competition for resources. Our case studies identify resilient forms of collective action in East Timor's customary property systems even after the extreme displacement events of Indonesian occupation. The following part discusses adaptive resilience to in-migration through game-theoretic accounts of collective action in cases of resource competition. We highlight, in particular, the potential role of rules of first possession in facilitating collective responses to population displacement and in-migration. Rules of first possession provide a focal point for strategies of cooperation in a game of resource competition, in a manner analogous to principles of origin in Timorese customary systems. As with the contextualized complexity of origin principles in East Timor, we argue that customary rules of first possession take on interpretive complexity in order to reduce the enforcement costs of property where cooperative respect for property is threatened by in-migrant encroachment. In other words, rule complexity supports resilient forms of collective action that responds to risks of costly racing for property rights after armed conflicts.

Game theory explains cooperation in a context of resource competition by reference to stylized hypothetical encounters between two property claimants (Trebilcock and Veel 2008: 412–13). Each party is not sure whether the other will adopt an aggressive approach (a 'hawk' strategy), or a passive approach (a 'dove' strategy). Where expectations of success are symmetrical, the two parties will settle into a war of attrition in which they both attempt aggressive hawk strategies in a calculated effort to test the endurance of the other party, while leaving open the option of surrendering to the other claimant at any stage of the resource competition (Sugden 1986: 62, Krier 2009: 152–3). Whenever there is an asymmetry of confidence, the parties will move to adopt hawk and dove strategies that reflect their mutual perceptions of likely success. Competing claimants are likely to surrender in order of confidence in their claim. The greater the prominence of the asymmetry the more likely it is that respective hawk-dove strategies will emerge early in the prospective war of attrition (Krier 2009: 152–3, Sugden 1986: 65–86, McAdams 2000). Moreover, because wars of attrition can be costly in net terms, both parties would prefer a property rule that assigns the roles of dove and hawk a priori, particularly if the rule means that each player has a good chance of winning in at least half of their confrontations (McDowell 2004: 795).

Possessory rules are said to lend themselves to asymmetrical understandings of likelihoods of success, because possession provides a clear and understandable sign of an ongoing connection with a resource (Sugden 1986: 83–6, 97, Krier 2009: 155). Those who have incurred costs to obtain possession may be expected to assert their possessory relationship with a resource more fiercely than those who simply wish to obtain possession (Sugden 1986: 101). This leads to mutually reinforcing expectations of relative success, with first possessors more likely to defend their claims with confidence and aggression, and prospective dispossessors more likely to forgo their own claims in order to search for possessory claims elsewhere. Property rules that protect the rights of first possessors provide the parties with a shortcut to avoid a war of attrition, particularly when there is uncertainty as to respective prospects of success in the game of resource competition (Zerbe and Anderson 2001: 134). Once both parties expect the other to follow a possessory rule, there is a natural tendency towards cooperation as it is costly to break the cooperative pattern (Epstein 1980: 672–3, Sugden 1986: 52–4, 62, 70–71, McAdams 2000). This argument owes much to Hayekian notions of spontaneous order, which posit that social order can emerge autonomously through decentralized expectations of behaviour rather than through imposition of state-based law and authority (Hayek 1979).

## Possession and Order in the Californian Goldfields

An iconic example of Hayekian ordering is said to be the development of order without law in the Californian goldfields between 1848 and 1849 (Clay and Wright 2005: 177, McDowell 2004, Leshy 1987, Morriss 2005). The nineteenth-century Californian gold rush involved large numbers of miners entering an area that had recently been annexed by the United States from Mexico. There were no courts, police or jails, and only a small military force (McDowell 2004: 771, Morriss 2005: 47, 1998). Mexican law did not apply as from 12 February 1848, and there was no US federal mining law until 1872. Between 1848 and 1849 rapid increases in the gold mining population served to create an unregulated race for control of resources (Clay and Wright 2005: 160, McDowell 2002: 4–5, Morriss: 2005: 47–8). Then, throughout 1849, American miners developed mining codes that established a high degree of order despite the absence of legal order and the competitive nature of the rush for gold itself (McDowell 2002: 4–5, McDowell 2004: 771).

Umbeck argues that mining code order was underpinned by violence or the threat of violence, particularly in the form of widespread gun ownership (1981). McDowell, and Zerbe and Anderson, take a different view: they contend that the mining conditions of relative order had little to do with sanctions and were examples of spontaneous ordering (McDowell 2004: 773, Zerbe and Anderson 2001: 114). According to McDowell (2004: 801), the mining rules did not require internalization as norms or enforcement by implicit sanction. They were simply 'rules of the game', created and if necessary cast off as items of convenience in a game of resource competition. Zerbe and Anderson (2001: 115–16, 128) similarly assert that American cultural norms of fairness and democracy, including Lockean notions of reward for possessory efforts, provided focal points that guided initial patterns of behaviour and predictions of behaviour, which then served to establish cooperative alternatives to costly resource conflict. Focal points are shared expectations or understandings that allow prospective resource claimants to shape strategies of cooperation or conflict around predictions of respective likelihoods of success (McDowell 2004: 77, Sugden 1986: 87–97, Zerbe and Anderson 2001: 116). They encourage one claimant to forgo the option of conflict based on the assessment that he or she is likely to lose a game of resource competition.

Almost all the Californian mining codes had a rule of first possession that granted rights to the first person to dig a hole and stake a claim (McDowell 2002: 27–8, Zerbe and Anderson 2001: 133–5). The claim extended to an area surrounding the hole, and was maintained by leaving tools in the hole, or meeting requirements to continue working the claim (McDowell 2002: 15). The right to jump claims was also defined by reference to loss of possessory entitlements, including various types of failure to meet work requirements (McDowell 2004:

778–9, Zerbe and Anderson 2001: 132, Clay and Wright 2005: 164). Zerbe and Anderson (2001: 133) characterize the first possession rule as a game-theoretic focal point because American miners shared cultural beliefs in reward for labour and the merits of associative democracy. McDowell (2004: 796) also adopts game-theoretic analysis to suggest that the first possession rule created asymmetrical expectations of success in the event of competition, while providing new entrants with the option of obtaining new rights by digging a claim elsewhere.

Neither McDowell nor Zerbe and Anderson examine the interpretive content of first possession rules in the Californian goldfields. Yet it is significant that the rules did not lead to rights of private property in perpetuity, but to possessory entitlements that were subject to rules of abandonment. The first possession rule had complex interpretive elements as it required determination of failure to meet work requirements. An alternative bright-line rule in the goldfields, involving rights in perpetuity rather than the possibility of abandonment, may have slowed the process of extraction, as claims were left unworked, but would not have reduced the total gains from extraction of a finite resource (Clay and Wright 2005: 177). Clay and Wright (2005: 157) persuasively argue that the inclusion of rules to legitimize claim-jumping was a response to the competitive racing nature of the gold mining activity itself. Each miner quickly worked a site to determine its potential, before digging new holes elsewhere in search of a more productive site. As new entrants filled the mining camps, the right to work unworked claims became a major flashpoint for potential social disorder. The need to minimize newcomer/latecomer conflict provided the basis for abandonment rules that allowed new entrants to obtain rights to unworked claims (Clay and Wright 2005: 162–3).

Clay and Wright (2005: 178) conclude that the mining codes of California provided order, in the sense that they minimized conflict, but failed to provide secure forms of property rights. The requirements to maintain the working of a claim were complex and ambiguous. They compelled mining associations, and later the courts, both to define 'work' and to identify legitimate reasons for non-work, which served to generate a high level of disputes and litigation from 1851 onwards (Clay and Wright 2005: 162–4). The rules relating to possession and abandonment were not necessarily enforced by the miners themselves, who were reluctant to intervene in *inter partes* conflicts (Clay and Wright 2005: 168). The mining associations dissolved in circumstances of disputation relating to the possessory rule, and its application to claims of abandonment (McDowell 2004: 801). Somewhat ironically, the system of order without law in California led to a degree of disorder, not only because of the increased numbers and heterogeneity of miners, but also because of the complex nature of the rule on which order was initially based (Clay and Wright 2005: 178).

Game theorists argue that rules of first possession were important to circumstances of order without law in the Californian goldfields as they provided bright-line signals of likely success in the event of competition for a mining claim (for example, Zerbe and Anderson 2001: 133–4). However, the Californian first possession rules had complex elements because they allowed the possibility of abandonment based on failure to meet work requirements. The rules had a social ordering imperative: they sought to maintain cooperative first-comer/latecomer relations by meeting the demands of new entrants for rights to unworked claims (McDowell 2004: 771–2). We argue that rule complexity in California evolved to promote social order, in circumstances of competitive racing for rights to resources, while also sowing the seeds of future disorder because competing claims of dispossession and abandonment, involving contested interpretations of ambiguous work requirements, led to a proliferation of disputes over mining entitlements. The system of order without law created by the Californian mining associations did not last long before it dissolved in part under the weight of disputation over the interpretation of the complex possessory rule itself.

## Possession and Efficiency: The Development of Complexity in Whaling Norms of Capture

The Californian goldfields example suggests a relationship between complex possessory norms, involving determinations of abandonment, and social ordering imperatives in circumstances of competitive racing for resources. While, as we have seen, the literature on collective action and resource management largely focuses on responses to customary pool problems, including preventing the so-called 'tragedy of the commons' (see Ostrom 1990), we highlight the relationship between collective action and the interpretive complexity of norms that respond to social ordering imperatives in a close-knit community context. We suggest that complex norms of resource capture can develop as a direct response to the potential for violence, and not necessarily as a direct consequence of collective efforts to ensure resource use efficiency (see also North 1990: 38. This re-framing of the debate on complex norms and collective action, to take into account relationships with social order, is important in a conflict-affected context. In particular, it helps to explain the resilience of complex norms in societies affected by fears of violent conflict, as resource users evoke shared norms to avoid the potential costs of conflict, and also the resistance of complex norms to translation into law, because of their embeddedness in local formulations of authority and social order.

In the Californian goldfields there were correlations between rule complexity and reductions in property enforcement costs. The rule on abandonment, in particular, reduced property enforcement costs by reducing the risks of violent property conflict between first-comers and latecomers. Ellickson (1989) explores the development of interpretively complex rules in terms of reward for resource use efforts rather than social ordering, or reductions in the enforcement costs of property. Interpretively complex rules may develop in close-knit community contexts to exploit potential gains from trade. His examples include nineteenth-century British and American whaling communities, which developed different norms to govern the acquisition of property rights in particular types of whale (Ellickson 1989). While all these norms were based on notions of first possession, they differed significantly both as to the interpretation of capture – when first possession was deemed to arise – and as to the determination of loss or abandonment of possessory entitlements. Ellickson (1989: 84, 1991: 167, 169) hypothesizes that, in close-knit circumstances, the development of more complex norms, involving greater transaction costs in the form of interpretive specialization and potential for disputation, ordinarily takes place if these increases in the costs of transacting are outweighed by reductions in deadweight losses (that is, under-rewarded resource use efforts) arising from failures to exploit potential gains from trade. Close-knit community rules trend towards wealth-maximization by reducing the objective sum of transaction costs, including the costs of rule interpretation, and losses caused by under-rewarded resource use efforts (Ellickson 1989: 87).

Prior to 1800 British whalers operating in the Greenland fishery developed a 'fast-fish/loose-fish' rule, in which a claimant owned a whale so long as the whale was fastened by line to the claimant's boat. As long as the harpoon held fast to the whale and remained connected by a line to the boat, the owner of the boat had exclusive ownership of the whale. If the whale was to break free, dead or alive, it was treated as a loose fish and was again free to be claimed (Deal 2010: 204–7). The fast-fish/loose-fish rule was relatively bright-line in nature: it created an easily understandable commencement point for a property claim, based on the visible and ascertainable nature of a connecting line between the whale and the boat. Property entitlements were acquired, and lost, by reference to this clear possessory act. The rule also encouraged resource use efficiency as it rewarded the first whaler to lodge a harpoon, which was 'the hardest part of the hunt', while allowing for loss of possession (that is, loss of the connecting line), which rewarded those who expended effort on finding unattached dead whales (Ellickson 1989: 89–90, 1991: 191–206).

In American fisheries, where the sperm whale predominated, local whalers developed an 'iron-holds-the-whale' rule. While this rule also conferred a right of property on the whaler to first harpoon a whale, it did not require the line to remain connected to the boat. The property entitlement would subsist so long as the claimant remained in fresh pursuit of the harpoon-bearing animal. The entitlement could be lost if the whaler were no longer in fresh pursuit, or another whaler had begun to 'cut into' the captured carcass (Ellickson 1989: 90). Ellickson (1989: 91) suggests that the difference in possessory norms, as between British and American whalers, may be explained by the fact that the right whales hunted by British whalers off Greenland were relatively slow and docile compared to the sperm whales hunted by the Americans. The American 'iron-holds-the-whale' rule responded to the increased likelihood that the harpoon line would have to be cut in order to save the boat from sinking under the pressure from a fast-moving sperm whale. The rule increased the relative efficiency of resource use by reducing the risks of death or injury to sailors, and damage to the boat.

The 'iron-holds-the-whale' rule provided American whalers with the incentive to make the first strike on a sperm whale, while encouraging innovations such as drogues (floats separated from the boat and attached to the whale by line) and waifs (poles planted into dead whales to signify ownership and collected later).

At the same time, the norm required determinations of 'freshness of pursuit' and therefore was more complex and open to interpretive contestation than the fast-fish/loose-fish rule (Ellickson 1989: 91–2). Consistent with his hypothesis of wealth-maximizing norms, Ellickson (1989: 94) suggests that the 'iron-holds-per-whale' rule developed in American fisheries, because of its advantages in terms of greater efficiencies of resource use, including reduction of risks and encouragement of innovation, outweighed the disadvantages of increased ambiguity and potential for disputation. Close-knit communities of whalers – the primary audience for property norms relating to captured whales – were able to understand and apply relatively complex rules of possession because they were expert in matters relating to whaling, and were subject to informal sanctions in the form of reputational loss or ostracism. Even beachcombers, happening upon the beached carcass of sperm whales, could understand and follow whaling rules of capture because of their own links with local groups of whalers.[1]

## Possessory Customs and Social Order in Traditional Timorese Culture

Social ordering considerations are implicit in Ellickson's analysis because social order allows reward for resource use efforts, which may then serve to outweigh the increased costs of rule complexity.[2] However, the correlation between rule complexity and reductions in deadweight losses may involve more than net gains from trade. There were no markets for goods when norms of ancestral first possession developed in the subsistence economies of customary parts of East Timor (Clamigarand 1980, Forman 1980, Hicks 1976, Traube 1986). Interpretively complex norms of ancestral first possession have evolved in response to fears of social conflict, in a context of regular in-migration, rather than as a direct response to potential gains from trade in agricultural products (Fitzpatrick and Barnes 2010). The East Timor example suggests that, viewed from a historical perspective of property rights evolution across different stages of economic complexity, the cost–benefit calculus of rule complexity may have a broader canvas than gains from trade and include reductions in property enforcement costs through maintenance of social order. In the absence of third-party sources of property enforcement, the

1 Wilson et al. (2012) establish through experiment that communities of resource users will not choose between the two rules of capture unless they are 'civil-minded', in the sense that community members are predisposed to cooperation. Their findings suggest that, in a similar manner, complex rules of first possession will only evolve in a close-knit community context if there is a sufficient degree of predisposition to avoidance of costly conflict. In relation to East Timor, this predisposition may arise from the existence of kinship relations among close-knit communities of resource users.

2 For example, Ellickson's description of a 'good neighbor' norm in Shasta County, California suggests an underlying relationship between norms and social order (Ellickson 1991: 52–62).

customary groups of East Timor developed complex rules of first possession to manage in-migration and the risks of violent property encroachments.

In Chapter 2 we described complex mythologies of ancestral first possession among the customary groups of East Timor, where authority over land is claimed by lineages or 'houses' that trace descent to a founding ancestor and a common source of identity. Ancestral first possession norms in East Timor support socio-political control over relatively large areas of ancestral domain, which allows swidden cultivation techniques that remain the predominant form of resource use in rural East Timor (Metzner 1977). Swidden cultivation requires the assertion of control over a relatively large area, to allow movement of plots, and hence tends to be associated with collective rather than private property systems (Fitzpatrick 2006: 1027, Baland and Platteau 1998: 645–6). There is limited direct correlation between complex aspects of first possession norms in East Timor and gains from trade, or incentives for innovation, in relation to swidden cultivation. Our case studies illustrate the fact that, in remote customary districts, there is little by way of cash economy, no markets in rights to land, and no practice of bartering agricultural surpluses with other groups. In these circumstances, the consequences of rule complexity may be an orderly environment to undertake mobile cultivation techniques, but the long-standing driver of complexity is a desire to reproduce authority and maintain orderly social relations in circumstances of in-migration, exogamous marriage relations, and tribal warfare (Fitzpatrick and Barnes 2010: 222–3).

Timorese narratives of origin are analogous to principles of first possession as they provide a baseline point of reference for calculating priority in relation to land. Local narratives of origin are well-known to in-migrants. They have the potential to generate patterns of compliance and anticipated compliance because in-migrants know they can avoid costly forms of conflict, and obtain access to land by incorporating themselves into customary order through marriage alliances and traditional agreements. As with rules of first possession in the Californian goldfields, origin principles in East Timor have helped to provide a focal point for the maintenance of social order in a context of potential racing by first-comers and late-comers for rights to resources (Fitzpatrick and Barnes 2010: 217–18). Yet, also as in California, customary principles of first possession have a high degree of interpretive complexity because of their role in reducing the enforcement costs of property. Timorese principles of ancestral first possession are not so much matters of objective historical fact as mythical events in the establishment of cosmological order (Fox 1996: 132). They establish complex hierarchical distinctions between firstcomers and latecomers (Fox and Sather 1996, McWilliam 2002, 2009). As a result, there is no simple customary rule in East Timor that physical acts of first possession give rise to property entitlements, because the possessory significance of acts of clearing, cultivation and residence is calculated by reference to the possessory authority of customary elders.

The customary groups of East Timor could have developed a simple rule of possession that granted rights to in-migrants who engaged in clearing and cultivation, without the need for agreement from origin group elders, or inter-marriage with an origin group lineage. Of itself a simple rule of possession would not create conflict with possessory claimants from the local origin group because historically land was not scarce in remote customary districts. Outsiders could claim land without impinging on the actual or prospective plots of origin group members. By comparison with complex principles of origin, a simple rule of possession would reduce the transaction costs of rule interpretation while allowing the same marginal rates of output from shifting cultivation. So why did a simple rule of possession not evolve in the customary societies of East Timor? The answer seems to be that complex principles of origin serve to reproduce social authority, in the absence of a state or law, and provide a system of allegiance to mobilize forces in circumstances of regular tribal warfare. Rule complexity allows the community to remain close-knit, which is a question of social order, in ways that could not be achieved by a simple rule of possession.

Our case study chapters provide numerous examples of the complexity of traditional principles of possession in East Timor, including distinctions between the possessory entitlements of in-migrants and the underlying rights of origin groups. Viewed through a common law lens, the rights of in-migrants are analogous to the rights of actual possessors that are subject to the legal or constructive possession of the land owner.[3] In-migrants have physical custody or control of the land. Their rights are good against all save the 'owner', which is the origin group. As a general rule, distinctions between actual and legal possession emerge in property systems without significant threats of group violence where there are reductions in deadweight losses from the separation of ownership from possession, as for example in relation to contracts of bailment or lease. However, in circumstances of in-migration and threats of violent conflict over property, distinctions between actual and legal possession also provide a mechanism to reduce the enforcement costs of property by allowing rights to land to in-migrants, while retaining exclusionary authority over land in a pre-existing group. We provide a theoretical discussion of the interpretive complexity of possessory rules and the provision of land to in-migrants in the following section.

The customary societies of East Timor suggest that the development of rule complexity in close-knit community contexts has a degree of correlation with the reproduction of social order, particularly in circumstances of potentially costly racing for rights to resources. This suggestion does not necessarily contradict Ellickson's hypothesis of efficiency-oriented trade-offs between rule complexity and simplicity. Among the whaling communities of North America, complex rules of first possession minimized risks to life and limb, and facilitated an environment that allowed increased rewards for resource use efforts. In the Californian goldfields, complex rules of first possession reduced the potential for wasteful conflicts over rights to mining claims. The significant implication from East Timor is that there may be different rule complexity/simplicity trade-offs in different circumstances

3 For a discussion of legal or constructive possession and its potential separation from actual possession see *United States v. Derose*, 74 F.3d 1177 [11th Cir. 1996]).

of social ordering. Just as a simple rule of possession may have promoted efficient resource extraction in California, in the absence of concerns relating to competitive racing for mining rights, so too would a simple rule of possession in East Timor encourage efficient agricultural production in the absence of concerns relating to migration and warfare. Rules that would have a degree of interpretive simplicity in stable environments may thus trend towards complexity in unstable contexts. Moreover, as we argue in Chapter 9 with reference to chronic possessory conflicts in some parts of East Timor, if there is no trend towards complexity, simple rules of possession may exacerbate underlying conditions of socio-political instability.

## Frontier Rules of First Possession: The Development of Interpretive Complexity

We hypothesize that, all else being equal, the development of interpretive complexity in rules of first possession is more likely in 'frontier' circumstances where the state is unable or unwilling to engage in generalized enforcement of property rights in land.[4] The use of 'frontier' terminology is not intended in a pejorative sense, as it refers only to areas in which customary systems, rather than the nation-state, are the primary mechanism for enforcing property rights. Moreover, the heuristic reference to a legal frontier for property rights enforcement does not deny the possibility of state influence over customary property arrangements, through recursive and mutually constitutive interactions of the kind identified by legal anthropological analysis (see Merry 1988). The reference to a property frontier, as an ideal type for heuristic analysis, speaks only to the potential for coercive enforcement of property claims, and not to porous interactions across the enforcement frontier. The use of frontier analysis provides a basis for exploring the development of rule complexity in customary systems, without discounting the possibility of strategic attempts to shift the enforcement frontier through recourse to the state, or even co-option by the state of customary symbols, processes and sources of legitimacy (Moore 1998).

The hypothesis that possessory rule complexity tends to develop in frontier settings where the state does not enforce property rights, and customary systems for property enforcement are subject to threats from in-migration, is based on a distinction between an economic frontier, where property rights first form, and a legal frontier where the marginal benefits of state enforcement of property outweigh the costs (Alston, Libecap and Schneider 1996: 31–4, Alston, Harris and Mueller 2009: 4). The economic frontier is the margin between the time or place where resources have no value, and the time or place where they have positive

4 This definition of the legal frontier for property rights enforcement does not preclude the state engaging in selective enforcement of entitlements that suit the interests of state actors, including the grant of licences or concessions for agri-business development over the objections of customary land holders.

value (Anderson and Hill 2004: 10). At the economic frontier individuals make decisions to seek property rights on the basis that their benefits will outweigh the costs of acquisition and enforcement (Demsetz 1967, Alston, Libecap and Schneider 1996: 27). If unowned resources increase in value, or become cheaper to claim, there are incentives for migration to the frontier (Alston, Libecap and Schneider 1996: 32, Alston, Harris and Mueller 2009: 5–6). When resources are abundant, an influx of migrants does not reduce the income or benefit levels of existing users, and there is no need for a rule to protect possession because all resource users may exploit a resource without creating significant negative effects on fellow users (Fitzpatrick 2006: 1016). Not only are there no costly races for possession or consumption, there are no costs in enforcing possessory claims to a resource.

As resource values rise and induce further migration, a user of land at the frontier may rely on self-help remedies alone to protect her possession. She may erect signs and a fence to send signals to potential encroachers. She may engage in violent acts of defence against actual encroachers. Yet self-defensive mechanisms tend to lead to dissipation of resources that could have been put to more efficient use if they were applied as investments in the resource itself (Fitzpatrick 2006: 1023). The dissipation of resources in self-help defence of possession, in circumstances of rising resource values, will encourage all property claimants, including current possessors, to seek assistance from second party coalitions of supporters, or third-party sources of socio-political authority (Ellickson 1991: 127). As people migrate to the frontier, in circumstances of relative resource abundance, the first social cost of relevance will be the threat of encroachment rather than the risk of over-consumption of resources (Smith 2002: S482–85). In the absence of third-party enforcement authority, usually in the form of the state, a resource claimant will tend to seek coalitions with compatible users to reduce the costs of property enforcement (Alston, Harris and Mueller 2009: 5–6, 8, Anderson and Hill 2004: 167, 172, 175, Fitzpatrick 2006: 177–78, 1028). In economic terms the coalition will form when the transaction costs of agreement, including group numbers, stability and homogeneity, are low enough to allow cooperative efforts to exclude outsiders (Libecap 2003: 146–50). Second party coalitions for enforcing property claims provide a mechanism to reduce the risk of encroachment by restricting the numbers of eligible claimants (Alston, Harris and Mueller 2009: 8).

Where the primary threat to resource rents is encroachment the second party coalition may supplement its exclusionary activity with a simple rule of possession, which allows rights to cleared or cultivated land without reference to more interpretively complex rules of property allocation. A simple rule of possession provides a low-cost mechanism for property allocation within the group, while also allowing users to capture returns from investment in acts of possession. Yet a simple rule of possession may also encourage costly racing within the group as group members make greater efforts to obtain possession in order to appropriate resources before other group members (Lueck 1995: 406–07). As a result, the coalition has incentives to agree rules on the use of resources, as well as mechanisms to monitor and enforce compliance with the rules (Fitzpatrick 2006: 1028). In response to further in-migration and the rising value of resources, members of a second party property system may respond in a consensual manner by allowing more exclusionary forms of internal property distribution, to reduce the externality of resource over-consumption, or by increasing the complexity of governance mechanisms for monitoring and enforcing rules of resource use (Smith 2002: S480–1).

Where in-migration poses a threat to the exclusionary capacity of the second party coalition, the coalition may supplement its rules of resource governance with a rule on abandonment, which removes rights from prior possessors to make land available for new claimants.[5] The rule on abandonment represents an attempt by the coalition to reduce the enforcement costs of property in the absence of third party sources of property enforcement authority.[6] The second party coalition may also develop a distinction between actual and legal or constructive possession, which allows in-migrants rights to land while retaining exclusionary authority in the hands of the group. The distinction between actual and legal or constructive possession also reduces the enforcement costs of property, by maintaining the conditions for collective action and preventing in-migrants from inviting in other claimants, without reference to group rules on claimant eligibility. In both cases – abandonment and actual possession – there is a grant of rights early in the process of racing for rights, which is consistent with Dean Lueck's analysis (1995: 422–30) of first possession rule design to minimize wasteful acts of competitive racing.

## Conclusion

In this chapter we have suggested that origin principles – reproduced through ritual and symbolized by sacred houses – act as resilient sources of social ordering in East Timor because they provide a visible signal of relations with land, which are interpreted by in-migrant property claimants as focal points to avoid costly conflict and secure access to resources. In game-theoretic terms, principles of respect for prior possession provide a common focal point to encourage strategies of resource

5 In a similar manner to the Californian gold mining districts, the 'squatters' of eastern Australia also developed a rule on abandonment to manage land relations beyond the line of settlement: see Alston, Harris, and Mueller 2011: 13.

6 Whether or not the rule on abandonment provides marginal reductions in enforcement costs of property will turn on the extent to which the rule itself induces marginal increases in acts of encroachment. Marginal reductions in the enforcement costs of property, as a result of the rule on abandonment, may be outweighed marginal increases in encroachment as a result of the incentives established by the rule: see Alston, Libecap and Mueller 2000. However, when developing the rule on abandonment, members of the second party coalition will not know whether it will create marginal increases in encroachment, as the calculus of encroachment will also include the value of the land, the demand for land, and the opportunity cost of migration to the frontier.

use cooperation. Respect for possession is said to provide a low information cost response to the potential for disorderly resource competition. Game-theoretic analysis suggests that social order can emerge autonomously from spreading patterns of respect for possession, without a necessary need for interpretation or enforcement of possession from sources of public authority (Sugden 1989, 1986). In Hayekian terms possessory norms develop as a result of mutually reinforcing expectations of respect for possession.

There is a potential analogy between origin principles, which incorporate notions of ancestral first possession, and game-theoretic treatment of the relationship between possessory principles and social order. However, while our thesis is that origin principles have been focal points for social ordering in East Timor, we do not suggest that the relationship between possession and social order can be understood without reference to the interpretive content of possessory rules and their relationship with systems of public authority. Focal points such as principles of first possession should be understood in a contingent sense, as autonomous precursors to game-theoretic decision-making by resource claimants. They are resilient because of their potential to maintain social order in contexts of heightened fears of social disorder. But they remain constructed arrangements, and the ambit of public land authority established by first possession narratives is a matter of negotiation, in a context of local power relations, rather than a necessary ordering consequence of the first possession principles themselves. As constructed arrangements for social ordering, focal points such as first possession are constrained by the potential for contestation over their interpretation and the presence of multiple institutions of public authority, which can act as alternative sources of legitimacy, expectation and enforcement for property claimants.

In the next chapter we discuss the legal regulation of resilient customary property systems after armed conflicts. On one view, the appropriate regulatory response to customary resilience is to provide legal space for self-organized customary property systems. This view is consistent with the work of Elinor Ostrom (1990). On another view, the best legal response is to allow for transition from custom to law, as population pressure and rising resource values create incentives for individuated resort to law. This view is associated with the work of Harold Demsetz (1967). We argue that both regulatory approaches, involving either recognition or replacement of customary systems, need to account for the development of customary rule complexity as an institutional mechanism to reduce the enforcement costs of property, at least in circumstances where third party enforcement systems are not present or able to impose bright-line rules of allocations on all prospective users. Ostrom-inspired policy approaches assume relatively static models of legal space for local collective action, involving identification of community 'rules', and can overlook the constructed, contextualized and inherently complex nature of community custom (Berry 2009, Peters 2004). Conversely, Demsetzian attempts to replace or standardize custom through law assume a ready transition from custom to law, under the influence of competitive institutional conditions, and a stable context of social order underpinned by legitimate and capable forms of state authority. In both cases, we suggest that there are complexity/simplicity trade-offs in the interpretive content of legal responses to custom that are affected not only by considerations of resource use efficiency but by imperatives for social ordering.

## References

Abudulai, S. 2002. Land Rights, Land-Use Dynamics and Policy in Peri-Urban Tamale, Ghana, in P. Delville, C. Toulmin and S. Traore (eds), *The Dynamics of Resource Tenure in West Africa*. UK: Heinemann.

Adger, W.N. 1999. Social Vulnerability to Climate Change and Extremes in Coastal Vietnam. *World Development*, 27(2), 249–269.

Adger, W.N., Huq S., Brown, K., Conway, D. and Hulme, M. 2003. Adaptation to Climate Change in the Developing World. *Development Studies*, 3(3), 179–195.

Adger, W.N. 2000. Social and Ecological Resilience: Are they Related? *Progress in Human Geography*, 24(3), 347–364.

Adger, W.N., Hughes, T., Folke, C., Carpenter, S.R., and Rockström, S. 2005. Social-Ecological Resilience to Coastal Disasters. *Science*, 12 August 2005, 1036–1039.

Alchian, A. and Demsetz, H. 1973. The Property Right Paradigm. *J. Econ. Hist*, 33(16).

Alston, L., Libecap, G., and Schneider, R. 1996. The Determinants and Impact of Property Rights: Land Titles on the Brazilian Frontier. *Journal of Law, Economics and Organization*, 33: 177–97.

Alston, L.J., Harris, E. and Mueller, B. 2011. Property Rights, Land Settlement and Land Conflict on Frontiers: Evidence from Australia, Brazil and the U.S., in K. Ayotte amd H.E. Smith (eds), *Research Handbook on the Economics of Property Law*. UK: Edward Elgar.

Alston, L., Libecap, G. and Mueller, B. 1999. *Titles, Conflict, and Land Use: The Development of Property Rights and Land Reform on the Brazilian Amazon Frontier*. Ann Arbor, MI: University of Michigan Press.

Axelrod, R. 1984. *The Evolution of Cooperation*. New York: Basic Books.

Anderson, T. and Hill, P.J. 2002. Cowboys and Contracts. *J. Legal Stud.*, 31: S489, S499.

Bailey, J. 1992. Approximate Optimality of Aboriginal Property Rights. *Journal of Law & Economics*, 35(1), 183.

Baland, J.M. and Platteau, J.-P. 1998. Division of the Commons: A Partial Assessment of the New Institutional Economics of Land Rights. *Am. J. Agric. Econ.*, 80: 644, 647.

Renard-Clamagirand, B. 1982. Marobo: Une société ema de Timor. Langues et Civilisation de L'Asie du Sud-Est et du Monde Insulindien 12. Paris: SELAF.

Clay, K. and Wright, G. 2005. Order without Law? Property Rights during the California Gold Rush. *Explorations in Economic History*, 42: 155.

De Soto, H. 2000. *The Mystery of Capital Why Capitalism Triumphs in the West and Fails Everywhere Else*. Basic Books.

Deal, R. 2010. Fast-Fish, Loose-Fish: How Whalemen, Lawyers, and Judges Created the British Property Law of Whaling. *Ecology Law Quarterly*, 37: 204–7.

Deininger, K. 2003. Land Policies for Growth and Poverty Reduction. In *World Bank Policy Research Report*. Washington: Oxford University Press/World Bank, 47.

Demsetz, H. 1967. Toward a Theory of Property Rights. *Am. Econ. Rev.*, 57: 347.

Eggertsson, T. 2003. Open Access Versus Common Property, in T.L. Anderson and F.S. McChesney (eds), *Property Rights: Cooperation, Conflict, and Law*. Princeton: Princeton University Press, pp. 73, 74.

Ellickson, R.C. 1993. Property in Land. *Yale L.J.*, 102: 1315, 1322.

Ellickson, R.C. 1991. *Order Without Law: How Neighbors Settle Disputes*. Cambridge, MA: Harvard University Press.

Ellickson, R.C. 1989. A Hypothesis of Wealth-Maximizing Norms: Evidence from the Whaling Industry. *Journal of Law, Economics, and Organization*, (5)83.

Epstein, R. 2002. The Allocation of the Commons: Parking on Public Roads. *J. Legal Stud.*, 31: S515, S516, S519.

Feeny, D. 1988. The Development of Property Rights in Land: A Comparative Study, in R.H. Bates (ed.), *Toward a Political Economy of Development*. Berkeley: University of California Press, p. 272.

Fitzpatrick, D. 2006. Evolution and Chaos in Property Systems: The Third World Tragedy of Contested Access. *Yale Law Journal*, 115: 996–1048.

Fitzpatrick, D. 1997. Disputes and Pluralism in Modern Indonesian Land Law. *Yale Journal of International Law*, 22: 171.

Fitzpatrick, D. and Barnes, S. 2010. The Relative Resilience of Property: First Possession and Order without Law in East Timor. *Law and Society Review*, 44(2).

Forman, S. 1980. Descent, Alliance and Exchange Ideology among the Makassae of East Timor, in J.J. Fox (ed.), *The Flow of Life: Essays on Eastern Indonesia*. Cambridge, MA: Harvard University Press, pp. 152–77.

Hardin, G. 1968. The Tragedy of the Commons. *Science*, 3: 1243.

Hayek, F.A. 1979. *Law, Legislation, and Liberty.* Chicago: University of Chicago Press.

Heller, M. 1999. The Boundaries of Private Property. *Yale L.J.*, 108: 1163, 1193–4.

Hicks, D. 1976. *Tetun Ghosts and Kin: Fieldwork in an Indonesian Community*. Palo Alto, CA: Mayfield.

Holling, C.S. 1973. Resilience and Stability of Ecological Systems. *Annual Review of Ecology and Systematics*, 4: 1–23.

Knetsch, J. and Trebilcock, M. 1984. Land Policy and Economic Development in Papua New Guinea. Inst. of Nat'l Affairs, Discussion Paper No. 6, 32–3.

Krier, J. 1992. The Tragedy of the Commons, Part Two. *Harv. J.L. & Pub. Pol'y*, 15: 325, 337–9.

Krier, J.E. 2009. Evolutionary Theory and the Origin of Property Rights. *Cornell Law Review*, (95)139, 151–2.

Leshy, J. 1987. *The Mining Law: A Study in Perpetual Motion*. Washington: Resources for the Future.

Libecap, G. 2003. Contracting for Property Rights, in T. Anderson and F. McChesney (eds), *Property Rights: Cooperation, Conflict and Law*, at 142, 155–56.

Lueck, D. 1995. The Rule of First Possession and the Design of the Law. *Journal of Law and Economics*, 38: 393.

Lund, C. 2002. Negotiating Property Institutions: On the Symbiosis of Property and Authority in Africa, in K. Juul and C. Lund (eds), *Negotiating Property in Africa.* Portsmouth: Heinemann, p. 107.

McAdams, R. 2000. A Focal Point Theory of Expressive Law. *Virginia Law Review*, 86: 1649.

McDowell, A. 2002. From Commons to Claims: Property Rights in the California Gold Rush. *Yale Journal of Law and Humanities*, 14(1).

McDowell, A. 2004. Real Property, Spontaneous Order, and Norms in the Gold Mines. *Law & Social Inquiry*, 29.

McWilliam, A.R. 2007. Customary Claims and the Public Interest: On Fataluku Resource Entitlements in Lautem, in D. Kingsbury and M. Leach (eds), *East Timor: Beyond Independence.* Melbourne: Monash Asia Institute Press, pp. 168–75.

Merrill, T. 2002. Introduction: The Demsetz Thesis and the Evolution of Property Rights. *J. Legal Stud.*, 31: S331, S331.

Merrill, T. and Smith, H. 2000. Optimal Standardization in the Law of Property: The Numerus Clausus Principle. *Yale Law Journal*, (110)1.

Merry, S.E. 1988. Legal Pluralism. *Law and Society Review*, 22: 870.

Metzner, J. 1977. *Man and Environment in Eastern Timor: A Geo-Ecological Analysis of the Baucau-Viqueque Area as a Possible Basis for Regional Planning.* Canberra: Australian National University.

Moore, S.F. 1998. Changing African Land Tenure: Reflections on the Incapacities of the State. *European Journal of Development Research*, 10(2), 33.

Morriss, A.P. 2005. Hayek and Cowboys: Customary Law in the American West. *N.Y.U. J. L. & Liberty*, 1: 35, 48.

North, D. 1990. *Institutions, Institutional Change and Economic Performance.* Cambridge: Cambridge University Press.

Nugent, J.B. and Sanchez, N. 1998. Common Property Rights as an Endogenous Response to Risk. *Am. J. Agric. Econ.*, 80: 651.

Olson, M. Jr. 1965. *The Logic of Collective Action: Public Goods and the Theory of Groups*. Cambridge, MA: Harvard University Press.

Ostrom, E. 1990. *Governing the Commons: The Evolution of Institutions for Collective Action.* Cambridge and New York: Cambridge University Press.

Ostrom, E. 2005. *Understanding Institutional Diversity*. Princeton, NJ: Princeton University Press.

Otsuka, K. and Place, F. 2001. Introduction to Land Tenure and Natural Resource Management: A Comparative Study of Agrarian Communities in Asia and Africa, in K. Otsuka and F. Place (eds), *Land Tenure and Natural Resource Management: A Comparative Study of Agrarian Communities in Asia and Africa.* Baltimore: Johns Hopkins University Press.

Paavola, J. and Adger, W.N. 2006. New Institutional Economics and the Environment: Conceptual Foundations and Policy Implications. Working Paper. Centre for Social and Economic Research on the Global Environment.

Platteau, J.-P. 1992. Land Reform and Structural Adjustment in Sub-Saharan Africa: Controversies and Guidelines. Food and Agriculture Organization of the United Nations. Econ. & Soc. Dev. Paper.

Platteau, J.P. 2000. *Institutions, Social Norms and Economic Development*. Oxford and New York: Routledge.

Posner, R. 1980. A Theory of Primitive Society, with Special Reference to Law. *J.L. & Econ.*, 23: 1.

Richard, P.R. 1993. *Economic Analysis of Law (6th edition)*. Aspen Casebooks.

Sahlins, M. 1999. Two or Three Things that I Know about Culture. *JRAI*, 5(3), 399–421.

Smith, H. 2002. Exclusion Versus Governance: Two Strategies for Delineating Property Rights. *J. Legal Stud.*, 31: S453, S463.

Sugden, R. 1986. *The Economics of Rights, Cooperation, and Welfare*. Oxford: Blackwell.

Sugden, R. 1989. Spontaneous Order. *Journal of Economic Perspectives*, 3(85), 88–90.

Taylor, M. 1987. *The Possibility of Cooperation.* Cambridge: Cambridge University Press.

Traube, E.G. 1986. *Cosmology and Social Life: Ritual Exchange among the Mambai of East Timor*. Chicago: University of Chicago Press.

Trebilcock, M. and Veel, P. 2008. Property Rights and Development: The Contingent Case for Formalization, University of Pennsylvania *Journal of International Law*, 30: 397.

Umbeck, J.R. 1981. *A Theory of Property Rights with Application to the California Gold Rush.* Ames: Iowa State University Press.

Wilson, B., Jaworski, T., Schurter, K., Smyth, A. 2012. The Ecological and Civil Mainsprings of Property: An Experimental Economic History of Whalers' Rules of Capture. *J. Law Econ. Organ.* (doi:10.1093/jleo/ewr024).

Zerbe, R.O. and Anderson, C.L. 2001. Culture and Fairness in the Development of Institutions in the California Gold Fields. *Journal of Economic History*, 61.

# Chapter 4
# Contested Transitions from Custom to Law: Property Rights in a Weak State

## Introduction

In the preceding chapter we set out the hypothesis that different complexity/simplicity trade-offs in the interpretive content of property rules apply in different circumstances of social ordering. The hypothesis provides a fresh perspective on Robert Ellickson's well-known hypothesis (1989) that in close-knit community contexts more complex rules may emerge where the increased costs of their interpretation are outweighed by increased gains from trade. Our case studies suggest that rule complexity may emerge where the increased costs of their interpretation are outweighed by reductions in property enforcement costs, at least in environments where there are risks of costly racing for rights to resources. Complex norms of ancestral first possession have evolved in East Timor as a response to fears of property conflict, in a context of population mobility, rather than as a direct response to potential gains from trade in agricultural products. While social order creates conditions for gains from trade, East Timor's complex systems of customary resource governance suggest a correlation between possessory rule complexity and reductions in property enforcement costs through maintenance of social order, in circumstances of potentially costly racing for rights to resources.

This chapter considers whether a relationship between social order, and the interpretive complexity of possessory rules, applies when possessory rules move beyond a close-knit customary context. Henry Smith (2009) suggests an information cost trade-off in matters of custom and law: where complex customs are recognized by law, either the process of communicating property information is made more costly for remote third parties, or standardization is required to strip the custom of its informational complexity. The East Timor example suggests that standardizing customary rules of first possession may reduce information costs, but may also create conflict in frontier areas where the state is unable or unwilling to engage in coercive enforcement of legal claims over longstanding customary claims. The analysis builds on Lee Alston, Edwyna Harris and Bernardo Mueller's hypothesis (2009: 6; 2011: 5) that violent land conflicts may emerge at a property enforcement frontier when a state is unable to enforce *de jure* property rights against competing customary claims developed by frontier mechanisms for private ordering. In these conflict-affected circumstances, there is a potential trade-off between the greater information costs of recognising complex customary rules of first possession, and the capacity of complex customary rules to reduce the enforcement costs of property.

## Simplicity and Complexity in Legal Rules Relating to Custom

Property rights theorists draw distinctions between 'bright-line' and 'fuzzy' rules of property. Bright-line rules involve *ex ante* identification of permitted and proscribed behavior. Fuzzy rules involve levels of ambiguity or discretion that may require *ex post* interpretation by a source of adjudicative authority (Krier 2009: 155–6, Dukeminier and Krier, 1993: 103–21, Penner 1997: 148). Merrill and Smith (2011: 31–4; 2001: 39) argue that bright-line rules are the appropriate baseline for property regulation because property information is costly in nature (see also Smith 2003: 1108–1113). Unlike *in personam* rights, which are limited to specified parties to a contract or Court judgment, the *in rem* rights of property establish duties of non-interference in a broad class of potential violators. The cost of compliance with duties of non-interference is prohibitively large where the permitted range of uses of a resource varies from 'place to place, thing to thing, or even person to person' (Merrill and Smith 2011: 10). The alternative is a simple rule of exclusion: If A is the owner, and the message is 'don't touch', there is a low-cost solution to the problem of compliance with property (Merrill and Smith 2011: 35–6). Hence the common law limits the range of rights that an owner may create to bind third parties, through the doctrine of *numerus clausus*, to ensure low-cost messages to a broad property audience (Merrill and Smith 2000). Correspondingly, the common law allows much greater flexibility for contracting parties to create context-specific *in personam* rights, as the cost of information remains comparatively low relative to the audience (that is the parties to the agreement) (Smith (2003: 1110–11).

Rule simplicity reduces costs for potential property transactors as well as violators. Merrill and Smith (2011: 28) put this point through a simple metaphor: if the applicable rule grants A the right of exclusion in relation to a car, then everyone knows that they must strike a deal with A. If 'all the world' has the right to use a car, and A wishes to use a car, then A will have to strike a deal with all the world. A rule that provides for ownership – the simplest form of exclusionary entitlement -facilitates transactions and establishes an incentive to invest in a resource, which serves to maintain it and prevent over-consumption, because the owner captures the benefit of her investment. This is why the law prefers simple 'winner-take-all' rules for the initial acquisition or allocation of property (Merrill and Smith 2011: 6). The rule of first possession grants exclusive rights to the first person to engage in acts of control over an unowned resource, available for claim, because it provides a low-cost mechanism for allocating ownership (Epstein 1979). Even a rule of adverse possession, which transfers rights from an owner, is justified by cost/benefit considerations because it removes the need for potential violators or transactors to search for old titles in the hands of a person not in possession, and provides a low cost mechanism for determining ownership when other means of proof are lost or costly to establish (Merrill 1984).[1] It follows that a legal rule allowing context-specific disaggregation of rights in a resource – implicit in the standard 'bundle of rights' metaphor for property – is justified where increased transactional gains from disaggregated rights outweigh the increased information costs of identifying, delineating and enforcing multiple interests in a resource (Merrill and Smith 2000).

Merrill and Smith (2007) argue for optimal rather than maximal standardization of property rules. In information cost terms the calculus of rule design tilts towards interpretive complexity where the efficiency benefits of complexity outweigh the increased costs of information, taking into account the size and nature of the audience (Smith 2003: 1109–11). The legal treatment of custom illustrates the baseline implication for property rules: all else being equal, the larger the audience the less likely a rule allowing for interpretive complexity (Smith 2003: 1117–21; 2009). As a general rule, custom can be adopted without a great deal of standardization when the audience is limited, or there are low informational demands on the prospective audience (Smith 2009: 13, 30). However, in cases of customs relating to property, the potential audience is often extensive as those interested in purchasing, valuing or using resources can extend far beyond the members of a local community, and can include state interests in taxation or the provision of services or infrastructure. This broad audience will incur significant costs in identifying property interests under customary regimes (Smith 2009: 21–22). According to Smith (2009: 23–24), where efficient but information-rich customs are recognized by law, either the process of communicating property information is made more costly for remote third parties, or the custom must be stripped of its informational complexity through a process of modification and standardization.

Smith's illustrations of the relationship between custom and law include the legal treatment of customary mining rules in the United States (Smith 2009: 32–33). The 19th century Californian mining rule of first possession was adopted by the US courts as the doctrine of *pedis possessio*, which applies to mining exploration before discovery of minerals and acquisition of a patent under the General Mining Law of 1872 (Finberg 1982). As with its customary predecessor, the *pedis possessio* doctrine includes the possibility of abandonment: possessory rights are lost once a prospector stops work and moves to another claim, at which point another prospector may obtain a property interests through the taking of possession. This aspect of mining custom has been criticized on the basis that under modern mining conditions there are benefits in multiple exploration of claims, and significant costs that prevent simultaneous exploration of those claims (Smith 2003: 1036–37). Nevertheless, in *Geomet Exploration, Limited v. Lucky Mc Uranium*

1 While some rules of adverse possession have complex interpretive elements, such as requirements of good faith, these may be justified where the benefits of incentives against 'bad faith' possession, with intent to deprive ownership through forced rather than voluntary transfer, outweigh the increased interpretation costs of rule complexity (Merrill 1984).

*Corporation*,[2] the Supreme Court of Arizona applied the *pedis possessio* rule to recognize rights to claim the workings of a mining company that had moved on to another exploration area. Smith (2009: 34) suggests that the court did not relax the customary requirements for ongoing work of a claim during the exploration phase, because in circumstances of absence of the possessor the informational demands of ascertaining property entitlements were too great for prospective users to bear. A rule modification allowing for abandonment would create greater information costs because possession would not set the visible and measurable limits of entitlement, in circumstances where there was no other low cost mechanism for ascertaining entitlement (such as a register for mining exploration claims).

Whaling customs provide a similar example of legal adoption of possessory customs without a significant degree of standardization or reduction in interpretive complexity (Ellickson 1989: 89–90, Deal 2010: 207, 216–19, Smith 2009: 28–29). For example, in *Glen* v *Rich* the Court determined entitlement to a dead whale, found on a beach by a beachcomber, on the basis of localized whaling custom that favored the first whaler to harpoon the whale.[3] There were efficiency benefits to the custom, which rewarded investment in the hunt (Ellickson 1989: 89–90). Moreover, the whaling rules of capture were relatively settled and the applicable audience remained whalers and at times beachcombers only. Unlike the case of land, remote third parties were not generally interested in determining ownership rights to dead or captured whales. In information costs terms, the interpretive demands of whaling customs, in the light of their prospective audience, were not such as to require their modification and standardization through law (Smith 2009: 20–29). Smith (2003: 1121) cites Judge Lowell in *Swift* v *Gifford*,[4] another case favoring whaling custom over a general rule of possession:

> While some [cases] represent great rules of policy, and are beyond the reach of convention, others may be changed by parties [including] … by usage, which, if general and long established, is equivalent to a contract.

In other cases the US courts have modified or replaced custom in order to reduce information costs for community outsiders. For example, in the fox-hunting case of *Pierson v. Post* the court declined to follow the hunting custom favoring the first hunter to find and pursue a fox. The majority formulated a possessory rule that granted rights to the first hunter to take possession of the carcass. Carol Rose (1985: 77) suggests that the adoption of a rule of capture, rather than the norm of fresh pursuit, arose from the majority's preference for a 'clear rule' that also provided reward for labor in most cases (see also Krier 2009: 77). Smith concludes (2003: 1118) that the majority sought to establish a rule for a broad audience, 'not all of whom … concerned with foxes'. While hunting custom may have rewarded

2 601 P.2d 1339 (Ariz. 1979).

3 U.S. District Ct., Dist. of MA (1881).

4 23 Fed. Cas. 558 (D. Mass. 1872).

in all cases the hunter who expended effort on finding the fox, and engaged in fresh pursuit, the interpretive costs of judicial determination of fresh pursuit, and the relative simplicity of the alternative possessory rule, outweighed the reward for effort incentives of the adoption of custom.

These US examples suggest a number of information cost principles for the design of property laws relating to customary rules of first possession. Customary rules of first possession may not require modification either when the prospective audience remains small and close-knit, the modification would provide net increases in informational complexity, or the custom itself has a high degree of invariance to context. Custom may require modification where it is rich in contextual complexity, and the prospective audience extends beyond the originating community. If custom is not modified, in these circumstances, there will be increased costs of information transmission to remote third parties. Where custom does require modification to reduce information costs, Smith (2009: 27–8) argues that relatively simple default rules, such as a bright-line rule of first possession, have a 'gravitational pull' once the audience for property information extends beyond a community of connected resource users. This baseline preference for bright-line rules of possession arises from their characteristics as lower cost mechanisms for the transmission of property information.

In East Timor the rationale for standardizing custom through law seems even greater than for the fox-hunters of the United States. In East Timor, customary rules of ancestral first possession are information-rich and context-specific. The development of new land law involves the basis for ownership in a new nation-state. As a response to high rates of poverty, the government plans to encourage outside investment in rural districts.[5] The law applies not only to a customary audience but to all citizens of East Timor. While customary audiences (the rule-followers) may have comparatively low information-processing costs, owing to their familiarity with customary principles and processes, both the courts (rule-enforcers) and outside investors (potential transactors) will have high information costs owing to the contextualized information-rich nature of custom. In information cost terms, these circumstances suggest a baseline preference for standardized legal rules that strip customary rules of their informational complexity, unless there are reductions in deadweight losses arising from legal recognition of complex customs. We argue that in East Timor there are efficiency benefits to the legal recognition of interpretively complex custom as rule complexity/simplicity trade-offs must take into account the weak state/resilient custom context, which includes a frontier for state enforcement of legal claims to land. As our case studies illustrate, at the legal frontier for property enforcement there are customary mechanisms for managing the social costs of resource governance, as long as localized transaction costs – including issues of group size, homogeneity and stability – remain low enough to allow collective

5 In 2009 approximately 41 per cent of the population lived below the poverty line (World Bank 2009). For a summary of the government's plans for rural development see Government of Timor Leste (2010: 9).

action. In East Timor the social costs of resource governance primarily include the risks of costly racing for rights to resources as a result of population displacement, rather than 'tragedies of the commons' arising from open access to resources. Legal intervention by the state, including attempts to standardize customary principles of land allocation, will increase the transaction costs of collective responses to post-conflict racing for rights to resources when the law provides opportunities for resource claimants to exit customary mechanisms, by providing alternative pathways for property claims (Trebilcock and Veel 2008: 447). If the state is unable to enforce legal claims, increases in the transaction costs of collective action, and degradations in customary system capacity to manage costly racing for rights to resources, may create increased social costs that outweigh the reduced costs of interpretation and information under a standardized legal rule.

## Rule Complexity and Reductions in Property Enforcement Costs at the Legal Frontier

Alston, Harris, and Mueller (2009: 4–6, 2011: 4–5) hypothesize four stages of settlement at the legal frontier for enforcement of property rights. In the first stage, cost/benefit calculations lead to initial assertions of property rights with little or no potential for conflict due to the relative abundance of resources. In the second stage, further migration to the frontier creates incentives for coalitions to protect possession and regulate resource use. In the third stage, customary claimants petition the state for *de jure* rights in order to maintain income levels and reduce the costs of property enforcement (see also Alston, Libecap and Schneider 1996: 33–4). Yet the state may provide legal recognition to claimants other than customary frontier claimants for reasons of its own, including the satisfaction of constituency interests. In this third stage of settlement, the state is unable to enforce *de jure* claims, which creates the possibility of violent conflict between customary and *de jure* claimants, unless customary claimants have a large violence advantage due to their pre-existing physical and economic presence (Alston, Harris and Mueller 2009: 47). In the fourth stage, the frontier settles and there is little potential for conflict because the state has a comparative advantage in violence and is willing and able to enforce *de jure* claims over customary claims.

Morriss (2005: 62) argues that private ordering examples in the American West, including the gold mining codes of California, did not survive as the frontier settled because the state had a 'competitive advantage in providing law, derived from its ability to cross-subsidize the production of services'. Unlike private ordering systems, the costs of which are borne by users, the state was able to spread the costs of legal order over the general taxpaying populace by funding police, prosecutors, courts, military outposts and the like (Morriss 2005: 62–63). Yet the frontier may not settle where there are longstanding customary mechanisms for managing social costs relating to property, and the state lacks the fiscal, technical and adjudicative capacity – or even the internal cohesion – to enforce legal claims over customary claims. At this legal frontier the marginal costs of enforcing property rights are high because second party frontier systems divert resources from production to defence, and the state must engage in processes of forced eviction in order to uphold *de jure* claims. These circumstances correspond with the penultimate stage of frontier settlement identified by Alston, Harris, and Mueller (2009: 6, 2011: 5). As noted, they tend to create a functional form of institutional complexity, where property claimants 'shop' their claims across different fora for property enforcement and legitimation.

The state may reduce enforcement costs at the frontier through laws that promote settlements that are easier to defend against customary claimants. For example, Douglas Allen (1991) argues that homesteading policy in the United States sought to reduce the costs of enforcing property rights at the frontier in the face of native American Indian resistance. Homesteading provided an alternative to the costly use of military force to enforce encroachment on Indian land (Allen 1991: 2). Allen (1991: 11) argues that the design of the Homestead Act 1862, in particular, sought to maximize the property enforcement value of frontier settlement. Homesteading was based on a rule of first possession, but was only available on surveyed lands, which opened the land in sections. It restricted homesteads to not more than 160 acres, which created denser forms of settlement. It required 5 years' residence after grant, and improvements to the land, which reduced the potential for speculation and ensured an ongoing settler presence for the purposes of defense (Allen 1991: 6, 10–11). Unlike the contrasting cases of Canada and Australia, where Allen (1991: 21–2) suggests there was less threat of dispossession as a result of violent indigenous resistance, homesteading policy in the United States had elements of administrative and interpretive complexity, which were directed at developing denser settlements, maintaining settler populations, and facilitating military defence against Indian attack.

The state may reduce the enforcement costs of property through another mechanism: by recognising customary systems of frontier ordering. While there is now considerable literature on the efficiency benefits of custom, in terms of tenure security (for example Bruce, 1998) and sustainable resource management (for example Ostrom 1990), customary land systems may also provide an efficient mechanism to reduce the enforcement costs of property, particularly by comparison with high cost state alternatives. Generally speaking, as we have suggested, the legal recognition of custom will have complex interpretive elements because of the contextualized nature of traditional authority, restrictions on eligibility for possessory claims to group members, and distinctions as to the property significance of acts of possession according to status within the group. Yet, in circumstances of state weakness, the legal recognition of complex customs may provide the lowest objective sum of transaction costs notwithstanding the relative costs of their interpretation. Moreover, the fact that customary arrangements of the kind seen in East Timor are embedded in complex kinship relations, and provide an ordering mechanism in circumstances of state weakness, means that any attempt to standardize them through law may itself involve substantial costs of institutional transition (Benda-Beckmann, 1995,

Binswanger et al., 1993, Platteau, 1992: 30–1, 41–2, 64, 232–44; Trebilcock and Veel 2008: 447–48).

Even with support from the state, customary mechanisms for reducing enforcement costs may degrade due to in-migration, as increased numbers and heterogeneity increase the transaction costs of agreement among groups of resource users. For example, the order reportedly established by the Californian mining codes of 1848–49 soon gave way to extensive litigation as the number of miners per claim increased, technological changes allowed more capital-intensive mining that used wage labour, and there was a further 'influx of miners with different cultures' (Zerbe and Anderson 2001: McDowell 2004: 793). Similarly, the self-organized property allocations of the Amazon frontier came under pressure from increased numbers and heterogeneity of settlers, leading many to seek formal titles to land from the Brazilian state (Alston, Libecap and Schneider 1996: 33–4; Alston, Libecap and Mueller 1999: 98–152). These circumstances suggest that, even where the legal recognition of complex customary rules of possession provides the lowest objective sum of transaction costs at the frontier, the law must also allow for the degradation of custom as rising resource values undermine conditions for collective action and create incentives for land claimants to exit customary systems (Fitzpatrick 2006: 1033–38, Trebilcock 1984: 401–06). In this phase of frontier settlement, it is not possible to enforce a simple legal rule as the costs of transition from custom to law remain high, and yet a high degree ofinstitutional complexity develops as a result of degradations in customary property systems.

## Bright-line Rules at the Legal Frontier: The Development of Institutional Complexity

As the East Timor example suggests, the state may specify legal rights through a legal rule of possession even though it lacks the capacity to enforce legal rights over customary claims. This possibility arises from the political incentives of legislative development. Even democratic governments may not support efficient local claims when they are contrary to the interests of political constituencies, particularly as state agencies do not engage in direct cost-benefit calculations relating to reductions in deadweight losses. State agencies are more likely to pursue their own interests by pandering to a constituency, increasing tax revenues, or implementing a rent-seeking development agenda (Anderson and Hill 2002: 512, McChesney 2003: 227–28). Alston, Harris, and Mueller (2011) argue that these incentives may lead to specification of *de jure* property rights that are inconsistent with customary rights. In these circumstances, complexity arises not from the interpretive content of the legal rule, but from competitive interactions among formal and informal rules of property allocation. This form of institutional complexity correlates with the failure of the state to reduce the enforcement costs of property, either through co-opting of customary systems or increasing its capacity for violence.

Morriss (2005: 42–6) suggests that the decline of frontier ordering systems in the American West occurred in part because they did not serve the interests of political groups. Interest groups took advantage of political power to develop laws and institutions that furthered their own interests, which at times included rent-seeking attempts to appropriate the wealth generated by frontier institutions. For example, in Montana and Wyoming cattlemen's associations created private rules that governed most aspects of their business, including branding, roundups, sales and the like. However, whereas in Wyoming cattlemen had sufficient political power to incorporate their rules into state legislation, in Montana the political power of homesteaders led to laws that enclosed open grazing ranges. Anderson and Hill (2004: 159–76) similarly point to laws in the American West that favoured homesteaders over ranchers, leading to inefficient results when they encouraged homesteaders to engage in costly racing for rights to land newly made available by the government. In their comprehensive study of the Amazonian frontier, Alston, Libecap and Mueller (1999: 17–22) also describe the decisive role of political considerations, including constituencies for land reform, in determining whether land titles granted to groups that occupied unused land belonging to a private owner. In all these cases, the process of property system change, and the extent to which one group of frontier claimants was favoured over another, was largely driven by political processes and interactions among interest groups competing for political power.[6]

All else being equal, changes in property rights are costly because they require a degree of collective action (Banner 2002: S366–71; Wyman 2005). While collective action can be inhibited by the costs of organizing a political coalition, and incentives to free-ride on the organizational efforts of others, it can also be facilitated by decision-making structures that provide significant net benefits to property-changing coalitions, as for example when an interest group takes political control over the law-making authority and collective enforcement machinery of the state. The state, in particular, can drive property transitions at low cost to beneficiaries by spreading the cost of change across the taxpaying populace, and exercising its coercive capacity to enforce changes against existing property-holders without necessarily compensating them for any loss of rights (Banner 2002: 368, Epstein 2002: S516). The enhanced opportunities for legislative changes during the formation of a new nation-state increase incentives for minoritarian coalitions to race for control of the state in order to drive property transitions for the benefit of the dominant coalition (North, Wallis and Weingast 2009: 59). Conversely, extension of the voting franchise can create majoritarian incentives to intervene in frontier systems of property ordering on the basis of constituencies that favor notions of distributional fairness (Alston, Harris, and Mueller 2011). In either event, there are incentives for legal intervention in frontier customary systems on the basis of cost/benefit calculations that do not include the costs of property enforcement and competitive racing for rights to resources.

6 Alston, Harris, and Mueller (2009) also show that the nature and sequencing of group migration to the frontier affects political processes for the supply of property rights.

## Contested Transitions from Custom to Law: The Development of Legal Pluralism

Economic explanations for transitions from custom to law tend to assume that resource users will migrate to standardized legal versions of custom as a result of their relative institutional efficiency. For example, Posner (1980: 10–19) argues that customary systems act as efficient institutional responses to environmental risks, in circumstances where no other social insurance mechanism is available. This efficiency explanation implies that the introduction of more efficient arrangements, including state systems of law and public administration, will lead to a decline in the use of customary mechanisms. Users of non-state mechanisms will migrate to state institutions because they provide a low-cost means to enforce rights of contract and property, while also providing alternative forms of social insurance (Cooter 1991: 771–80 but see Trebilcock 1984: 388–90). Morriss (2005: 62) thus argues that private ordering examples in the American West, including the gold mining codes of California, did not survive as the frontier settled because the state had a 'competitive advantage in providing law, derived from its ability to cross-subsidize the production of services'. Unlike private ordering systems, the costs of which are borne by users, the state was able to spread the costs of legal order over the general taxpaying populace by funding police, prosecutors, courts, military outposts and the like (Morriss 2005: 62–3).

An informational approach to property highlights the fact that members of a customary community will face barriers to calculating the costs and benefits of resort to law, particularly where the interpretive costs of a law are high relative to the cognitive frameworks of custom itself. While there will be situational attempts to take advantage of new legal opportunities, there will also be an aversion to uncertainty that creates a form of social entropy, a residual loyalty to the familiar (Fitzpatrick and Barnes 2010, Moore 1978). In these circumstances, customary group members may variably interpret or misinterpret the standardized custom offered by state law, notwithstanding its low-cost and bright-line characteristics, because there are social, cultural, linguistic or geographic obstacles to accessing legal information (Luhmann 1985, Tuebner 1998: 15–25). Even in circumstances where cognitive understandings of custom and law have a degree of consonance, group members may continue to pursue their own information-rich versions of custom, notwithstanding attempts at legal standardization, because of the self-interest of influential actors in the community, or a collective interest in the continuation of custom or customary forms of authority as an alternative to imposed state authority. The result may be diverse interpretations of standardized custom, at multiple levels of resource and public governance. We discuss this possibility further in Chapter 10, which considers the potential implementation of East Timor's draft land law in rural districts.

Where the state is unable to impose a unitary system of property adjudication and enforcement, and customary systems retain a degree of social authority, disputants may resort to multiple sources of interpretive authority, and multiple formulations of custom, to maintain their claims of property rights in land (Lavigne Delville 2000: 97, Fitzpatrick 2006: 1040). This phenomenon is described in the literature on postcolonial land relations as legal forum shopping (Fitzpatrick 2006: 1015),[7] although it also often involves a degree of legal principle shopping, including as to the formulation of 'rules' of custom (Fitzpatrick 1997). At the same time, there may be 'shopping forums' where sources of authority – state and non-state – compete for interpretive and adjudicatory influence over contested property claims (Benda-Beckmann, von K. 1981). In these competitive circumstances, authority is constituted by the capacity to attract, interpret and purport to resolve matters relating to the control of resources (von Benda-Beckmann, von K. 1993: 127–30). Property and authority have mutually constitutive aspects, which is important as more efficient property institutions may not evolve through institutional competition where volatility in authority structures leads to instability and cyclical conflict in property arrangements (Lund 2002).

Simple legal rules can reduce transaction costs once the frontier settles, and the state has the legitimacy and capacity to enforce legal titles to land. Yet, where the frontier does not settle, attempts at standardizing custom through law may fail to achieve their objectives of reducing costs associated with property (Baxter and Trebilcock 2009: 101–11, Knetsch and Trebilcock, 1981: 32–3; Trebilcock and Veel 2008: 447–53). In postcolonial contexts, for example, numerous attempts at replacing complex customs with simple laws have increased transaction costs by overlaying formal institutions on informal arrangements, which allows disputants the opportunity to manipulate competing property enforcement mechanisms through legal forum shopping. The *in rem* nature of property creates zero-sum considerations that may lead some claimants – who would otherwise lose in a state-administered system – to assert the continuing legitimacy and relevance of customary institutions (Fitzpatrick 2006: 996). As predicted byAlston, Harris, and Mueller (2011), the result can be violent conflict where there is a degree of equivalence in the violence advantages of customary and *de jure* claimants. Alternatively, however, there may be a form of negotiated indeterminacy, where the quantum of property rights clarity is agreed at a low level, for fear of provoking costly conflict over attempts at crystallising rights. This phenomenon of negotiated indeterminacy, notwithstanding simple legal rules of property, is also much-observed in postcolonial contexts (see, for example Berry 1993, 1997, Bourdieu 1990, de Sardan 1999, Moore 1986, 1998).

---

7 The literature on 'legal forum shopping' in Third World environments is vast: for examples see Bruce, 1998, Fitzpatrick, 1997: 184, Knetsch and Trebilcock, 1981: 40, Lavigne-Delville, 2000: 108, Simpson 1976: 236, Toulmin and Quan, 2000: 219, Platteau, 1996: 41–6, Toulmin et al., 2002: 13.

## Customary Systems and the Evolution of Property Rights

The potential for incomplete and contested transitions from custom to law challenges economic accounts of autonomous evolution from collective to private property. Inspired by Harold Demsetz's 1967 article, 'The evolution of property rights', some economic explanations for the evolution of property rights tell an optimistic story: more crystalline delineations of property emerge as an efficient response to rising resource values (for example Alchian and Demsetz 1973). In Demsetzian terms, property definition is an efficient institutional response to problems of resource scarcity and over-exploitation (Demsetz 1967). As 'tragedies of the commons' develop, where rising resource values encourage unsustainable use of scarce resources, the benefits of asserting property rights may increase to the point where they outweigh the costs of establishing, measuring and enforcing the property right itself. According to some economists, these processes of degradation in collective property systems lead inevitably to a legal system of individuated private property rights (for example, Binswanger and McIntire 1987: 73).

Demsetz's example of autonomous evolution of property rights involved a transition from 'tribal-based collective ownership' to 'family-based private ownership' among the Montagne Indians who inhabited large regions of modern-day Québec. Prior to the arrival of Europeans, a system of collective ownership allowed any tribal member to hunt beaver within tribal territory. Because the demand for beaver fur was relatively low and internal to the tribe itself, the system did not lead to over-hunting. However, as the French began to buy furs from the Montagne, the rising value of beaver furs eventually led to over-hunting by tribal members and a reduction in net fur-trading income for the tribe as a whole (Demsetz 1967: 351–3). In Demsetz's words, '[p]rivate rights to land provided a practical way to ameliorate this problem' (Demsetz 2002: S656). As a number of scholars note, Harold Demsetz did not specify the mechanism for transition in his cost–benefit model of evolving property rights. His case study of the Montagne Indians simply provided 'before and after snapshots' of transition (Epstein 2002 S515–6, S519, Banner 2002: S360–61, Krier 1992: 325, 337–9, Merrill 2002: S333, 336, Heller 1997: 678). At one stage of their history, the Montagne Indians had a common property system. At a later stage, once demand for fur had increased, they appear to have moved to family-based private ownership of land.

Demsetz's analysis speaks only to demand for property rights. Changes in cost–benefit conditions may lead individuals to assert property rights, including through acts of possession. Yet there is no guarantee that these rights will be enforced 'against the world' as entitlements of property. As Merrill and Smith (2001: 358–9) note, much of the law and economics literature on property has overlooked the significance of exclusion – of enforcing rights against the world – in analysing the nature and function of property rights. Modern economists define property not in classical legal terms, as rights that attach to a thing and are good against the world, but as authorized rights to use a resource (without analyzing the source of that authority). Merrill and Smith (2001: 398) speculate that the distinctive, *in rem* characteristic of property 'is an idea that looms largest at a relatively early stage in social and economic development, when a society has not yet solved the problem of order'. In pluralist post-conflict contexts such as East Timor, the problem of social order, and its effect on transitions from custom to law, requires attention to sources of property enforcement authority at state and non-state levels (Fitzpatrick 2006). In other words, just as social ordering imperatives can explain the emergence of interpretive complexity in community-generated rules, so too can social ordering in plural property enforcement environments explain contested or incomplete transitions from custom to law.

Imagine a possessor who possesses without reference to any prevailing system of authority. She intends to rely on self-help remedies alone. She erects signs and a fence to send signals to potential encroachers. She values the resource highly, so she is prepared to divert time, money and effort from production to defence of her resource. Yet her rights of property will not be secure. There are always risks that other potential encroachers will value the resource even more highly than her, or at least calculate that the benefits of dispossession, combined with the potential value of the resource itself, are greater than the costs of dispossession efforts. These risks will increase as new entrants to the area become aware of the self-help reliance of the possessor. As Krier notes (2009: 155–6), even under game-theoretic conditions resource claimants will engage in violent acts of dispossession when the rewards of obtaining possession exceed the costs of violence. In these circumstances, Hayekian expectations of respect for possession will not necessarily prevent the emergence of resource conflict. Self-help acts of possession will not of themselves drive a transition to settled social patterns of exclusive rights of property. What is required is not only a rule that recognizes entitlements derived from possession, but a system of authority to enforce *in rem* aspects of the possessory entitlement (see also North 1990: 58; Platteau 2000: 283–4).

Those who desire a valuable resource held by a self-help possessor will not necessarily be limited by self-imposed enforcement constraints. The imperative to defend possession will encourage all property claimants, including current possessors, to seek assistance from coalitions of supporters, or intervention by socio-political authority (usually the state). While a possessor may assert an exclusionary claim when anticipated benefits exceed anticipated costs, possessory conflicts will develop where the mechanisms for enforcing property rights either are not available, or interact in an incompatible fashion. Enforcement mechanisms relating to property can be incompatible when the state purports to replace customary systems while lacking the capacity or local legitimacy to enforce new claims based on law. In these circumstances, there will be competing legal and customary systems, which may lead property claimants to affiliate with competing sources of property authority. This pattern of contested property pluralism is a common phenomenon in a number of postcolonial contexts (Fitzpatrick 2006). It is far removed from the clear property rights predicted by Demsetzian analysis, and yet is a plausible scenario as East Timor moves to legislate and implement a new law on private rights to customary land. In circumstances such as East Timor, the legal standardization or replacement of custom may exacerbate rather than resolve uncertainty, because customary 'rules' of property are contextualized and complex, and because customary systems have displayed a powerful capacity for resilience, even in circumstances of mass population displacement.

## The Structures of Constrained Resilience: State Encroachment and Degradation in Customary Systems

Incomplete or contested transitions from custom to law may produce a worst-case scenario: the degradation of local ordering mechanisms without replacement by the state. This situation arises because the phenomena that motivate resort to the state – rising resource values and increased interaction with outsiders – also tend to degrade the capacity of customary property systems to engage in collective action (Fitzpatrick 2006: 1033–7). As resource values rise, members of a common property system have a greater incentive to capture resource rents (which are benefits above ordinary returns from control of an asset). A common property system may respond in a consensual manner by allowing more exclusionary forms of internal property distribution or by tightening its governance mechanisms to resolve or prevent disputes caused by these inflationary pressures (Smith 2002: S480–81). Alternatively, it may deteriorate as group members defect in order to capture the gains of asserting increasingly exclusionary rights. In relation to land, for example, primary rights-holders may engage in acts of exclusion against other group members and the group as a whole by reclaiming fallow plots, purporting to pass property down to direct descendants, or even pledging or leasing land to other group members. Increased resource values and contact with outsiders will further lead to the commoditization of rights to land and attempts to sell or lease those rights to outside interests (Fitzpatrick 2006: 1033–4). In all these circumstances, those who stand to gain from asserting exclusionary rights may well calculate that the benefits of success outweigh the costs of defection and conflict with other members of the group (Smith 2002: S480–81). This phenomenon is illustrated by a number of our case studies of East Timor, particularly in relation to peri-urban areas and areas cleared by colonial governments for irrigated rice cultivation.

Whether a common property system can manage defection incentives caused by rising resource values depends on structural questions of social resilience. We have noted that, absent external methods of enforcement, the maintenance of collective action in a common property system generally requires relatively minor stakes and a group that is sufficiently small, homogenous and egalitarian. This creates reciprocity in power relations and low-cost information flows to encourage cooperation and provide sanctions against defection. However, even resilient collective property systems will deteriorate as rising values put increasing pressure on internal governance mechanisms. As our case studies also illustrate, demographic growth will lead to competition for authority and resources among constituent lineages of a customary group. Opportunities for formal education and organized religious instruction will reduce attendance at customary ceremonies and rituals. Sanctions such as ostracism will lose efficacy when members have opportunities for off-farm income. Collective trust may deteriorate if group leaders opportunistically appropriate benefits that would otherwise accrue to the group as a whole (Platteau 1992: 203–4). Most importantly, the sale or transfer of rights to outsiders will undermine the kinship, resource use, and behavioural requirements necessary to maintain cooperative arrangements and a system of informal sanctions (Fitzpatrick 2006: 1036–7).

Over time, a common property system can lose control over land use within its territory as individuals assert ever-increasing rights of exclusion, transfer and alienation. Yet the question remains: By what mechanism will these individuated rights be enforced? Some Demsetzian proponents argue that increased conflict – resulting from degradations in non-state systems – leads the state to intervene in the form of systems for dispute resolution, demarcation of boundaries, and registration of individualized titles (Feeny 1988: 286–90, 294). An oft-cited example is Lee Alston, Gary Libecap and Bernardo Mueller's study of land titles in the Amazonian frontier. The study discusses the ways in which successful private ordering arrangements at the frontier broke down as new settlers appeared with different expectations and greater heterogeneity of experience, which created incentives for individual settlers to travel to state land offices in order to obtain formal titles (Alston et al. 1999: 98–152). Yet Alston, Libecap and Mueller (1999: 17–22) also highlight the fact that in Brazil, for reasons of incapacity or self-interest, political institutions largely failed to provide secure land titles in response to demands from frontier land-holders. This issue of political responses to demands for property rights certainty is the subject of the next chapter.

## Conclusion

Our hypothesis that different rule complexity/simplicity trade-offs apply in different circumstances of social ordering is not necessarily inconsistent with the baseline preference of economic analysis for low information cost rules of property. In stable circumstances of social order, standardized legal rules of first possession may emerge from interpretively complex norms of possessory entitlement as a result of information cost considerations. For example, the US Mining Act of 1872 adopted customary rules of first possession but standardized claim sizes and work requirements. It also removed the possibility of abandonment, through deemed loss of possession, after grant of a mining patent. Similarly, the Court in *Pierson v. Post* adopted a rule of first possession but preferred interpretively simple acts of possession – taking control of the fox carcass itself – over the more complex hunting custom of hot pursuit. This preference for simplicity arose even though the hot pursuit custom minimized unproductive racing for control by granting rights at an earlier stage of the hunt. In both these cases, the state had the legitimacy and coercive capacity necessary to ensure respect and enforcement in relation to its legal standardization of custom. There was not, as in East Timor and other postcolonial contexts, a combination of weak state authority and resilient tribal systems that can lead to incomplete, indeterminate or contested application of legal attempts at standardizing custom (see further Chapter 11). Where there is state weakness, in particular, attempts to impose a bright-line mechanism for property allocation may increase the transaction costs of customary property systems, and channel claimants into extra-legal attempts at asserting entitlements, which may create persistent forms of institutional complexity notwithstanding the presence of simple legal rules of property. The analysis further illustrates the importance of enforcement authority, and its relationship with social order, for institutional complexity in a conflict-affected environment.

## References

Abudulai, S. 2002. Land Rights, Land-Use Dynamics and Policy in Peri-Urban Tamale, Ghana, in P. Delville, C. Toulmin and S. Traore (eds), *The Dynamics of Resource Tenure in West Africa*. UK: Heinemann.

Alchian, A. and Demsetz, H. 1973. The Property Right Paradigm, *J. Econ. Hist.*, 33: 16.

Allen, D.W. 1991. Homesteading and Property Rights: Or, 'How the West was Really Won'. *Journal of Law and Economics*, 34: 1–23.

Alston, L., Libecap, G. and Schneider, R. 1996. The Determinants and Impact of Property Rights: Land Titles on the Brazilian Frontier. *Journal of Law, Economics and Organization*, 33: 177–97.

Alston, L.J., Harris, E., and Mueller, B. 2011. Property Rights, Land Settlement and Land Conflict on Frontiers: Evidence from Australia, Brazil and the U.S., in K. Ayotte and H.E. Smith (eds), *Research Handbook on the Economics of Property Law*. UK: Edward Elgar.

Alston, L., Libecap, G. and Mueller, B. 1999. *Titles, Conflict, and Land Use: The Development of Property Rights and Land Reform on the Brazilian Amazon Frontier*. Ann Arbor, MI: University of Michigan Press.

Axelrod, R. 1984. *The Evolution of Cooperation*. New York: Basic Books.

Anderson, T. and Hill, P.J. 2002. Cowboys and Contracts. *J. Legal Stud.*, 31: S489, S499.

Anderson, T. and Hill, P.J. 2004. *The Not So Wild, Wild West: Property Rights on the Frontier*. Stanford, California, Stanford Economics and Finance.

Banner, S. 2002. Transitions Between Property Regimes. *J. Legal Stud*, 31: S359.

Baxter, J. and Trebilcock, M. 2009. Formalizing Land Tenure in First Nations: Evaluating the Case for Reserve Tenure Reform Indigenous. *Law Journal*, 7(2), pp. 45–122.

Berry, S. 1993. *No Condition is Permanent: The Social Dynamics of Agrarian Change in Sub-Saharan Africa*. Wisconsin: University of Wisconsin Press.

Berry, S. 1997. Tomatoes, Land and Hearsay: Property and History in Asante in the Time of Structural Adjustment. *World Development*, 25(8), 1225–41.

Bourdieu, P. 1990. *The Logic of Practice*. [trans. Richard Nice.] Cambridge: Polity.
Demsetz, H. 1967. Toward a Theory of Property Rights. *Am. Econ. Rev.*, 57: 347.
Cooter, R.C. 1991. Inventing Market Property: The Land Courts of Papua New Guinea. *LAW & SOC'Y REV.*, 25: 759.
Dukeminier, J. and Krier, J.P. 1993. *Property. 3rd ed.* New York: W.W. Norton.
Ellickson, R.C. 1993. Property in Land. *Yale L.J.*, 102: 1315, 1322.
Ellickson, R.C. 1991. *Order Without Law: How Neighbors Settle Disputes*. Cambridge, MA: Harvard University Press.
Ellickson, R.C. 1989. A Hypothesis of Wealth-Maximizing Norms: Evidence from the Whaling Industry. *Journal of Law, Economics, and Organization*, 5(83).
Epstein, R.A. 1979. Possession as the Root of Title. *Georgia Law Review* 13: 1221–1243.
Epstein, R. 2002. The Allocation of the Commons: Parking on Public Roads. *J. Legal Stud.*, 31: S515, S516, S519.
Feeny, D. 1988. The Development of Property Rights in Land: A Comparative Study, in R.H. Bates (ed.), *Toward a Political Economy of Development*. Berkeley: University of California Press, p. 272.
Fitzpatrick, D. 2006. Evolution and Chaos in Property Systems: The Third World Tragedy of Contested Access. *Yale Law Journal*, 115: 996–1048.
Fitzpatrick, D. 1997. Disputes and Pluralism in Modern Indonesian Land Law. *Yale Journal of International Law*, 22: 171.
Fitzpatrick, D. and Barnes, S. 2010. The Relative Resilience of Property: First Possession and Order Without Law in East Timor. *Law & Society Review*, 44(2), 205–238.
Haddock, D.D. and Kiesling, L. 2002. The Black Death and Property Rights. *Journal of Legal Studies*, 31: S545.
Heller, M.A. 1997. The Tragedy of the Anticommons: Property in the Transition from Marx to Markets. *Harvard Law Review*, 111: 621.
Knetsch, J. and Trebilcock, M. 1981. Land Policy and Economic Development in Papua New Guinea. Inst. of Nat'l Affairs, Discussion Paper No. 6, 32–3.
Libecap, G. 2003. Contracting for Property Rights, in T. Anderson and F. McChesney (eds), *Property Rights: Cooperation, Conflict and Law*, at 142, 155–56.
Lueck, D. 1995. The Rule of First Possession and the Design of the Law. *Journal of Law and Economics*, 38: 393.
Luhmann, N. 1985. *A Sociological Theory of Law*. [trans. E. King; ed. M. Albrow.] London: Routledge.
Lund, C. 2002. Negotiating Property Institutions: On the Symbiosis of Property and Authority in Africa, in K. Juul and C. Lund (eds), *Negotiating Property in Africa*. Portsmouth: Heinemann, p. 107.
McAdams, R. 2000. A Focal Point Theory of Expressive Law. *Virginia Law Review*, 86: 1649.
McDowell, A. 2002. From Commons to Claims: Property Rights in the California Gold Rush. *Yale Journal of Law and Humanities*, 14(1).

McChesney, F.S. 2003. Government as Definer of Property Rights: Tragedy Exiting the Commons? in T. L. Anderson and F.S. McChesney (eds), *Property Rights: Cooperation, Conflict, and Law*.

McDowell, A. 2004. Real Property, Spontaneous Order, and Norms in the Gold Mines. *Law & Social Inquiry*, 29.

McWilliam, A.R. 2007. Customary Claims and the Public Interest: On Fataluku Resource Entitlements in Lautem, in D. Kingsbury and M. Leach (eds), *East Timor: Beyond Independence*. Melbourne: Monash Asia Institute Press, pp. 168–75.

Merrill, T. 1984. Property Rules, Liability Rules, and Adverse Possession. *Northwestern University Law Review*, 79: 1122.

Merrill, T. and Smith, H. 2001. What happened to property in law and economics?

Merrill, T. 2002. Introduction: The Demsetz Thesis and the Evolution of Property Rights. *J. Legal Stud.*, 31: S331, S331.

Merrill, T. and Smith, H. 2000. Optimal Standardization in the Law of Property: The Numerus Clausus Principle. *Yale Law Journal*, 110: 1.

Merry, S.E. 1988. Legal Pluralism. *Law and Society Review*, 22: 870.

Metzner, J. 1977. *Man and Environment in Eastern Timor: A Geo-Ecological Analysis of the Baucau-Viqueque Area as a Possible Basis for Regional Planning*. Canberra: Australian National University.

Morriss, A.P. 2005. Hayek and Cowboys: Customary Law in the American West. *N.Y.U. J. L. & Liberty*, 1: 35, 48.

North, D. 1990. *Institutions, Institutional Change and Economic Performance*. Cambridge: Cambridge University Press.

Ostrom, E. 1990. *Governing the Commons: The Evolution of Institutions for Collective Action*. Cambridge and New York: Cambridge University Press.

Ostrom, E. 2005. *Understanding Institutional Diversity*. Princeton, NJ: Princeton University Press.

Platteau, J.-P. 1992. Land Reform and Structural Adjustment in Sub-Saharan Africa: Controversies and Guidelines. Food & Agriculture Organization of the United Nations. Econ. & Soc. Dev. Paper.

Platteau, J.-P. 2000. *Institutions, Social Norms and Economic Development*. Oxford, New York: Routledge.

Posner, R. 1992. *Economic Analysis of Law*. 4th ed. Boston: Little, Brown.

Sardan, de, O. 1999. A Moral Economy of Corruption in Africa? *Journal of Modern African Studies*, 37(1), 25–52.

Simpson, S.R. 1976. *Land Law and Registration*. Cambridge: Cambridge University Press.

Smith, H.E. 2003. The Language of Property: Form, Context, and Audience. *Stanford Law Review*, 55: 1105.

Teubner, G. 1998. Legal Irritants: Good Faith in British Law or How Unifying Law Ends Up in New Divergences. *Mod. Law. Rev.*, 61(15).

Trebilcock, M. 1984. Communal Property Rights: The Papua New Guinean Experience. *U. TORONTO L.J.*, 34: 377, 382–83.

Wyman, K. 2005. From Fur to Fish: Reconsidering the Evolution of Private Property. *N.Y.U. L. Rev.*, 80: 117.

# Chapter 5
# Solving the Problem of Violence: Land Law in a New Nation-State

## Introduction

In Chapter 1 we noted that the 2012 draft land law of East Timor provides for ownership rights if a claimant has been in long-term peaceful possession of land since 31 December 1998, or is a holder of a statutory ownership title issued either by the Portuguese or Indonesian administrations. Importantly, the definition of possessors includes those who use land claimed under ancestral customary domain (art. 10(3)). The application of possessory principles to areas of ancestral customary domain takes place in conjunction with two new legal categories: community protection zones and community property. In a community protection zone, the state has a number of protective obligations, including to ensure participatory and non-discriminatory customary practices, and to protect community ways of life. These protective obligations apply irrespective of the nature of land ownership in a community protection zone. In addition to individual rights based on possession or prior regime statutory ownership, land in a community protection zone may be owned by the state or collectively by a community. Community-owned land is defined as land of common and shared use, organized in accordance with local practices and customs (article 25). There is thus a complex, if not confusing, mosaic of legal land-holdings in rural districts, which is overlaid by a wide-ranging set of protective obligations vested in the state.

The draft 2012 land law allows individual, state and community ownership of land within a community property zone. While it establishes a category of 'community property', it does not provide for explicit recognition of customary forms of tenure or authority relating to land. This approach may be contrasted with other countries with Austronesian heritage, such as Fiji or the Solomon Islands, which provide legal recognition of customary land tenure without standardization through legal constructs such as possession and alienable ownership (AusAid 2010). In Chapter 11 we argue that the application of standardized legal constructs to socially embedded custom in East Timor will be incomplete, hybridized and contested, particularly in areas where the state lacks the administrative, financial and coercive capacity to enforce legal claims to land. The argument is an East Timor-specific application of the argument presented in Chapter 4: that conflict or chronic uncertainty may develop at the frontier for state enforcement of legal rules of private property in land. In this chapter we analyse the development of land law in East Timor to illustrate the interests and incentives that produced a standardized rule of possession in customary areas, with complex overlays of state land, community property and community protection zones.

Our analysis further explores the hypothesis that different rule complexity/simplicity trade-offs correlate with different circumstances of social ordering. All else being equal, relatively simple rules of property are less prone than complex rules to high-cost forms of variable or contested interpretation. Yet, as our analysis of the development of land law in East Timor suggests, simple rules may not arise because of the nature of the resource and its histories of occupation and claim, or because of political economy considerations relating to the balancing of competing interest groups. This inability to develop simple rules is often the paradox of property policy in a post-conflict state. Even if bright-line rules of possession reduce information costs once property information moves beyond a close-knit interpretive context, the political and social ordering implications of rule-making may result – as in East Timor – in a complex layering of rules that respond to state-stabilization imperatives through compromises among interest groups. These interest group compromises will have negative aspects: including enhanced opportunities for rent-seeking by state actors, increased likelihood that investment money will flow through state land leases rather than impersonal exchange of private rights, and delay or paralysis in the determination of private title by courts with limited post-conflict capacity. Yet the emergence of complex legislative compromises will have a degree of inevitability due to the conflict-affected environment.

## Rule Formation and the Dynamics of State Stabilization

In 2009 we published a policy note on the legal recognition of customary property systems in East Timor, which concluded that the starting point for legal regulation of rural land should be a default or presumptive position that custom governs land outside city boundaries (see further Chapter 11). While the policy note recommended legal space for customary property systems in East Timor, it did not adopt Ostrom-like recommendations for delineation of customary system boundaries, or identification and enforcement of community 'rules' of resource appropriation. As the case studies in this book illustrate, notions of customary 'boundaries' and 'rules' in East Timor are highly resistant to legal definition because of their context-specific informational complexity. We recommend recognition, and where appropriate enforcement, of traditional agreements between customary elders and in-migrants, as these are essential to localized management of legacies of relocation. In Chapters 10 and 11 we also explore the potential for extension of a rule of possession to lowland areas first cleared under colonial supervision, where there are a number of chronic land conflicts that are not amenable to customary resolution.

We argue that the efficiency benefits of custom in East Timor outweigh its high information costs for outsiders, not only in terms of tenure security and natural resource management, but as a result of the social ordering role of custom in a context of potentially violent racing for control over resources (see Chapter 3). This is an instrumental conclusion that applies an information cost approach to law and custom. As a practical matter, however, the draft 2012 land law of East Timor does not adopt our recommendations of a default rule of recognition of custom in rural districts. It applies standardized legal constructs of possession, community property and community protection zones to areas of customary domain. The following section discusses the way in which property rule formation relating to custom, in fragile states emerging from armed conflict, is shaped by incentives for state stabilization. The discussion provides a further application of our hypothesis that there are different rule complexity/simplicity trade-offs in different circumstances of social ordering. In other words, just as the imperatives of social ordering in a customary environment lead to the instrumental conclusion that custom should be recognized in East Timor, the imperatives of state stabilization in a conflict-affected context helps to explain the interests and incentives that led to complex draft land laws, which included a rule of possession in areas of customary domain.

Our account of the development of land law in East Timor illustrates correlations between configurations of rule complexity and simplicity, and the imperatives and incentives of state-strengthening in a post-conflict environment. The case study supports the hypothesis of a relationship between state-stabilization and design choices in the initial development of land law. These issues of legal design responded, in different ways, to a social ordering environment characterized by risks of violent racing for control over resources. Our analysis draws on recent work by North, Wallis and Weingast (2009a, 2009b) on social order and state formation in circumstances of violence. It also illustrates the pivotal role of a group outside the political elite – international legal advisers – which supported complexity/simplicity configurations in the new law not to obtain privileged access to rents, but as a result of cognitive preferences for imported legislative models, and professional incentives for legislative compromise. We argue that a confluence of incentives among the two interest groups– the political elite and international legal advisers – led to a default rule of state title to land, and a complex layering of community property and protection concepts over a rule of possession. In the case of East Timor's draft land laws, therefore, rule complexity takes the form of multiple potential bases for establishing ownership of rural land.

## Flexible Property Rights in a Limited Access Order

North, Wallis and Weingast (2009a: 57–8) describe social order in terms of managing 'the central problem of violence'. They distinguish between three basic types of social order: foraging order, limited access order, and open access order. Foraging order applies to small social groups characteristic of hunter-gathering societies. Once social organization moves beyond small groups the initial institutional response to violence is a limited access order, which forms through elite coalition with privileged access to rights and rents from resources. Limited access orders are fragile where realignments in power and access to means of violence affects the pay-offs of violence versus the benefits of membership of the elite (North, Wallis and Weingast 2009a: 59–64, Zartman 2005). While limited access orders are the 'natural state' of institutional development, some societies have evolved into open access orders with equal access to privileges, resources and organizations, including the police and military, on the basis of minimal and impersonal criteria such as citizenship. Impersonal property exchange is a hallmark of open access orders.

Regimes or states such as East Timor are likely to have characteristics of a limited access order, because of the social ordering imperatives of a conflict-affected environment. As discussed in Chapter 1, armed conflicts that cause regime change and large-scale population flight can create conditions that favour violent races for rights and authority over resources (Fitzpatrick and Barnes 2010). The opportunity to obtain possession and the incentive to claim property may create struggles for possession and violent conflicts over acts of possession. The opportunities created by regime change will also encourage racing for public authority relating to land, particularly as control over the machinery of the state will allow privileged access to rents from land and natural resources. In these conflict-affected circumstances, groups and individuals that retain access to means of violence, through non-state patrimonial networks (Zartman 1995), may calculate that the net pay-offs of political violence outweigh the net benefits of non-violent forms of competitive racing for public authority (Brinkerhoff 2005). Violent races for political authority may interact with disputes over the possession of land to cause further outbreaks of armed conflict and state instability (Brinkerhoff 2005: 4).

Limited access orders respond to the threat of group violence by co-opting individuals and groups with access to means of violence (North et al. 2009a: 55, 59). The imperative to stabilize the state leads to co-option of actors who could otherwise destabilize or de-legitimize the state (Zartman 1995). The co-option process is facilitated by inducements based on privileged access to rents, which are benefits above ordinary returns from control of an asset (North, Wallis and Weingast 2009a: 108). As North, Wallis and Weingast (2009a: 59) put it, privileged access to rents in a limited access order is not 'simply a method of lining the pockets of the dominant coalition … [but] the essential means of controlling violence'. The elite formation process includes incentives to control the development and application of new laws on land. And the incentive to extract rents from minoritarian control of the state is heightened where members of the dominant elite have obligations to deliver state largesse to their sources of non-state authority, including the patron-client networks that provide them with the capacity to exercise or threaten group violence, and even more so where their position as privileged agents is precarious because of elite competition in an unstable socio-political environment (North, Wallis and Weingast 2009b: 42–3).

North, Wallis and Weingast's typology of social ordering provides a framework for analyzing institutions that emerge in response to threats of group violence. In relation to property, they note the conflicting interests of a limited access elite.

While secure rights makes resources more valuable for the elite, flexible property rights may serve to balance competing elite interests, particularly in the early phase of elite coalition-forming as the balance of power shifts among members of the elite (North, Wallis and Weingast 2009b: 77–8). The development of land law in England provides an example. After the Norman Conquest in 1066 there was a problem of social order where a distinct social group, the Normans, now controlled a new political entity, England (North, Wallis and Weingast 2009b: 75). The Normans avoided forced evictions by overlaying a feudal structure on the pre-existing system of landholdings. Landholders owed service, homage and fealty to new feudal landlords, who in turn owed service, homage and fealty to superior landlords or to the King himself. Initially the elite coalition of feudal landlords had a military purpose: to stabilize Norman control through obligations of military service to the King in exchange for the grant of land. The grant of land was personal as on death there was no inter-generational transfer and the land reverted to the control of the King. This flexible property arrangement facilitated royal control and capable military commanders. However, over time the lords demanded greater security of tenure through the right to devise land, first to a legal male heir, and later on trust or testamentary disposition to a choice of heirs (North, Wallis and Weingast 2009b: 80– 86). Importantly, as the lords crystallized their property rights, the bulk of the population retained relatively insecure formal rights to land, at least until feudal tenants (in their various forms) obtained rights to prove their (better) title in the Royal Courts through the action of ejectment (North, Wallis and Weingast 2009b: 84–5).

The following case study of land law development in East Timor explores the relationship between state stabilization and property rules in a contemporary setting. It argues that, in a broad sense, the East Timorese analogue to flexible grants of feudal title is a default rule of state title to land, combined with complex rules of private property in land. The orthodox legal baseline of state (allodial) title to sovereign state territory suits elites seeking to extract rents from state control over resources. In particular, a rule that the state holds title to land without an owner places the burden of proving private title on private claimants, and creates opportunities for extraction of rents from the grants of rights to public land, including grants of licenses and concessions to commercial interests. Equally, while the proposed rules of private property in East Timor are not flexible – in the early feudal sense of *in personam* grants – they are complex because of the competing demands of groups with the capacity to destabilize the state, or disrupt the dominant coalition. The proposed private property rules reflect legislative compromises to accommodate competing interest groups, with access to means of violence, by establishing multiple pathways of argument, and leeways of adjudicatory choice, for respective sets of claim. The complex result, in a post-conflict state where determinations of contested title are likely to be slow, increases the likelihood that investment funds will flow through (rapid) personalized grant of state titles rather than impersonal exchange of (uncertain) private rights.

## Land Law Development and Social Ordering in East Timor

Portugal held Timor as a colony from 1701 to 1974, interrupted by Japanese military occupation between 1942 and 1945. In 1975 the Indonesian military invaded East Timor, shortly after Portugal withdrew from all its colonies. In 1999 the Indonesian government agreed, over the objections of its military command, to hold a popular consultation on independence for East Timor. Almost 80 per cent of East Timorese voted for independence, notwithstanding a campaign of intimidation planned by Indonesian military forces and executed by pro-Indonesian militia groups (Fitzpatrick 2002: 1–2).

Following the vote, the Indonesian military and its militia proxies carried out a 'scorched earth' campaign of property destruction and forced population displacement. Most land title offices and records were destroyed. More than half the housing stock was seriously damaged or destroyed. Over 400,000 people were internally displaced within East Timor itself, and a further 300,000 fled or were forcibly transported across the border to West Timor. This widespread displacement—more than 75 per cent of the population—created a humanitarian crisis, while also reawakening cycles of land conflict as some took advantage of displacement or abandonment to repossess lands allegedly lost as a result of dispossession in either the Portuguese, Japanese and Indonesian periods of control of East Timor (Fitzpatrick 2002: 5–7). Not surprisingly, in the capital city of Dili there was a rush to occupy habitable houses when displaced people returned to seek shelter. Much of the housing subject to ad hoc occupation had been held by Indonesian citizens, who fled once order was established by a UN-led military force (INTERFET) (Fitzpatrick 2002: 6).

As a result of the war-torn history of East Timor there are multiple bases for land claims, and a legacy of contestation over past events of possession and dispossession. The potential bases for private claims to land in contemporary East Timor include custom, possession, Portuguese title documents, Indonesian title documents, and eminent domain (Fitzpatrick 2002: 136). According to Indonesian government records, the colonial Portuguese Timor administration issued and registered 2,843 land titles between 1900 and 1974 (Da Cruz 1999: 44). Between 1976 and 1996 the Indonesian administration issued and registered a total of 34,965 Indonesian property titles, covering approximately 10 per cent of East Timor's total land mass. Most titles issued by the Portuguese and Indonesians took the form of limited term in leasehold interests rather than indefinite ownership interests (Fitzpatrick 2002: 88–9, 158–60). By 1998, according to Pedro de Sousa Xavier (2000: 2), the total number of Indonesian titles had increased to 44,091 titles. In theory, these Indonesian titles included converted Portuguese titles pursuant to conversion regulations issued by the Indonesian government for East Timor. However the number of converted Portuguese titles was relatively small, as Indonesian government files record that only 142, out of a possible 1,503 in the capital city, Dili, were converted; and that, moreover, there was never any application for conversion by non-Indonesian citizens (that is East Timorese exiles in Portugal or Australia) (Da Cruz 1999: 11, 49).

On 25 October 1999 the United Nations Security Council passed Resolution No 1272, establishing the United Nations Transitional Authority in East Timor (UNTAET). Article 1 vested all legislative and executive authority with respect to East Timor, including the administration of justice, in the hands of UNTAET. After democratic elections East Timor attained independence in March 2002. The Fretilin party, which had been closely associated with the armed (Falantil) resistance to Indonesian occupation, formed the new government with a majority of ministers drawn from a group of Portuguese-speaking Timorese that had been exiles in Mozambique or Portugal during the Indonesian occupation (Kingsbury 2008). In 2006 political conflict between the Fretilin Prime Minister and the President, a former Falantil military leader, degenerated into circumstances of temporary state failure, as elements of the police and army engaged in armed combat, and latent tensions over post-1999 land occupations escalated into large-scale house burning and evictions in Dili (Harrington 2007). In the lead up to the violent events of 2006, supporters of the Prime Minister and President had armed and funded competing private militia, which were associated with martial arts gangs and elements of the police and military (Scambary 2006). The conflict soon took on so-called 'Easterner-Westerner' distinctions, which contributed to violent housing conflicts in Dili as 'Westerners' – long-term residents of Dili – took advantage of widespread lawlessness to engage in tit-for-tat forced evictions of 'Easterners', who had occupied houses largely owned by Indonesians before their departure in late 1999. The return of UN-led military and police forces led to restoration of order in 2007, the resignation of the Prime Minister, and the election of the President as Prime Minister under a coalition of parties known as the Association with a Parliamentary Majority (AMP). Fretilin is now the major opposition party.

The tragic events of 2006–2007 highlighted the fragility of the East Timorese state, and the relationship between state stability and post-displacement disputes over the possession of land and housing. The conflict over housing, in particular, increased appreciation among legal advisers and the political elite of the risks of disorder if the state attempted mass evictions as part of a program of restitution of pre-Independence titles to land. Until 2006, most international legal advisers advocated a simple rule of restitution of possession as at 5 October 1999 (to facilitate the return of displaced persons). Subsequently, a draft 2009 land law replaced restitution of titles with recognition of rights based on possession. East Timorese citizens could claim ownership on the basis of possession since 31 December 1998, even where there was a competing claim based on titles issued by the Portuguese or Indonesian administrations. The recognition of possession represented an acknowledgement of the likelihood of violent resistance to eviction by possessors, and the effects of further housing violence on state stability. However, the next year amendments to the draft re-introduced an element of restitution, as a result of recommendations by Portuguese legal advisers, while retaining a primary focus on recognition of possession.[1] Subsequent amendments also introduced concepts of community protection and community property, which were derived in part from Mozambican law. The following description of draft land laws for East Timor suggests that this layered complexity of private property rules is largely a product of concerns for state stability, including the need to accommodate possessory interests that may otherwise destabilize the state. It also reflects the complex political economy of legislative development in a fragile state, which requires compromises among diverse interests – including international legal advisers – in order to increase the prospects for legislative approval.

*The Draft UNTAET Regulation of 2000: Qualified Recognition of Indonesian Era Titles*

On 25 October 1999, as the pro-Indonesian militia rampaged after the vote for East Timor's independence (Fitzpatrick 2002: 5–6), the United Nations Security Council passed Resolution No 1272, which established the United Nations Transitional Authority in East Timor (UNTAET). Article 1 vested all legislative and executive authority with respect to East Timor, including the administration of justice, in the hands of UNTAET. UNTAET Regulation No. 1 established a governing law for East Timor that maintained 'the law as applied in East Timor prior to 25 October 1999', subject to certain international human rights standards.[2] This phrase was interpreted as a reference to Indonesian law, which had purported to adopt Portuguese law in East Timor after the Indonesian invasion in 1975 (Strohmeyer 2001: 58–9). In other words, UNTAET Regulation No. 1 applied Indonesian law – which had purported to apply and amend Portuguese law – as at 25 October 1999 rather than Portuguese law in East Timor as at April 1974. The primary drafter of UNTAET Regulation No 1 was a judge from Germany, who had been the legal adviser for the United Nations mission in Kosovo (Strohmeyer 2001: footnote a1). The decision to adopt Indonesian law was motivated by practical considerations – to maintain a degree of legal continuity – and was evidently not persuaded by arguments that Portugal retained sovereign authority over East Timor because Indonesia had a status as a belligerent occupier (Fitzpatrick 2002: 44–76, Strohmeyer 2001: 59).

In June 2000 the Land and Property Unit of UNTAET formulated a draft regulation to establish a land commission. The regulation was prepared by lawyers from Australia and Canada, who at that time predominated in the Land

1 Copies of all the draft regulations are held on file with the authors.

2 These standards included the Universal Declaration on Human Rights, the International Covenant on Civil and Political Rights, the International Covenant on Economic, Social and Cultural Rights, the Convention on Elimination of all Forms of Discrimination against Women, and the International Convention on the Rights of the Child (arts. 2, 3). UNTAET Regulation No. 1 is available at http://www.un.org/en/peacekeeping/missions/past/etimor/untaetR/etreg1.htm , accessed on 5/6/2011.

and Property Unit. The regulation provided that applications for the registration of land rights, where there was no objection, were to be determined by reference to UNTAET Regulation No 1, subject to obligations to reject an application where the right had not been acquired in good faith. The reference to UNTAET Regulation No 1 favoured claims based on Indonesian titles, with the qualification that land commission officers were to observe the international human rights standards set out in UNTAET Regulation No 1. The regulation did not allow for registration of customary claims to land, at least those that were inconsistent with Indonesian law, but did provide for the noting of boundaries and any other information about land that was the subject of a traditional communal right. In effect, the draft regulation recognized Indonesian titles to land while adding a number of interpretive considerations relating to good faith and compliance with international human rights standards.

The recognition of Indonesian era titles to land was based on a lawyer's approach: the draft 2000 regulation simply implemented the qualified recognition of Indonesian law in UNTAET Regulation No 1. Proponents of the draft regulation noted that Indonesian law recognized and converted pre-1975 Portuguese titles in East Timor, which meant that Indonesian law would not necessarily prejudice claims based on Portuguese titles (Wright 2004). At the time, proponents of the regulation were not aware of the failure to convert most Portuguese titles into Indonesian titles (see above). In theory, therefore, the draft UNTAET regulation adopted a relatively bright-line approach to private property based on restitution of pre-displacement rights to land. However, in relation to customary rights to land, the adoption of Indonesian law restored ambiguous and highly interpretive rules that favoured state development interests over local land-holders. Indonesian land law 'acknowledges' collective customary rights to land but does not recognize them as a form of property right. Moreover, although custom (I: *adat*) purportedly forms the basis of Indonesian land law, it may be overridden on the basis of a number of vague criteria, including 'national unity' and 'Indonesian socialism'. State officials have discretionary authority over application of these criteria, with little in the way of effective oversight or constraint from the judiciary (Fitzpatrick 1997).

On its face, the restitution of pre-displacement rights to land provides a simple response to the problem of population displacement. There is no great interpretive complexity to a rule providing that those who were displaced should go home. In countries affected by ethnic cleansing or systematic racial discrimination – such as Bosnia-Herzegovina, Kosovo, and South Africa – there have been simple categories of displaced claimants with entitlements to restitution of property rights in land (Williams 2005: 448, Cox 1998: 599, Rosand 1998: 1128–9, Atuahene 2007: 1419, Attuahene 2010: 765, Carson 2007: 394). However, in East Timor there are multiple categories of potential claimants, including customary groups displaced by the Portuguese, Portuguese era title-holders dispossessed by the Indonesian administration, and Indonesian era title-holders displaced as a result of independence for East Timor (Fitzpatrick 2003: 1–21). While the law could focus on the most recent event of nationwide displacement – in 1999 when the pro-Indonesian militia embarked on its campaign of violence – this restitutionary focus would restore titles to Indonesian citizens and pro-Indonesian East Timorese, and confirm the denial of rights to customary land through acts of legal acquisition or unlawful land grabbing by the Indonesian administration. It would also challenge state capacity to implement a restitutionary programme because of the large numbers of post-1999 occupiers of land who did not hold titles to that land in the Indonesian era. In the event, these considerations led to rejection of the draft regulation by the United Nations Transitional Administrator in September 2001 (notwithstanding the obligations of the UN Guiding Principles on Internal Displacement) (Wright 2004). Over time, as we shall see, they also lead to consideration of a rule of adverse possession, as an alternative to restitution of pre-1999 titles to land.

### *Law No 1 of 2003: The Bright-line Rule of State Title to Land*

East Timor became an independent state in March 2002. In 2003 the National Parliament of East Timor approved Law No 1 of 2003 on the regulation of state land and abandoned land. This law is most significant for its definition of state land. The law defines land held under the 'private domain' of the state to include unclaimed private land without an identifiable owner. This provision provides a bright-line default: the burden of proving private title lies with the claimant. It seems that there was no trend towards complexity in the definition of state land because the interests of key regulatory agents – the political elite and international legal advisers – converged on the need to strengthen the state (Buchanan et al. 1980). The then governing party Fretilin, in particular, had a long-standing ideological preference for state control over land, as a result of its socialist revolutionary history as the party of resistance to Indonesian occupation and to the concentration of landed property ownership under Portuguese rule (Braithwaite et al. 2010: 17). International advisers were also comfortable with default presumptions of state title, both because of their legal training and because of international aid donor concerns for state viability.

Land laws that strengthen the state are consistent with aid donor objectives relating to international security and development (McAuslan 1998). Land law can be central to the territorialization of state power as it includes certain projections and assumptions of state sovereign authority (Peluso 2009). In James Scott's well-known expression government officials 'see like a state' and interpret complex social relations with land through a legal lens of abstraction and objectification, as rights enforceable in autonomous terms, without the necessity of reference to cultural context or originating systems of authority (Scott 1998; McDougall 2005). In similar vein, international legal advisers may also 'look for a state' to facilitate strategies of exit and the achievement of programme outputs. The East Timor example suggests that the resulting focus on state-strengthening, including presumptive views of sovereign control over land, can interact with oligarchic processes of elite coalition formation to produce relatively well-defined forms of public property and more complex or interpretable rules of private property. This conclusion is consistent with the working hypothesis we derived from North, Wallis and Weingast's analysis of social ordering responses to the problem of violence. The East Timor example is not the same as North, Wallis and Weingast's example of early feudal England, which involved flexible *in personam* grants of private rights to land rather than a complex layering of legal bases for *in rem* rights to land. Nevertheless it does illustrate a similar relationship between state stabilization incentives and the initial development of legal rules on property rights in land.

Default presumptions of state ownership lie within orthodox common and civil law conceptual frameworks. Yet, in post-conflict circumstances of competitive racing for control over resources, there are considerable incentives and opportunities for government officials to claim large areas as un-owned land to facilitate rent extraction from the grant of state land leases. There will likely be widespread uncertainties of private ownership because of population displacement, destruction of records, and undocumented forms of land-holding. There may be investor interest in agribusiness developments. There will be economic pressures to generate employment and investment. In all these circumstances, a bright-line rule on state land may provide a low-cost interpretive pathway for government actors to obtain rents and grant land concessions to investors, who would otherwise face uncertain negotiations with purported groups of private landowners (Alden Wily 2009: 36–8). Law No 1 of 2003 allows this result as officials from the Land and Property Directorate may determine that an area of land lacks an identifiable owner and is therefore, subject to proof of ownership by a private claimant, available for grant to an outside investor. The interaction between default rules of state land, and complex yet-to-be-legislated laws on private rights to land, means that most commercial interests will acquire rights to land through state grant rather than private transfer. We explore this possibility further in Chapter 11, which considers the potential application of the draft 2012 land law in rural districts.

### *The 2005 Draft Law on Private Land: Restitution and Recognition of Custom*

In September 2005 international legal consultants prepared a draft law on private land ownership, under the auspices of a USAID technical assistance programme, and in consultation with the Ministry of Justice. In general terms, the 2005 law continued the restitutionary approach of the UNTAET draft regulation. While the 2005 draft limited restitution to ownership titles issued under the Portuguese or Indonesian administrations, it provided for limited term Portuguese or Indonesian titles to act as evidence for claims to 'first adjudication' of ownership. Unlike the UNTAET draft regulation, the 2005 draft law also allowed for first adjudication of ownership based on 'possession and customary rights of ownership', provided there was no applicable Portuguese or Indonesian title claim (art. 29(3)). This basis for claim provided a degree of standardization, as it required proof of occupation for at least 20 years, but did not establish a bright-line rule as the occupation had to follow 'the practices of the community', and possessory rights were subject to 'no well-founded opposition from the community'.[3] The draft law also allowed communities to hold collective title to land and apply customary rules in administering their land, while respecting the principles of equality established in the law (art. 3). These provisions provided the first substantive legislative reference to customary rights and authority relating to land, and arose from increased awareness among international legal advisers of the social reality of customary land-holdings in rural East Timor.

The references to custom in the draft law were controversial as almost all members of East Timor's political elite – including leaders of the Fretilin Party – are opposed to including the traditional authority of customary elders in the new institutional landscape of independent East Timor. In part this elite consensus reflects a 'modernizing' desire, common to many decolonizing contexts, which is justified by reference to developmental needs and opposition to the perceived feudal and discriminatory aspects of custom. It is also significant that in East Timor – unlike countries such as Afghanistan or Sudan – there are no 'warlords' representing powerful tribal interests with access to violent means of destabilizing the state. As the violence of 2006–07 indicates, the 'violence entrepreneurs' of East Timor are not identified with particular customary groups, but are members of political parties that armed and encouraged private militia within the police, military and the country's large and well-organized martial arts gangs (Scambary 2006). Most importantly, in the specific historical context of East Timor, the desire not to recognize customary authority reflects long-standing antagonism to the role of some customary leaders, who were represented in a now-defunct political party known as APODETI, in calling for Indonesian intervention in East Timor in 1975 (Braithwaite et al. 2010: 38. These historically contingent political ordering circumstances rendered approval of the draft law highly unlikely, even though its qualified reference to custom increased the prospect of understanding and acceptance among rural landholders.

### *The Draft Law of 2006: Possessory Rights outside a Customary Context*

East Timor's then Minister of Justice rejected the 2005 draft law prepared under the USAID technical assistance programme, and commissioned a further draft in 2006, not long before the outbreak of violent conflict in May 2006. The 2006 draft law was prepared with the assistance of a lawyer from Brazil. It provided much weaker recognition of customary relationships with land, as a result of

3 Draft Land Law 2005, article 16. Eligible ownership titles must also have been the subject of registered claim by 10 March 2004, pursuant to Law No. 2003, and also have 'evidence of legitimacy' (articles 28, 43).

explicit drafting instructions from the Prime Minister.[4] The draft law did not refer to custom but did recognize a 'communal right of use'. The draft did not define the incidents of a communal right of use. However, it stated that land subject to a communal right of use fell within the public domain of the state (art. 9(2)). Moreover, 'traditional institutions' had a right of participation – but by implication no right of veto – relating to natural resource exploitation (art. 9). It seems that the communal right of use was intended as an *in personam* interest, akin to a common law license. The flexibility reflected the government's desire for control over the allocation of rural land for investment projects.

As with the 2005 draft, the 2006 draft law provided for the restitution of ownership titles issued by the Portuguese or Indonesian administrations (art. 41). However, the law stated that restitution would not take place if there was a third party in possession of the claimed property, who had exercised peaceful possession for at least 10 years or peaceful and undisputed possession in good faith for at least 5 years (art. 46). For the first time, then, the 2006 draft law privileged some possessory claims over restitution of Portuguese or Indonesian ownership titles. While some members of the Fretilin elite stood to benefit from restitution of Portuguese land titles, as their families had large land-holdings in colonial times (Fitzpatrick 2002: 141–66), it seems that the political calculus began to favour possession because of the emerging belief of the Prime Minister and the lead Brazilian legal adviser, in particular, that restitution of Portuguese or Indonesian titles would result in large numbers of forced evictions and substantial risks of social conflict over possessory claims to land and housing. This belief proved somewhat prescient given the violent conflict over urban housing that erupted in 2006–07.

### *The Draft Law of 2009–10: Possessory Principles and State Stability*

The violence of 2006–07 led to the fall of the Fretilin government and its replacement by a coalition government headed by Prime Minister Xanana Gusmao (the former President) (Braithwaite et al. 2010: 91). The coalition includes a number of former combatants. Most notably, the Prime Minister was the head of the armed resistance to the Indonesian occupation, whereas the Vice Prime Minister until September 2010 – Mario Carrascalao – was the governor of East Timor under the Indonesian administration (Leach 2009). The coalition has had some success with social and political stabilization through promotion of economic activity, including cash transfers to groups capable of violence such as demobilized veterans of the independence conflict. In terms of land, there have been significant increases in rural land allocations to investors, notwithstanding the continuing absence of a law on private ownership of land. For example, in January 2009, the Ministry of Agriculture purported to allocate over 100,000 hectares of rural land for bio-fuel

4 Pers. Comm., 9 September 2011 Ibere Lopez, Legal Adviser, USAID Strengthening Property Rights in Timor-Leste Project.

developments under Memoranda of Understanding with foreign investors, even though the Minister of Justice has legal authority to grant leases over state land not the Ministry of Agriculture (Anderson 2008). Tellingly, in terms of our hypothesis of conflict and uncertainty at the frontier for state enforcement of property claims, the lease purportedly granted by the Ministry of Agriculture in 2009 has not been implemented in the area purportedly subject of the grant.

There are persistent allegations of rent-seeking associated with the grant of state land leases.[5] For example, the former Minister of Justice was accused of corruption in an official report by the Provedore (a corruption ombudsman) in 2010. The corruption accusations encompass alleged text messages in 2008 between the Minister and potential bidders for Justice Ministry tenders.[6] Yet the Prime Minister did not suspend or dismiss the Minister until 2012. Moreover, the current head of the Land and Property Directorate, which makes initial determinations on the legal status of land (that is whether state or private), allegedly was the head of a leading martial arts gang (PSHT) implicated in the violence of 2006–07 (International Crisis Group 2010: 17); and yet he (Jaime Xavier Lopes) has been elevated to the status of Secretary of State for Land and Property since the 2012 parliamentary elections. The appointment as the Secretary of State to Land and Property, in particular, illustrates the relationship between control over state land leases and the incorporation of potential 'violent entrepreneurs' into current government order. In 2006, a survey of gangs in Dili stated that (Scambary 2006: 15):

> Also known Nehek Metan (Black Ants), PSHT are one of the biggest and most controversial groups, and are alleged to have been closely linked to the current violence … . [T]heir leader, Jaime Xavier Lopes, is Timorese … [T]hey are widely perceived to be close to … the Partido Democratica (PD) and Social Democratic Party (PSD), although PSHT themselves deny any links to any political parties … They are said to have heavily infiltrated the security forces, and to have received weapons from the police and army.

The coalition government rejected the draft 2006 land law prepared by the Fretilin government, and commissioned a further draft under the auspices of a second USAID technical assistance project, which again worked in conjunction with the Ministry of Justice. Ironically, the lead drafter was the Brazilian lawyer who had worked on the 2006 Fretilin draft. The first version of the current draft law was issued in June 2009. It did not allow for restitution of Portuguese or Indonesian titles at all, and provided for ownership based on 'special adverse possession'. A claimant would receive an ownership right if she peacefully took

5 For a discussion see the NGO blog post: 'Disputa Rai ho Estabilidade Nasional Iha Timor-Leste' ['Land Disputes and National Stability in Timor-Leste'], Mahein Nia Lian, No. 8, (fundasaunmahein.blogspot.com ), 12 July 2010.

6 'Minister for Justice gives herself and friends projects', Tempo Semanal Online, 12 October 2008.

possession of a vacant property before 26 April 2006, without the authority of the previous possessor; and maintained possession in good faith for at least five consecutive years (art. 13). While the draft law privileged possessory claims over ones of restitution, it did provide that where there was no special adverse possession, a claim based on Portuguese or Indonesian titles – including long term use rights – would be entitled to conversion to a registered ownership right.

The privileging of possession over restitution in the draft 2009 law had an orthodox policy rationale: to reduce the costs of proving title. As in stable socio-political environments, the rule of adverse possession reduced the costs of proving rights in circumstances where other mechanisms of proof were lost or costly to establish (Merrill 1984: 1122). Yet there were context-specific issues of social ordering affecting the design of the possessory rule, including a desire to minimize the likelihood of forced evictions, which would strain the enforcement capacity of a fragile and emergent state. Tom Merrill (1984: 1131) notes that this interest in preserving the peace, in circumstances where a possessor is more likely to resist re-occupation, has 'distinct echoes of a frontier society'. In East Timor, the peace-preservation imperative also stems from the fragility of the state, where conflict over housing can intertwine with competitive racing for public authority among members of the political elite. Its effect on legal design involves a social ordering trade-off: the greater the risks of violent resistance to evictions, and the greater the fragility of the governing elite, the more likely a preference for rules favoring possession over remedies for prior dispossession (restitution).

### *The 2010 Draft Law: A Partial Return to Restitution*

In early 2010, the Minister of Justice commissioned Portuguese lawyers to review the 2009 draft law. The Portuguese legal advisers highlighted the importance of state fragility concerns, noting that the attribution of ownership to long-term possessors 'avoids mass dispossessions (and therefore the social tensions that could arise)' (Belmarco and Moucheira 2008). However, the advisers also noted the importance of meeting expectations of ownership, which suggested restitution of Portuguese or Indonesian era ownership titles. They recommended restitution of pre-independence ownership titles while retaining ownership rights based on long-term possession. This result favors members of the Portuguese-speaking elite that had received ownership rather than limited term titles under the Portuguese administration.[7] The draft law as approved by the National Parliament of East Timor in February 2012 combines restitutionary and possessory principles. Claims of ownership may be based on Portuguese or Indonesian ownership titles and, where there is no such title, on continuous, peaceful, and notorious possession that commenced on or before

7 Portuguese ownership titles were only granted to senior members of the indigenous colonial elite, including members of large landholding families that retain political influence in contemporary East Timor.

December 31, 1998.[8] Under this formulation, the great majority of ownership claims will be based on possession rather than restitution as Portuguese and Indonesian ownership titles were relatively small both in number and areas covered, with most pre-independence titles limited term leasehold interests. In Dili, for example, 88 per cent of all titles issued under the Indonesian administration were limited term in nature *(hak guna bangunan*) (Fitzpatrick 2002: 88).

On 20 March 2012 the President refused to assent to the law, and referred it back to Parliament with a list of proposed revisions. The veto reasons included concerns over the definition of state land, and a lack of consultation with civil society groups.[9] The Parliament did not have time to consider the proposed revisions of the President before parliamentary elections due in June 2012. As a result of the elections, the AMP coalition has formed government again and, with a new President after Presidential elections in April 2012, it is likely the draft law will be submitted without revision to the Parliament and submitted for assent by the President in late 2012 or early 2013.

### *Applying the Rule of Possession to Areas of Customary Domain*

In Chapter 1 we noted that, under the 2012 draft land law, 'mere occupants' cannot acquire ownership rights to land by means of special adverse possession. Mere occupants are defined to include people using land with no intention of acting as owners, people 'who took advantage of the tolerance of legitimate possessors', and representatives and agents of the legal possessor (art. 10(1)). These categories establish distinctions between actual and legal possession that are common to civil and common law systems. They allow possessory doctrines to accommodate transactions such as bailment, leases and licences. Unfortunately, and somewhat surprisingly, the draft 2010 law does not extend the distinction between mere occupants and legal possessors to customary districts. Article 10 (3) defines possessors to include those who reside in, have erected buildings on, or have cultivated land claimed by another party based on the belief of ancestral customary domain, even when rent is being paid to that party. This definition potentially allows large numbers of relocatees to claim alienable ownership of land within ancestral customary domains, even though they might otherwise fall within the definition of 'mere occupant'.

---

8 *See* Art 22. It seems that the decision to push the commencement date of possession back to 31 December 1998 was motivated by a desire not to reward ad hoc occupiers of land after 1999, in part because of fears of renewed possessory conflicts in Dili. It may also be that the current coalition government was concerned not to recognize post-1999 claims to valuable coastal land by Fretilin-connected actors.

9 The reasons for the decision of the President are set out in President Vetoes Three Land Laws, http://www.laohamutuk.org/Agri/land/2012/12PNpassPRveto.htm. The other two laws subject to presidential veto were the Expropriation Law and the Real Estate Financing Law.

There are large numbers of relocated peoples living on land claimed by a customary group in East Timor. Many have occupied the land since before 31 December 1998, which entitles them to claim statutory ownership of land provided they have remained in possession. The application of a rule of possession to areas of customary domain will be highly contestable as a result of multiple events of population displacement in the history of East Timor. Our case studies indicate that there are two broad categories of persons relocated to customary land during Portuguese or Indonesian times: those who have access to land pursuant to traditional agreement with the origin group; and those who occupied land during the war-torn years of the Indonesian occupation without contemporaneous agreement from origin house elders. While these categories are subject to a number of fine distinctions, and an evolving spectrum of relations between latecomers and first comer landholders, it is clear that entitlement to ownership on the basis of individual possession alone, with unrestricted powers to sell land to other Timorese citizens, will be inconsistent with localized understandings of relocatee rights and, in some cases, will lead to violent conflict should relocatees claim alienable rights of ownership.

Reportedly, East Timor's Council of Ministers debated extension of a relatively bright-line rule of possession to customary districts at some length. The decision to apply the possessory rule, without reference to mere occupant distinctions, was made with one dissent – a Minister from the Socialist Party (pers. comm. Ibere Lopez). The Socialist Party is a member of the governing coalition. In essence, the decision reflects a consensus among the political elite – including leaders of the opposition Fretilin Party – that the traditional authority of customary elders should not be recognized in the new institutional landscape of independent East Timor. As noted above, there is long-standing elite antagonism to political acceptance of customary authority in rural areas in East Timor (Fitzpatrick 2002: 24–42). While it seems that members of the Council of Ministers are aware of the risks of conflict should relocatees claim ownership of customary land, it also appears that rural land conflict does not pose a sufficient threat to state stability to generate the development of a more complex rule that includes the retention of distinctions between mere occupancy and legal possession.

### *Chapter V of the Draft Land Law: Community Protection Zones and Community Property*

The legal regulation of customary land in East Timor will be affected further by Chapter V of the draft land law, which creates legal categories of community property and community protection zones. Article 21 defines community protection zones as areas protected by the state for the purpose of safeguarding common interests of local communities. A community protection zone does not take the form of a right to property. Individuals, communities and the state may own land in a community protection zone, with the ordinary rights and incidents of ownership, subject only to the protective safeguards set out in Articles 22 and 25. The nature of state protective obligations in community protection zones includes responsibilities to ensure that all customary practices conform to the Constitution and are participatory, non-discriminatory and respect gender equality; promote environmental and socio-cultural sustainability in the uses of natural resources and the way of life of each local community; and protect immovable property in the community from real estate speculation (art. 22). Article 25 further provides that economic activity by a third party in a community protection zone is subject to a number of conditions, including requirements that the activity be preceded by consultation with the local community; benefit the local community as a whole in an inclusive and non-discriminatory fashion; be performed in a sustainable way from environmental and socio-cultural points of view; and respect community ways of life and access to natural resources.

At this stage, all domestic land actors in East Timor are unfamiliar with the notion of a 'community protection zone' (World Bank 2010). The notion of a community protection zone was taken from Mozambican law, primarily as a result of conversations among international legal advisers. There was a belief among international actors that key political and bureaucratic figures in East Timor would not support explicit recognition of customary structures, that a reference to Mozambique would provide legitimacy and a cognitive shortcut for East Timorese political figures who were exiles in Mozambique during the Indonesian occupation, and that the experience in Mozambique would provide a useful template for the implementation of Chapter V in East Timor. The development of land law in Mozambique involved similar circumstances to East Timor of a former Portuguese colony emerging from war, and a political elite antagonistic to recognition of customary authority (Tanner 2002). As is possible for community protection zones in East Timor, the state in Mozambique may grant state land leases to investors in rural areas subject to requirements of community consultation and partnership. The aim is not to grant bright-line collective rights of exclusion to customary landholders through recognition of customary rights to land, but to encourage 'fuzzy' local processes of discussion and participation in development projects (Tanner 2002).

The importation of Mozambican legal concepts by foreign advisers had little to do with indigenous East Timorese processes of elite-formation. Community protection zones are not compatible with rent-seeking models of legislative development and their relationship with limited access orders. Their incorporation into the law reflects a conscious effort by foreign legal advisers to work within political constraints on recognising customary rights to land, and elite desires for broad definitions of state land. However their implementation will be influenced by the rent-seeking incentives of key actors in the state. In particular, at present there are no incentives for Land and Property Directorate officials to identify or demarcate community protection zones, in a timely or expansive manner, as that will trigger costly consultation and protection measures, and reduce the opportunity for rent-seeking gain from rapid grant of leases over state land.[10] A lower cost interpretive pathway will involve declaration by the Land and Property Directorate that an area sought by an investor is state land outside a community protection zone. This will allow the direct grant of rights to an investor, without incurring community protection zone obligations, including in particular the requirements of consultation prior to third-party economic activity.

*The New Category of Community Property*

The first version of the 2010 draft law did not provide for customary ownership of land, whether individual or collective. After some debate, and criticism by a former UNTAET property lawyer, a second version included the possibility of collective ownership of land through incorporation as a cooperative. After further advice that customary groups were unlikely to form cooperatives, in circumstances of limited access to legal information, the draft law was amended to establish communities as juridical entities for the purposes of community property. A community may hold and register ownership of community property without the need for legal incorporation. Community property is defined as land acknowledged by the community as being of common and shared use, by a group of individuals or families, organized in accordance with local practices and customs (article 25 (1)). The reference to local practices and customs is significant as the notion of community property is intended to apply in customary districts.

Article 26 provides that the Land and Property Directorate shall assist each local community in the process of community property demarcation and consult with local and community authorities, as well as the elders residing locally, as sources of essential information. However, even more so than is the case with community protection zones, Land and Property Directorate staff have few incentives to identify and demarcate areas of community property in a timely or expansive manner. In conversations with one of the authors, senior Land and Property Directorate officials also interpreted the notion of community property by reference to restrictive Indonesian conceptions of customary land (that is limited to areas of actual residence and cultivation). There is little funding, capacity and political will to undertake any process for demarcating areas of community property. Wherever possible, the state is likely to grant rights directly to investors through claims of state land, or compulsory acquisition of private land, rather than facilitating agreements between a community and an outside investor. In these

10 The 2012 draft land law does not define the process of identifying community protection zones, or the line agency responsible for demarcating their boundaries. These lacunae will be filled by separate regulation or legislation. Based on conversations with a legal adviser in the Ministry of Justice, it is likely that the Land and Property Directorate will take responsibility for identifying and delineating community protection zones. This responsibility would be consistent with Land and Property Directorate authority over the demarcation of state land.

circumstances, the category of community property will likely not be a bright-line right of exclusion vested, in a customary community and enforced by agencies of the state, but a symbolic legal artefact – a product of compromises in the drafting of the law – that at best acts as an element in the localised negotiation of entitlements to customary land, and at worst contributes to widespread uncertainty and confusion surrounding the effects of private property rules in the draft law. This also is an example of functional institutional complexity, as described in Chapter 1.

## Conclusion

An emerging body of literature considers the initial development of institutions and their path-dependent effects on economic growth (North 1979: 1319–32; Robinson, Acemoglu, and Johnson 2005: 386–472). Other literature analyses the origin of property institutions in small group settings (Ellickson 1993: 1333–34). Yet there is little on the initial development of property legislation, notwithstanding its path-dependent effects on economic development. While economic analysis asserts a baseline preference for simple legal rules of property, to reduce transaction costs for a broad audience, there is little understanding of the variables affecting initial configurations of interpretive simplicity and complexity in the drafting of foundational property legislation. This chapter identifies incentives for social and political ordering, to avoid violent conflicts over scarce resources, as a key factor in the initial development of laws on land. In particular, the chapter describes incentives for initial property legislation, in systems emerging from violent conflict, to develop simple default rules of state title to land, and complex rules relating to private rights to land. In East Timor, complex private property rules include rules of possession, community property, and restitution of prior regime ownership titles, nested within notions of 'community protection zones'.

The chapter suggests that the path-dependency of post-conflict property systems may be explained by tensions between elite processes of state stabilization, and the challenges of broad-based development of property legitimacy. Simple default rules of state title to land, and complex rules relating to private rights to land, may manage the problem of group violence but will do little to establish a system of secure private property rights. The analysis suggests that societies with histories of violent conflict may have legacy rules of private property complexity that developed in response to imperatives for state-stabilisation. These legacy rules may be sub-optimal in the sense that they have higher information costs than a correspondingly simple rule. They may also prevent or inhibit the development of simple private property principles that are conducive to the emergence of a broad property consensus. Yet interpretively complex rules of private property may be difficult to revise because they form part of the process of elite-formation that negated the threat of group violence in the first place. As a result, while there will be economic incentives to trend towards rule simplicity, there may also be historical episodes of group conflict that explain the divergent paths of different property systems.

We argue that understanding path-dependent choices of property rule complexity and simplicity requires attention not only to preferences for efficiency and equity but to foundational mechanisms to solve the problem of violence and social disorder. Our analysis suggests a number of hypotheses for understanding initial choices of rule complexity and simplicity in the formation of social order. First, as argued in Chapter 3, complex rules may develop in close-knit community contexts to manage the potential for violent disorder arising from competitive racing for resources. These rules may be resistant to legal translation because of their role in the maintenance of social order. Second, as argued in Chapter 4, the legal regulation of complex custom in unstable socio-political environments involves not only the potential benefits of custom for tenure security and sustainable resource management, but also the role of customary mechanisms for managing processes of population displacement, return and resettlement. Appreciating the social ordering role of custom may lead to policy conclusions that the benefits of legal space for custom outweigh increases in information costs for outsiders. Third, as argued in this chapter, the imperatives of social and political ordering in nation-states emerging from armed conflict may lead to complex rules of property that would not emerge in stable socio-political conflicts. The following chapters provide case-study material that allows further exploration of these hypotheses in the contemporary context of East Timor.

## References

Alden Wily, L.A. 2009. Tackling Land Tenure in the Emergency to Development Transition in Post-conflict States: From Restitution to Reform, in S. Pantuliano (ed.), *Uncharted Territory. Land, Conflict and Humanitarian Action.* Warwickshire: Practical Action Publishing.

Anderson, T. 2008. Privatizing Land in Timor Leste. Available online at: <http://www.etan.org/et2008/9september/20/15land.htm> [accessed 11 August 2012].

Arraiza, J.M. and Moratti, M. 2009. Getting the Property Questions Right: Legal Policy Dilemmas in Post-Conflict Property Restitution in Kosovo (1999–2009). *International Journal of Refugee Law*, 21: 421.

Atuahene, B. 2010. Property Rights and the Demands of Transformation. *Michigan Journal of International Law*, 31: 765.

Atuahene, B. 2007. From Reparation to Restoration: Moving Beyond Restoring Property Rights to Restoring Political and Economic Visibility. *SMU Law Review*, 60: 1419.

AusAid 2010. Making Land Work: Reconciling Customary Land and Development in the Pacific. Commonwealth Government of Australia.

Belmarco, A. and Moucheira, J. 2008. Work Mission in East Timor of the Technical Team from the Institute of Registers and of Notary of the Ministry of Justice of Portugal (Copy on file with author).

Binswanger, H.P. and McIntire, J. 1987. Behavioral and Material Determinants of Production Relations in Land-abundant Tropical Agriculture. *Econ. Dev. & Cultural Change*, 36: 73.

Braithwaite, J., Dinnen, S., Allen, M., Braithwaite, V. and Charlesworth, H. 2010. *Pillars and Shadows: Statebuilding as Peacebuilding in Solomon Islands*. ANU E-Press.

Brinkerhoff, D. 2005. Rebuilding Governance in Failed States and Post-Conflict Societies: Core Concepts and Cross–Cutting Themes. *Public Administration and Development*, 25: 1, 4.

Bruce, J.W. 1998. Learning from the Comparative Experience with Agrarian Reform, in J. Barry (ed.), *Proceedings of the International Conference on Land Tenure in the Developing World.* Cape Town: University of Cape Town.

Buchanan, J. 1980. Rent Seeking and Profit Seeking, in J. Buchanan, R. Tollison and G. Tullock (eds), *Toward a Theory of the Rent Seeking Society.* Texas: A&M Press, p. 3.

Cardinoza, M. 2005. Reviving Traditional NRM Regulations (*Tara Bandu*) as a Community-based Approach of Protecting Carbon Stocks and Securing Livelihoods, in D. Murdiyarso and H. Erawati (eds), *Carbon Forestry: Who Will Benefit?* Proceedings of a Workshop on Carbon Sequestration and Sustainable Livelihoods, CIFOR Bogor: Indonesia.

CARE International Timor Leste, pp. 197–210.

Carson, A.O. 2007. East Timor's Land Tenure Problems: A Consideration of Land Reform Programs in South Africa and Zimbabwe. *Independent International & Comparative Law Review*, 17: 395.

Cox, M. 1998. The Right to Return Home: International Intervention and Ethnic Cleansing in Bosnia and Herzegovina. *International and Comparative Law Quarterly*, 47: 599.

D'Andrea, C., da Silva, O. and Meitzner Yoder, L. 2003. The Customary Use and Management of Natural Resources in Timor Leste. *Oxfam Timor Leste and GTZ–German Technical Cooperation and DTP, Directorate of Land and Property Timor Leste.*

Da Cruz, P. 1999. *Studi Tentang Penguasaan dan Penggunaan Tanah Bekas Hak Portugis yang Ditunda Konversinya Dengan PP No. 34 Tahun 1992 di Kabupaten Dili Propinsi Timur-Timur*, ('Study concerning the Control and Use of Former Portuguese Title Land that was Converted under Presidential Decision No. 34 of 1992 in the Dili Region of East Timor Province'), Thesis completed at Sekolah Tinggi Pertanahan Nasional Yogyakarta, ('National Land College, Yogyakarta') 44. Copy on file with author.

Deininger. K. 2003. Land Policies for Growth and Poverty Reduction. In *World Bank Policy Research Report*. Washington: Oxford University Press/World Bank, 47.

Dodson, A. and Heiskanen, V. 2003. Housing and Property in Kosovo, in S. Leckie (ed.), *Returning Home: Housing and Property Restitution Rights of Refugees and Displaced Persons.* New York: Transnational Publishers, pp. 223–5.

Ellickson, R.C. 1989. A Hypothesis of Wealth-Maximizing Norms: Evidence from the Whaling Industry. *Journal of Law, Economics, and Organization*, 5: 83.

Fitzpatrick, D. 2002. *Land Claims in East Timor.* Canberra: Asia Pacific Press.

Fitzpatrick, D. 1997. Disputes and Pluralism in Modern Indonesian Land Law. *Yale Journal of International Law*, 22: 171.

Fitzpatrick, D. and Barnes, S. 2010. The Relative Resilience of Property: First Possession and Order without Law in East Timor. *Law and Society Review*, 44(2).

Fitzpatrick, D. and Monson, R. 2009. Balancing Rights and Norms: Property Programming in East Timor, the Solomon Islands and Bougainville, in S. Leckie (ed.), *Housing, Land and Property Rights in Post–Conflict United Nations and Other Peace Operations.* Cambridge: Cambridge University Press, pp. 124–52.

Fukuyama, F. 2004. State-Building: Governance and World Order in the 21st Century, in F. Fukuyama (ed.), *State–Building: Governance and World Order in the 21st Century*. Ithaca, NY: Cornell University Press, pp. 6–7.

Harrington, A. 2007. Ethnicity, Violence, and Land and Property Disputes in Timor-Leste. *East Timor Law Journal*, 2.

Hicks, H. 2007. Community and Nation-State in East Timor: A View from the Periphery. *Anthropology Today*, 23(1), 13–16.

Independent Special Commission of Inquiry for Timor-Leste. 2006. *Report of the United Nations*, Geneva.

Kingsbury, D. 2008. East Timor's Political Crisis: Origins and Resolution, in D. Mearns (ed.), *Democratic Governance in Timor-Leste: Reconciling the local and the national*. Darwin, NT: Charles Darwin University Press.

Leach, M. 2009. The 2007 Presidential and Parliamentary Elections in Timor-Leste. *Australian Journal of Politics and History*, 55: 219–32.

McAuslan, P. 1998. Making Law Work: Restructuring Land Relations in Africa. *Development and Change*, 29: 525–7.

McDougall, D. 2005. The Unintended Consequences of Clarification: Development, Disputing, and the Dynamics of Community in Ranongga, Solomon Islands. *Ethnohistory*, 52: 81–3.

McWilliam, A.R. 2003. New Beginnings in East Timorese Forest Management. *Journal of Southeast Asian Studies*, 34(2), 307–27.

North, D. 1979. Institutions and Economic Growth: An Historical Introduction. *World Development*, 17(9), 1319–1332.

North, D., Wallis, J. and Weingast, B. 2009a. *Violence and Social Orders: A Conceptual Framework for Interpreting Recorded Human History*. Cambridge; New York: Cambridge University Press.

North, D., Wallis, J. and Weingast, B. 2009b. Violence and the Rise of Open-Access Orders. *Journal of Democracy*, 20: 55, 59.

Office of the Prime Minister. 2010. *On the Road to Peace and Prosperity: Timor Leste's Strategic Development Plan 2011–2030*, pp. 4–197 to 4–201.

Palmer, L. and Amaral de Carvalho, D. 2008. Nation Building and Resource Management: The Politics of 'Nature'. *Timor Leste, Geoforum*, 39(3), 1321–32.

Platteau, J.-P. 1996. The Evolutionary Theory of Land Rights as Applied to Sub-Saharan Africa: A Critical Assessment. *Development and Change*, 27(1), 29–86.

Platteau, J.-P. 1992. Land Reform and Structural Adjustment in Sub-Saharan Africa: Controversies and Guidelines. Food and Agriculture Organization of the United Nations. Econ. & Soc. Dev. Paper.

Prado, M. and Trebilcock, M. 2009. Path Dependence, Development and the Dynamics of Institutional Reform. *University of Toronto Law Journal*, 59: 341–79.

Robinson J., Acemoglu, D. and Johnson, S. 2005. Institutions as a Fundamental Cause of Long-Run Growth, *Handbook of Economic Growth* 1A: 386–472.

Rosand, E. 1998. The Right to Return under International Law following Mass Dislocation: The Bosnia Precedent? *Michigan Journal of International Law*, 19: 1091, 1128–9.

Scambary, J. 2006. A Survey of Gangs and Youth Groups in Dili, Timor-Leste – A Report Commissioned by Australia's Agency for International Development, AusAID. *East Timor and Indonesia Action Network (ETAN)*, 15 September <http://www.etan.org/etanpdf/2006/Report_Youth_Gangs_in_Dili.pdf> Accessed 1 October 2012.

Science Direct. Available online at: <http://www.sciencedirect.com/science/article/pii/S0016718507001522> [accessed 11 August 2012].

Scott, J.C. 1998. *Seeing Like a State: How Certain Schemes to Improve the Human Condition have Failed*. New Haven: Yale University Press.

Tanner, C. 2002. Law Making in an African Context: The 1997 Mozambican Land Law. Rome, FAO, FAO Legal Papers Online No. 26.

Toulmin, C., Delville, P. and Traore, S. 2002. Introduction, in P. Delville, C. Toulmin and S. Traore (eds), *The Dynamics of Resource Tenure in West Africa*. London: Heinemann, p. 1.

Williams, R.C. 2005. Post-Conflict Property Restitution and Refugee Return in Bosnia and Herzegovina: Implications for International Standard-Setting and Practice. *New York University Journal of International Law and Politics*, 37: 441, 448.

Zartman, I.W. 1995. Introduction: Posing the Problem of State Collapse, in I.W. Zartman (ed.), *Collapsed States: The Disintegration and Restoration of Legitimate Authority*. Boulder, CO: L. Rienner Publishers.

Chapter 6

# Controlling the Domain, Sharing the Land: Customary Land Tenures in a Naueti Community

This chapter explores how customary claims to land are reasserted in post-independence Timor Leste. The focus is on a predominantly *Naueti*-speaking community in the southeastern district of Viqueque.[1] The chapter begins with a brief overview of the social and political organization of communities living in village Babulo, Uatolari sub-district. This is followed by an exploration of how customary claims to land are predicated on interrelated histories of origin and migration. Customary claims within the Darlari domain revolve around the emplaced rights of 'origin' groups and the commonly held belief in the interdependent nature of relations between people and the land. Traditionally, access to land has been granted to in-migrant groups through processes of negotiation and accommodation. The chapter furthers the discussion of the impact of in-migration, war and displacement on customary tenures and the capacity of 'origin' groups to maintain control over access to land and natural resources. Finally, it describes some ways in which 'origin' groups have sought to reassert their claims to land in the post-independence environment, and reveals some of the ongoing processes of negotiation between 'origin' and in-migrant groups and customary and local government authorities.

The case study supports our thesis that customary property arrangements have retained a high degree of resilience notwithstanding the displacement and disruption of Indonesian occupation. Through a description of a ceremony of ritual communication with the ancestors performed on completion of the reconstruction of communal sacred houses, we illustrate the way in which ancestral origin narratives have served to re-establish an orderly system of social and moral relations without engaging in a significant degree of conflict or post-displacement competitive race for rights or authority relating to land and natural resources. At the same time, we describe land tensions in Babulo involving migrants from the neighbouring village of Afaloicai, who have remained relative outsiders in spite of at times lengthy periods of occupation, because village government structures initially introduced by the Portuguese have affected traditional mechanisms for

1 Alternative spellings: Nauheti, Nauhete and Nauoti. According to Census (2004) statistics the total number of Naueti speakers in Timor Leste (over 6 years of age) is 11,361 of which 9,832 reside in Viqueque district.

incorporating newcomers into customary hierarchy. This description highlights the constrained nature of customary resilience in East Timor, as the capacity of customary principles to maintain social order, in a context of relocation and associated land tensions, has been limited by the emergence of state-affiliated sources of public authority and the potential for contested interpretations of possessory authority itself.

## The Setting:
## Babulo Village

The village of Babulo is located in Uatolari sub-district, Viqueque district on the southeastern coast of Timor Leste. Map 6.1 shows the location of Babulo in a context of the language groups in Viqueque district.

Babulo village has a total population of 4,531 (Census 2010), the majority of whom are of the *Naueti* ethno-ligustistic group. A minority of inhabitants of Babulo are of *Makassae* origin and some individuals and families are of mixed ethno-linguistic descent. The majority of the population are subsistence farmers. Agriculture is based mainly on the swidden cultivation of maize, cassava, legumes and root crops. Irrigated rice is cultivated in the lowland areas close to the Bee Bui River and dry land (rain-fed) rice is also cultivated in the upland areas. Coconut and candlenut plantations provide many families and individuals with an important cash income. Hunting and fishing are also part of local subsistence strategies. While a limited number of families possess livestock such as water buffalo (*karau-*

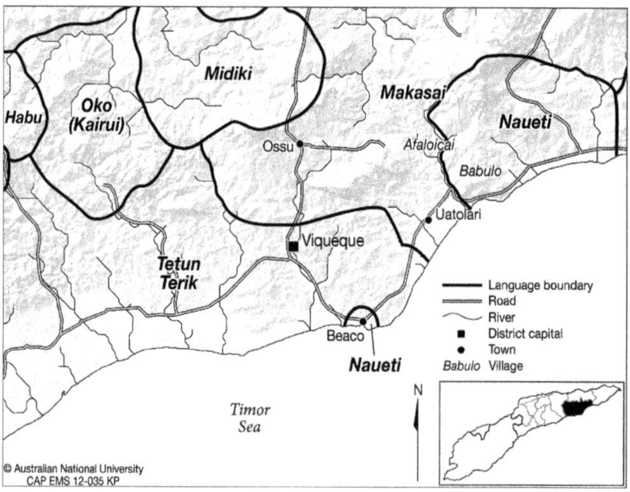


**Map 6.1 Language communities in Viqueque**
*Source*: ANU Cartography 2012

*Timor*) and cows (*karau vaca*), many keep pigs, goats and chickens. Livestock is generally considered to be a valuable household asset and holds an important role in the patterns of reciprocal exchange that are at the heart of rural social relations.

Prior to the Indonesian invasion the people of Babulo lived in dispersed upland settlements or *baha*.[2] It was common for these settlements to comprise a group of agnatically related males, their in-married spouses and children. As a result of Indonesian strategies of control the majority of the population is now settled along main roads or the former administrative *posto* buildings in Uatolari Leten.[3] However, since independence there has been a gradual trend towards re-establishing pre-1975 upland settlements. In particular, the older members of the community have chosen to return to these settlements while a younger generation continue to live in Indonesian period villages. The choice to remain is often dictated by considerations regarding access to services such as education and health care or investments made in existing housing. Many people also maintain simple temporary shelters in their swidden gardens where they might stay during planting or harvesting season.

Administratively, Babulo is divided into eight hamlets: Beli, Darlari, Aha Bu'u, Kotanisi, Roma, Liasidi, Abadere and Asamuta. All but one of these hamlets was established and named during the Portuguese period, and little was done during the Indonesian occupation or since independence to alter these administrative units other than change their name from *povação* (Portuguese) to *kampung* (Indonesian) and, most recently, *aldeia* (Portuguese). Each hamlet broadly corresponds to a descent group sharing common ancestors and centred on a common *uma luli* (sacred house). Each descent group is subdivided into a number of lineages and sub-lineages (*uma kain*), each of which has their own 'branch' or subsidiary cult-house. In the past, these sub-groups formed the core of *baha* settlements and each subsidiary cult-house was associated with a specific function and role within the ritual and social organization of the broader descent group. Members of each branch of a common descent group are typically classified as *kaka* (older) and *wari* (younger) in relation to one another.[4] The members of 'older' houses are considered to be more closely related to the common ancestors of the group and therefore have authority over 'younger' houses. The senior male members of the 'eldest' house of each decent group are often referred to as *Na'i* (Tetun: master) or *Bu Dato* (Naueti: grandfather lord), and are considered to be the direct descendants of the group's ancestors.

2 In Naueti *baha* can mean both mountain and settlement.

3 *Posto* denotes a Portuguese era administrative centre.

4 Three broad social sub-categories are found in Babulo and across Naueti speaking communities. These are *liurai*, *reinu* and *ata* (noble, common and slave). *Liurai* represents the senior lineage of a descent group. *Reinu* (sometimes *povo* or people) groups are subordinate houses of each lineage or sub-lineage within a descent group. *Ata* (Naueti: slaves) groups are the lowest social category whose ancestors were former slaves or war captives. Inter-marriage between these groups was traditionally forbidden.

Complex dynamics of kinship, marriage and long-term alliance bind the principal descent groups around which hamlets are structured.[5] However, it is unclear how long these groups have considered themselves to form part of a larger unit such as a village. The village headman (*chefe suku*) of Babulo has traditionally been 'selected' from the senior houses of the hamlets of Aha Bu'u and Kotanisi.[6] These hamlets represent two lineages of the same descent group originally called Burmeta. Informants suggest that the ancestors of the *Burmeta* emerged as political leaders in the area by threat of force and through strategic marriage alliances with local house-based descent groups. Their political leadership was consolidated by the Portuguese authorities who relied on pre-existing social structures and hierarchies for territorial control, labour recruitment and revenue extraction, and chose the Burmeta as representatives of colonial authority.

Despite a history of considerable in-migration during the late colonial period, followed by massive displacement and forced relocation of the population from the upland areas surrounding Matebian Mountain during the Indonesian occupation, hamlet and village composition based on group membership has remained unchanged. As a consequence, approximately 50 per cent of the population currently residing in Babulo are originally from the neighbouring village of Afaloicai and remain under the jurisdiction of their own hamlet and village heads. Although many of the people from Afaloicai have long been settled in the area, they continue to maintain physical links with their ancestral lands and make a clear distinction when speaking about their place of residence and place of origin. By the same token, while there is a long history of social interaction between the people of Afaloicai and Babulo, in particular through marriage alliances, many local groups continue to view people from Afaloicai as in-migrants with limited and sometimes temporary rights to access land and other natural resources. This apparent administrative anomaly is not uncommon in Timor Leste. In the case of Babulo, it reflects the way in which the administrative units of hamlet and village were established and fixed during the Portuguese period. And it calls attention to the way in which attachments to land are linked to local discourses of origin and precedence that underpin imposed colonial structures.

5 Traditionally, members of each descent group are exogamous and must seek marriage with members of other groups. Marriage establishes the basis for reciprocal relations between groups that become wife-givers (*umana*) and wife-takers (*oa sae*) in relation to one another. In practice, marriages do occur between members of lineages and sub-lineages although these are often frowned on. Members of *liurai* (noble) lineages cannot marry their subordinates and must *buka liurai* (seek marriage with other noble groups).

6 While 'democratic' elections for the positions of village and hamlet head were held in 2004–05, as in other parts of East Timor, in Babulo informants suggested that candidates had to be members of a noble family of Aha Bu'u or Kotanisi (descendants of Burmeta), in accordance with the ancient oath that existed between the Burmeta and Darlari. During the 2010 local elections new legislation required village heads to candidate themselves as part of a local governance 'package' or slate. The current village head is only related to the Burmeta by marriage. This has caused some tensions with the Darlari traditional landowners.

Tables 6.1 and 6.2 show a breakdown of population per hamlet for the villages of Babulo and Afaloicai respectively. The vast majority of the population of Afaloicai live outside their traditional village lands. Most in-migrants from Afaloicai live in and around Kampung Baru, Uatolari Leten (the ex-administrative *posto*) or in Naedala along the main road towards Darabai where Uatorlari sub-district administration is now located. Today, Naedala is considered to form part of the administrative village of Uaitame. However, elders from Babulo argue that originally this was part of their domain.

**Table 6.1 Population figures for Babulo village**

| Hamlet | Households | Male | Female | Total |
|---|---|---|---|---|
| Liasidi | 51 | 166 | 176 | 342 |
| Abadere | 54 | 158 | 146 | 304 |
| Asamuta | 45 | 136 | 147 | 283 |
| Aha Bu'u | 52 | 155 | 132 | 287 |
| Kota Nisi | 22 | 81 | 76 | 157 |
| Roma | 35 | 107 | 99 | 206 |
| Beli | 66 | 182 | 192 | 374 |
| Darlari | 54 | 140 | 138 | 278 |
| | 379 | 1125 | 1106 | 2231 |

**Table 6.2 Population figures for Afaloicai**

| Hamlet | Households | Male | Female | Total |
|---|---|---|---|---|
| Lena† | 107 | 326 | 394 | 630 |
| Buibela†† | 54 | 141 | 142 | 283 |
| Uatulata† | 58 | 153 | 142 | 295 |
| Kailake† | 49 | 136 | 139 | 275 |
| Kai Tau† | 48 | 134 | 136 | 270 |
| Lari† | 76 | 212 | 219 | 431 |
| Ossocaiua†† | 103 | 273 | 268 | 541 |
| Uaicai†† | 112 | 272 | 287 | 559 |
| Dassuate†† | 80 | 188 | 214 | 402 |
| Lorosae††† | 47 | 107 | 99 | 206 |
| | 734 | 1942 | 1950 | 3892 |

*Note*: † Afaloicai population currently settled in the village of Babulo. †† Afaloicai population currently settled in the village of Uaitame. ††† Afaloicai population currently settled in areas of origin

*Source*: Data presented to the author by the village headmen of Babulo and Afaloicai in January 2007

## *Rea Luli* – Sacred Land

In Babulo, hamlet and village administrative units and, the concomitant offices of hamlet and village head, are considered to be relatively 'new', foreign structures, associated with 'external' relations between the community and outsiders, in particular the state. The underlying community of house-based groups, on the other hand, are 'old', autochthonous structures dealing with the 'internal' management of collective social and ritual relations within and between house-based groups (Trinidade 2008).

Within the traditional community members recognize the authority of specific 'origin groups' over defined territories or domains. 'Origin group' status is predicated on interrelated notions of ancestry, attachment to place, histories of migration and settlement and networks of alliance. In Babulo, one such group is composed of the 'eldest' houses, or senior lineages, of the hamlets of Beli and Darlari.[7] These groups represent the lineages of two brothers who were the direct descendants of the mythical founders of an ancient kingdom called *Bubulu*.[8]

According to local *tete bo'ona* (Naueti literally: oldest stories), the sibling ancestors of Beli and Darlari lived together near Baha Liurai, the ritual centre of their land and burial site of their ancestors. The elder brother was the forefather of Beli and the younger of Darlari. Both were entrusted with the custodianship of their ancestors' sacred land (*rea luli*) and sacra (*sasan luli*). However, owing to the neglectful actions of the Beli ancestor, the descendants of the Darlari ancestor now carry this responsibility alone.

> One season, when the time came, the brothers agreed that they would take turns to harvest their portion of the rice fields at *Lia Kakeu*. One would go to the fields while the other guarded over the sacred land and ancestral sacra at Baha Liurai. The elder brother went first, while the younger brother waited in silent vigil. The elder brother's harvest was plentiful and when he had finished he returned happily to Baha Liurai to relieve his younger brother. When the younger brother

---

7 The origin names of the descent groups that comprise the hamlets of Beli and Darlari are deemed sacred and cannot be spoken. In everyday exchange and even during communal rituals these groups are referred to using their hamlet denominations. The principal cult-houses of Darlari are commonly referred to as the *um buti* (white house) and *um ita* (black house). Beli on the other hand have a single principal cult-house referred to simply as *um luli* (sacred house). The 'real' names of these houses are linked to the descent-group genealogies seldom disclosed to outsiders.

8 Local informants believe that the Portuguese derived the name Babulo. In Darlari origin narratives, Bubulu is presented as encompassing the whole world 'over which the sun reigns'. Most commonly, the narrative focuses on the exploits of the offspring, the 'seven brothers' of the founder-parents – a human female and a crocodile male who came from the sea. Although these narratives are presented as 'historical', 'time' is fragmented and non-linear. They are open to contestation and have incorporated the influence of Christianity and adapted to the historical realities in which they continue to be placed.

left to harvest his portion of the fields the elder brother was unable to contain his joy at the success of his harvest and began celebrating with his people.

In the meantime the younger brother reached the rice fields but his crops had disappeared and there was no rice left for him to harvest. Wearily he returned to Baha Liurai. When he found his elder brother dancing, singing and playing drums, he flew into a fit of rage, grabbed the drums and other instruments and broke them. The younger brother chastised his older brother and blamed him for the loss of his harvest. By neglecting his duties to the ancestors and prematurely celebrating the harvest, the elder brother had caused his younger brother's harvest to disappear. The brothers quarrelled and decided that they would separate. The elder brother was banished from the sacred land of his ancestors and obliged to settle on land belonging to his wife-givers. However, before parting the brothers made a blood oath and promised that they would meet regularly to pay tribute to their ancestors at the summit of Baha Liurai.[9]

Members of the senior Beli and Darlari houses continue to acknowledge their sibling status through the use of the terms *kaka* and *wari* (elder and younger), while other groups living on their ancestral lands related through marriage or long-term alliance refer to them collectively as *Ina Ama Beli Darlari* (Mother and Father, Beli Darlari).

The transgression of the elder brother and his exile to the territory of his *wife-givers* serves to justify the reversal of common concepts of authority based on genealogical precedence. As a consequence of the actions of their ancestors, the descendants of the elder (Beli) brother forfeited their right to claim their status as heirs to the domain of their mythic founder-settler ancestors the *Mane Hitu* (seven brothers). This privilege was bestowed and retained uniquely by the male-line descendants of the younger (Darlari) brother who remained at Baha Liurai. In recognition of their senior status, the senior lineage of Darlari is accorded the title of *rea bu'u* or 'lord of the land'; also expressed as *rea mumu, rea uato* (rod of the land, rock of the land) in formal ritual speech. Today, the authority of the 'lord of the land' is embodied in a former hamlet chief of Darlari. He shares this responsibility with two other senior Darlari members, one of whom 'sits and watches' over the ancestral sacra placed in the main Darlari cult-houses the *um buti* and the *um ita* (white house and black house).

9 Two versions of this narrative were presented to the author by Darlari and Beli elders on separate occasions. Both original narratives conform to this summary. They differ only with regards to the significance of objects that the elder (Beli) brother took with him to his exile. In the Darlari version of events the elder brother left with no ancestral sacra. In the Beli version the elder brother took with him the drums and instruments that were the cause of his exile. In time these objects have become sacralized in their own right.

## The Emplaced Nature of Ritual Authority

As 'lord of the land', the Darlari elders are the chief stewards of their ancestral lands.[10] Darlari elders claim that the 'original' boundaries of their domain extend far beyond current hamlet or even village boundaries. They argue that these boundaries were established long ago (before the arrival of the Portuguese) often as a result of conflict with neighbouring groups and agreed upon by means of sacred oaths, or *juramento*.[11] However, they also recognize that throughout the colonial period their land was slowly being encroached upon as the colonial authorities extended their control over the territory, in a way that often favoured powerful neighbouring kingdoms.

While the Darlari elders continue to contest the boundaries of their domain in private, they are reluctant to make these claims public, as they believe this may stir up unnecessary and perhaps even violent conflict with neighbouring groups. To legitimize their claims, they refer to ancestral histories and name specific sites where the ancestors are believed to have landed, settled, farmed, fought, died and were buried. These sites are often marked by physical features such as rocks, springs and specific areas of old growth forest as well as symbolic structures such as stone altars, ancestral graves and particular *um luli* (sacred houses) where ancestral sacra are stored. The memory of these histories and the significance of these sites is preserved through local *tete bo'ona* (histories) and reinforced through specific rituals associated with place. Many of these sites are considered to be *luli* (sacred) and access is restricted, or must be mediated through communication with the ancestors and *bu'u* (spirits) that guard them.

### *Land, Knowledge and the Sacred*

The authority of Darlari elders as 'origin group' representatives rests in their position as legitimate heirs of the founder-ancestors and is sustained by their intimate knowledge of their land and its history. Local informants claim that only the Darlari elders have the full knowledge from 'trunk to tip' (*la'a-na, rae-na*) of the arrival and settlement of the founding ancestors, the establishment of local houses and eventual arrival of in-migrant groups. They know the history of conflict, past treaties, alliances and *juramento* (oaths) within and between local and neighbouring groups. They know the history of land use, the boundaries of their domain and the way land was allocated to local and in-migrant houses. But, most importantly, they know the names of the various spirit and ancestral guardians that control access to forest, fields and water sources of their domain. Knowledge

10 In the past lord of the land status also gave rights to demand labour and services from other kin-group members.

11 These *juramento* took the form of 'blood-oaths and are considered to be *luli* (sacred), broken on pain of death or some other form of ancestral retribution.

of this ancient and therefore sacred time is not accessible to all members of the community.

Knowledge is considered to form part of the legacy of the ancestors and is usually passed on from one generation to the next. Darlari elders describe the knowledge bestowed on them by their ancestors as both a privilege and a burden. Only the elders 'may speak' and therefore pass judgement on what is considered to be *luli* and what is not.[12] Through this knowledge they have become the privileged intermediaries between the 'light' and 'open' world of the living and the 'dark', 'hidden' world of the ancestors. However, this knowledge also means they are bound to 'service' regardless of whether or not they receive any support – material or otherwise – from the community.

Darlari elders are keen to point out that they do not worship *uato no kai* (rock and tree) but rather they insist that, even prior to the arrival of the first Catholic missionaries, they believed in a creator-god entity called *Ulu Lara* (Moon Sun).[13] According to the elders, *Ulu Lara* created the world and then placed certain people on earth to 'control' (*ei*) and 'tame' (*masi*) the land. Before the arrival of these 'chosen' people the inhabitants of the earth lived like 'people with no rules and regulations' (*ikuteme, garateme*). As the chosen people took control of the land they established behavioural norms and practices that form the basis of the social and moral order. As descendants of these 'chosen' people, the Darlari elders have a duty to ensure that the social and moral order is maintained through the continued application of these norms and practices.

Behavioural norms and practices have developed over time and as such they have also been shaped by interaction between individuals, groups and the land. In time some have gathered strength and others have weakened. Often presented as *luli* (sacred), these norms and practices regulate everyday ritual and social life. The most sacred/dangerous of these norms are those associated with the arrival and settlement of the founding ancestors. In settling the land the ancestors were responsible for naming the physical landscape – hills, rocks, rivers, streams, springs, forests and fields. They also began to exercise control over nature. They cleared and burned the land to make way for fields and gardens, they used natural resources from the forests to build shelters, provide food and fuel, and they used water from various springs to wash, cook and cleanse themselves. In taking control of the land and its natural resources, the ancestors are believed to have set the precedent for interaction with the *bu'u,* the original 'owners' or guardians that inhabited the earth.

12 The term *luli* has a range of meanings and applications. In Naueti, the term *ba'ina* is also used to describe what is prohibited or considered to be 'un-tamed' or out of control. Something that is *ba'ina* or *luli* may become *masi* (tame or sweet) through ritual transformation. The word *luli* is frequently used to denote all that is sacred but at the same time all that is dangerous or prohibited. There is a direct correlation between time and the sacred (*luli*) objects, names, places and norms that increase in value or potency across multiple generations.

13 Also sometimes spelt *Wula'Lara.*

Among the population currently living on Darlari lands, there continues to be a strong belief, among both young and old, in the existence of an 'unseen' or 'hidden' dimension inhabited by various forms of *bu'u*. The most powerful *bu'u* are independent or untamed 'owners' (of the land or natural resources) who can take on human or animal form. In general, it is believed that *bu'u* have the power to control natural processes and influence the relationship between people and the land. Many believe that failure to respect the *luli* proscriptions governing interaction with the *bu'u* has negative consequences. It is therefore customary to 'follow in the footsteps' of the ancestors by performing specific rituals, invocations and offerings in order to placate the *bu'u* and gain safe access to the resources they guard.

A number of informants recounted stories of individuals who failed to respect prohibitions associated with specific locations such as areas of forest or bodies of water, and either became gravely ill or, in some instances, died as a consequence. It is common for people to interpret accidents, illness or some form of personal tragedy as a sign that they, or a member of their family, has somehow done something *luli* or prohibited. Those who survive or are able to overcome their difficulties are able to do so because they seek to make amends by consulting the elders on how best to placate the angered *bu'u*. The widespread belief in sanctions for transgressing customary prohibitions accounts for the relative resilience of customary systems in Babulo village, not standing population growth and the in-migration of large numbers of people from the neighbouring village of Afaloicai.

In time the ancestors themselves have been 'spoken into' the landscape. Numerous places and locations across the Darlari domain where ancestral spirits are believed to congregate are deemed *luli* (see examples cited above). Through their actions and deeds, sometimes involving great personal sacrifice and even death, various named ancestors are remembered for having provided the first harvest, or securing the borders of the domain, or protecting the land from natural disasters.[14] The principle of reciprocity underpins the relationship between those living on the land and the ancestors. The seasons are punctuated with communal and smaller house-based rituals during which invocations and offerings are made to the ancestors to ask for their continued protection and bounty.

Behavioural norms and practices are not limited to interaction with the land and natural resources but extend to the nature of relations between male and female members of the community, preferred paths of alliance/marriage and social ranking within and between house-based descent groups. Critical to the production and reproduction of these norms and practices are historical narratives (*tete bo'ona*) and regular ritual communication with the ancestors. Today, Darlari elders lament the fact that many people living on their land, including members of Darlari houses, do not perform the necessary rituals to ensure the continued fertility of their land and prosperity of its people. They also claim that many

14 Part of the Darlari 'origin' narrative that deals with the arrival of the ancestors and the trials and tribulations of the *Mane Hitu* deals with the personal sacrifice made to secure the 'first' harvest of the founder-ancestors.

people do not know the history of the land or the correct invocations to be made, and that some 'outsiders' continue to invoke ancestors from their places of origins rather than the local emplaced *bu'u*. According to the elders this 'chaotic' situation has been the cause of many trials and tribulations, particularly in the period during and after the Indonesian military occupation.

## Histories of Incorporation and Accommodation

Ancestral itineraries and histories serve not only to reinforce the emplaced nature of claims to authority and territory but also reaffirm the order of arrival and settlement of various descent groups living within these territories. These narratives provide a guide to understanding the dynamics and processes whereby subsidiary groups were formed and in-migrant groups were incorporated into the social order (Lewis 1996). At the same time they reveal the historical impact of political change within the Darlari domain and strategies employed to share land with incorporated groups while retaining overall control. Darlari elders offer two interrelated and recursive narratives to determine precedence and explain the nature of social relations within their territory. One explains the delegation of tasks or duties to subsidiary houses and in-migrant groups and the other is concerned with the history of land allocation within the Darlari domain. Both illustrate our argument that origin principles provide a focal point for managing in-migration and potential resource conflicts.

### *Delegation of Tasks*

The Darlari elders represent the highest ritual or spiritual authority within a domain incorporating numerous house-based descent groups. Although Darlari elders claim that in the past their ancestors held both ritual and jural power over the territory and people of their domain, they acknowledge that, at some stage in their history, their forefathers began to 'retreat into darkness', delegating specific tasks to members of other house-based groups. Ostensibly, the elders state that this 'retreat into darkness' was a conscious decision in order to keep the secrets of their land from 'outsiders', in particular the colonial authorities (and the Catholic Church).[15] However, they also acknowledge that the delegation of tasks to other groups was also a means of appeasing subsidiary lineage-houses and in-migrant groups that represented a potential threat to their authority.

---

15 The *makaer* (spokesperson) for the senior Darlari house explained that their forefathers delegated these tasks to other houses because they wanted to be 'above' the everyday matters of managing their 'kingdom'. Rather than a sign of weakness or loss of power this 'retreat' into darkness becomes a source of strength. In the context of independence – having resisted 'outsiders' and maintained their identity – this has become a means to legitimize attempts of the Darlari elders to re-impose their authority.

Of one of the subsidiary lineage-houses of Darlari called the *uma kabo*[16] the elders state that their ancestors delegated the task to monitor the use of land and natural resources, *lai bosa, lai wai*, to guard the fields, guard the water. Later, according to local histories, the main representative of the *uma kabo*, the *kabo rea*, asked the lord of the land to grant his house a token of office so that those under their jurisdiction would have something to 'believe in' or 'fear'. As a result, a ritual specialist called the *makaer luli* (keeper of the sacra) was appointed to assist the *kabo rea* in their task. The *kabo rea's* function is practical – to monitor land use and access to natural resources, including the application of seasonal prohibitions on the harvesting of various products, collecting tributes for collective ceremonies and/or exacting fines for the infringement of prohibitions. Representatives of two other subsidiary houses of Darlari, *asu rati reino* and *asu rati liurai*, assist them in these practical tasks.[17] The role of the *makaer luli* on the other hand is more spiritual; to preside over collective rituals, acting as an intermediary with the spirit world, and 'watching over' the sacra held in the *uma luli* at Burlalu.

To the Burmeta, ancestors of the people of Aha Bu'u and Kotanisi, the Darlari ancestors gave the prescriptive title of *ana bo'ona, ana tadana*, the eldest and wisest son. This group was designated the task to *lai reinu, lai rea* (guard the people, guard the land) to rule over the people and protect the borders of the domain. More specifically, this group became known as the *ita mata, kai hene* (door and gate), gatekeepers between the traditional 'inner' community and 'outsiders', in particular the colonial authorities. Such a narrative is consistent with the notion of 'stranger kings' found throughout the Austronesian world, outsiders who are incorporated into local hierarchy to manage relations with the outside world. While status as the 'lord of the land' is retained by origin group lineages, political authority for the purposes of external relations may reside in senior members of an affiliated 'latecomer' house (Fox 1995).

The Portuguese colonial authorities granted the title of *tenente coronel* to the head of the Burmeta clan and traditionally village headmen are chosen from this group.[18] Members of this group stress that they were granted authority to *ukun* (Tetun: rule or govern) over the people of Babulo village when they received a *rota* (cane often used as a symbol of office) from the rulers of Viqueque. They describe their role in terms of local governance in relation to the state. In the past this entailed specific duties and responsibilities regarding the settlement of local disputes, the collection of taxes (for the colonial authorities) and the recruitment of labour for

16 Although local informants insist this is an autochthonous title *kabu* appears to be derived from the Portuguese military rank Cabo.

17 It seems likely that the term *asu rati* is a corruption of the Portuguese term *ajudante* or assistant.

18 During the eighteenth and nineteenth centuries the Portuguese colonial authorities granted military titles to local potentates. Ranked beneath the *dom* or *coronel*, a *tenente coronel* was considered to be the second in command of a *regulado*. On the coastal plain of Uatolari the rulers of the Kingdom of Vessoru/Uaitame were given the rank of *dom*.

colonial or state projects. Today the village headman continues to be viewed as the principal intermediary between the local community and the state, or other 'external' parties such as national or international non-governmental organizations.

Often described as the right and left hand of the lord of the land, the descendants of the Burmeta and the combined offices of the *kabu rea* and *makaer luli* have come to represent jural and ritual power respectively within the Darlari domain. The delegation of authority to these groups and dualistic structures of authority created in the process reflect common patterns and themes observed throughout Austronesian societies (Fox 1996). However, Darlari elders are keen to point out that the power of these groups is always subordinate to the authority of the lord of the land. As proof of their seniority, the Darlari elders explain how they gave the Burmeta and the *kabu rea*/*makaer luli* a number of sacred objects believed to have belonged to the Beli/Darlari ancestors. The objects given to the Burmeta are stored in a scared house at a place called Burosoba. To ensure that the political leaders of Burmeta did not try to usurp the ritual authority of the lord of the land by attempting to handle and harness the power of these sacred objects a second *makaer luli* was appointed to guard the objects and control access to this house. The sacred objects given to the *kabu rea* and *makaer luli* on the other hand were placed in a sacred house built at Burlalu.

### *Land Allocation*

Historically, new arrivals to the Darlari domain have been granted land on which to settle and farm by the lord of the land by means of various 'traditional' contracts, including *juramento* (oaths) or marriage, aimed at incorporating the in-migrants into local social and political structures. These traditional mechanisms for incorporation have been weakened by the emergence of state-affiliated village government structures, which – most likely as result of the Portuguese head-tax system – linked hamlet and village administration to people rather than territory. As a result, in-migrants retain affiliation with their source village rather than their village residence. In more recent times, the systematic rclocation of people following the Indonesian invasion has fostered a trend for in-migrants to claim land based on possession and input of labour rather than through incorporation into customary order.

Today, Darlari elders claim that within their domain there remains no 'unused' or 'unallocated' land. They state that long ago their land was divided into five areas corresponding to the five main *uma kain* (houses/families) or lineages of the Darlari descent group. Darlari informants state that territorial divisions within the Darlari domain are well known and marked by physical features such as streams, rocks and hills. These demarcations do not represent five distinct units representing the five main houses of the Darlari group but a patchwork of holdings across the Darlari domain – reflecting traditional farming practices based on shifting cultivation and histories of settlement. The type and size of land-holdings depends on labour, resources and time invested in land. In other words there is a principle of actual possession, as a basis for property entitlement. However, the entitlements created by possession and input of labour are contextualized and subordinate to the overarching claims of Darlari authority to the ancestral domain.

Members of the Darlari houses gain access to land by virtue of their genealogical relation to the common Darlari founder-settler ancestors. The obligation to participate in regular communal ritual is essential to the production and reproduction of discourses of origin on which social organization of the community is structured. To continue to benefit from the land and natural resources, members of these houses are expected to fulfil their ritual and social obligations to members of superior houses and the ancestors. Failure to do so is believed to incur the wrath or displeasure of the ancestors and may result in some form of misfortune, illness or death. These internalized norms and sanctions have been central to social organization and co-operation as Darlari numbers have increased and dispersed across the constituent houses. One of the principal in-migrant groups comprises the descendants of Burmeta. Today, this group is divided into two lineages corresponding to the hamlets of Aha Bu'u and the other Kotanisi. Darlari describe the descendants of Burmeta as *asuwain* (warriors) and claim they arrived in the area some eight generations ago. The origins of the Burmeta are contested. Some claim they are *liurai* (rulers/noble) who came from the east of Matebian Mountain in search of land, while others claim they are members of a group banished from their ancestral lands for cattle hustling. Darlari elders claim that the Burmeta stopped and camped on land close to Baha Liurai on their way to offer vassalage to the much larger and more influential kingdom of Luca. Rather than let these warriors join forces with their strong neighbour, the Darlari ancestors offered the Burmeta some land on which to settle and in exchange asked them to protect the borders of their domain.

Another in-migrant group closely associated with the Burmeta lineages consists of a group that now makes up the majority of people of the hamlet of Roma.[19] Many Darlari and Aha Bu'u informants refer to this group as 'the hamlet without land'. According to local histories, the people of the hamlet of Roma represent a group of *ata* (slaves) originally from Quelicai who traditionally served the senior lineages of Aha Bu'u and Kotanisi. According to one history of the origins of this group, the Laka Roma served a member of the chiefly house of the Burmeta descent group who lived in exile near Quelicai. When members of his family asked him to return to Babulo and become the *liurai* (ruler), he agreed on conditions that he could bring 'his people', who were 'stuck' to him like the 'seeds of a long-grass' called *laka roma* in Makassae.

The Laka Roma were not granted specific areas of land on which to farm or settle by the Darlari lord of the land but became servants to the chiefly houses of Aha Bu'u, Kotanisi and Darlari. In the past one of the main tasks of the Laka Roma was to watch over the buffalo of their masters. Local informants state that in time the Laka Roma started farming land near the animal enclosures or land where

19 The hamlet of Roma was established post-independence.

they regularly took the animals to pasture. Many members of this group now claim these areas of land as their own, based on long-term occupancy. These claimants are likely to seek support from the proposed rule of possession in the land law of East Timor. In this event, the question for local social ordering purposes will be the relationship between Laka Roma entitlements, including future claims based on acts of clearing and cultivation, or even attempts to lease or sell land to customary 'outsiders', and Darlari claims to land authority in the ancestral domain.

### *The Challenge of Afaloicai Migration*

The third, most recent and largest group of in-migrants are originally from the neighbouring village of Afaloicai. Locally, people broadly distinguish between three movements of people from Afaloicai to Babulo. The first group, mainly from the hamlets of Buibela and Lena, arrived sometime in the 1930s in search of land. The second group came during the post-war period, at first seasonally, to work in the rice fields that were being 'developed' on the Uatolari coastal plain, and later settled more permanently in the area. The third group were forcibly displaced from their villages of origin as a result of the Indonesian invasion and 'relocated' following the 'surrender' of civilians from the resistance stronghold at Matebian Mountain in 1979.

The way in-migrants from Afaloicai gained access to land on which to farm and settle depended on the circumstances of their arrival and the level of engagement with the Darlari 'origin group', their kin and affines. However, in-migrants from Afaloicai do not appear to have been incorporated into the local social order in the same way as the descendants of the Burmeta. They were not 'installed on the inside' (Fox 1995) by taking up a specific role or rank within the social hierarchy of the Darlari domain.[20] They remained organized according to their own house-based descent groups, hierarchically ranked and ordered in accordance with their own histories of origin and precedence. Their permanence on Darlari lands is often viewed as temporary and in the context of communal rituals the people of Afaloicai are often referred to as 'the people who use the land for farming and gardening'.

Some suggest that in-migration in the 1930s was triggered by constant conflict between petty-kings around the area of Matebian, which led to the fragmentation of Afaloicai into three distinct villages (Afaloicai-Baguia, Afaloicai-Uatolari and Afaloicai-Uatocarabau) and forced some people to leave their land. Others believe that the newly appointed village head of Afaloicai-Uatolari, who was not of the 'ruling' houses of Afaloicai, wanted to move closer to the Portuguese colonial

20 One could speculate numerous reasons why the people of Afaloicai were not fully integrated into the local social order, for example, timing – migration occurred post-wars of pacification. The local power of the Darlari 'lord of the land' was waning and the Portuguese were firmly in control and installed in the *posto* at Uatolari. It is possible that an alliance was made between the rulers of Afaloicai and the descendants of the Burmenta. The leaders of these ruling groups were later embroiled in the 1959 rebellion against the Portuguese.

authorities at the *posto* that had recently transferred from Tualo on the coast to Uato-U-Lari near Babulo Mountain. Still other informants, such as the village head of Afaloicai (2005–2009), state that increased population pressure, poor soils and difficult farming conditions in the rocky foothills of Matebian all contributed to the decision to migrate towards Babulo and other locations near the coast.[21]

Local informants recall that *liurai* Gregorio, originally from the hamlet of Lena, arrived sometime before the arrival of the Japanese.[22] The Darlari elders claim that *liurai* Gregorio and his people arrived with some fanfare – accompanied by drums and whistles – and set camp on *rea luli* (sacred land) near Baha Liurai. However, it was not long before they started falling ill because they had not respected the prohibitions associated with this land. As a result *liurai* Gregorio approached the Darlari elders and asked them for some land on which to settle and farm. A marriage alliance was established between the two groups. *Liurai* Gregorio was 'given' a bride from the senior houses ofBabulo, and through this marriage the group from Afaloicai were offered land on which to farm and settle. They settled at a place called *Tua Rae Laleo* (shelter of palm wine leaves) and were also given land on which to farm at a number of sites around present-day Uatolari Leten and Kampung Baru.

Access to this land is mediated and managed within the framework of *oa-sae/umana* relations (wife-taker/wife-giver relations). Throughout East Timor, marriage alliance establishes a set of reciprocal social and moral obligations between families and groups. Through marriage, *liurai* Gregorio and his followers were integrated into the broader community by entering into local networks of alliance and exchange. As *oa-sae* (wife-takers), Gregorio and his followers were expected to contribute goods and services to their *umana* (wife-givers), in exchange for being allocated specific plots of land on which they were permitted to farm and build their houses. Over time other marriage alliances were formed between families from Afaloicai and the local houses of Babulo in general and Darlari in particular.[23] However, Darlari elders insist that according to the original *juramento*, oath or agreement with *liurai* Gregorio, land was not (and could not) be transferred outright but rather remained under the ultimate control of the lord of the land. In the contemporary peace-building circumstances of independent

---

21 Local informants also claim that during this pre-war period people from Afaloicai began to settle beyond the boundaries of Babulo. Some state that the village head of Uaitame, Dom Umberto, and his successor Gaspar from Sana invited people from Afaloicai to come and work on their land around present-day Darabai and west of the Bee Bui river. Much of this land has been subject of an ongoing dispute between individuals and groups from Afaloicai and of Makadiki and Matahoi (see Chapter 8 for more details).

22 The use of *liurai* by informants suggests that Gregorio was of the senior lineages of Lena.

23 For example, land at a place called Kai Oris was given to the *oasae* (wife-takers) from Afaloicai of the house of the *kabo rea*.

East Timor, a critical legal question is the status and enforceability of traditional agreements between origin and in-migrant groups.

The movement of people from Afaloicai to closer to the coastal region of Uatolari sub-district was not limited to Babulo village or the Darlari domain. Informants from Afaloicai also describe how during the 1930s the *dom* of Vessoru-Uaitame 'invited' people from Afaloicai to work on land close to the present-day Darabai, the seat of Uatolari sub-district administration since the Indonesian occupation. And after the Second World War, people from Afaloicai continued to work on the coastal plain opening up rice fields and digging irrigations to the east of Darabai towards the Bee Bui River. Today, informants from Afaloicai claim to 'own' land within the ancestral domains of the *dom* of Vessoru-Uaitame and Darlari-Babulo (da Silva 2004). These claims and ongoing tensions over productive land in the Uatolari plain will be discussed in detail in Chapter 10. They illustrate the tension implicit in property claims based on prior acts of possession, where entitlements claimed through mythical acts of ancestral first possession conflict with entitlements claimed through clearing and cultivation by recent forebears.

## The Impact of the Indonesian Invasion and Occupation

The Indonesian invasion and occupation of East Timor layered another round of displacement, dispossession, re-possession and relocation on to the histories of population movement in Viqueque district. Indonesian troops are reported to have advanced towards Uatolari sub-district from the port at Beasu in mid to late 1976. Local informants describe both erratic and systematic patterns of displacement between 1976 and 1979. Some informants report taking part in group movements or 'evacuations' organized by local Fretilin (*Frente Revolucionária de Timor-Leste Independente*) delegates to specific sites. In other cases individuals and families state that they made their way over a period of two to three years towards the Matebian mountain range, either on their own or in groups with their hamlet and village heads. Sometimes people sheltered for a few days in a particular area while at other times they stayed for a few months, often building temporary housing and finding time to plant crops.[24]

Informants from the hamlet of Darlari describe how the area 'emptied' out. People left even the more remote settlements fleeing the Indonesian troops, looking for shelter from the aerial bombardments. Most informants described reaching Matebian in mid to late 1979 and staying there until the Fretilin leadership 'ordered' the 'surrender' of the civilian population.[25] Conditions on Matebian

24 Most informants claim that political violence within Babulo was contained as a result 'traditional' alliances and oaths. The perpetrators of violence were often described as 'outsiders' from groups who were displaced to Babulo as a result of the internal armed conflict between UDT (Uniao Democratica Timorense) and Fretilin, and the Indonesian invasion.

25 Generally this is dated around 23 November 1976.

Mountain were traumatic. Informants describe how they lived in fear of the aerial bombardments, taking shifts to sleep in cramped conditions with little food or water. Many informants attribute their survival during this period to the fact that the Darlari elders (and their sibling Beli elders) did not abandon their ancestral sacra but carried them to Matebian.[26]

The 'surrender' and return of the civilian population to areas under the control of the Indonesian military began in late November 1979. As elsewhere in East Timor the inhabitants of Babulo were ordered to report to internment and resettlement camps while the troops conducted military mop-up operations in the area (CAVR 2005). The main internment camp in Uatolari sub-district was established at the old *posto* at Uatolari Leten. People from all six villages of Uatolari, as well as the sub-districts of Baguia and Quelicai, were 'contained' within a restricted area around the *posto.* For the first few months the Indonesian military and East Timorese collaborators surrounded the encampment and people were not permitted to leave unless accompanied by an East Timorese or Indonesian guard. Informants describe how during this time people had little or no shelter and they had to sleep, eat, wash and go to the toilet within the guarded perimeter. Food was scarce and they had restricted (and sometimes no) access to fields and gardens beyond a specified distance.

In the early 1980s the Indonesian military began relocating the population. Most of the population residing in the village prior to the invasion were relocated from isolated upland settlements to linear settlements along the main road networks. Some informants claim that East Timorese who collaborated with the Indonesians had considerable influence over where people should be relocated.[27] Within the Darlari domain some degree of homogeneity was retained as members of the various house-based groups tended to be relocated together. Today, members of the principal houses of Darlari, Beli, Aha Bu'u and Kotanisi all agree that the village head of Babulo at the time consulted with the elders as to where groups should be relocated. For example, members of the Beli and Darlari houses were relocated to Aliambata on the coast. Elders argue that this site was chosen as it was close to a number of important ancestral *luli* sites, including the off-shore gas seep located some 100 metres from the settlement at Aliambata.[28] However, the vast majority of the population appear to have remained close to the *posto* at Uatolari Leten or moved to the new settlement of Kampung Baru.

---

26 Both Beli and Darlari claim that few of their own people were killed during this period. However, this generally regards people who had died as a result of bombing or later executions, rather than deaths owing to illness and hunger.

27 Some (but not all) of the East Timorese collaborators in Uatolari had previously been involved – directly or indirectly – in the anti-colonial uprising of 1959. Others had suffered at the hands of Fretilin during the internal conflict and saw their opportunity for pay-back.

28 The village head originally from Aha Bu'u, and his family also relocated to Aliambata. Some suggest that this was in order to control access to the Aliambata gas seep and ensure that 'outsiders' did not try to exploit these resources without consultation.

Continued restrictions on movement during the 1980s and early 1990s meant that fields and gardens in more remote upland locations remained 'off limits'. Some informants claim that these restrictions were 'self-imposed' – as people feared attacks by the armed resistance, or of being suspected of collaborating with Falintil. Darlari elders claim that increased population pressure and limited access to land meant that people just went ahead and farmed whatever land was available in order to survive, circumventing any 'traditional' principles and processes of land allocation.

## Contemporary Tenures

The following section describes contemporary tenure arrangements in order to illustrate the effects of return and reconstitution of property rights after the Indonesian occupation. Entitlements to land and access to natural resources have been negotiated and renegotiated over time between the Darlari *rea bu'u* (lord of the land) and in-migrant groups. Within the Darlari domain entitlements to land have historically been linked to ancestral histories of arrival, settlement and land allocation. While incorporated groups such as Aha Bu'u and Kotanisi enjoy broad rights to land and natural resources, traditionally in-migrant groups such as those from Afaloicai have been granted 'temporary' or revocable usufruct rights to land. Over time, experiences of migration, war and displacement have challenged these customary processes of negotiation and accommodation giving rise to multiple and multi-layered claims to land.

At present, what might be described as private and communal tenures co-exist within the Darlari domain. Certain types of entitlement are rooted in notions of ancestral attachments to land; others derive from long-term usufruct rights based on agreement with Darlari elders; and others still are based on claims of long-term occupancy and/or land use. Types of entitlement or tenure are also dependent on the history of the land, type of land and land use as well as attitudes towards the relationship that exists between people and the land.

### *Sacred Sites and Communal Resources*

Informants from Babulo declare that some areas of land and natural resources within the Darlari domain may never be individually owned. Typically, these areas and resources are of symbolic importance and/or value to the entire community. Some of these sites are deemed *luli* and may be completely 'out of bounds' such as the area of old-growth forest surrounding the summit of Baha Liurai. Others may be accessed as long as the necessary prohibitions and proscriptions are upheld and the relevant authorities informed. This includes important communal resources such as water springs but may also be applied to areas of secondary forest or agricultural land. For example, the *luli* rice fields of *Lia Lakeu* (see history of Beli and Darlari brothers above) are currently being farmed by members of the Afaloicai community, and land surrounding the natural gas seep at Aliambata, which is believed to be protected by a particularly unpredictable *bu'u* (guardian), is also being farmed.

Nominally, the *kabu rea* is responsible for the oversight of these communal resources. However, in practice it is impossible for the *kabu rea* to physically monitor access to all these areas. Often individuals or groups will report an infraction to their own 'house' level authorities (the senior males of the house-based lineage group), the hamlet head or directly to the Darlari elders. Typically, infractions are not reported immediately and sometimes may only be reported if and when the person or persons who committed the offence fall ill or suffer some kind of misfortune. In this case, the Darlari elders, the *kabu rea* or the *makaer luli* will determine a sanction to be 'paid' by the offender. Sanctions usually take the form of a fine or sacrificial offering to be made to the ancestral guardians and spirits associated with the site or resources where the offence was committed. These sacrificial offerings may be presented at the principal Darlari sacred houses, the *uma buti* and the *uma ita*, during communal ceremonies such as the maize and rice harvests or at the site the infraction took place – this usually requires the attendance of a house elder or ritual specialist.

### *Swidden Gardens, House Plots and Rice Fields*

While most individuals, families and groups claim to 'own' land within the Darlari domain, understandings of 'ownership' do not necessarily reflect legal concepts of 'private property rights'. More specifically, while many inhabitants of the Darlari domain – both Darlari and in-migrant groups – claim to have individual inheritable rights to land they stop short at claiming the right to sell, transfer or freely administer this land. It is possible that these attitudes to 'ownership' reflect a knowledge of Indonesian concepts of land rights such as *hak adat pribadi* (private property rights to customary land) and *hak adat masyarakat* (common property rights to customary land). These Indonesian legal notions encompass restrictions on alienation (Fitzpatrick 1997). However, the interpretation of property rights in the Darlari domain also reflects local understandings of the emplaced authority of the lord of the land and their claims to overarching territorial control. The restriction on alienation, in particular, reflects local understandings of collectivity, as a source of resource use cooperation in a context of population movement.

Given the virtual absence of a local land market it is likely that most Darlari and their affines have never been confronted with the possibility of selling land. Many informants felt that selling land outright was irresponsible and failed to provide for the well-being of future generations. However, the notion of transactions within the framework of reciprocal exchange between families, for example as part of a bride-wealth exchange, was not viewed in the same way. In general, a distinction was also made between *to'os* (swidden gardens) and *natar* (rice fields). Rice fields were generally regarded as highly individualized land-holdings and important household assets that might be transferred or transacted – either as dowry or under some type of share-cropping or renting agreement. In contrast, Darlari informants found it unlikely that anyone would want to buy land used for swidden gardens since locally most people had access to their ancestral lands or could negotiate usufruct rights from local landowners.

In relation to rice fields, entitlements do not necessarily derive exclusively from group membership but are also linked to labour, time and resources invested in land. Rice fields provide an illustration of interactions among principles of origin, possession and input of labour in Darlari property matters. For example, Darlari informants claimed that many members of the various Darlari house-based groups did not have access to rice fields because they (or their relatives) were not involved in 'opening' the land. Often it was suggested that this was because they were 'lazy'. However, given it was the duty of village and hamlet heads to organize the population to open this land, injustices regarding land distribution may have more to do with power than the 'effort' of individuals and families. In particular, the power of colonial village government officials over eligibility to contribute acts of possession and labour in newly cleared coastal areas shaped ensuing understanding of entitlement to rice field lands. It should also be noted that some former village and hamlet heads from the Portuguese period tended to 'own' more land on the coastal plain, not because they were harder workers but because they were able to requisition labour and/or allocate more land to themselves.

It seems logical that many of those who migrated or were relocated to land within the Darlari domain, with no ancestral claims to negotiated rights to land, base their right to 'own' land on histories of land clearance and use. For example, one informant from Afaloicai claimed he owned several plots of rice paddy on the coastal plain. He stated that he had purchased some of these plots from local landowners but he had inherited most from his father who had been involved in the work groups established to 'open' the coastal plain for rice cultivation. He declared that he had the right to sell, transfer or use/manage the land according to his own needs. However, he also added that he acknowledged the overarching claims of the local lord of the land.

This example from Afaloicai illustrates some of the ways in which in-migrant groups seek to nest their possessory entitlements within the general framework of origin principles. It represents an attempt to accommodate notions of actual possession and ancestral first possession. However, despite these attempts to reconcile claims to land and histories of land use, tensions remain, in particular in relation to the use of natural resources and feelings of encroachment. We discuss these tensions further in Chapter 10.

### *Inheritance*

When discussing entitlements to land, informants claim to have inherited land from their fathers and grandfathers, which they, in turn, will bequeath to their own children. In most cases, the right of in-migrant groups to inherit land is also recognized, notwithstanding that their entitlements rests on agreement with Darlari elders.[29] Usually, land is passed on to male sons. Unmarried daughters have access to their father's land-holdings until they marry, after which they are expected to move to their husband's family, 'house' and ancestral lands. In the absence of male heirs, a daughter might be named the prescriptive 'eldest son' in order for her to inherit her father's land. Informants claimed that it was crucial in such cases that male relatives – from the immediate family and the extended house-based lineage group – witness the will of the father in his lifetime. They suggested that in such cases male relatives from both the father's (*oa-sae*) and mother's (*umane*) side become embroiled in disputes over inheritance. For example, a brother or cousin of the deceased may claim that they are the legitimate heir through the male line. While, the male relatives of the wife of the deceased may claim that the land formed part of the bride-wealth agreements between the two families. Informants also suggested that disputes over inheritance sometimes emerge during mortuary rituals. For example, a relative who has provided either in cash or in kind a considerable amount to the mortuary rituals of the deceased may expect to 'inherit' part of the deceased relative's land in return.

### *Land and Produce*

There is a clear distinction between claims to land and claims to produce from the land. Within the Darlari domain all groups recognize the right of individual cultivators to their produce, for example swidden garden crops, rice and fruit trees. Traditionally, this right is upheld by means of regular participation in communal rituals and the maintenance of social and political obligations towards the lord of the land and the ancestors.

Since independence, some individuals and families displaced during the Indonesian occupation have returned to their places of origin. In doing so many have left behind fruit trees that they planted locally. Darlari elders claim that those responsible for planting the trees continue to have rights to the produce/fruits. However, they do not necessarily retain usufruct rights to the land. In an attempt to retain some control over the land that they farmed during the Indonesian occupation some displaced families have sought to form alliances with local families. For example, one informant described how a family from the hamlet of Liasidi displaced to Darlari lands during the occupation approached the Darlari elders to arrange a marriage between their families in order to continue farming land within the Darlari domain. This type of agreement – which we found in all our field sites – illustrates the resilience of local responses to displacement through agreements based on shared acceptance of the organizing principle of origin. It illustrates our argument that peace-building requires legal facilitation of local agreements between customary groups and relocated persons notwithstanding the high degree of information intensiveness.

---

29 This might be a reflection of the notion of inheritable *hak pakai* (usufruct rights) under Indonesian land law.

## Reassertions of Territorial Control

Histories of colonization, war and occupation have all had an impact on behaviours and practices associated with land. In particular, processes of 'voluntary' and 'involuntary' migration, which began in the inter-war years and intensified during the Indonesian occupation, have had a lasting impact on population and settlement within the Darlari domain. A key response to the potential for land conflict caused by migration has been ritual re-affirmation of Darlari claims to precedence based on proximity to the source of ancestral origin.

Since independence the diverse house-based descent groups of Babulo have been engaged in the process of returning to their pre-1975 settlements and rebuilding their ancestral cult-houses. Darlari elders, and members of the Darlari descent group in general, consider the return to their settlement of origin at Baha Liurai an important and necessary step in re-establishing their credentials as lords of the land. The Baha Liurai is the most sacred of all sites in the Darlari narratives of origin. It is considered to be the burial place of the *ina ama* (mother and father) of the *Mane Hitu*, the founder ancestors of *Bubulu*. Access to the summit is absolutely prohibited unless accompanied by ritual authorities. Symbolically, Baha Liurai serves not only to legitimate Darlari precedence in relation to other groups living in the area but confirms the emplaced nature of their authority. Informants reported that during discussions as to whether or not the settlement should be rebuilt on its original site, closer to the summit of the Baha Liuari, or on a more accessible site, the elders agreed that it should be moved closer to the main road (from Uatolari to Quelicai) so that people would be made aware that they were 'passing through sacred land'.[30]

As early as August 2000 work began on rebuilding the main Darlari ritual houses, the *um buti* and the *um ita*. Elders describe the *um buti* as the principal sacred house. It 'belongs' to the whole community – understood as all those living within the Darlari domain – but is 'owned' by the Darlari. More specifically, this structure symbolically represents the 'origin' house of the Darlari ancestors. The *um ita,* on the other hand, is described as an *uma ukun* or ruling house where Darlari headmen traditionally stored symbols of political power called *rota*, which they distributed to subsidiary houses and allied groups. Both structures retain sacred heirlooms believed to have belonged to the ancestors and passed down from generation to generation. It is believed that the essence of the ancestors continues to live through these objects and inhabit specific spaces within the sacred house. During collective rituals, food offerings, water, *bua* and *malus* (areca nut and betel pepper) are placed within these sacred spaces and emerge transformed to be redistributed to members of the community. Betel nut and leaves stored in these houses are believed to have special protective qualities. They are used in collective

30 Younger members of the family stated that they felt the site should be moved closer to the road and to the water source given the age of those who would be returning to the settlement.

ritual as a marker of membership of the group but also to protect visitors to the area or in healing rituals.[31]

Following the completion of the *um buti* and *um ita*, representatives of all the house-based descent groups living on Darlari lands, including people from Afaloicai, and neighbouring allies, were invited to take part in a rare ceremony of ritual sacrifice to the ancestors on the summit of Baha Liuari.[32] The elders explained that the purpose of the ceremony was threefold: to visit the burial site of the ancestors and communicate within them; to thank the ancestors for watching over the people living on their sacred land; and to ask for their continued protection and generosity. This ceremony last took place immediately prior to the community's displacement towards Matebian in late 1976. Prior to 1976, the Darlari elders stated that the ceremony took place every five to ten years or 'when it was deemed necessary'. During the initial stages of the ceremony there was considerable debate and negotiation regarding various aspects of the 'order of things'. While in part this debate reflected the fact that none of the elders who had directed the last ceremony are now alive, the degree of contestation also forms an integral part of the nature of relations between the various house-based groups now living on Darlari lands.[33]

### *Description of Ceremony*

In essence, the ceremony represented the re-enactment and representation of key discourses of origin and precedence that account for the social organization of house-based descent groups within the Darlari domain. The ceremony began at the *um buti* and the *um ita*. During this first stage of the ceremony, the main sacrificial offering, rice, betel nut and 'holy' water were taken from inside the *um buti* and handed to the senior members of the diverse Darlari lineages, sub-lineages and their affines. The *kabu rea* then directed those participating in the ceremony to form into single file according to rank with senior members of the 'elder' houses preceding the 'younger' house members. Once the group was assembled they began the procession to the summit of Baha Liurai.

Representatives of the sibling Beli and Darlari descent groups approached Baha Liurai from their separate domains. At a location called *ita mata, kai hene*

31 Unlike the *um ita*, the *um buti* is not used as a meeting house and is not permanently lived in.

32 Only representatives from senior *liurai* (noble) lineages were included in the procession to the summit of Baha Liurai. However, a large gathering of people remained at Uatosoba where the sacred houses are located.

33 To a certain extent the ceremony at Baha Liurai provides a space for a degree of 'theatre' where representatives of different groups attempt to redefine their role within the broader group. Once such discussion involved the placing of the ex-*nurep* in relation to the former village head. During the Indonesian occupation the *nurep* represented a covert counterpart to the Indonesian-installed village leadership, the *kepala desa*.

(door and gate), they were met by representatives from the Burmeta clan, who had made their way there from their principal cult-house at Burosoba. Together the group continued their 'pilgrimage' to the ancestral burial site on the summit of Baha Liurai. The *makaer luli* from Burlalu and Darlari elders were responsible for 'opening the door' to the summit before all others could pass through.[34] The *makaer luli* carried sacra from the sacred house at Burlalu while acolytes from the houses of *asu rati reino* and *asu rati liurai* led the way towards the summit of Baha Liurai. They were followed by the Beli and Darlari elders and the former village head of Aha Bu'u and Kotanisi. Other senior members of the community followed carrying animals and rice that were offered up to the ancestors and shared amongst all those present during the course of the vigil. Sacred betel nut, betel leaves and water drawn from one of the *ue mata luli* (sacred springs) were also carried.

On reaching the summit an area of forest was cleared and preparations for the night-long vigil and communal feast began. Two altars were prepared where food was laid out for the *ina ama* Beli Darlari (mother, father Beli Darlari) the mythical 'original' couple. Once the food was prepared, it was laid out on the altars. According to custom all those present were required to stay awake and alert throughout the night, in solemn vigil remembering the ancestors and members of the community who could not be present. There were strict rules regarding behaviour throughout the ceremony, including no alcohol, no betel nut, no smoking, no defecation, no swearing and no inappropriate conduct between men and women. Throughout the night representatives of the Darlari sub-lineages ensured that no one fell asleep or broke these prohibitions. Every so often men from the houses of *asu rati reino* and *asu rati liurai* would beat the sides of the altar with bamboo sticks to keep malignant spirits away.

At sunrise, following the sharing of food that was distributed according to precedence, the spokesperson for the Darlari elders supported by the *kabu rea* reminded all those present of their social and moral obligations to the ancestors and the *rea mumu, rea uato* (lord of the land). This proclamation included behavioural norms and practices regarding social interaction between men and women, and descent groups. It also reiterated any prohibitions regarding access to certain areas of land, forest or other natural resources and reminded those present of protocols pertaining to land use such as those determining the season for certain agricultural tasks like clearing, burning, planting and harvesting. Once these rules collectively known as *luli* (Naueti) or *bandu* (Tetun) were declared, all the participants prepared to leave the Baha Liurai in single file and in silence without turning back. The last to leave was a Darlari ritual specialist who 'closed' the *ita mata* (door) through which the participants had passed the day before.

During the course of the ceremony key notions of ancestry, attachment to place, histories of migration and settlement and networks of alliance were all acknowledged within a single visual narrative. The ceremony at Baha Liurai

---

34 This door is an invisible 'threshold' marking the division between the visible world and the realm of the ancestors.

provided a vivid and visual medium for understanding the role, function and status of each house-based group and the nature of the relationships that bind house-based groups to cooperative action within a single domain. Critically, the ceremony at Baha Liurai also constituted a 'renewal' or 'reaffirmation' of the bond that exists between the ancestors and members of the different house-based groups living within the Darlari domain. Darlari elders believe that the ritual (re) connection with the founding ancestors is indispensable for the restoration of the 'proper order of things' after 24 years of war, occupation and displacement.

The time, effort and resources invested in the ceremony at Baha Liurai suggest that the community is committed to maintaining the social and moral order within which the different house-based groups are situated – including the rights, duties and obligations that this implies (McWilliam 2005). The ceremony provides an example of mechanisms for the reproduction of collective action after the social disruption of war and displacement. However, not all members of the community take part in these ceremonies and the reassertion of emplaced authority and social hierarchies based on precedence has coincided with calls for 'outsiders' who were displaced or relocated during the Indonesian occupation to return to their ancestral lands. As a result there are tensions arising from the reaffirmation of customary authority, between incentives for displaced groups to accommodate their claims through incorporation into customary order, and the exclusionary and dispossessory potential of failure to reach agreement with customary elders.

## The Constrained Nature of Customary Resilience

Members of the various Darlari house-based groups expressed concern regarding the growing numbers of people from Afaloicai living on their ancestral lands. While some people from Afaloicai have chosen to return to their hamlets and villages of origin many have chosen to remain in the lowland, coastal settlements. At present, people from Afaloicai account for 49 per cent of the total population residing in Babulo.[35] Despite the fact that many individuals and families from Afaloicai have lived in Babulo for decades they have not been integrated into local hamlet and village structures. In 2007 the headman of Darlari hamlet, who is the son of one of the senior elders of Darlari, stated that the people of Darlari (and Babulo in general) did not want to incorporate the people from Afaloicai into their administrative hamlet and village. The reason he gave was that the Darlari wanted to maintain control of their territory. He feared that, given their growing numbers, if the people from Afaloicai were incorporated into local hamlet and village structures, the balance of power would be tipped in their favour as they would out-number the autochthonous populations, including the Darlari, during local elections. In the short-term, at least,

35 Population living on Darlari lands in 2007: Aha Bu'u 287, Kotanisi 157, Roma 206, Darlari 278, Afaloicai (6 aldeias) 2,184.

the numbers of Afaloicai on Darlari land challenge traditional mechanisms to incorporate in-migrants through marriage and customary agreements.

While Darlari elders acknowledge that their ancestors granted usufruct right to certain groups from Afaloicai, they too feel that land and natural resources (forest products and fuel in particular) available to their own people are becoming scarcer. Elders also expressed their concern regarding access to land and natural resources by suggesting that some 'outsiders' donot partake in communal thanksgiving rituals andmaintain strong links with their own ancestral settlements outside the Darlari domain. One elder commented that many people from Afaloicai who had been displaced during the Indonesian occupation were now prospering and as a consequence taking over more land. He felt that more and more people from Afaloicai were building houses on Darlari land out of concrete blocks and zinc roofs, which suggested they planned to stay permanently. The same elder stated that the presence of people from Afaloicai on Darlari was not the issue but rather that, little by little, the Darlari themselves were being 'pushed out' of their own land and in the future might have to look for land elsewhere.

Some younger informants betrayed a sense of jealousy towards people from Afaloicai, claiming that they had prospered under the Indonesian occupation and continued to do so since independence. They commented on the fact that people from Afaloicai appeared to have plenty of livestock, were building houses and were able to afford buses or motorbikes. For their part, informants from Afaloicai claimed that part of the social jealousy between Afaloicai and Babulo in general (not just Darlari) was based on the fact that the people of Afaloicai worked harder on their land and therefore were able to prosper. However, informants from Afaloicai, including the village head, stressed that they respected the agreements made with the Darlari lord of the land and the *dom* of Vessoru-Uaitame and claimed that whenever people from Afaloicai sought to expand their land-holdings they always negotiated with local *rai na'in* (Tetun: landowners). This acknowledgement is significant because it illustrates attempts to maintain social order, even in circumstances of in-migration and increased competition for land, through reference to broad historical agreements between origin elders and in-migrants relating to land entitlements.

For example, during the course of fieldwork one of the authors attended a rice harvest ritual at which a settler family from Afaloicai presented a large pig for sacrifice. The pig was a tribute to the ancestors and the Darlari lord of the land to 'heal the wound of the earth', and make a customary 'payment' for having built a permanent structure on Darlari land. It is believed that when building the foundations of a house the earth is 'wounded' (halo kanek rai), and the tribute serves to redress the balance. This example supports our conclusion that to date most people from Afaloicai have made strategic attempts to nest their claims within the overarching normative framework provided by the emplaced land authority of the Darlari lord of the land.

Although the Afaloicai generally recognize the emplaced land stewardship of the Darlari, at least within the territory of Babulo itself, there is little doubt that most

Afaloicai also hope for long-term support from the new land laws of East Timor, through recognition of property claims based on possessory acts of residence and cultivation. Afaloicai recognition of Darlari land authority certainly does not extend to acknowledgment that the Darlari could evict Afaloicai migrants from their land, or prevent them from building 'permanent' housing and transferring those houses to their children. While ancestral origin principles have proved resilient mechanisms for social (re)ordering after the Indonesian occupation, this does not mean that they offer bright-line solutions to all problems of property allocation in Babulo itself. No precise delineation of entitlements arises from the broad nature of historical agreements between origin elders and in-migrants, particularly in terms of revocability and inter-generational transfer. The precise nature and status of Afaloicai rights to Darlari land is a question of social construction and power, rather than topics that are autonomously resolvable by origin principles, including agreements with origin elders. Within the rubric of respect for origin there is considerable scope for asserting and contesting entitlements.

Since the time of *liurai* Gregorio the people of Afaloicai have been associated with 'development' and 'progress' in Uatolari sub-district. Many Afaloicai informants expressed with pride the role that members of their community played as catechists, teachers and nurses. For example, a former village head of Afaloicai, killed by the Indonesian forces in 1991, is said to have been the driving force behind the Catholic Church in Uatolari Leten.[36] It is possible to suggest that, constrained in their position as 'outsiders' within the Darlari domain, certain individuals and groups from Afaloicai have sought social advancement through education and economic development rather through 'customary' or 'traditional' structures.

Relations between Darlari landowners and Afaloicai settlers are in general cordial. Many individuals and families from these communities are bound by networks of reciprocal exchange and alliance through marriage and also remember the agreements (*juramento*) made between their forefathers regarding land allocation. Nevertheless, since independence, tensions over access to land and natural resources have increased. Whenever these tensions have surfaced the Darlari local leaders and elders have tended to reassert their rights as lords of the land. In some instances this has been done by recourse to 'strategies of resistance' aimed at retaining control over resources, while at other times more direct action has been taken to 'enforce' customary rights.

36 Adelino Carvalho became the village head of Afaloicai in 1960. He replaced Abilio Menezes who was killed in the aftermath of the 1959 rebellion. Adelino became a prominent Fretilin delegate immediately prior to the Indonesian invasion. At the time of the invasion he fled to the mountains and joined the armed resistance. It was reported that in 1980 Adelino's wife was brutally tortured, raped and killed by pro-Indonesian elements. Adelino was killed in 1991 by members of Battalion 321. He was replaced by Agustino Ribeiro. Abilio Menezes was preceded by *liurai* Feliciano and *liurai* Gregorio.

### *Strategies of Resistance*

In 2001–02, the village head of Afaloicai was involved in promoting a community-development project aimed at channelling water from a water source in the Darlari domain called *Kabu Rea* to a public water tank in Kampung Baru. The main beneficiaries of the project were people from Afaloicai who had been relocated to Kampung Baru during the Indonesian occupation. This case study illustrates the way in which interventions of the new state and other external actors can put pressure on fault lines created by displacement and relocation during the Indonesian occupation. The discussion also identifies strategies used at local level to manage these tensions.

The village head and an elected community council submitted a proposal and were granted funding through the World Bank funded Community Empowerment Project. People from Afaloicai living in Kampung Baru were involved in laying down the water pipes, building the water tanks and connecting the pipes to the source. However, once the project was complete they found that every night the pipes were being tampered with – either cut off, diverted or stolen. Stories began to circulate that an old lady with white hair was seen roaming the fields of *Tuku Besi* (literally, banging the iron or iron smith's fields) just below the *Kabu Rea* spring. Darlari elders and other members of the community claimed that this old lady was a *bu'u,* the spirit owner of the spring who was angry because the people of Afaloicai had not sought permission to use the water source. However, people from Afaloicai claimed that people from Darlari did not have the initiative to organize themselves to collaborate with the project and once the project was complete they expected to benefit from it.

Eventually, tensions between the two communities came to a head and it was agreed, since the water project mainly services the Afaloicai community of Kampung Baru, that water from a source within Afaloicai ancestral lands would be channelled into Babulo and serve the community of Liasidi. The fact that this second project has never materialized is considered by some members of the Afaloicai community as evidence of a Babulo lack of initiative and organization. The Darlari strategy of passive resistance and (possible) recourse to sabotage could also be interpreted as an attempt on the part of the Darlari customary landowners to make their voices heard from a position of weakness in relation to external structures such as the state and international funding agencies (see Scott 1985).

### *Enforcing 'Customary' Rights*

More recently, some leaders within the Darlari community have sought to 'enforce' rights to land and natural resources, not through ritualized reaffirmation of origin and precedence, but through local governance structures and with reference to national legislation. These efforts have been led by a younger generation of local government officials and have been met with suspicion and resistance by some of the elders. Although there has been a long history and tradition of incorporation and accommodation between the two systems of authority (customary and village government), there is a sense that these initiatives represent an attempt to undermine customary authority. This development illustrates the vulnerability of origin, as a social ordering principle, to recourse by members of the origin group itself to the state and state-based forms of property authority.

For example, in Feburary 2007 a man from Uai Cai, Afaloicai, who had long been settled in Kampung Baru, approached the hamlet head of Darlari to complain that some Darlari youths had destroyed a number of his coconut trees. The youths had been building a house for a widow from Darlari but in the process had cut down leaves and fruits from a number of his trees. According to custom, trees and their fruits belong to whoever planted them and even though this man's plantation was on Darlari land he was well within his rights to complain.

The hamlet head acknowledged that he had organized the work group to build the house and had arranged with another Darlari member to use palms from his plantation to build the house. However, the work group found that these trees were too tall and therefore took some palms from nearby trees. The hamlet head proposed that there should be a community meeting between the people of Uai Cai and Darlari to resolve the issue. However, other Darlari elders and senior house members present at the meeting were not so accommodating. They made comments to the effect that the man from Uai Cai was a 'visitor' on their land and should be grateful he was even permitted to plant trees. One suggested that if he had a problem he should take it to court.

Despite these comments, a community meeting was called. The village heads of Afaloicai and Babulo attended as did some of the Darlari elders, the local police and representatives from the sub-district administration. The outcome of the meeting went far beyond resolving the original dispute between the man from Uai Cai and the youth work group and resulted in the proclamation of a 'new' *tara bandu* between the two communities.[37] The general terms of this agreement as described by the hamlet head of Darlari hamlet were as follows:

1. Public acknowledgment of the Darlari as '*rea bu'u*' or traditional owners of the land and natural resources in the hamlet. '*Rekonese ami nia riko soin, ai, fatuk, raihenek, bee matan*' (Acknowledge our natural resources, our forests, rocks, sand and water sources).
2. Acknowledgement of the fact that Darlari had 'allowed' people from Afaloicai to farm land to feed themselves ('*aprovieta fo hahan ba Afloicai iha ami nia area*').
3. Acknowledgment that any trees or crops planted by people from Afaloicai on Darlari land belonged to whoever planted them.

37 Tara Bandu is a Tetun expression that literally means 'hanging the prohibition'. While the term is often used to describe prohibitions or 'rules' regarding access to land and natural resources it actually applies to a much broader set of behaviours and practices – such as those presented to the participants of the ceremony at Baha Liurai.

4. Ban on Afaloicai people resident on Darlari land from planting new trees.
5. Ban on taking firewood from the roadside etcetera. Afaloicai residents can only use wood from their own trees.
6. Ban on both Darlari and Afaloicai from cutting down any trees in the area – unless with express permission from the hamlet head and village head.
7. A total ban on cutting down old-growth forest.

The last two points of the agreement were considered by the hamlet head to be a reaffirmation of the state ban on logging that has been in place since 2002. The hamlet head felt that these measures were necessary to safeguard Darlari land and reduce environmental degradation. He specifically mentioned recent landslides in Naedala suggesting that these had been caused by over-farming by people from Afaloicai. The hamlet head's actions appear to have been influenced by his participation in training for local government officials on new forestry legislation, which included examples of successful community-based natural resource management solutions based on *tara bandu.*

Although a verbal agreement was made between the two communities and the meeting was concluded with the sharing of food, not all members of the community were satisfied with the results. A number of senior Darlari members refused to attend the meeting. They argued that the original complaint from the man from Uai Cai should have been handled differently by the hamlet head. They referred back to the original *juramento* between the Darlari 'lord of the land' and the people of Afaloicai and suggested that the youths responsible for destroying the trees should have been held accountable for their actions. With regards to the 'new' *tara bandu* agreement between the two communities the Darlari elders and senior house members were angry with the hamlet head, suggesting he had undermined the authority of the elders by overriding the solemn proclamation of the *tara bandu* made during the course of the communal ritual held at Baha Liurai.

The examples of the dispute of the water project and the 'new' *tara bandu* agreement between Afaloicai and Darlari reveal some of the ongoing tensions between these communities regarding access to land and natural resources. Although historically there has been a relatively high degree of accommodation between customary systems of authority and the village structures initially introduced by the Portuguese, these case studies expose some of the tensions that can emerge between the two systems under the influence of displacement and relocation pressures.

They also touch on some internal tensions within the Darlari community itself. While Darlari elders and senior Darlari house members seek to reassert their authority over their domain by recourse to ancestral narratives of 'origin' and migration reinforced through the rebuilding of sacred cult-houses and renewed participation in communal ritual, the actions of the hamlet head suggest that other sources of authority or legitimacy are also being engaged as a means to assert control over land, resources and population within the Darlari domain. The intervention of the hamlet head is consistent with a growth in the importance of village government authority. Yet the hamlet head was ultimately unable to enforce the *tara bandu* agreement, suggesting that the challenges of Afaloicai displacement cannot be easily resolved by village government actors operating as alternative sources of public authority to customary elders.

## Conclusion

Communities throughout Timor Leste experienced considerable loss and social upheaval as a consequence of war, displacement and policies of resettlement and relocation, restrictions on movement and cultural practice during the Indonesian occupation. Since independence many Timorese communities have (re)turned to 'traditional' symbols and structures to provide a sense of social and moral order (Babo-Soares 2004, Hicks 2007, Meitzner Yoder 2005, Ospina and Hohe 2002). The most visible sign of this 'resurgence' of custom (*lisan*) has been the rebuilding of sacred ritual houses (*uma lulik*), which were were either destroyed by the Indonesian military or fell into disrepair after their keepers were forced from their lands. The process of reconstituting these symbolic structures has involved the re-articulation of the social relations and hierarchies they encompass, including those governing access to land and natural resources.

There are many commonalities between the principles and practices associated with customary claims to land within the Darlari domain and other communities throughout Timor Leste. Traditionally, individuals and groups lay claim to rights to land and other natural resources by invoking histories of 'origin' and migration. These narratives are often inscribed in the local landscape in the form of sacred sites and reproduced during periodic participation in communal rituals (Reuter 2006). Narratives and ritual performances reveal a concern with the impact of social and political change. They provide an understanding of the dynamics and strategies employed by 'origin' groups to retain control over their territory through the incorporation of in-migrant groups into the local social order and sharing the land.

The experience of communities living within the Darlari domain offers an example of how customary claims to land are currently being reasserted and renegotiated in post-independence Timor Leste. The time, effort and resources invested in rebuilding community *uma luli* and the organizing communal ceremonies such as that held at Baha Liurai suggest that the community is committed to maintaining the social and moral order within which the different house-based groups are situated – including the rights, duties and obligations that this implies. However, the reassertion of the emplaced authority of the 'lord of the land' is not occurring in isolation from the wider social and political context but is likely to be shaped and transformed by interaction within competing sources of power and social influence.

**References**

Babo–Soares, D. 2004. Nahe Biti: The Philosophy and Process of Grassroots Reconciliation (and Justice) in East Timor. *The Asia Pacific Journal of Anthropology*, 5: 15.

CAVR 2005. Chega! Report of the Commission for Reception, Truth and Reconciliation of Timor Leste. Dili: CAVR.

Census 2010. Census of Population and Housing. Dili: Direcção Nacional de Estatística and United National Population Fund.

Da Silva, A.B. 2004. Potential of Education for Conflict Transformation and identity reconstruction in the cultural context of Uato-Lari and Uato-Carbau. Paper to Instituto Católico Para Formação de Professores, 20 September 2004.

Fox, J.J. 1996. Introduction, in J.J. Fox and C.A. Sather (eds), *Origins, Ancestry and Alliance: Explorations in Austronesian Ethnography*. Canberra: Australian National University, pp. 1–17.

Fox, J.J. 1995. Installing the 'Outsider' Inside: The Exploration of an Epistemic Austronesian Cultural Theme and its Social Significance. Paper to the First Conference of the European Association for Southeast Asian Studies: Local Transformation and Common Heritage in Southeast Asia, 29 June to 1 July 1995.

Hicks, H. 2007. Community and Nation-State in East Timor: A View from the Periphery. *Anthropology Today*, 23(1), 13–16.

Lewis, E.D. 1996. Origin Structures and Precedence in the Social Orders of Tana 'Ai and Sikka, in J.J. Fox and C.A. Sather (eds), *Origins, Ancestry and Alliance: Explorations in Austronesian Ethnography*. Canberra: Australian National University, pp. 157–78.

McWilliam, A.R. 2005. Houses of Resistance in East Timor: Structuring Sociality in the New Nation. 15 Anthropological Forum, 27–44.

Meitzner Yoder, L.S. 2005. Custom, Codification, Collaboration: Integrating the Legacies of Land and Forest Authorities in Oecusse Enclave, East Timor. PhD Thesis: Yale University, pp. xviii, 370.

Ospina, S. and Hohe, T. 2002. *Traditional Power Structures and Local Governance in East Timor: A Case Study of the Community Empowerment Project (CEP)*. Geneva: Graduate Institute of Development Studies.

Reuter, T. 2006. Sharing the Earth, Dividing the Land: Land and Territory in the Austronesian World, in T. Reuter (ed.), *Comparative Austronesian Studies*. Canberra: ANU E Press.

Trindade, J. 2008. An Ideal State for East Timor: Reconciling the Conflicting Paradigms. Paper to Democratic Governance in Timor-Leste: Reconciling the National and the Local Conference, Darwin, 7 and 8 February 2008.

# Chapter 7
# The Unsettling Histories of Ponta Leste

## Introduction

The district of Lautem is the most easterly administrative region of Timor Leste and provides the setting for the second case study on comparative customary land practices, dynamics and disputes. In the decade or so since the withdrawal of the Indonesian government, local Fataluku communities have been gradually restoring social life after many years of disruption and repressive state control. This process has included the restoration of customary land tenures and social hierarchies of emplaced precedence within which land entitlements are negotiated and inherited. The comparatively smooth reinstatement of these arrangements among Fataluku settlements reflects the fact that the influence of Indonesian law surrounding land appropriation and its transfer has had surprisingly little lasting impact on underlying Fataluku customary tenure patterns. It also highlights the slow progress of the new government of Timor Leste over the last decade, to reinstate land administration and regulatory arrangements. In the absence of clearly defined parameters, customary practices are flourishing in the gaps arising between the intention and implementation of government policy.

Each of our case study regions illustrates a range of common historical experiences of adjustment and adaptation to colonial intrusions that have set in motion a diverse set of culturally specific assertions of land attachment and claim. While Lautem has its own patterned forms of customary revival and resilience, particularly since the end of the Indonesian occupation, its indigenous land relations are influenced strongly by the consequences of colonial intervention arising from Portuguese and Indonesian occupation over the last 100 years. Principal among these effects is, firstly, a gradual but sustained historical trend of population displacement and concentration into more closely settled residential communities adjacent to sealed roads. These relocations have typically been justified on the basis of internal security and more efficient provision of services, but the effect is an unsettling one that serves to depopulate extensive portions of the landscape in favour of more intensive utilization within designated settlement areas. The process has been a gradual one across Lautem, initiated by the Portuguese colonial government and reinforced under Indonesian rule. Secondly, the more recent neo-colonial experience with that of Indonesia, introduced processes of secular modernity and popular education along with the possibility of alternatives to the comparatively closed life-worlds of subsistence agriculture and customary exchange economies. These processes are being sustained during the early years of national independence and are likely to accelerate as young people increasingly seek opportunities beyond the farm. They therefore represent a challenge to established ideas and practices surrounding customary land tenures; one that is likely to see a trend towards a growing acceptance of land as an alienable commodity of value, especially in settlement areas with higher populations and increased pressures on available land.

Against this broader background, this chapter presents aspects of customary land tenures and patterns of historical displacement in Lautem, especially as they relate to the principal ethno-linguistic grouping in the district, the Fataluku language community. Following an overview of the post-independence environment and the general features of Fataluku land access and attachment, we present an extended case study of the social history of one small settlement (*aldeia*) named Vero in the village of Tutuala. The experience of Vero households reveals something of the complex historical pattern of displacement and resettlement that has affected many small farming communities in Lautem and contributes to contemporary patterns of uncertainty or ambiguity over land claims in the post-independence environment. The study highlights both the resilience of customary systems as they adapt and adjust to external shocks over time; and at the same time identifies the inherent and contradictory tensions that arise between claims to customary authority over land resources, and areas asserted by government authorities to be legally the property of the state and recognized officially as state land (*rai estado*). These tensions raise questions around issues of access, compensation, entitlement and management of natural resources across the region.

## Ecology and Economy in Lautem

Lautem is a triangular shaped territory that covers the far eastern corner of Timor Island. Historically referred to as Ponta Leste[1] (the eastern point of Timor), the region is highly diverse ecologically despite being little more than 30 kilometres across at its widest point. Much of the coastline is unpopulated with an extensive forested hinterland rising sharply from the beachfront along the northern and southern coastal fringe. Inshore waters are rich in marine life and coral reefs and the forested limestone island of Jaco (F: *Totina*), separated from the mainland by less than a kilometre, is the easternmost land of Timor Leste.

The hinterland of Lautem forms an elevated plateau (300 metres) comprising an expansive grassland, ringed by forested hills, that slopes gently to the east, draining into Ira la Laru, the largest freshwater lake in Timor. The lake is perennially replenished with monsoon rains and is bounded on its southern reaches by the prominent and heavily forested Paicao mountain range (to 925 metres). In the

1 Ponta Leste refers to the general region to the east of the great mountains of Matebian located in the neighbouring district of Baucau.

centre of this plateau is the main town of Los Palos,[2] the rather sleepy and semi-rural capital of the district with a population of around 10,000 residents. Los Palos serves as an administrative, marketing and services hub for the surrounding region and has been slowly rebuilding infrastructure and services since the destructive departure of the Indonesian government in 1999.

The most populous ethno-linguistic community of Lautem are the Fataluku who number around 35,000 resident native speakers (based on Census 2010). Lautem itself is composed of five sub-districts (*sub-distritu*) and Fataluku speakers form the principal resident communities of the three most easterly of these (namely Tutuala, Lautem-Moro and Fuiloro, see Map 7.1). There are reportedly up to seven dialects of Fataluku, all of which are mutually intelligible, although definitive linguistic research on the issue remains incomplete.

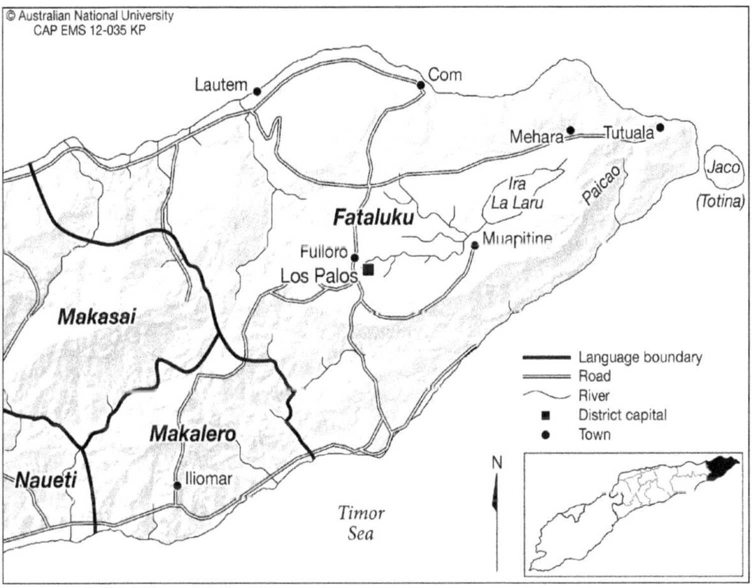


**Map 7.1 The Fatuluku language area of Lautem**
*Source*: ANU Cartography 2012

2 The name Los Palos is a Portuguese corruption of the local Fataluku language name, *Laos Pala*, which has a variety of contested etymologies – including that it translates as 'fertile garden', that it derives from the phrase *Loho Pala* (corral and garden) referring to an early settlement site, or even that it represents a version of the phrase *Loiasu Pala* (garden boat).

In the remaining sub-districts a number of other indigenous languages are spoken. They include Makalero, primarily in the sub-district of Iliomar (southwest Lautem), and a Makasai language dialect form known as *Sa'ané* in the mountains of Luro (western Lautem). All these languages are non-Austronesian in morphology and linguistic origin, but share many cultural affinities with their Austronesian speaking neighbours (see McWilliam 2007).

A feature of Lautem and one that is consistent with trends across Timor Leste as a whole, is a high degree of population mobility, both within the district itself as illustrated by the 21.7 per cent increase in resident population of Los Palos (2004), as well as the drift of population, particularly among young adults, beyond the district to other urban centres such as Baucau and the national capital Dili, where economic and educational opportunities are more readily available. Many younger Fataluku men and women are also pursuing opportunities overseas, including Indonesia and Europe.[3]

Lautem grew in population over the period 2001–04 but at a much lower rate (7.5 per cent) than the burgeoning growth of districts in the central west of the nation, such as Dili, Liquisa, Ermera and Ainaro where population growth over the period averaged 23 per cent (Census 2004).

**Table 7.1 Population figures for Lautem**

| Sub-district | Households | Population | | Total | % difference since 2001 |
|---|---|---|---|---|---|
| | | Male | Female | | |
| Los Palos | 6,045 | 13,559 | 14,066 | 27,625 | 21.7 |
| Lautem | 3,345 | 6,426 | 6,576 | 13,002 | -9.7 |
| Iliomar | 1,606 | 3,101 | 3,497 | 6,598 | -3 |
| Luro | 1,596 | 3,501 | 3,435 | 6,936 | 9.9 |
| Tutuala | 790 | 1,587 | 1,705 | 3,292 | 1 |
| **Total** | 13,382 | 28,174 | 29,279 | 57,453 | 7.5 |

*Source*: National Census 2004

Given that fertility rates are assumed to be uniformly high (7.8 births per fertile woman) across the nation this contrast in growth rates highlights two further trends evident in Lautem. Firstly there is a continued drift of younger people out of the district, and a corresponding increase in the dependency ratio of those families remaining (that is, the number of dependent children per household). Secondly, population densities in the eastern regions of Timor (T: *lorosae*) remain significantly lower than their counterparts in the west (*loromonu*) and, as

3 There is a well-worn sponsorship pathway for young Fataluku from Los Palos enabling them to access residential work opportunities in a variety of destinations especially in the United Kingdom where they work in a variety of low wage shift work.

a consequence, access to land is relatively abundant with little direct competition over land resources.

The region also receives two distinct periods of monsoon rain, a short intense rainy season in December–March (F: *aia varat*) and a second period of often heavy rain in May–June associated with the southeast monsoon (F: *temuru pala*). This climatic pattern provides favourable conditions for agriculture and rapid regrowth of forest vegetation. Consequently most Fataluku households rely on forms of mixed agriculture for income, combining seasonal maize and secondary food crop cultivation with dry season horticulture and smallholder livestock production. Buffalo (*arapou*) and pigs (*pai*) hold important and reciprocal roles in local livelihoods, especially in the complex ceremonial exchanges that mark life cycle transitions and the making and remaking of social alliances. Livestock numbers, especially buffalo, have increased significantly since the destruction and loss of herds in the late 1990s.

Coconut production has been a significant source of income for farmer households in Lautem following concerted efforts by the Portuguese colonial government to establish the tree crop from the early 1900s (Lencastre 1929: 44–46). Coconut gardens are usually developed out of dryland food gardens cropped over several seasons. Much of the settled landscape of Lautem is thus a mosaic of active and fallowed food garden sites with coconut palms representing material markers of past occupation and contemporary claim. Copra is sold in small quantities to traders and coconuts (*oco*) are also consumed locally as food, cooking oil or livestock feed. Other significant sources of income include red onions, which are cultivated along the north coast during the dry season, and the production of palm wine and distilled spirits (*tua piti* and *tua haraki*), which are widely consumed products.

Lautem is a diverse and comparatively well forested district, and this feature, along with the fringing coastal reefs and warm tropical waters, provides an abundant array of foodstuffs and other resources that help sustain the domestic economies of Fataluku households. Apart from firewood, timber and other building materials (bamboos, rattan and thatch for roofing), local residents draw on a whole range of plant species for fibres, ropes, baskets, gums and vegetable supplements such as tubers, wild beans, leaf vegetables, saps, honey, and forest fruits. An extensive pharmacopoeia is also recognized and drawn upon from the plant world (see Collins et al. 2007), while hunting is a livelihood activity throughout the year, and the use of various poisons, traps, spears and dogs provides a regular supply of game meat and seafood.[4]

4 This diversity of harvestable food includes fish (*api*), clams (*saka)*, sea turtles (*ipitu*), sea eels (*suanu*) crabs (*capuku*) and sea urchins (*tiri*), as well as freshwater shrimp (*asi*) and turtles (*veu*), bats (*maca*), monkeys (*lua*), civet cats (*loh*), cus cus possums (*acuru*), deer (*vaka*), feral pigs (*pai hoto*) and birds (*olo*). Reef gleaning (*meti fai, tono fai*) for shellfish, seaweed and other edible marine creatures is practised along the foreshore during low tide in selected locations (see also Pannell 2011).

## Fataluku Customary Relationships to Land: Fundamentals of Practice

A starting point for appreciating Fataluku customary attachments and claims to land in Lautem is to recognize that they are embedded within dynamic relationships of reciprocity. These relationships provide access to a diverse range of resources and labour that may be deployed and managed to support the material conditions of social life. Claims to resources including land are therefore simultaneously assertions and statements about particular kinds of emplaced social relationships. Within this conceptual framework, the idiom of exchange and reciprocity encompasses both the living world of clan and familial allies, as well as the less immediate but no less significant realm of ancestors and the spirit world that is thought to animate and influence events in the natural environment (see McWilliam 2008, 2011).

Fataluku households engage in a wide variety of exchange relationships in everyday social life, but within this diversity two related but complementary networks of exchange are accorded high priority. The first of these networks is located in the relationships between the agnatic members of 'origin groups', known generically in Fataluku by the term *ratu.* All Fataluku people are affiliated to one or another of these enduring social groups that are constituted around paternal lines of origin.[5] Fataluku women generally relinquish membership to their natal *ratu* upon marriage and enter that of their husbands, raising their children within the marital house. Across Lautem there are dozens of residentially dispersed *ratu*, the local members of which assemble from time to time to celebrate their shared ancestral origins in ritual communion and commensality.[6] An important component of *ratu* identity over time is the need to maintain the narrative histories and founding myths of the group, as well as ancestral regalia and forms of clan-specific ritual knowledge and spatial claims. Protecting, nurturing and expanding the collective resources of the agnatic *ratu* is a key motivation in social life.[7]

5 Namely, one's father's father, father's father's father and so on. Fataluku recognize and name five ascending generations of paternal ancestors (*Palu, Calu, Papu, Cuci* and *Macua*) beyond which the names of ancestors become taboo (*tei*) and are known collectively as *Cal(u) arafura.*

6 A key element of commensality is the shared consumption of sacrificial meat, known as *leura tei,ipilu tei*, among attendant male members and agnatic affiliates of the ratu.

7 This general statement glosses a rather more complex social context in which historically defined status differences have produced three sets of inherited social classes, castes, or what Lameiras-Campagnolo and Campagnolo have termed *ensembles endogames* (1984: 84). These three status classes are known as *ratu, paca* and *akanu* and reflect a common eastern Indonesian distinction between high born (*ratu*), ordinary citizenry (*paca*) and a slave category (*akanu*). Slaves (akanu) represent the descendants of war captives or people bankrupted into slavery in colonial times. These distinctions remain significant influences on social life especially in terms of marriage relationships, while the generic form of the term *ratu* remains an appropriate description for the origin group as a whole.

A second category of exchange relationships derives from the complex social alliances that intersect and evolve between different exogamous *ratu* origin groups. In the present discussion the most significant of these group relationships are affinal alliances created through marriage; alliances that provide the reproductive basis of *ratu* groups over time. These negotiated relationships of blood and marriage engage different claims and entitlements to resources over time including the extensive fallowed regrowth forests utilized by Fataluku farming communities for swidden agriculture. Formal Fataluku marriage has a reputation for requiring complex negotiations and large numbers of buffalo and other resources as bride-wealth (*fai'in[u]).* In return negotiated arrangements around marriage exchange and alliance provide a key cultural mechanism for securing access to arable land, especially for in-marrying men. The mosaic of marriage agreements among 'wife-giver' and wife-taker' lineages not only creates *in personam* rights between the married parties, but inter-generational and inter-group obligations of exchange and alliance.

The particular pattern of *ratu* land ownership and the relative size of their respective territories across Lautem derive from the mythic origins of settlement and the inherited customary entitlements of ancestral spatial practices. Further adjustments and modifications reflecting complex and mobile histories of inter-group warfare and shifting political alliances have also informed boundary-making processes over time. Today, the limits of these ancestral common property lands are more or less fixed, their meandering edges marked variously by prominent trees, ridge lines or marker stones, as well as crumbling stone walls (*lutur mataru*) of fallowed garden sites, creek lines and other topographic traces. The fixing of group boundaries, after a pre-colonial history of inter-group warfare, appears to reflect the 'peace' imposed by Portuguese colonisation, which increased the costs of inter-group conflict. The knowledge of group boundaries (*kai kai ho varuku*) is retained as part of the heritage of the *ratu* agnatic community especially among the senior male affiliates of the group. One consequence of this pattern of settlement history is that, in cultural terms, there is no surplus or 'free' land where customary attachment does not apply, even though the demographic decline of some groups associated with particular tracts of forested land has left this matter unresolved and subject to cautious and invariably contested succession in a number of areas. Wrongfully assuming or appropriating the rights of the landed property of other *ratu* is a risky activity that is likely to result in spiritual sanctions manifest as misfortune or illness for the households of those who make the attempt. These overarching attachments to land and the question of spiritual sanctions will be relevant both to claims of state land, and implementation of principles of community property and community protection zones under the 2012 draft land law (see further Chapter 11).

In describing the authority and relationship of a *ratu* group to its ancestral lands, use is made of an honorific title, *mua ho cawaru* (lit: land and lord, Tetun: *rai na'in*). The title refers to the status of a *ratu* group over the land in question, one that confirms and honours their precedence, or mythic 'first settler' status, in the area and their emplaced ritual ties of intimate association. In Fataluku ritual speech this relationship is expressed by the phrase:

| | |
|---|---|
| *Mua cao vele ocawa* | Land head skin lord |
| *Horo cao vele ocawa* | Gravel head skin lord[8] |

The reference speaks to the Fataluku conceptual distinction between the 'body' of the earth and its covering 'skin' (*vele*). People may cultivate the skin (*vele*) of the land for food crops or to hunt game, but only the 'lord of the land', the *mua ho cawaru*, asserts a pre-eminent authority over the whole of the land in question. This is an enduring relationship reaffirmed through sustained ritual engagement and means that, in one general sense, all land across Lautem is held as forms of common property by the collective members of discrete agnatic groups (*ratu*) who share 'one blood, one serum' of origin (*vehe ukani, ahi ukani*). Their territory is said to form part of the 'sacred land and the sacred garden' (*mua tei ho pala tei*)[9] of the *ratu*; a phrase that links contemporary members to the early settlements of their ancestors, the autochthonous spirits of the land (McWilliam 2008) and the long history of cultivation and food production that has provided life and sustenance to *ratu* households over generations. In this sense the relationship of the *ratu*, and the land to which they are ancestrally connected, may be said to be consubstantiated; that is to say, mutually constitutive and deeply interconnected (McWilliam 2011).

These ideas surrounding the collective property of the *ratu* continue to inform decisions about activities on the land, but in practice most of the common property of the group is internally divided among the constituent lineages of the origin kin group. These internal distinctions reflect the historical development and expansion of the group and its division into elder (*kaka*) and younger (*noko*) sibling lineages whose members lay claim to different portions of the common landed inheritance. Here, use rights to land will depend on the strength of the agnatic relationships involved, while overall ritual authority for the territory remains the responsibility of the *ratu* leadership, which typically is one of the oldest men of the *ratu* and referred to in ritual language as the *laficaru* or 'the master of chants, the master of words' (*nololonocawa*: *luku-lukunocawa*) [Tetun: *lian na'in*]. In contrast to the relatively fixed nature of external *ratu* boundaries, the internal boundaries of lineage authority have a degree of fluidity, which manifests in endemic processes of negotiation among origin-affiliated lineages. The fluidity of internal boundaries most likely reflects the relatively low costs of strategic attempts to enhance entitlements within the negotiating 'umbrella' of affiliations based on origin,

8 The word *horo* in Fataluku refers to the coraline rubble that litters the ground in many areas and is used to construct sturdy food garden fences, the remnants of which are distinctive markers of former swidden fields.

9 The term *tei* or (pl) *teinu* may be glossed as sacred or taboo and has a similar sense as the Tetun word *lulik* (see McWilliam 2008, 2011).

which minimizes the potential for costly forms of violence. The result is a nested – and at times contested – series of lineage-based common property arrangements within a broader collectivity based on principles of descent from a mythical source of ancestral origin.

## Patterns of Land Access

The history of Fataluku land relations and the complex consequences of shifting political alliances and marriage exchange over generations have given rise to a range of arrangements for subsidiary groups to gain access to occupied *ratu* lands. Use rights to cultivate the 'skin' (*vele*) of the *ratu* land are dependent on the particular histories of association articulated through negotiated entitlements of settlement and claim. Affiliated households to the land owning *ratu* may be referred to as *i na maunu* (those who come later) or more prosaically as *olo ca maunu* (lit: 'birds' coming from afar).[10] This category includes both allied *ratu* lineages with long-standing relationships of marriage exchange, as well as newcomers with shallow histories of engagement. For reasons of etiquette and social propriety, however, direct reference to these phrases is considered impolite, and subsidiary households and groups are more typically referred to either as 'sisters and children' (*leren ho moco*) designating households deriving directly from the agnatic group, or as *lan(u) ho tava* (friends and acquaintances) referring to groups more distantly associated. Alternatively, in the highly metaphoric language of Fataluku relation, the botanical trope of the tree describes the respective entitlements between permanent *ratu* landowners of the 'trunk and branch' (*ara ho pata*) and settler cultivators who receive rights to the 'flowers and fruit' (*i cipi i mana*). Marriage allies and politically aligned resident households of landowning *ratu* enter into permanent reciprocal relationships that generally confer lasting entitlements to cultivate land and draw sustenance from its bounty.[11] These relationships and benefits are mutually and morally self-affirming, protected from arbitrary removal or denial by spiritual sanctions and customary ethics.

10 Fataluku exhibits a prevalence for paired ritual speech, known as canonical parallelism. The genre is a form of highly stylized poetic speech expressed in couplets as synonyms. The complement of *olo co maunu* is *aca co maunu* (lit: chickens that come from outside). Another version of the relationship between founder groups and in-marrying settlers is *a'a la lunu*: *a'a ca unu* (to add to the foundation: to pile on top of the base).

11 Fataluku recognize various forms of land transfer between marrying groups. A gift of land in marriage for example may be referred to with the ritual expression *leo amire, poke amire*, meaning to offer a 'wooden pillow' to rest the head of the recipient and provide for their well-being. These entitlements are only lost if the recipient and their descendants expressly relinquish their claims to the land in question through abandonment or the demographic demise of the lineage.

In practice there are two categories of subsidiary or settler group land entitlement within Fataluku customary land practices. The first of these categories confers a status approaching 'ownership,' namely, land that has been devolved or transferred from an origin settler *ratu* to an in-marrying affinal group as part of the former marriage exchange and settlement negotiations (the *leren ho moco*: sister and children connection). These arrangements appear to have been more commonplace in pre-modern days when the need to attract (male) labour and co-residential political allies was a compelling factor. In these instances of nested ownership, the subsequent settler group controls access and inheritance decisions over the land granted to their ancestors, but issues of alienation or sale to third parties are usually said to require explicit permission from the pre-eminent 'landlord' (*mua ocawa*). In reality, to date at least, the sale of *ratu* land remains largely hypothetical, particularly outside townships where alienation of land from the ancestral inheritance would be considered disrespectful and risk spiritual retribution in the form of illness or economic misfortune. Over time in any particular area, land tenure arrangements reflect the negotiated histories of settlement, cultivation and political alliance in a mosaic of usually well-recognized and differentiated origin group land portions.

In recent times, and particularly as a consequence of the Indonesian occupation of Timor Leste, issues of land entitlement and opportunities to secure notional ownership of land from affinal allies have undergone some transformations, including by taking on a more contractual (*in personam*) character. Specifically, it is quite common these days for in-marrying males or relocated households to obtain access rights to arable land for cultivation or house plots from the resident landowner (*mua ocawa*), but to be explicitly denied 'ownership' or entitlements for inter-generational transfer. In common law terms, these arrangements are more akin to a revocable licence to occupy than an *in rem* interest in land. Fataluku sometimes describe this situation as one of being merely 'passengers' (I: *penumpang*), temporary settlers, on the land of others. The generic phrase 'friend and acquaintances (*lan(u) ho tava*) may be extended to these households with less secure tenures. Typically they apply these ideas to situations of forced relocation as a consequence of external factors. In these circumstances the conventional protocols governing in-migration have been bypassed and the resident groups obliged to give ground to the newcomers under situations of duress. Over time there is often a degree of accommodation to these situations of reluctant resettlement, including moves to normalize relationships through marriage between members of resident *ratu* and settler households, but to date, at least, these processes of adjustment and adaptation have not extended to offering permanent or transferable land entitlements. The status and claims of the respective parties therefore remain somewhat ill-defined and often characterized by a degree of latent resentment. While we argue that agreements to manage relocation through inter-marriage are highly significant, as context-specific responses to the problem of displacement, the status and claims of the contracting parties were not agreed with *ex ante* precision and are thus vulnerable to conflict, which is likely to crystallize should relocated groups on customary lands claim alienable ownership of land, as envisaged by the rule of possession in the draft 2012 land law.

In both these categories of land relation, the patterns of land use and settlement choices reflected in contemporary Lautem have been informed by successive waves of colonial occupation and the often disruptive politics and resettlement programmes that accompanied them. The consequences and implications of these displacements have created a complex legacy of inter-group land relationships and local politics that continue to inform claims to land and contested jurisdictional authority. To illustrate something of this legacy of displacement, we present a case study focusing on the social history of just one Fataluku community, the small hamlet (*aldeia*) of Vero, and the processes of adaptation and change that have so influenced settlement choices for Vero households over a number of generations. Vero is one example among many, but its case history offers insights into broader historical processes at work in Lautem through the lens of one particular set of experiences.

## Unsettling Histories: A Case Study of Vero

The contemporary settlement of Vero comprises one of the four constituent hamlets (*aldeia*) of *suco* Tutuala, the most easterly village in East Timor. With a population of around 254 people (Census 2010), Vero forms a closely settled compound of some 35 thatched and metal-roofed houses adjacent to the main road that winds down into the centre of the village (total population 1,539). Tutuala itself is an administrative centre of government in the region (*sub-distritu*) and largely escaped the excesses of the Indonesian-backed militias and their destructive rampage following the historic vote for independence in 1999. Still, a decade on, social services remain rudimentary, with a police station, health clinic and school in operation, but only intermittent electricity, a failed water supply system and few employment prospects for residents. In Vero, most people pursue forms of swidden agriculture on surrounding land, cultivating maize and cassava with a range of secondary food crops. Households also raise livestock, especially chickens and pigs for consumption and participation in the community exchange economy. Market prospects remain limited, and high transport costs to other centres such as the district capital, Los Palos, some 35 kilometres away constrain small-scale commercial trading opportunities. Commerce tends to be conducted around local household kiosks, offering for sale limited quantities of copra, garden produce, domestic livestock and a lively trade in distilled liquor (F: *tua haraki*) fashioned from extensive sugar palm groves (*enau* and *lontar*). Small-scale trading in seafood and hunted game secured from the surrounding forests and coastal foreshores is also pursued. These activities provide supplementary cash incomes to cover school fees and basic household consumption needs.

The location and composition of present-day Vero is in one sense the product of 24 years of Indonesian occupation of Timor Leste. Certainly, Vero residents are well established in their current site, with some households demonstrating their commitment to place by constructing more permanent concrete block housing. However, like other settlements across Lautem, Vero is a displaced community whose origins and the ancestral lands to which most of its members lay claim lie at a distance from the present-day settlement. In this case, the historical origins of Vero derive from the lower reaches of the Vero (River) Valley and the heavily forested southern slopes of the Paicao mountain range, a few hours' walk to the south. These lands and the abundant natural and symbolic resources they contain are regularly accessed along well-defined walking trails by members of the Vero community, but for at least a generation they have been unable to farm the arable lowlands of former garden areas such as *Alaera lafae* and *Aleara moko* where by the 1970s they were cropping irrigated rice. Their access to land resources both in the current Vero settlement and the immediate surrounding fallowed fields is therefore something of a compromise; namely an agreement with resident customary landowners (*mua ocawa*), the clans Cailoro Ratu and Kukulori Ratu in particular, to remain in place and to retain enduring entitlements to settlement and nearby fallowed farming land, but always subject to the permissive authority of the landowners.

Heuristically the historical displacement of Vero may be characterized by three, more or less, distinct phases of external intervention played out over a century from the early 1900s. Each phase had the effect of drawing Vero households more closely into the sphere of state surveillance and control, and, for most, geographically more removed from their ancestral lands. The three phases coincide with (1) the pacification campaigns of the Portuguese colonial government at the turn of the twentieth century, (2) the return of the Portuguese government following Japanese wartime occupation, and (3) the Indonesian military occupation of the territory after 1975. The pattern of displacement for Vero households was one mirrored in similar strategies implemented across Lautem and which continues to influence Fataluku livelihood choices and land attachment into the post-independence period.

### *Phase 1: Origins and Intervention*

The origins of Vero settlement are retained in the mythic narratives of key *ratu* groups who trace their ancestors to founding settlements in the Vero Valley (the term *vero* is Fataluku for rivercourse). The general consensus among local Fataluku is that the founding settlers of the area are associated with the mythical sailing exploits of four allies or four 'siblings' who subsequently took the clan (*ratu*) names Renu, Marapaki, Keveresi and Paiuru. The recorded landing site at *Teluo'o* near the mouth of the Vero (river) is marked to this day with a sacrificial altar post (*ia mari tuliya*: ancestral footprint) that also serves as a site of periodic invocation and sacrifice.[12]

12 Members of the Vero settlement in Tutuala gather annually at Telu o'o, to participate in the *meci* (sea worm, *Eunice virides*) harvest on the full moon in March. Sacrificial invocations are conducted at the altar post at this time.

Nearby on the Aleara plain a prominent limestone outcrop covered in tangled vegetation is venerated as the fossilized 'stone' boat (*loiasu mataru*) of the seafarers that beached on Timor and became embedded in the land. These and other signs of ancestral presence provide the material evidence of the mythic origins of settlement and the basis for claiming landed entitlements. As 'archives of past habitation and sociality' (Fairhead and Leach 1996: 113), the origin landscapes of Vero families are simultaneously sites of spiritual agency and moral authority (see McWilliam 2007c).

An early and prominent settlement of the founding settlers is linked to the fortified mountain site known as Haka Paku Leki, located in the upper reaches of the Paicao[13] mountains immediately southwest of the Vero River overlooking the valley. As the settler population grew, however, feuding and warfare is said to have broken out between the established groups, leading to an acrimonious division between Keveresi and Renu, each of whom subsequently established separate areas of landed authority. The boundary of the disputed territory was formed by the Vero River and its adjacent beachfronts (*Sere lafai* – 'great' Sere to the east, and *Sere moko* – 'little' Sere to the west). The northern cliff bordering the mouth of the Vero River is known as Pati Patinu (meaning to divide [the land]). Keveresi took lands to the east and established a stone-walled settlement on the hill overlooking the beach front, while Renu assumed control over the lands extending from the Vero mouth to a rivercourse known as Vekase Ver some 15 kilometres to the south and west.[14]

Taking precedence as the founding group, Renu Ratu is referred to by the title, *mua ho cawaru* (lit: land and lord) a seniority and pre-eminence reproduced over time as newcomers settled in the area and married into the Renu group. In this respect Renu Ratu may also be described as the 'great mother' (*nalu lafae*) who, in the marriage of their daughters to immigrant husbands, provide the *susu ho ami*[15] (white sap and milk) that enables their households to prosper and grow. In the process migrants gained residence rights and access to portions of the forested estate of Renu Ratu for cultivation. To this day the Renu group is accorded the senior status among each of the subsidiary groups who assert historical connection to the area. Clan groups such as Serelau, Mainoh, Paiuru, Tana, Aca Cao and Pai'ir Ratu, among others, forged alliances with Renu and secured entitlements to forested land. Today Snr Sidonio da Cruz, a resident of Vero settlement in Tutuala,

13 In Fataluku orthography the letter 'c' is pronounced 'ch' as in modern Malay or Indonesian.

14 The precise boundaries of this traditional domain have not been mapped, but in general terms the Vekass ver boundary between the coast and the hinterland is associated with the senior clan of Muapitine settlement, Latu Loho Ratu and in the higher elevations including the mountains, with the Pai Cao Ratu group whose members reside in the contemporary settlements of Malahara and Pitilete (Tutuala). Mention is also made of a group known as Kuamai Ratu that held lands on the great mountain Pua Loki itself, and are also linked to the abandoned stone fortification of Pariloho, but no longer have any known living members.

15 *Ami* is the Fataluku word for breast milk while *susu* is the name given to the white sap of the forest fig tree (*hama*) that grows in abundance in the lowland forests and is often the site of ritual veneration (somewhat ironically given that this is the Malay/Tetun term for milk).

is the senior representative of the now dwindling clan group, Renu, and the leading ritual authority for the domain. The local membership of both Keveresi and Renu is now reduced to a small number of male-headed households. Some attribute this demographic misfortune to the fact that the groups have never undertaken the required peacemaking ceremonies to acknowledge the wrongs of the past. As a result the lingering blood guilt of those ancestral events debilitates the fortunes and fertility of the two groups.[16]

Subsequent to the establishment of the mountain stronghold, Haka Paku Leki, a series of stone-walled fortifications (*pa'amakolo*) was constructed at strategic locations along the eastern foothills of the Paicao Mountain range within the jurisdiction of the Renu *mua ocawa.* The dates of these fortified settlements are not recorded, but recent archaeological work on fortified settlements in Tutuala indicate that they were built and operating by at least the late sixteenth century (O'Connor et al. 2012). Given their prominent locations on strategic hilltops with extensive defensive stonework employed to secure the perimeters of the structures, it is evident that mutual warfare and the fear of attack were abiding concerns (McWilliam 2011, see also Forbes 1885 for comparison). Within the structures themselves, stone graves and old house platforms offer mute testimony to earlier residents who exploited surrounding forests and cleared patches for seasonal food gardens.

Among the more prominent fortified settlement sites are those of Ili Haraku (a massive rocky outcrop beneath the imposing Pua Loki Mountain). Ili Haraku is one of the former principal settlements of the Renu Ratu group and its allies. Several kilometres to the southwest and deep in the forest is the smaller barricaded hilltop settlement known as Maiana linked to ancestral allies Pai'ir Ratu and Aca Cao, while a third hill fort known as Pai Lopo is located near the western boundary of Renu Ratu territory at Vekasse Ver- Ili Mimiraka.[17] The principal group associated with this site is also Aca Cao Ratu who, according to clan histories of the area, was appointed by Renu to defend the western boundary. In ritual terms the role of Aca Cao is referred to as a peacemaker or enforcer, the *ece moron: aka moron* (to cover and stop the fighting). A large clump of bambu (*petenu*), known as *ratu varuk* (ratu boundary), demarcates a site where the ancestors of Aca Cao Ratu concluded a land settlement with Pai'ir Ratu to mark out the border between the two groups and settle the hostilities that had broken out between them.

The four defensive hilltop settlement sites of Haka Paku Leki, Ili Haraku, Maiana and Pailopo appear to have been occupied until the early twentieth

16 The unresolved enmity between Keveresi and Renu as a result of mutual atrocities that occurred in the past means that they continue to maintain an avoidance relationship known as *nita tana tei* (lit: our hands are *tei*), which precludes the sharing of food and marriage exchange. The Marapaki group is said to have settled the northern reaches of Sere lafai at Lulu Vero.

17 The boundary bears no relation to the current administrative borders of the village, Tutuala and Muapitine, although it is widely recognized among local clans.

century.[18] Older Vero resident Martinho dos Santos, for example, is very familiar with the grave of his paternal grandmother and the stone base of her house site at Ili Haraku. While he never met his grandmother, who died soon after the birth of his father, personal attachments to the site such as these and the graves that populate its confines remain important markers of cultural connection and personal geographies. Martinho regularly utilizes bamboo groves and taro patches cultivated at springs in the area.

All this was to change, however, when in 1902, after years of indifferent Portuguese colonial government attempts to control and tax the recalcitrant populations of Lautem, a concerted military effort was initiated to establish administrative control. The campaign utilized Timorese militias (*moradores*) from the districts of Manatuto, Baucau and allied groups from the domains of Faturo, Sarao and Sama in western Lautem. These former domains were notionally loyal allies of the Portuguese colonial government from as early as the eighteenth century (see Leitao 1948: 1250) but it is not clear that their jurisdictions had effective control over the settled eastern regions of Lautem. Oral history suggests that for long periods of time the former kingdom of Luca in present-day Viqueque was the stronger political influence. Either way, Pélissier notes that the Lautem region had not seen a campaign of such size since 1889 when the Portuguese had previously attempted to assert their authority and put an end to the 'illegal trade' in sandal(wood), goats and sheep trading as well as guns and gunpowder with the offshore Dutch controlled islands of Wetar, Kisar, Leti and Tepa (1996: 210).

In a series of violent clashes the military campaign was able to vanquish Fataluku resistance, which ushered in a new period of Portuguese military rule over the district[19] and the gradual but not particularly successful introduction of a range of government development initiatives (McWilliam 2007b).[20] Included in these programmes were attempts by the Portuguese district command to gradually bring the scattered populations of Lautem into more accessible and concentrated settlements. In Lautem, as elsewhere in East Timor, a perennial motivation of the Portuguese administration was to encourage more efficient taxation of the local population; a task made much easier if they could be concentrated into a smaller number of accessible centres.

18 The old fortified settlement of Muapitine on the densely forested northern slopes of the Paicao range was occupied until 1975 when all residents were ordered out on to the plains of the lake, Ira Lalaru.

19 Fataluku refer to this period as *Monargia rua* (lit: the second Monarchy) and use the term 'savarika (scorpion) in relation to the colonial Portuguese government. The term derives from a Fataluku version of the name of the Portuguese commander of the campaign, Francisco Xavier.

20 Gunn has observed of the colonial economy that 'there is no question […] that the colonial state in Timor presided over an economy of extremely low productivity where development was a highly restricted concept based upon low levels of technical inputs and accountability' (1999: 187).

The extension of Portuguese administrative control over Lautem initially had little impact on the forest-dwelling inhabitants of Vero. But the combined effects of a lessening of inter-communal feuding and warfare that accompanied more peaceful times appears to have encouraged Vero residents to move out of the fortified settlements and settle in a series of garden areas scattered within the forest. Named locations such as Pitilete, Laivai, Cara Cipi Lori and Ira Romonu among others, all now covered with forest regrowth, reveal traces of previous occupation in the form of remnant coraline garden fences, old graves and house foundations. These settlements took the form of small clusters of households known as *otu* whose residents cultivated the sloping forest land for maize and secondary food crops, shifting their sites periodically as yields declined and fences succumbed to termite infestation and dry rot. Settlement, in other words, tended to be highly dispersed, small-scale and mobile.

On the forested slopes between the mountains and the coast in 1915 the Portuguese military government, according to local history, established a sub-district (*posto*) administrative centre at a site known as Roka Hala, but which became popularly known as Malae Laca or Kota (GR S08.48873: E127.19991). Here the Portuguese constructed a small walled compound and residential structure on a mounded site, and called people in from the surrounding forests to register their names for an initial census of the population. The first administrator or *chefe do posto,* recalled as Commander Francisco Zemente, would visit on horseback from the colonial garrison in Tutuala. According to Fataluku correspondents, Roka Hala was the first site of the Postu of Tutuala but was subsequently moved to the north coast at Loiqueiro. I have not been able to corroborate these details with official Portuguese sources but the rectangular shape of the compound and remnant structures including a kitchen at Malae Laca are strikingly at variance with remnant Fataluku structures.

Over time the scattered population was gradually concentrated into one designated area known as Ira Cao Piti on the orders of the Portuguese military command. This directive may have also been associated with preparation of another census in Timor Leste during the early 1930s. Sidonio Da Cruz, the senior representative of the *mua ocawa*, Renu Ratu, was born in Ira Cao Piti around this time as the population grew and the settlement prospered on the sloping plateau overlooking the coast.

### *Phase 2: Post-war Relocation*

During the Japanese wartime occupation of Timor, Vero households continued to live in the forests and coastal hinterland of their domain in the shadow of the Pua Loki and Paicao Mountains. Possibly coincident with the rise of population by this time, the Japanese directed the construction of a walking path and horse trail, lined with stones, that connected the settlement of Tutuala in the northeast with (old) Muapitine in the southwest as well as to Pehe Fitu-Lupuloho on the southern coast. Remnants of this *caminho*, as it is described on Portuguese maps, formed the main communication link through the area, and portions of the walking trail are still used by contemporary hunters and passers-by.[21]

The return of the Portuguese colonial government at the end of the warbrought another significant phase of settlement displacement for the households of Vero. As part of a more general strategy to promote greater economic development and taxation revenue for the colony, following the ravages of Japanese occupation (Dunn 1983),[22] the people of the Vero Valley were ordered to move away from the forested zone to a location close to the main road at Tutuala. At that time the forest-dwelling population is estimated to have been in the order of 40 households and, according to Fataluku colleagues, the area had been officially declared an administrative village (*suco*) known as Laivai after one of the settlement sites. Laivai village was composed of nine administrative *aldeia* or hamlets whose names were drawn from former settlement sites in the area. They comprised Haka Paku Leki, Ira Pata (above Aleara lafai), Ili Haraku, Mai Ana, Pailopo, Keveresi, Pitilete, Lai Vai and Lu Kenu (near Ira Romonu spring and creek).

The demands of the new Portuguese government were reportedly not well received. The community was reluctant to abandon their gardens and ancestral lands and had to be coerced to move by the colonial government. Some households of the village withdrew into the forests or dispersed to alternative locations such as the settlements of Mehara and Malahara near the shores of Lake Ira lalaru, an area that offered extensive grasslands for buffalo herds and where existing family connections could facilitate the move. Eventually just 12 households settled at the new site at Tutuala, selecting a ridge adjacent to the main road to construct basic housing and calling the new settlement Vero. Here they remained until the Indonesian military invasion in 1975.[23] The new location lay within the customary lands of two resident landowning clan groups (*mua ocawa*), Cailoro and Kukulori Ratu, who granted permission for the displaced households to reside on the land and establish their community.

The Dos Santos family of the Serelau origin house was one of the settler households. Their family history exemplifies the cultural processes of adaptation and incorporation that characterize patterns of Fataluku mobility. The father of

21 An undated Portuguese map has this track marked but without documentation of its construction; see Carta Militar de Timor: Serviços Cartográficos do Exercito. n.d. Sociedade de Geographica de Lisboa [received by the Geographical Society 1946].

22 By 1945 East Timor was an economic ruin. Most of the population was close to starvation, there was virtually no commercial activity, the plantations of coffee, cocoa and rubber – the colony's most prosperous economic sector – had nearly all been abandoned and most had degenerated into bushland, while Timor's livestock population had been reduced to a third of its pre-war level (Dunn 1983: 27). Dunn estimates that more that 40,000 Timorese had perished as a result of the war.

23 The process of transplanting old place names into new areas is a common practice across Timor Leste. In these circumstances, the process involves animal sacrifice and invocations to ancestors (*calu ho papu*) in order to secure their blessings and agreement.

contemporary resident Mario Dos Santos Loyola came of age in the new settlement of Vero and married the daughter of the senior Kukulori landowner, gaining access and cultivation entitlements to a sweep of nearby fallowed forest land. Mario and his siblings maintain a continuing close and interdependent relationship with their affinal Kukulori relatives, who as *ara ho pata* (base and post: wife givers) provide life cycle services and protection for their sister's children (*tupurrmoko*). They also continue to maintain cultivation rights to Kukulori land, and have assumed the former food gardens worked by their late father. In discussions over the tenure status of the land in question, Mario is quick to state that he and his brothers have 'ownership entitlements' – using the Indonesian term, *hak milik*, an ownership right but he added that his brother-in-law (*vaien ara ho pata, Kukulori*) has ultimate say on matters of land division or divestment. Dos Santos entitlements are expressed by the phrase *ira ho oco, i cipi ho i mana* – water and coconut, flowers and fruit. In other words they are only authorized to take the 'fruits' of the land controlled by Kukulori, but this is a strong and continuing authorization, effectively one in perpetuity that reflects the continuing inter-generational social alliance that informs the reproduction of the customary community.

The process of relocating forest-dwelling households and whole settlements to main arterial roads was one replicated in many areas of Lautem following the re-establishment of Portuguese colonial rule in 1945. Although there is little documentation of these processes, it is evident from interviews with Fataluku farmers in different areas that the post-war period was marked by concerted attempts to draw the scattered rural populations into more concentrated settlements. Many of the contemporary hamlets and villages along the Tutuala road from Los Palos, for example, have their origins in the post-war decade. Mehara, Poros, So Moco, Bauro and Asalaino, and Sepaerara among others were all settled by households that had previously occupied settlements in the northern forested plateau. Similarly, the whole of the settled highlands of Nari (Planalto de Nari in the central north) were emptied out and its residents relocated to contemporary roadside settlements on lower slopes such as Pairara, Punu, Moro, Ipairira and Soekili among others.[24]

### *Phase Three: Matebian and Back*

The Indonesian military invasion of East Timor in December 1975 ushered in a new period of uncertainty and displacement for residents of Vero and their compatriots in the region. In Lautem, however, for a number of years through 1977 the Indonesian military controlled little more than the main settlements and road corridors in the district, and rarely ventured beyond these confines. This allowed

24 It is only in recent years that groups of households (15 in 2008) have returned to Nari and opened new gardens (*pala miri*) and house sites with a view to re-establishing their presence in the area.

the Falintil (Fretilin) armed resistance, along with substantial numbers of Fataluku combatants and sympathizers, to elude capture in the dense forests of Lautem, even securing food crop harvests over a number of seasons in select locations. By late 1977, with increasing pressure from Indonesian military forces, most of the forest-dwelling resistance along with their civilian charges had worked their way along the southern coastal hinterlands behind the Paicao mountain range to Lore and Iliomar in the southwest, eventually seeking refuge in the massive mountains of Matebian and the neighbouring coastal plains of Natarbora in the district of Baucau. Under Falintil protection an estimated 90,000 Timorese had sought refuge in the region by early 1978, the massive numbers all but overwhelming conventional protocols governing land access.

In that year, however, the Indonesian military intensified their operations against the 'rebels' and initiated a sustained campaign of aerial bombardment and intimidation (Operation Encirclement and Annihilation (Taylor 1999). Shell-shocked and weak from inadequate food, by September 1978 the battered Timorese resistance forces succumbed to the pressure and surrendered *en bloc* (Budiardjo and Liong 1984: 33), with survivors straggling back to their respective regions under Indonesian military supervision.

From this time the populations of Lautem were subject to a strict internal security regime. Many communities were relocated and concentrated into crowded settlements around the main town and other regional administrative centres (former *posto*) such as Lautem, Luro, Com and Tutuala. Here they were subject to close military surveillance and restrictions on movement and congregation that severely constrained opportunities to plant food crops and tend livestock, much of which was by then lost to or confiscated by the military.[25] A Fretilin report from 1983 referring to the 'temporary residential camp' in Tutuala hints at the great difficulties people suffered during this time. 'In Tutuala, on the eastern tip, conditions are appalling; many people die of hunger. Little land is available for food production by people in the camps who can produce only small amounts of corn' (cited in Budiarjo and Liong 1984: 93).[26]

This was the experience for Vero residents whose settlement had been burnt to the ground in 1976 by Indonesian military forces. They were subsequently housed in a 'temporary residential camp' (*Campo de Concentração*) in Tutuala before being directed in due course to reconstruct their settlement in its present site aligned with the main road. As part of the process, senior members of the Vero

25 Edmundo da Cruz, a witness to events in Com and Moro-Lautem, provided testimony to the CAVR (Reception Truth and Reconciliation Commission) about this period. He commented that 'in the concentration camp in Com we suffered a lot [...] not allowed more that 100m from the camp. Anyone who did was immediately shot dead. Because of this rule we couldn't get any food, and many of us died of starvation' (CAVR 2005: 22).

26 Based on a mid 1983 Fretilin report of conditions in Lautem compiled by the village clandestine leadership known as the *nurep* (*nucleos de resistencia popular*) and covering 61 camps in 8 districts.

group made representations to the customary owners of the land, Cailoro Ratu, for permission to settle on the land in question. But their suffering was compounded in 1983 where Fretilin resistance forces torched their new settlement as a sign of defiance and resistance, and the process of rebuilding started once again.

These deprivations gradually receded in Lautem as the Indonesian military forces gained greater authority over the territory. But they never entirely disappeared, as Lautem remained a region of armed resistance throughout the occupation, provisioned and protected by a growing network of clandestine support drawn from the surrounding settlements and farming communities. The area was long known among Fretilin supporters as the 'land of continuous warfare' (*rai funu sei nafatin*), and provided a key refuge for the armed resistance throughout the period of occupation. Under these circumstances, many Fataluku settlements remained targets for repressive actions against perceived subversive involvement in the clandestine resistance movement.

The difficulties for Vero residents were compounded by the resurgence of Fretilin armed resistance after 1981. From that time the forests and the now depopulated hinterland of Lautem became a key refuge and resistance base for the independence struggle. Over many years in the ensuing cat and mouse insurgency, Indonesian military patrols regularly engaged armed guerilla resistance and its clandestine civilian networks in a protracted and ultimately untenable attempt to assert Indonesian sovereignty and control. Many residents of Vero were active participants in supporting 'the people in the forests' and came under constant surveillance because of it. Government suspicions of their complicity were influenced by the knowledge that the settlement was the natal home to one of the military heroes of the struggle, Nino Konis Santana, who led the national Falintil armed resistance between 1993 until his death in 1998. Former head of the hamlet (Kepala RT) Mario Loyola recalls having to report daily on the residents' whereabouts to the Indonesian military authorities down the hill in Tutuala. A certain amount of risky, creative subterfuge allowed hamlet members to work the forests without detection while maintaining outward signs of accommodation to Indonesian modes of security requirements.

The impact of these restrictions and constraints on the former wide-ranging agricultural and hunting activities meant that much of the arable land held under customary entitlements underwent a period of extended fallow. During the 1980s and 1990s the continuing guerrilla warfare in the forests precluded attempts to reopen former swidden garden areas for cultivation and much of the farming land has since returned to dense monsoon rainforest where traces of old settlement sites such as Ira Cao Piti and Laivai are marked by the decaying rubble of house foundations, old garden walls and scattered graves.

Over the last few years Vero residents have discussed the possibility of reopening former garden areas, and extensive use of the forests is made for regular hunting and gathering of livelihood resources, but to date no specific attempts have been made to reoccupy the land, much of which is now regarded as having returned to the communal jurisdiction of the customary steward, the clan group Renu Ratu.

But at the very time that Vero residents were considering returning to take up their ancestral landed legacy, the national government of Timor Leste moved to establish an extensive conservation park that encompasses the now emptied lands of the Vero community (McWilliam 2007c). Named in honour of freedom fighter Nino Konis Santana, the new national park was ratified in August 2008. But in the process of establishment and despite a series of consultations between government and community, the question of customary rights enjoyed by Vero residents has been brought into question by a renewed assertion of state sovereignty and governmental authority to manage the conservation zone in the national interest. These and related issues bring into counterpoint the respective scope and rights of customary land-holders on one side and the definition and extent of state land (*rai estado*) under government regulatory authority on the other. In Lautem, at least, the question of the commons and the authority of custodial authorities still looms as a significant policy question in post-independence Timor Leste. Issues arising around the management regime for the Nino Konis Santana National Park are taken up in more detail below. It provides an illustrative case study for the potential application of land law regulation, including implementation of the legal categories of community property, community protection zone and state land, in Chapter 9.

## The Post-independence Environment

The history of displacement and adaptive resettlement exemplified in the case study of Vero is one replicated in multiple ways across the enculturated landscape of Lautem. The local Director of the Land and Property office for Lautem, for example, estimated that as many as 90 per cent of the population were forcibly displaced during the Indonesian occupation (pers comm. 2008). The effects on any particular settlement may vary but all reflect similar local adjustments to successive waves of occupation over the last century. The result is a complex pattern of customary landownership claims and contested positions that form a durable legacy of colonial intervention and the present grounds for negotiation of claims to property. In this section we explore examples of post-independence negotiation of rights to property given the contested legacies of colonial intervention.

There are winners and losers in this process of property negotiation. One of the consequences of historical displacement and the gradual concentration of scattered Fataluku residential groups into larger settlements is permanent reconfiguration of relations to land among Fataluku clans. A small number of groups have remained on their ancestral lands and retained secure customary authority and ownership entitlements. In these circumstances older patterns of customary practice tend to be maintained including protocols for securing access and use rights to land. Boundary markers and the material evidence of ownership are well known, retained and reproduced in the orderly social relationships of community.

By contrast a much larger group of historically displaced populations now find themselves living on other people's land, as 'passengers' (I: *penumpang*) or 'refugees' (I: *pengungsi*) as Fataluku sometimes put it, and all are dependent upon the permissive authority of resident landowners (*mua ocawa* and their long-standing affines) for continued access and use. This grouping includes those who have been displaced locally or within village boundaries and are close enough to continue to cultivate their own customary held lands while continuing to reside in resettlement sites. The incentive for some displaced households to claim possessory entitlements under the proposed land law is reduced by the relative security of their relocation agreement with the landholding *ratu* group. However, other displaced groups in Lautem have less security of tenure – as 'passengers' (I: *penumpang*) or 'refugees' (I: *pengungsi*) on other people's land – and have greater incentive to claim possession because of the enhanced benefits of legal entitlements relative to their customary status. The Fataluku settlements of Mua Pusu and Lohomatu on the north coast of Lautem are cases in point. Both groups were resettled by the Indonesian government on the beach front at the port of Com in the late 1970s where they were initially directed to farm the rocky coralline soils in the near vicinity. In time they were permitted to reopen farmland in their former settlement areas 3 to 5 kilometres to the east, and in the post-occupation period this trend has intensified. Men and women leave their houses in Com in the early morning to tend the gardens, check on grazing livestock, harvest tree crops or tap sugar palm, returning to their houses in Com in the evening, the plaited baskets of the women laden with firewood and vegetables.

For members of Mua Pusu and Loho Matu, customary patterns of landownership and landed authority are retained on ancestral lands despite the relocation of the residential elements of the settlement. In Com itself, however, members of the two communities, who live there in separate residential groupings, have no such entitlements to land under customary arrangements. The senior landowning group in Com and *mua ocawa* for port area *Kon(u) Ratu* permits the residential arrangements created under occupation to continue, but will not freely transfer ownership or recognize any form of enduring entitlement for those households forcibly relocated to Com. This is despite over a generation of residence and a degree of intermarriage between the communities. The recent 2009 government funded rehabilitation of a graded road to Mua Pusu and Loho Matu has thus been warmly welcomed and offers a new opportunity for return and rebuilding. To date,few have actually taken that option as their well-established contemporary residences preclude any immediate relocation.

For dozens of other communities in Lautem, however, the impact of the historical relocations has meant that they find themselves settled in areas many kilometres from their homelands. The distance and the cost of re-establishing settlements in areas now far from social services mean that many settlers are also somewhat ambivalent about the prospects of return, especially having invested their savings in housing and grown accustomed to life in the resettlement environment. Examples of these long-range displacements include the whole population of Homé village, most of whom still live along the main road on the outskirts of the district capital, Los Palos, and some 10 kilometres from their ancestral lands to the west. They still work their coconut and tree crop fields and farm seasonal maize, but wholesale relocation appears to remain a distant possibility. Further examples include the urban communities of Ira Ara and Lere Loho. Relocated to Los Palos from their forested settlements in the hills to the east during the late 1970s, the residents were subject to harsh surveillance regimes under Indonesian governance owing to their strong support for the armed resistance struggle. Many now live permanently in Los Palos, while others (around 40 households) have elected to return to their former settlements sites where ancestral lands and proximate forest resources offer livelihood security.

The small settlement of Lupuloho, located on the main road to Muapitine village some 10 kilometres from Los Palos, was initially forcibly moved from the southern coast by the Indonesian military to a concentrated compound in Los Palos in the late 1970s. Subsequently, they were permitted to develop a new residential site (named Pehe Fitu after their former origin settlement) on the grasslands near Lake Ira La laru. Here members have constructed basic thatch housing and are gradually fashioning rain-fed food gardens nearby with the support of the Muapitine village head and the local customary land-holder. But they complain that their entitlements to arable land in the area are simple usufruct and many people continue to express a desire to re-establish their old settlements on the coast where they retain an abiding interest in arable land, tree crops and ancestral cultural sites (see McWilliam 2007c: 173). The site now lies within the boundary of the national conservation park and the possibility of return remains uncertain. Should this land be classified as state-owned, on the basis of the absence of possession since 1998, the people of Lupuloho will be left with the alternative of claiming ownership on the basis of possession in their place of relocation.

Each of these communities of displaced households has had to reach an accommodation with their landowning hosts. In some cases this has been achieved by activating family relationships constituted through kin or affinal links. Some have sought to regularize their presence through the conventional means of marriage alliance while still other households maintain temporary or limited use rights to arable land and house sites with the permission of landowners. To date there is little evidence in Lautem of an emergent land market and opportunities for selling land to outsiders, although informal transactions especially in urban contexts such as Los Palos are said to occur.[27] Thus for the majority of displaced householders across the district, the formal tenure status of the land on which they live and draw livelihood remains dependent upon the goodwill of others, an indeterminate status in the continuing absence of any formal state regulatory mechanisms and recognition.

27 The practice of so-called 'black exchanges' has been reported by Land and Property Staff. Fataluku use the phrase *upata nitutuare* to exchange goods in this context, usually among people who are very familiar with one another.

## State Land and Fataluku Jurisdictions

A key issue for new land law in East Timor will be the status of land that falls within customary jurisdictions of the kind described above for Fataluku communities, but that is not subject to active cultivation or residential occupation claims. This includes large areas of forested and savanna areas as well as the grasslands of the Los Palos plateau that lie within the customary authority of clans recognized as 'the lord of the land' (*Mua ocawa*). These areas may or may not have been cultivated in the past and may not contain physical markers of former settlement, but they constitute the living inheritance of the clan members in question, a privileged ancestral commons constituted in myth and oral history, and for this reason may not be arbitrarily alienated to outsiders, including state agents seeking to appropriate the land for development purposes. When we consider that, historically and culturally speaking, all land across Lautem has long been divided among the constituent clan groups and their affinal allies with boundary markers and distinctive topographies ritually demarcated, the issue of defining broad acre land that is the property of the state, the *rai estado*, presents a problem for Fataluku farmers and state officials alike.

Just what exactly constitutes the location and extent of state land remains subject to debate. One viewpoint, which might be described as a government land and property position, takes as its starting point the concept that the default status of all land in Timor Leste is *rai estado*, land belonging to the state by virtue of the acclamation of sovereignty. This position is evident in the new 2012 land law. However, the state recognizes that individuals and groups may hold forms of subsidiary entitlement to land that are demonstrated through evidentiary claims of attachment and use. This would include categories of property such as buildings, cultivated food gardens and fallowed fields where there is material evidence of past or present activity connected to the claimant. Under the 2012 land law these forms of land activity may provide evidence either for a claim of individual possession-based ownership, or for community property on the basis of 'local practices and customs'. In either case, there are interpretive pathways in the law for government officials to claim that the land is state land and free of the possibility of private planes. We consider these potential bases for legal claim further in Chapter 9.

Government staff in Lautem draw a distinction between that which is law (T: *lei*) and that which is culture (T: *kultura*). Following this line of reasoning, the oral traditions and mythic histories of Fataluku, their customary protocols and practices, ritual jurisdictions and sites of sacrificial veneration do not constitute the basis for legal entitlements to landownership. Rather, they represent forms of cultural heritage, elements of which may well be subject to legal protections under appropriate legislation, but, according to this prevailing view, cannot form the basis for sweeping claims to broad acre landownership.

In this respect the position of the Timor Leste government is not dissimilar to that of the earlier Portuguese colonial governments and the Indonesian state that followed. Native tenures in East Timor were notionally recognized by colonial officials but only to the extent that land was under cultivation or used for housing purposes. Customary lands outside these areas were variously defined at different times by the Portuguese colonial state as 'land without a master', 'unused land' or 'empty lands' and subject to various forms of state-determined appropriation and dispossession (see Fitzpatrick 2002: 146–7).

Similarly, the Indonesian government approach to customary land tenures drew upon earlier Dutch formulations and asserted a right to control all lands not under statutory title. Customary lands that were not accorded individual or ownership or cultivation rights were known as 'free state land' (*tanah negara bebas*) (Fitzpatrick 2002: 128) and were very often appropriated in the national interest (*kepentingan umum*) without incurring obligations to pay compensation. In these and a range of other ways (Fitzpatrick 2002: 126–30) the Indonesian state, under the new order government of Suharto, marginalized and undermined customary land tenures (*hak ulayat*), especially in those areas deemed reserve such as the forestry estate (McWilliam 2003).

There is a similar reluctance on the part of the government of the independent East Timor to embrace customary rights over reserve lands, but this is clearly at odds with broad sections of the Fataluku resident community, who continue to place significant store in the authority of ancestors, and the ritual standing of the local 'lord of the land', the *mua ocawa* under whose authority households are able to secure productive land-based livelihoods. Informally, Land and Property staff, who are in many cases Fataluku community members themselves, understand and may well be sympathetic to these views, even if they are reluctant to attribute any formal status for these various attributions of attachment. The result may well be an incomplete and hybridized application of the law in areas where the state lacks the capacity or legitimacy to enforce legal claims to land. We address this possibility further in Chapter 9.

One recent example of the capacity of government to negotiate and effectively acknowledge customary claims was the case of a planned 50 hectare industrial zone ratified on the north coast of Lautem in an area known as Tenu. Once the extent of the zoning was made clear, it sparked a flurry of protests from local community representatives concerned that a highly significant ancestral site, known as *Lutur(u) vaci*, would be damaged in the development process. *Lutur(u) vaci* is a key mythic landing site of numerous clan ancestors where a series of sacrificial altar posts (*ia mari tuliya*: ancestor footprints) cluster on the beach front and serve as sites for periodic sacrificial invocation. As a result of negotiations between land and property staff and the senior clan representatives for the cultural site, it was agreed to excise a 5 hectare portion of the coastal strip encompassing *Lutur(u) vaci* from any future development activity. There is no current legislative protection for the agreement, however, and the integrity of the site is largely dependent upon the continued goodwill of developers. Nevertheless, the example highlights government sympathies towards forms of customary claim even where there remains a reluctance to extend that recognition to the status of ownership.

The tension between formal assertions of state land and broader claims to clan land is likely to persist in Lautem for the foreseeable future. Perhaps the clearest example of this tension and uncertainty is the creation of the Nino Konis Santana National Park, which was legislated in the dying days of the Fretilin government in June 2007 but not officially declared until 3 August 2008. The park establishes an IUCN Category 5 multi-purpose region where livelihood activities, development and conservation values are designed to coexist. Covering some 123,600 hectares, it includes within its maximal boundary the dense monsoon rainforests of eastern Lautem, the Paicao mountain range and Lake Ira lalaru as well as a broad band of coastal waters, marine habitats and fringing coral reefs forming a national marine park. More significantly, perhaps, the park boundary fully incorporates the land area of six Fataluku villages (suco), namely Bauro, Com, Muapitine, Mehara, Lore 1 and Tutuala. Management of this extensive area of multiple settlements and its constituent diverse ecologies remains at a preliminary stage but the plan involves a zoning system that provides space for conservation reserves, economic development and opportunities for local communities to maintain approved forest and marine-based livelihood activities and cultural practices (McWilliam 2007c). A local management committee involving representatives of local communities and senior staff of government ministries was to be formed to guide and oversee the process (MAF et al. 2006).

At this stage (2011) of the development of the national park, however, no formal zoning agreements have been established, particularly around key conservation areas and 'no take' protected environmental reserves.[28] It is likely and logical that the most prospective areas for conservation are precisely those that have been emptied of their former resident populations and where tropical forest regrowth and reduced impact of coastal ecologies[29] have substantially increased biodiversity and natural environmental values in the intervening years. For those displaced communities who continue their cultural engagement with ancestral homelands and the ritual obligations and entitlements that accompany and sustain customary tenures, the question arises whether the creation of protected conservation zones in these areas will further undermine and marginalize their customary sovereignty. At this time there is no definitive answer. While park policy allows for the protection of cultural sites and tangible heritage within the conservation zone (McWilliam 2006), any further acknowledgement of historical tenures and legal authority over customary jurisdictional authority remains uncertain. Current legislation establishing the national park does not provide clarity on the legal status of the land in question or the respective entitlements of individuals, clans, communities or the state. In the interim, resident Fataluku communities will continue to draw livelihoods and resources from the proximate forests and inshore waters of Lautem,

28 See Mau 2010 for an example of how such an approach might look.

29 The cessation of reef bombing and other destructive fishing practices that flourished during the Indonesian period has allowed for the recovery of natural stocks.

balancing domestic economic imperatives against potential regulatory constraints, and pursing their customary interests and adaptive opportunities.

## References


Boggs, G. et al. 2009. Marine & Coastal Habitat Mapping in Timor Leste (North Coast) [Boggs, G., Edyvane, K., De Carvalho, N., Penny, S., Rouwenhorst, J., Brocklehurst, P., Cowie, I., Barreto, C., Amaral, A., Smit, N., Monteiro, J., Pinto, P., Mau, R., Amaral, J. and Fernandes, L.].

Budiardjo, C. and Soei Liong, L. 1984. *The War against East Timor*. London: Zed Books.

Carta Militar de Timor: Seviços Cartográficos do Exercito. nd. Sociedade de Geographica de Lisboa [received by the Geographical Society 1946].

CAVR 2005. Timor-Leste: Forced Displacement and Famine. National Public Hearing, Dili 28–29 July 2003.

Census 2004. Census of Population and Housing. Dili: Direcção Nacional de Estatística and United National Population Fund.

de Lencastre, J.G. 1929. *Aspectos da Administración de Timor*. Boletim de Agência Geral das Colonias, 54: 32–54.

Dunn, J. 1983. *Timor: A People Betrayed*. Milton, Queensland: Jacaranda Press.

Fairhead, J. and Leach, M. 1996. *Misreading the African Landscape: Society and Ecology in a Forest-Savanna Mosaic*. Cambridge; New York: Cambridge University Press.

Fitzpatrick, D. 2002. *Land Claims in East Timor*. Canberra: Asia Pacific Press.

Forbes, H.O. 1885. *A Naturalist's Wanderings in the Eastern Archipelago: A Narrative of Travel and Exploration from 1876–1883*. London; New York: Harper and Brothers.

Gunn, G.C. 1999. *Timor Loro Sae 500 Years*. Macao: Livros do Oriente.

Hajek, J., Himmelman, N. and Bowden, J. 2003. Lóvaia: An East Timorese Language on the Verge of Extinction. *International Journal of the Sociology of Language*, 160: 155–167.

Lameiras-Campagnolo, M.O. and Campagnolo, H. 1984. Les modes de caisson des Fataluku de L´orehe ´a Timor Oriental. 3(1–2) Garcia de Orta, Serie de Antropobiologia, 93–114.

Leitao, H. 1948. Os Portugueses em Solor e Timor 1515 a 1702. Lisboa: Tip.de Liga dos Combatentes da Grande Guerra.

McWilliam, A.R. 2011a. Fataluku Living Landscapes, in A. McWilliam and E.G. Traube (eds), *Land and Life in Timor-Leste: Ethnographic Essays*. Canberra: ANU E-Press, pp. 61–87.

McWilliam, A.R. 2011b. Exchange and Resilience in Timor-Leste. *Journal of the Royal Anthropological Institute*, 17: 745–63.

McWilliam, A.R. 2007a. Austronesians in Linguistic Disguise: Fataluku Cultural Fusion in East Timor. *Journal of Southeast Asian Studies*, 38(2), 355–75.

McWilliam, A.R. 2007b. Harbouring Traditions: Maginality in a Lowland Entrepôt. *Modern Asian Studies*, 41(6), 1113–43.

McWilliam, A.R. 2007c. Customary Claims and the Public Interest: On Fataluku Resource Entitlements in Lautem, in D. Kingsbury and M. Leach (eds), *East Timor: Beyond Independence*. Melbourne: Monash Asia Institute Press, pp. 168–75.

McWilliam, A.R. 2006. Fataluku Forest Tenures and the Conis Santana National Park, in T. Reuter (ed.), *Sharing the Earth, Dividing the Land: Territorial Categories and Institutions in the Austronesian World*. Canberra: ANU E-Press, pp. 253–75.

McWilliam, A.R. 2003. New Beginnings in East Timorese Forest Management. *Journal of Southeast Asian Studies*, 34(2), 307–27.

Mau, R. 2010. Ecosystem and Community Based Model for Zonation in Nino Konis Santana National Park, Timor-Leste, Thesis, Bogor: Institute Pertanian Bogor.

Ministry of Agriculture, Forestry and Fisheries (Republica Democratica de Timor-Leste), Bird Life International, NSW Dept of Environment and Conservation. 2006. Conservation Proposal for Nino Conis Santana Naitonal Park, Timor-Leste. Dili.

O'Connor, S., McWilliam, A., Fenner, J. and Brockwell, S. 2012. Examining the Origin of Fortifications in East Timor: Social and Environmental Factors. *Journal of Island and Coastal Archaeology* [in press].

Pannell, S. 2011 Struggling Geographies: Rethinking Livelihood and Locality in Timor-Leste, in A. McWilliam and E.G. Traube (eds), *Land and Life in Timor-Leste: Ethnographic Essays*. Canberra: ANU E-Press, pp.217–240.

Pélissier, R. 1996. *Timor en guerre: le crocodile et les Portugais, 1847–1913*. Orgeval.

Taylor, J.G. 1999. *East Timor: The Price of Freedom*. New York: Zed Books.

UNDP 2003. Timor-Leste: Poverty in a New Nation: Analysis for Action. Volume II: Technical Report [Co-authored with UMISET, ADB, UNICEF, JICA, World Bank, RDTL].

# Chapter 8
# Land, History and Politics in Maliana Sub-district

## Introduction

Maliana sub-district lies in the far west of East Timor nestled in the fertile upland plains of Nunura and enclosed by steep mountain ranges that form the western highlands of Bobonaro district. The region provides the setting for the next case study, which compares the impact of migration, displacement and return on land relations in two distinct communities: the Bunak-speaking mountain community of Saburai in the borderlands with Indonesian West Timor, and the Kemak-speaking community of Uat whose members are settled both near the upland origin settlement of Tapor and the neighbourhood of Ritabou in Maliana town in the lowlands (see Map 8.1).

Following a brief introduction to the setting of Maliana sub-district and town, the chapter turns to the first land study from Saburai village. Saburai experienced intense yet relatively brief periods of displacement during the mid-1970s and in 1999. The process of return and rehabilitation since independence has been

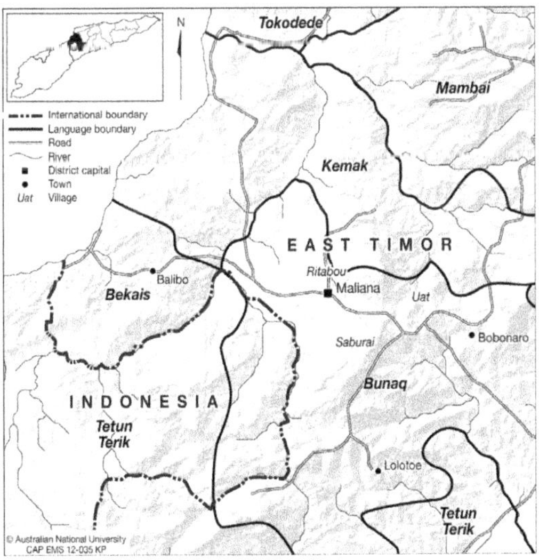


**Map 8.1 Bunak and Kemak language areas in Bobanaro district**
*Source*: ANU Cartography 2012

marked by a revitalization of cultural practices that has provided a strong sense of stability for the local community in times of change and uncertainty. Like the case of Babulo, Uatolari, customary institutions have proved to be remarkably resilient in the light of Portuguese and Indonesian era processes of encompassment and continue to provide a focal point for local land relations.

A contrasting experience is provided by the recent history of Uat. This study engages issues of relocation, possession and plural forms of authority that have developed since colonial times. The discussion tracks the emergence of translocal relationships in Uat between the upland settlement of 'origin' and a more recent settlement that developed in the lowlands where part of the community now resides. In the upland settlement, access to land and natural resources is inextricably linked to membership of one of the constituent houses of Uat. Ancestral attachments to land are regularly reinforced by reference to local histories of arrival, settlement and alliance, and specific markers and sites in the landscape. In the lowlands, where Portuguese and Indonesian era policies of relocation led to the establishment of a more heterogeneous community and competing sources of authority, highly individualized claims to land have emerged.

### *Background to Maliana Sub-district*

Maliana sub-district is one of six constituent regions of Bobonaro district. The sub-district has a total population of approximately 25,234 inhabitants (Census 2010) and comprises 7 administrative villages (see table for population distribution). Kemak and Bunak are the main ethno-linguistic groups present in the sub-district. While the people of the villages of Saburai, Tapo/Memo, Holsa and Odomau are predominantly Bunak-speakers, the villagers of Ritabou, Raifun and Lahomea are mainly speakers of Kemak. Generations of proximity and engagement mean that there are many bilingual individuals and families, and in Maliana town in particular there are numerous ethnically mixed families where the lingua franca, Tetun, is also widely spoken.

**Table 8.1 Population of Maliana sub-district by administrative village**

| Suku name | Population |
|---|---|
| Lahomea | 3,086 |
| Raifun | 2,011 |
| Ritabou | 5,441 |
| Odomau | 3,831 |
| Holsa | 5,520 |
| Tapo/Memo | 4,238 |
| Saburai | 1,107 |
| **Total** | **25,234** |

*Source*: Census 2010

The great majority of the population of the Maliana region are near subsistence farmers cultivating dryland swidden gardens (Tetun: *to'os*) with seasonal staples of maize, cassava and sweet potato mixed with supplementary taro, beans and pumpkin. Household vegetable plots are planted in house gardens (Tetun: *kintal*) and many households also tend fruit-tree groves including oranges, pawpaw, mango, jackfruit, banana, candlenut and coconut. In limited upland areas some coffee is grown. Cattle (Tetun: *karau vaka*) are raised in some upland areas where there are extensive natural pastures, while water buffalo (Tetun: *karau Timor*) are more common in the lowlands where they are used to prepare irrigated fields for rice cultivation. Most households also keep goats, pigs, and chickens. Animals are valuable household assets that may be sold in times of need, or slaughtered to fulfil family exchange obligations during mortuary rituals, weddings and other ceremonial events.

The Maliana plain is also well known for its irrigated rice production. During late Portuguese times and throughout the Indonesian period large tracts of the upland plateau of Nunura were converted into permanently irrigated rice fields. The climatic conditions in the area are such that farmers are able to benefit from two rice-planting seasons. According to official Indonesian statistics, by the mid 1980s the Maliana rice fields were producing as much rice as the rest of Timor Leste put together (Fox 2002). However, in the aftermath of the violence that followed Timor Leste's vote for independence in 1999, most of the agricultural subsidies collapsed and infrastructure, including warehouses for rice storage and production, was damaged or destroyed. Since independence, local communities, in partnership with the government and international development organizations, have been engaged in the process of repairing essential infrastructure and re-establishing rice production, but progress has been slow and crop yields much diminished owing to limited equipment and production inputs. The marketing of local rice is also hampered by a range of issues such as storage, transportation, seed quality and the competition from government-sponsored cheap imported rice and rice subsidies (Oxfam 2004).[1]

Maliana town is the administrative capital of the sub-district and the capital of Bobonaro district as a whole. The town was practically razed to the ground by pro-autonomy militia and elements of the Indonesian military and police during the violence that surrounded the UN-sponsored popular consultation in 1999.[2] Almost

1 During the Indonesian occupation, the rice industry was part of a national centralized collection and distribution system. This system began to breakdown in 1997/98 owing in part to political violence in Timor Leste but also to the broader socio-economic crisis affecting Indonesia. After the 1999 referendum, what remained of this system stopped operating completely. Today rice production levels generally remain at subsistence level (Oxfam 2004).

2 Levels of violence in Bobonaro district and Maliana sub-district were extremely high. Two of the worst incidents involved the killing of seven pro-independence supporters in Kailako on 13 April 1999, and the massacre of scores of people who had sought refuge at Maliana Police Station on 8 September 1999 (see CAVR 2005). At least three militia groups

the entire population of the sub-district, and Maliana town in particular, was displaced in the aftermath of the vote. The majority of the population was forcibly displaced to camps in Indonesian West Timor while others sought refuge on the slopes of Loelako Mountain or the mountain ranges between Saburai and Lolotoi. Although the majority of the displaced population returned in late 1999 and early 2000, a number of former members of pro-integrationist groups involved in the violence have not returned, and are not likely to return. The reconstruction and rehabilitation of public buildings and basic infrastructure has been slow. However, since independence in 2002, some progress has been made in the provision of key public services and Maliana has become an important regional centre. There are two senior high schools, an agricultural college, two junior high schools and ten primary schools, a regional hospital and the regional police command station. The town is also well connected to Dili with a number of daily bus services to the capital. Given its proximity to the Indonesian border, Maliana town has also benefited from cross-border trade and has a vibrant market. Although most market stalls are open throughout the week, there are also a number of shops and commercial businesses in Maliana town. The main market day is Saturday and it draws many traders from the surrounding region including people from more distant upland communities who come to sell their produce and buy domestic provisions such as oil, kerosene, sugar, and rice.

## The Stability of Saburai

For some communities beyond the more intensely settled lowlands in Maliana and the ribbons of sealed road that connect the town to other centres, the customary basis for patterns of land ownership have remained relatively unaffected by long-term migration or displacement to the lowlands. The Bunak-speaking village of Saburai located in the mountains between Maliana town and the Indonesian border is a case in point. Their experience illustrates the resilience of customary institutions and the persistence of practices among long-emplaced communities. They represent a 'coherent ritual community' where the rhythm of social life is tied to the ceremonial cycle of agriculture and local governance is very much in the hands of the customary leadership who provide moral and political guidance as well as decision-making on matters affecting the domain (*suku*) including the allocation and use of land and natural resources (McWilliam 2008). The following discussion presents a more detailed description of Saburai social relationships to land in their ancestral domain, including some of the considerations governing customary land management practice.

operated in Bobonaro district: Dadurus [Dadarus] Merah Putih militia (DMP, Red White Tornado), which was based in Ritabou and had a branch in Maliana town; Halilintar, which was established by the former *bupati* of Bobonaro, João Tavares; and Kaer Metin Merah Putih, which was based in Lolotoe.

Saburai village comprises three administrative hamlets (*aldeias*) scattered across the territory of the *suku*. These are Tas Massac (152 households), Cossal (132 households) and Mabil Oa (142 households) (Census 2010).[3] Right up until the 1970s the majority of the population of Saburai lived in dispersed settlements across the foothills of Mt Mali Toli and along the border region with West Timor, where they retain familiar and alliance relationships with neighbouring Bunak communities in the Lamaknen region.

Unlike other communities in Maliana sub-district, Saburai experienced intense yet relatively short periods of displacement during the second half of the twentieth century. During the internal political conflict and immediately prior to the Indonesian invasion in August 1975 supporters of UDT (União Democratica Timorense) and Apodeti (Associação Popular Democratica Timorense), including the *liurai* of Memo, who under the Portuguese administration had jurisdiction over Saburai, forced scores of villagers from Saburai and Tapo/Memo across the border to West Timor (CAVR 2005). More widespread displacement followed in October 1975, when the Indonesian troops began covert military incursions into the territory of then Portuguese Timor and the people of Saburai began to flee their settlements seeking refuge either farther up in the mountains or across the border.

During the early years of the occupation, as the Indonesian troops took control of the area and the civilian population began 'surrendering' from their places of refuge, the people of Saburai were forced to live in large camps under military supervision. The majority was held either at a 'displacement camp' in Memo on the Nunura plain, or in Maliana town. In the early 1980s the Indonesian authorities permitted the return of the population to 'secure areas' or arranged for resettlement to 'new' villages along sealed roads and urban clusters. The return to Saburai took place in 1982 and was coordinated by the newly appointed village head, the *kepala desa*, who had taken the place of the former village head (*chefe do suco*) appointed in Portuguese times. While some people chose not to return home but to 'seek out a living' in Memo or Maliana town, the majority of the population returned to live and farm on their ancestral lands. On return some restrictions to movement were in place. For example, areas close to the mountains and forests were out of bounds for security reasons, including Tas Massac, the main ritual site of Saburai, and the population was encouraged to settle in hamlet 'clusters' rather than dispersed settlements.

In the violence that followed the popular consultation in August 1999, the people of Saburai were displaced once again. For most of the population the displacement was short lived. Informants described how immediately after the ballot most of the men fled to the hills while women and children were transported on trucks to camps across the border in Indonesian West Timor by pro-integration militia. As early as October 1999 the majority of the displaced population had spontaneously returned to Saburai and begun the process of rehabilitation. Only one group, under the leadership of the Indonesian era village head, who was also

3 During the Portuguese period the village, together with Holsa and Tapo/Memo, the other predominantly Bunak *suku* of Maliana, fell under the jurisdiction of the *liurai* of Memo.

a commander in the local Dadurus Merah Putih (DMP) militia, remained in West Timor until mid 2001.[4] This group comprised mainly people from the former village head's own hamlet of Mabil Oa and included some members of the DMP militia. Their return involved intense negotiations with the local community and caused the former militia to voluntarily surrender to the UN Peacekeeping Force (PKF). While the former village head himself chose to resettle in Maliana town, most of this group has now returned to its ancestral lands.[5]

Today, there exists a degree of mobility between Saburai and more densely populated areas such as Memo or Maliana. However, this tends to be limited to students attending secondary school, or those employed as civil servants, teachers or nurses. Those who study or work in Memo or Maliana elect to walk the four-hour round trip to Maliana town on a daily or weekly basis rather than settle there more permanently.

### *Social and Ritual Organization*

One of the main reasons why the customary basis for patterns of land ownership has remained relatively unaffected by migration or displacement lies in the resilience of customary institutions and the persistence of cooperative practices that foster the interdependent nature of the relationship between people and the land.

Land relations and the organization of everyday social life are ordered around nine principal clan 'houses' of origin (*deu ginil*). Each house comprises a number of subsidiary houses or lineages. All people of Saburai belong, or are affiliated, to one or another of these ritual houses. Members of clan houses affiliate through their mothers and all clan land is held maternally and inherited through the mothers and daughters of the house. Sons of the ancestral house must marry out and cultivate the lands of their wives and affinal relatives, although they retain entitlements and obligations to their mother's and sister's in their natal house. The complex of practices is referred to collectively as the 'mother's law' and provides a set of conventions and protocols of practice to which all members of the community abide.[6]

A key site of cultural and ritual orientation in Saburai is the ancestral settlement of Tas Massac. Located high on the slopes of Mt Mali Toli the settlement forms an extensive stone fortification and spiritual centre for the nine clan houses that founded the first settlement of Saburai. These ritual structures were largely destroyed during the Indonesian military invasion but the layout and the megalithic

4 About 11 families chose to remain in West Timor or elsewhere in Indonesia. They maintain contact with their family in Saburai.

5 Later in 2003, a community reconciliation meeting that included a number of deponents who were part of this group was held under the auspices of the Commission for Reception, Truth and Reconciliation.

6 While women play an important role in the ritual life of the community the elevated status of 'the feminine' as source of all life does not necessarily mean that women are afforded greater decision-making power within the sphere of everyday social life.

focal points of the centre remain intact.[7] When Saburai households were able to return to the village in the early 1980s they were not permitted to rebuild the ritual complex in the old centre, but instead constructed a temporary or transitional complex (described as *uma simples* or *knua foun*) farther down the mountain that, in terms of its layout, mirrors that of the old settlement and provides the active focus for house-based rituals for the local community.[8]

**Table 8.2 Customary authorities in Saburai**

| | |
|---|---|
| 'Eme'<br>Deu hima pó bali | Female keeper or guardian of the ritual clan house. |
| Deu Gubul | Male head of the house. Responsible for decision-making regarding disputes between members of the house. |
| Lal Gomo | Ritual speaker/spokesperson equivalent to *lia nain* in Tetun. Determines sanctions for any infractions of the customary social and moral code. |
| Lolo Gomo | There are a number of different *Lolo Gomo* who are responsible for the oversight of different areas of land and natural resources. They also act as intermediaries between the people and the *Lal Gomo*. The *Lolo Gomo*'s role is similar to that of the Kabu or Cabo in other areas. |
| Ukon Gomo | The *Ukon Gomo* makes public announcements regarding seasonal prohibitions and together with the Lal Gomo determines sanctions for any infractions of the customary social and moral code. |
| Lokar Gomo | Equivalent to the *Kukun Nain* in Tetun, the *Lokar Gomo* retains special knowledge of the history of the land and its people. |

At each of the 'sacred' houses (*deu pó*) in the 'temporary' ritual complex, a woman from the respective clans takes the role of female guardian (*Deu hima pó bali*: the women who tend the sacred house) or 'mother' (*eme*) of the clan. Her role is to guard the ancestral clan heirlooms and sacra, tend the sacrificial hearth fire (Bunak: *hot giral*, Tetun: *ahi matan*) and participate in birth rituals for new members of the house community. Members of each house also choose a male head of house (*deu gubul*). His role is to safeguard the 'words of the ancestors' (sacred knowledge), provide leadership for all members of the house and have the authority to resolve conflicts that might occur within the house or between houses.

Five houses provide the ritual leadership of the *suku* community. These are Lo Nai, Mone Ichu, Siri Gatal, Los Lokar and Leo Ues. Members of each of these

7 The site includes stone altars, the stone base of the domain flag (*bandeira hun*) and of the former cult houses as well as gravestones and other elements of the ritual centre. Although people no longer live at the old centre, it is still used actively for major house ceremonies and as a vital (*pó*) location for cultural performance.

8 Other houses have also been constructed in the settlements of Mabiloa and Cossal. However, these are meeting houses and do not contain hearths. Tas is the ritual centre for all the community.

houses appoint a *lal gomo* (spokesperson or Tetun: *lia nain*) and together they represent the senior holders of local cultural knowledge and principal advisers on all matters of significant community interest. The *lal gomo* are assisted in both ceremonial and practical tasks by a series of customary officeholders who provide a policing and communicating role to maintain the cultural rules. Although the community duly elected a village head in 2006 (re-elected in 2009) in accordance with the national state system, the *chefe suco* is a young man and quite junior in the customary hierarchy. His authority is very much dependent on the advice and support he can garner from the customary elders of the domain. A view expressed in Saburai is that 'if the Government (*governu*) wishes to do something in the village, they have to go through the ritual leaders (Tetun: *lian nain*, Bunak: *lal gomo*, ritual speakers)'.

### *Ritual and the Agricultural Cycle*

Three of the nine clan houses are considered to be the founding houses of the Saburai community. During ritual ceremonies all other clan houses and their subsidiaries congregate around three distinct altars representing these founder houses:

**Table 8.3 Saburai founding houses**

| 'Feminine' lord | Mone Ichu Mil or Gamal Ichu | Ratu or Datu Mil/Gamal Dato/Deu Benu |
|---|---|---|
| Lo Nai | Mone Ichu | Siri Gatal |
| Ferrian Mau* | Loko Gatal (Loko Hatar) | Los Lokar (gate-keepers) |
| | Ma Belis | Los Chu |
| | Leo Ues | *Deu Ebi* |
| | *Leo Rawan* | |
| | *Leo Malis* | |

*Note*: The clan of Ferrian Mau no longer exists. The house of Lo Nai looks after the Ferrian Mau altar and Ferrian Mau lands

During the decades of Indonesian rule, the major ritual festivals that marked the agricultural cycle in Saburai fell into disuse, but they have been gradually revived from 1997 and further revitalized in the years following national independence. The ceremonial cycle that engages a series of collective domain-wide ritual events provides another example of the strength of the moral community of Saburai.

There are four main rituals undertaken during the year. The first is a ritual involving a public sacrifice (buffalo/pigs) and commensality with the ancestors undertaken at the 'old centre'' (*knua tuan*). The purpose is to 'feed' the dead, and restate the relationship of mutual interdependency that the living maintain with their forebears. Participants are expected to attend with clear consciences and no arguments are permitted on the day. Following this ceremony known as *Chubi Lai*, which marks the beginning of a new cycle, the community participates in a ritual known as 'burning the grass' (Bunak: *an ini*).

*An ini* is associated with the clearing and burning off of cleared gardens in preparation for planting. At this time over a three-day period of licence, young men of the village engage in ritual hunting, of pigs, deer, monkeys, and cuscus possum among other edible wild animals, bringing them to a designated site called *La Ta* below the old settlement for preparation of sacrificial offerings that will later be taken to the ancestral centre by the female house custodians and male ritual authorities.[9] Both men and women are active in the ritual process, but distinguished by gendered tasks.

Subsequent rituals include a post-planting ceremony invoking the fertility of the soil and strong growth of plants (Bunak: *ukur ho'on gio*, Tetun: *matak malirin*, cool green), and a closing public ceremony as a maize harvest celebration (Bunak: *paol gipi ge*, Tetun: *silu batar*: harvest maize) and an expression of gratitude to the ancestors and God. Each ceremony provides an occasion for the community to reinforce the spiritually sanctioned rules by which people are expected to live. The community-wide injunctions or prohibitions (Bunak: *ukon zikalkail*, Tetun: *Tara bandu*) apply to forms of harvesting and land use practices (periods of no burning, hunting or felling of trees) as well as to a range of proscriptions against social offences – no stealing, no adultery, no fighting and so on.[10] Transgression incurs fines (*ukon no golo*) and opens offenders to forms of spiritual or ancestral sanction such as illness, the death of children or other misfortunes. Within the traditional clan structures, a series of customary officeholders are recognized who provide a policing and communicating role to maintain the cultural rules. The *lolo gomo* for instance has a monitoring and reporting role across the domain and will report infractions to the *ukon gomo*, who is responsible for announcing the seasonal prohibitions (*ukon zikailkail*), and then to the *lokar gomo*, who is also one of the senior clan ritual leaders of Saburai (*lal gomo*) and has oversight over the agricultural cycle, if the issue is considered sufficiently serious

### *Marriage Prescriptions and Practice*

The practice of matrilineal kinship and matrilocal residence is a cornerstone of Saburai land relationships and distinguishes the Bunak-speaking people of Saburai

9 Older men and women also 'follow' the ritual hunt sometimes assisting in chasing down an animal but mainly in order to gather forest fruits and other natural resources. Only the female and male elders attend the ancestors in the old village. All other participants return to their own homes where they consume their portion of the sacrificial offerings and share it among family members who were unable to attend.

10 The prohibitions are opened and closed or reinstated through ritually sanctioned invocations.

from the majority of other ethno-linguistic groups across East Timor.[11] As a general rule members of the same 'house and hearth' (*deu gubul, hot giral* or *hoto deu*) may not marry. Sanctioned marriage patterns or relationships between houses are described as *malu ai*. There is no custom of *barlaki* or *hafoli feto* (bride-wealth or bride-price) in Saburai marriage practices. Elders stressed that equal value was placed on both men and women and that marriage gift exchange represented the effort and investment of the respective families in bringing up their children – not the 'purchase' of the bride.[12] *Malu* houses (bride's house) give feminine goods, while *ai* houses (groom's house) give masculine goods.[13] Gifts exchanged during the course of marriage negotiations are minimal in comparison to similar prestations among other groups found across East Timor.[14] On marriage the groom lives on land belonging to his wife's mother. He does not become a member of his wife's house, nor does his wife become a member of his own house. Any children will be members of their mother's house.[15] A newly formed family unit will farm the wife's mother's land and may also have access to the wife's mother's house land. If a man's wife dies he is no longer entitled to farm her mother's land and must return to his own maternal house land. In the case of the death of their mother, children often remain with their maternal relatives; typically a female sibling will take charge of her nephews and nieces if her sister dies. Informants suggested that whoever looks after the children has the right to cultivate land previously farmed by their parents but once the children are old enough they will farm this land.

If a man or woman from Saburai marries outside the community a degree of negotiation is required regarding place of residence, access to land, inheritance and house membership of the wife and children. Across Timor Leste the most common marriage pattern involves asymmetric exchange between wife-givers and wife-takers (Tetun: *fetosae-umane*), whereby the bride usually leaves her paternal home to form a new family unit on her husband's father's land and will usually

11 In Tetun speaking areas such as Suai/Kamenasa or Viqueque matrilineal clans are found but they are not necessarily matrilocal (see Hicks, 2004). In the case of the Kemak of Leosibe a form of temporary uxorilocal residence may occur until bridewealth exchange is complete (see Uat example).

12 This may be a relatively new concept but informants (including some of the elders) suggest that the Tetun phrase *uma folin* (house-price) rather than *feto folin* (bride-price) more accurately describes the spirit of this exchange.

13 In *malu ai* relations there is no sense that wife-givers are superior to wife-takers.

14 Usually this involves the simple 'symbolic' exchange of 'feminine' goods such as *tais* (cloth) and 'masculine' *belak* (gold plate) or money. One informant stated that for her 'traditional' (*lal adat*) marriage the cloth and money exchanges between houses probably had a value of around USD 100. This pattern of exchange is replicated during specific times of the year or events such as house building, funerals, etcetera.

15 Friedberg describes another type of marriage among the Bunak of Lamaknen where the bride is represented metaphorically as a cutting that is 'transplanted' to her husband's house. She and her children become members of her husband's house and inaugurate a line of descent called *dil* (Freidberg 1996).

– depending on the protocols regarding bride-wealth (Tetun: *barlaki*) – become a member of her husband's father's house. Of the mixed marriages observed in Saburai there was a tendency to accommodate the customs of the bride's family. Therefore, in the case where a man from Saburai married a woman from outside the community her family expected that she would leave her paternal home and that her husband's family would engage in the appropriate gift exchange.[16] The wife and any children from the marriage would remain members of the wife's father's house until the complete bride-wealth was exchanged.[17] The *deu gubul* and maternal uncles of the husband would be responsible for identifying and allocating house land to the couple. While the couple would not 'own' this land, their children would have the right to inherit the land through their paternal grandmother. In the case where a woman from Saburai married a man from outside the community there was a strong sense that the wife's marriage customs would prevail. Women are considered to be the source of all life. For many it is unthinkable that a woman would leave her maternal house and land as this would involve an obligation to take the source of life and 'wealth' (Tetun: *rikosoin*) of her house with her.

### *Land Allocations, Boundaries and Use*

Informants from Saburai described possessing a variety of entitlements to land for both farming and house-building based on ancestral and contemporary cultivation practices, type of land, type of crops and location. Most people farmed one to four plots of land measuring anything between 1 and 3 hectares on a rotational basis. Some plots were farmed exclusively by the farmer and immediate family, some farmed collectively with other house members or affines (*malu ai*), while others share-cropped. Few informants claimed to farm irrigated rice plots in the lowlands (see also Census 2010).

The nine clan houses of Saburai form the principle land-holding units of the domain. Informants typically stated that the ancestors were responsible for distributing land among the clan houses and that land allocation reflects ancestral cultivation practices. House land (*Echu Deu*) is usually demarcated by certain physical features in the landscape such as rocks, trees and river courses. The head of each house (*deu gubul)* is considered to be the authority on all house land history and boundaries. He is ultimately responsible for all important decisions regarding land including land allocation and land dispute resolution. The ritual speaker of the house (*lal gomo*) also retains communal knowledge of domain land and may be called upon to resolve any boundary disputes. Houses that are considered to be

16 Not all *fetosae-umanne* marriages have this requirement.

17 In the event that a husband dies before the 'bride-wealth' exchange is complete, his widow and children may return to her father's land. However, if the exchange is complete there is an expectation that the widow and children would remain on his mother's land. In the past, this meant that arrangements may have been made for a widow to marry her husband's brother or other male relative.

founder houses can have no distinguishing boundaries and access to land among these houses is fluid. For example, there are no boundaries between land belonging to the house of Siri Gatal and those of Lo Nai, Mone Ichu or Los Chu and similarly Loko Gatal shares land with Mone Ichu, Ma Belis, Leo Rawan and Leo Malis.[18]

House land is ultimately considered to be the common property of the clan, but it is held maternally and rights to individual plots are inherited through mothers and daughters. Nominally, any land previously farmed by the mother will pass to the eldest daughter. However, she may allow other members of her family to also farm this land. Her brothers and other male members of the house can ask permission to farm their sister's or their mother's land, but are generally expected to access land belonging to their wives and affinal relatives in the first instance. One area of house land is specifically reserved for the female guardian of the house and members of the house are expected to contribute time, labour or resources to farming this land. Although land is maternally held, husbands and brothers are considered to be the 'managers' of this land. Depending on individual dynamics between husbands and wives or sisters and brothers, women may have a greater role in land management. However, more often than not men will make important decisions regarding land management.[19]

Informants expressed conflicting views regarding sale, transferral or rental of house land. However, land transactions between members of different houses do occur. Once land has been transferred it can no longer be claimed by family members or house members of the original owner, if the land is sold to a member of a different house. Most informants agreed that no house land could be sold to outsiders. Any land transactions should involve the relevant customary authorities, principally the *deu gubul*, the *lolo gomo* charged with oversight over land, and in some cases the *lal gomo*, *chefe aldeia* and *chefe suco* as well.

Informants typically asserted that there was no un-allocated land within the domain.[20] However, they also stated that not all land was considered to be house land. Non-house land includes previously unused or abandoned land. Customarily, the *lolo gomo* must be informed prior to farming any unused or abandoned land within the domain. The *lolo gomo* (the guardian of land and natural resources) informs the *lal gomo* (ritual spokesperson) who will determine whether or not this land may be cultivated. This land is individually owned by whoever is responsible for fencing, clearing, burning and cultivating it. What distinguishes this land from house land is that it cannot be claimed by other house members but will pass

18 This reflects the three broad house groupings based around the founder houses described above.

19 One informant suggested that this was because during the Indonesian occupation the concept of male head of household was enforced for contractual reasons.

20 One informant suggested that the only 'unused' land left in the village domain was *rai manas* (sacred or haunted) and therefore could not be farmed or used to build houses. However, another informant described how he and his wife asked for permission to build their house on a plot of land that was deemed to be *rai manas* by the elders.

directly to the children of the individual owner and to subsequent generations through the female line.[21] The inter-generational entitlement arises from acts of possession subject to the permissive authority of ritual elders.

### *Rice Fields*

Included in this category of 'privately' or 'individually' owned land are also areas of irrigated rice paddy in the lowland areas close to the Nunura River. However, it is unclear the degree to which customary officeholders such as the *lolo gomo* and the *lal gomo* have been involved with the management of this land. One such area of land is called Zupal Galap. Informants stated that, during the 1960s, a workgroup of about 20 people from the hamlet of Tas Massac dug irrigation channels on this land in order to cultivate rice. They claim that this land belonged to the traditional domain of Saburai but had previously laid 'abandoned' and 'unused' because it was too far from the settlements. People from Tas Massac claim to have farmed this land right up until 2000 after which the irrigation system fell into disrepair. However, during the mid 1990s the land was the subject of a land-grab by the then district administrator of Bobonaro, Guilherme dos Santos from Tapo/Memo. Dos Santos claimed that the land originally belonged to his father the Portuguese-era *liurai* of Memo.

While further inquiry into the details of this dispute is required, it follows a similar pattern found in other areas of Timor Leste including Uatolari and Ainaro. Under Portuguese rule powerful *liurai* or *regulo* were able to draw on labor from the populations under their jurisdiction to work on agricultural projects that were in many cases initiated by the Portuguese administration. In the post-independence period disputes have arisen between those involved in working on these fields and family members of the former local authorities charged with establishing these projects. The case of Zupal Galap also has political undertones as the claimants from Saburai involved in the dispute were considered to be pro-independence supporters and Guiherme dos Santos was a prominent pro-integrationist, instrumental in the creation and support of pro-integration militia in Bobonaro district. These types of dispute, which are explored in detail in Chapter 10, illustrate the interaction between contested historical claims of possession and dispossession, and political changes in the state regime.

### *Plantations*

As in other areas of Timor Leste, informants from Saburai stated that fruit trees belonged to the person responsible for planting them (and their descendants) regardless of whether or not these were planted on house land. However,

---

21 Insufficient cases of this sort of individual land ownership were documented to draw any conclusions. However, it is possible to suggest that either this land will eventually become part of the broader house legacy and therefore become house land; or that this type of individual land ownership claim represents an evolving land-holding model.

informants also identified certain areas such as sacred betel nut groves that were considered to be communal resources. One such area, in a place called Soe Lelo, used to be harvested collectively once a year by the people of Saburai and Memo. But it seems that this is no longer the case.

### *Natural Resources*

Certain areas of land and natural resources within the domain of Saburai are subject to special injunctions or prohibitions (Bunak: *ukon zikal kail*, Tetun: *Tara bandu*). These include rocky outcrops, mountaintops and stone altars, many of which are associated with ancestral histories of origin as well as important communal natural resources such as areas of old-growth forest and water sources. Some of these sites are completely 'out of bounds' and transgression will not only incur a fine (*ukon no golo*) defined by the *lal gomo* but also expose the transgressor to 'unseen' forms of spiritual or ancestral sanction including illness or death. Other sites and resources may be accessed but one or more of the *lal gomo* must be involved and the correct invocations and animal sacrifices must be made to the ancestral or spirit guardians.[22] This applies in particular to certain areas of old-growth forest that may be accessed by members of the community, particularly when they require wood to build or rebuild their houses. Some sites, such as sacred springs, may be accessed at any time but particular 'rules' or behaviours must be observed. For example, from one water source called *Il Pó* (literally: sacred water) it is safe to fetch water as long as none of the surrounding trees or plants are damaged or broken and no water is spilt back into the source. Although they may not be recognized as such, many of these prohibitions and injunctions have clearly positive environmental outcomes. Conserving areas of forest and foliage around springs and water sources serves to create natural filters that keep the water fresh and potable. By acting as gatekeepers to areas of old-growth forest and imposing fines for infractions, the *lal gomo* manage access to this valuable resource and potentially ensure its sustainable use.[23]

### *Customary Dispute Resolution Mechanisms*

Any land disputes or infractions regarding the use of land and natural resources are dealt with in the same way as a range of social offences through a process called *pil*

---

22 Such statements by informants are usually accompanied by a 'cautionary tale' involving a well-known member of the community. For example, elders recounted the story of a former village head who was baptised and no longer believed in local customs and practices. He decided to open an area of old-growth forest in which to let his animals graze without undertaking the necessary rituals and as a result both he and all his animals started getting sick.

23 Some informants who had heard of, or were involved in, projects run by environmental NGOs commented that their ancestors understood the benefits of looking after their environment.

*gewen* (Tetun: *nahe biti boot*). In the case of a land dispute between members of the same house, the disputants meet with the *deu gubul* and other members of the house who know the history of the land. In cases involving disputants from different houses then the *deu gubul* of the houses involved will be present. The disputants, house elders and witnesses sit together to discuss the nature of the dispute. In most cases the *deu gubul* will try to negotiate a compromise between the disputants. However, in cases where a party to the dispute is found clearly in the wrong the *deu gubul* will settle the case in favour of the injured party and may impose a fine on the offender. The case will be 'closed' with some form of ritual sharing of food and drink. If a case cannot be resolved by the *deu gubul* he may call on the council of *lal gomo* to intervene and pass judgement (Bunak: *dato hol leki*). After listening to the parties to the conflict and witnesses the *lal gomo* will make a decision regarding the case, which again might entail some sort of compromise between the parties to the dispute, or, in cases where a person is found guilty of an infraction, a fine might be imposed and the offender may be publically admonished.[24]

Local dispute resolution mechanisms are favoured in Saburai, in part because people's experiences dealing with government institutions such as the Department for Land and Property, the police or the sub-district administration have been unsatisfactory. These institutions tend to be regarded as remote, inefficient or biased.[25] Consequently, the leadership of Saburai have instituted a local rule declaring that if anyone takes an accusation or dispute 'outside' the community and the charge is not made or found to be legitimate, then the accuser must pay a series of fines (at the river, the road, the edge of the settlement) by way of recompense for bringing members of the community and the name of the village into disrepute.

In many ways Saburai presents a largely self-regulating community where access to land is based on ancient clan histories, and use of land and other natural resources is regulated through the still influential cycle of sacrificial religious practice. This is not to say that the people of Saburai do not suffer discrimination and differential access to resources derived from entrenched social hierarchies, or that principles and practices regulating access to land and natural resources remain fixed in time, are non-negotiable or are free from external influences. But what is striking is the range of cultural practices that has been sustained and revitalized in the years since the Indonesian occupation, and the sense of stability that these have afforded the local community in times of change and uncertainty. For people

24 By way of example, for breaking the prohibition a person may be fined a pig or a buffalo if serious enough, by the clan leaders. At the hearing of the offence, the animal would then be slaughtered and its legs cut off and hung on a post or tree near the site of the offence. The rest of the meat would be carved up and distributed among the witnesses and participants to the process of judgement.

25 People's experience has been shaped during the Indonesian era and post-independence. Police or representatives have been found slow to respond or reluctant to travel to remote locations such as Saburai, which at the time this research took place was only accessible by foot (two hours' walk) or by 4X4 vehicle.

in Saburai the enduring authority of customary institutions provides a continuing and locally legitimate framework for understanding relations in land and for negotiating land use agreements between categories of kin, affines and outsiders (McWilliam 2008). It is evident that, while the external influence of the state in its various guises has introduced alternate forms of legitimation and regulation, these have yet to radically transform the nature of land-based transactions in Saburai. Saburai, in other words, provides a striking illustration of resilient and self-sustaining customary practices, notwithstanding the experience of displacement during the Indonesian military occupation.

## The Translocality of Uat

A very different experience is presented in the following discussion of the community of Uat. Here, under the pressures of late colonial development policies, and the impact of Indonesian occupation, the original settlement split and substantial member households now reside in the lowlands as a formal part of the village of Ritabou around the town of Maliana. The following discussion highlights the complications of translocal settlements and illustrates the limits of customary institutions in seeking to manage land relations in different settings. The context involves large numbers and heterogeneity, and greater plurality of public authority, than the case of Saburai. There is also much greater individuation of rights to land as a result of changing cultivation practices, increased involvement by the state (in its colonial and neo-colonial forms), and greater awareness of the commodified monetary value of land. In a number of cases, these individuated claims to land rests on histories of actual possession or narratives of dispossession.

Until the early 1970s, the *concelho* of Maliana was made up of 3 *reinos* (kingdoms), 6 *sucos* (villages) and 21 *povoção* (hamlets) (Sherlock 1983). However, these administrative divisions did not always match pre-existing or underlying social organization and political groupings. The people of the present-day villages of Raifun, Ritabou and Lahomea (and to a certain extent Odomau) consider themselves part of a broad *Kemak*-speaking kin group called *Leo Sibe* (literally: nine settlements).[26]

Today, Uat is one of the administrative hamlets of the village of Ritabou, which is the most heterogeneous of the seven villages of Maliana sub-district. Ritabou now includes populations that historically formed part of *Leo Sibe* as well as communities from Marobo (Atu-Aben, Soilesu, Bobonaro sub-district) and Hauba (Mali Ubu, Bobonaro sub-district) settled in Maliana town. However, during the Portuguese period, the composition of a village or *suku* was determined

26 The history of *Leo Sibe* is locally contested. Bunak people claim that Leo Sibe is derived from an earlier territorial grouping of Bunak lands. In Bunak, Leo Sibe is known as *Lamak Chiwe* (Lamak Nine). *Lamak Itchu* (Lamak Seven) is in West Timor and *Lamak Sogo* (Lamak Ten) is in Bobonaro.

by group membership rather than territory. Thus, regardless of whether they are settled in the uplands or lowlands, the people of Uat claim hamlet and village membership based on their relations to one of the constituent clans or houses of Uat that traditionally formed part of Ritabou *suco* (village).[27]

From a population of approximately 120 families, the hamlet head of Uat calculated that 56 families are currently settled in the lowlands around Maliana town, while 64 families have chosen to settle in the uplands close to Tapor, the now abandoned original hilltop settlement of the origin houses of Uat.[28] However, he stated that there was a high degree of mobility between the two locations. In general, he felt that older members of the community tended to prefer living in the upland village close to their ancestral houses and lands, while younger members, particularly those of secondary school age, tended to move with their parents or close relatives down to Maliana town to attend school. Nevertheless, there were some families who moved between the upland settlement and Maliana town.

According to local histories, the original founders of Leo Sibe came to the uplands between Bobonaro and Maliana in search of land. They were granted land and settlement entitlements through an alliance with the people of Marobo.[29] Leo Sibe was divided into two groups of ten 'houses' or clans, each corresponding to one of the two hilltop settlements of Usi and Uat. The two groups refer to each other in kinship terms as brother and sister (*na'an ho feton*). The 'female' houses of Usi, which is located at a higher altitude in relation to Uat, are also called *Sapulu Tete* (ten above), and the 'male' houses of Uat are known as *Sapulu Nera* (ten below). As the population of Usi and Uat grew, subsidiary or branch houses settled throughout the upland areas and down towards the Nunura plain just south of Maliana town.

### *The Upland Community*

The upland community of Uat is structured around nine (originally ten) lineages/houses.[30] Each house may have several branches or subsidiary houses – some have settled within their ancestral lands while others have settled farther afield

---

27 There is a long history of animosity between the community of Uat and the former *liurai* of Ritabou described in more detail in Chapter 8. During the Indonesian period this rivalry manifested itself in attempts by a village head from the *liurai* house of Ritabou to transfer the people of Uat under the jurisdiction of a village in the upland area close to Bobonaro township.

28 Current Census 2010 population figures, based on village of residence, place current population of Uat to be 99 households, 535 persons.

29 The houses of Leo Sibe are collectively 'Tai' (male) in relation to Marobo 'Sabe' (female). The houses of Uat are sometimes referred to as 'uma ai-ri'in mane' in relation to the houses of Marobo, which are described as 'uma ai'ri'in feto' in recognition of their traditional role as 'wife-takers' (Uat) and 'wife-givers' (Marobo).

30 The house of Nugu Luli is still remembered in ritual; the house of Bau Ubun has been 'exiled' and is no longer considered part of the ritual community.

but still carry the same name. House membership usually consists of agnatically related male kinsmen, their in-married spouses and children. However, there are exceptions. In some cases a person may be incorporated into, or 'adopted' by, a particular house because they have been chosen by members of a community of related houses to perform a specific ritual or political role historically associated with that house, or as a way of circumventing marriage prescriptions. Members of these nine core houses lay claim to land surrounding the historic settlement of Tapor based on ancestral cultivation practices.

Each house is associated with a specific responsibility and role within the community. Three senior houses have the authority to 'rule' over the community – these are Liko Loko, Bili Ubun and Lika Ubun. The *txu'uman* (head of the house) of Liko Loko has the power to pass judgement (Tetun: *tesi lia*, literally 'cut the words') within the community. Liko Loko is 'paired' to the house of Bili Ubun. Together these houses are referred to as *Lesu no Bane* (Tetun: *ai-lele* and *ai-nitas*).[31] According to local informants, the house of Bili Ubun was given a 'flag' as a symbol of office by the colonial Portuguese authorities and therefore the village head must be chosen from this house (or one of its subsidiary houses).[32] The third, 'founding' house of Uat is Lika Ubun. The main role of this house is to mediate the relationship between the community and the natural resources. The elders of this house provide ritual leadership to the community and are closely associated with the house of Lori Ubun, whose members are usually chosen to act as the *kabo* responsible for notifying the community of key stages in the agricultural cycle, monitoring the fruit trees and overseeing house yards and plots.

For the purposes of ritual, houses used to gather in one of three corporate groups: *Mane Munun, Mane Selala and Mane Morin* (translated as the eldest, middle and youngest men respectively). Elders from Uat also stated that these corporate groups represent work groups formed by their ancestors to labour on their ancestral lands. The distribution of houses into 'age' groups is consistent with a widely documented trend within Austronesian societies whereby ritual power and landed authority are associated with origins and precedence, while temporal or political power is associated with newcomers or in-migrant groups (Fox, 1995).

---

31 According to local custom the founder-ancestors of Uat planted Ai-lele (kapok) and Ai-nitas (Java olive tree) on the site of the origin village.

32 There is a long-standing dispute between members of the house of Bili Ubun, its principal subsidiary house Manephat and the 'exiled' house of Bau Ubun. According to local informants, the house of Bau Ubun previously held the office of *liurai* but sometime in the twentieth century the Portuguese transferred this power (*entrega bandeira*) to a member of the house of Bili Ubun because 'he knew about administration' (*hatene administrasaun*). The action of the colonial authorities appears to have exacerbated long-standing animosity between members of these ruling houses. Tensions between members of these houses underpin a long-standing land dispute considered in further detail in Chapter 8.

**Table 8.4 Uat houses division by 'age' group**

| Mane Munun (Eldest Men) | Mane Selala (Middle Men) | Mane Morin (Youngest Men) |
|---|---|---|
| Lika Ubun | Leo Boi | Liko Loko |
| Lori Ubun | Duas Mali | Bili Ubun |
| | Lua Laben | Manephat |

*Note*: Original houses of Uat not included here include Nugu Luli, now incorporated into a community of suku Manapa; and Bau Ubun, origin house of the liurai of Ritabou 'exiled' from the community of Uat/Sapulu Nera (see footnote 40)

The origin settlement located on top of Tapor hill was a stone fortification that enclosed the original ten houses of Uat (Sapulu Nera). In the past, members of the community were also buried within this enclosure, close to their ancestral houses. Following the Indonesian invasion, however, the site has been abandoned and no communal ceremonies have been performed there. Most houses were destroyed or burnt during the Indonesian invasion and many of the burial sites were looted. In the absence of a communal site for ritual focus, a number of the elders of the community lamented that the larger rituals associated with yearly ceremonial cycle were fading. Nevertheless, despite being abandoned and engulfed by the surrounding forest, the site at Tapor remains a key cultural reference point for the community.

Since independence, traditional structures representing the remaining houses of Uat have been built on land surrounding the original settlement. Members of the community describe these houses as *uma simples* (simple houses) in recognition of the fact that they have not been rebuilt according to customary prescriptions.[33] Each house structure is presided over and cared for by one of the senior male members of the house. Their role is to guard the ancestral heirlooms and sacra of the house. The house is both a symbolic and social structure and in many respects mirrors the customary arrangements in Saburai. In their panels, pillars and platforms Uat ritual houses preserve the memory of previous generations of house members, subsidiary houses and houses related through marriage.[34]

### *Marriage Prescriptions and Practice*

Houses of Uat are exogamous and therefore the members of each house must seek marriage with members from a different house. Within the Uat community

33 These prescriptions relate to the order in which reconstruction must take place, who should be involved, the sourcing of materials, etcetera.

34 For example, subsidiary houses take a wood-chipping from the central pillar of the origin house, which is then placed in the new house structure. Also, hanging within the house structure are horns of water buffalo received from 'wife-taker' houses or pig jaws received from 'wife-givers'.

of houses, as elsewhere in Timor Leste, preferred 'paths' of marriage alliance exist between houses (Clamagirand (-Renard) 1980, Forman 1980, Traube 1986). Within Uat, there are three main categories of marriage alliance. The first is between houses with whom the earliest marriage alliances were made – these are called *ai mea*. A second category consists of all subsequent marriages with in-coming groups; and a third category, called *bei-bei*, refers to marriages that are not sanctioned by custom, or do not fall within the preferred categories of *ai mea*. In order to circumvent marriage prescriptions, it is customary for the bride to 'pass through' the house of a traditionally accepted wife-giver house to that of the groom. That is to say that the prescribed wife-giver house acts as an intermediary between the houses of the bride and groom.[35] Today, marriage relations are not confined to the community of houses of Uat. Increased spatial mobility and interaction with other groups of houses (including related groups such as Usi, or subsidiary houses dispersed throughout the district, neighbouring groups and even foreigners) has led to the formation of new alliances that do not fit the customary prescriptions.

The houses of Uat have distinct marriage practices that set them apart from most other Kemak-speaking groups. In communities across Timor Leste, affinal relations involve the continual exchange of goods and services between 'wife-giver' (progenitor) and 'wife-taker' (progeny), not only at the time of the formal exchange of bride-wealth but at all events that regulate the social life between the houses. In most Kemak-speaking areas, a bride will move to her husband's house regardless of whether the fully agreed bride-wealth (*berlaki, folin*) has been exchanged between 'wife-giver' (*uma mane*) and 'wife-taker' (*uma mane foun*) houses. However, among the houses ofUat, it is often the case that the groom is expected to live and work on his wife's family land (sometimes called 'bride service') until the full bride-wealth has been exchanged. Until such time as the exchange between wife-givers and wife-takers is complete, any of the couple's children are considered to belong to their mother's house.

The practice of temporary matrilocal residence has direct implications for land and inheritance. According to local informants, if a man dies while he is still living on his wife's house land, this land will not be automatically inherited by his wife or their children but will revert to his wife's brothers (or male relatives). In such cases where the couple have purchased land outright (that is, the land does not belong to the wife's house) then it will be passed on to the man's wife and children.

### *Land Allocations, Boundaries and Use*

Informants resident in upland Uat described a mixture of individual and communal tenures. Types of entitlement are based on narratives of arrival and settlement, ancestral and contemporary cultivation practices, types of land and types of crop. Certain areas of land are linked directly to ancestral founding narratives of arrival and

35 Marriage prescriptions in Uat reflected many of the characteristics described in depth by Clamagirand in her work on the 'Ema' of Marobo; see (Clamagirand (-Renard) 1980).

settlement. These include areas of land believed to have been first cleared, burned and cultivated by the core houses of Uat. In the past, communal house land was subject to ritual prohibitions and farmed collectively by members of all the houses of Uat. Part of the harvest was used for communal rituals held at the site of the origin settlement or individual house-based ceremonies. This practice has been largely discontinued and one such 'communal' area was being farmed individually at the time of the survey. Nevertheless, communal rights and ritual prohibitions still applied to particular areca palm groves (two named groves were Ai-Mu and Dara-Abu).

According to the hamlet head of Uat and the village head of Ritabou (also originally from Uat), the upland community adheres to customary injunctions regulating access to certain natural resources and those related to the agricultural cycle. The *kabo* of Lori Ubun, for example, is traditionally responsible for notifying the community of these injunctions and together with senior members of the house of Lika Ubun may be called to deal with infractions by members of the community.

Most informants claim to have access to house land for the cultivation of staple crops (for example, maize, peanuts, cassava, and some upland dry rice). House land was generally described by informants as any land that was first cleared and farmed by members of their house. The senior members of each house retain the knowledge of house lands. House elders and the *txu'uman* (head of the house) are responsible for resolving any disputes that might arise concerning house land. When speaking of their house land, informants tended to trace back at least two or three generations to make their point. House land is generally passed from father to son and tends to be cultivated with other members of the family. Women are entitled to farm on their father's land or that of their house until they are married, or move to their husband's house lands. Given the lengthy nature of marriage exchange practices described above, it is not uncommon for children to be granted access to land through their mother's house. Also, if a wife-taker (*uma mane foun*) house is unable to provide a couple with land when they get married, then the wife-giver (*uma mane*) house may grant some land to the couple.

Although informants stated that house land belonged to all members of their house, they also recognize that this land is subject to individual inheritable rights. For example, if a man from the house of Duas Mali cultivates a plot, his children will have the right to inherit the land when he dies. It does not revert to the communal property of the house although it remains ritually part of the collective landed domain of the house. Thus, in the event that the children of this man decided not to farm the land, then other members of the house are entitled to seek permission from the head of the house to use the land.

Most people claimed that tensions or disputes regarding land tended to relate to inheritance. For example, one man commented that male siblings do not always respect their sister's claims to land. Another stated that when a man dies while he is still living on his wife's house land, male relatives of his widow might claim back this land.

It is generally agreed that fruit trees (apart from the sacred groves) belong to the person responsible for planting them (and their descendants) regardless of whether or not these are planted on house land. Most fruit trees, be they individually or communally owned, are subject to ritual prohibitions. Members of the houses of Lori Ubun inform the community when it is time to harvest the fruit of these trees. Penalties may be incurred for infractions of these prohibitions, usually in the form of a sacrificial offering to be made to the guardian spirits or ancestors who mediate the relationship between people and the land. Some informants stated that it was possible to 'get away' with breaking the rules by 'hiding away' or eating the fruits out of sight, surreptitiously.

Upland tenures are multilayered and complicated. They include notions of both communal entitlement based on ancestral histories of possession and individuated ownership based on inheritance and long-term cultivation. House members are entitled to farm their house land but may also farm areas of land belonging to other houses related through marriage. The principle of temporary matrilocal residence means that children may have access to their maternal house land but not their paternal house lands, and sometimes 'outsiders' are granted land through arrangements via 'adoptive' houses. Despite this complexity, informants stated that there were no members of the community who did not or could not gain access to land. Any land disputes arising within the community are usually dealt with at house level or between individuals and representatives of the houses involved in the disputes. However a number of people did raise the issue of encroachments from neighbouring groups who lay outside the jurisdiction of their house and community elders and were therefore more difficult to resolve.

### *The Lowland Community*

There is a high level of mobility and fluidity between the upland and lowland settlements of Uat. Individuals and families from the core houses of Uat who have long settled in Maliana town continue to participate in house-based activities, ceremonies and rituals in the upland settlement. Similarly, family members settled in the uplands will often travel to Maliana town to attend the weekly market, visit the health clinic or attend to matters at the sub-district or district administration. As members of core houses of Uat, lowland settlers continue to have rights to land in the uplands and in some cases may actively contribute to farming activities there. Some members of the community who previously lived in Maliana town and have chosen to return to the upland settlement continue to have rights to land in the lowlands and may actually share-crop this land with family members who remain settled in Maliana. The translocal character of Uat is a legacy of the past and represents a pattern that is widely experienced across Timor Leste.

There are multiple histories of how lowland settlers from Uat gained access to land in and around Maliana town and the Nunura plain, whether for house plots or cultivation. These histories date from the post-war period, the Indonesian occupation and post-1999. Many informants base their claims to land on family histories that describe a shift in livelihood practices from hunting to grazing, to shifting cultivation and finally to the more sedentary farming of permanent crops. These stories are often tied up with oral histories from Uat emphasizing the role members of certain houses played in clearing, burning and farming the land or digging irrigation channels.

Elders from Uat claim that in their father's day there were no permanent settlements of Uat people in the lowlands. They remember their fathers taking part in seasonal hunting parties to the lowland forests. At the time, the eucalypt forests of the Nunura plain were considered to be 'dangerous', untamed areas. Hunting parties would 'present' their horses and dogs to the ancestors before leaving Tapor (the original upland settlement) to ask for protection and a successful hunt. Later, the elders claim some people began to graze animals in the lowlands but it was not until after the Second World War that they began to clear land for farming.

Like many other migrants or 'latecomers' to the lowlands, informants from Uat acknowledge that the land on the Nunura plain originally belonged to groups from the areas of Saburai to the west, and Kailako to the east. In particular, they claim that in-migrant groups paid tribute to the land-holding houses of Achu and Achu Plaza (now part of the village of Manapa) in exchange for rights to use land in the lowlands.[36] In Uat oral histories, members of the houses of Duas Mali and Lua Laben (often referred collectively to as *asi no txua:* fields and palm wine) were the first to venture into the lowlands:

| | |
|---|---|
| *Balik ulu* | Open the path by throwing the spear |
| *Sesa be ka, dudu ma loa* | Spread out, open and broaden |
| *Sama teho, napa gh'e nu* | Tread and trample [the eucalypt] underfoot |

Members of these houses claim they were granted access to some land on the Nunura plain by the land-holding houses of Atchu and Atchu Plaza, and in exchange were expected to pay tribute:

| | |
|---|---|
| *Tere bale, lape bale* | We ask you, we give to you this land |
| *Datxu bale, prio bale* | This is the garden, this is the palm wine |
| *Dia Duas Mali, Lua Laben* | Duas Mali, Lua Laben |
| *Mara de'ena, m'ghen dia luro* | Use it, the end is ripe, the head is yellow |
| *Imi hodi tate, imi hodi toi* | When we come, give us part of the cob, pour us some of the wine |

Described in Uat narratives as an offering of palm wine and a portion of the harvest, this tribute is commonly referred to throughout Timor Leste as *rai te'en*, the 'waste' of the land (*kakata te'e, sura ra'a* in Kemak ritual language). Oral histories refer to general usufruct rights granted to members of the houses of Duas Mali and Lua Laben. However, many informants from Uat now settled in the lowlands claim highly individualized permanent rights to land.

36 Atchu and Atchu Plaza are also considered to be the custodians of the sacred water source of Kor-Luli on the Nunura plain.

A number of informants from Uat living in the lowlands link their claims to land to colonial 'development' programmes implemented during the post-war period. They claim that they themselves, their father or grandfather, were recruited by the local authorities to take part in work groups responsible for clearing areas of forest for farming. During the 1950s and 60s, the Portuguese colonial authorities urged the population to move into larger settlements in the lowlands on the fringes of the Nunura plain and work the land. These directives were usually given effect through the direction of local leaders (*liurai, chefe suco, chefe povoção*) and appear to have been implemented without the involvement of any customary groups claiming stewardship over lowland resources.[37] No formal documentation exists regarding the transferral of land to members of these work groups. However, the head of the district Land and Property Department stated that since independence a number of individuals have come forward to claim plots of land based on participation in these work groups. Indeed many claim that land they cultivated under these schemes was then appropriated by the Indonesian authorities or occupied by other individuals and families.

Despite the efforts of the colonial administration it appears that few people chose to settle permanently in the lowlands during this time.[38] Furthermore, according to informants from the Land and Property Department only a small number of individuals, mainly senior civil servants, wealthy business people or the Church, were ever issued any form of land title during the Portuguese era.[39] Informants recall that by the 1970s some coconut plantations had been established close to the administrative post of Maliana and a number of people from the uplands who owned livestock had cleared portions of land to build enclosures on the plain.[40] However, they also describe how, right up until the Indonesian invasion, much of the land on the Nunura plain was still uncultivated forest mostly used by upland populations for seasonal communal hunting.

More permanent settlement in the lowlands, and in particular Maliana town, was the direct consequence of the Indonesian invasion and occupation. During the months of political unrest that preceded the invasion in late 1975, there was a trickle of refugees into neighbouring West Timor, but it was the full impact military occupation that provoked massive displacement. Informants from Uat

37 In part, these directives were the result of a drive by the Portuguese authorities to make the colony more productive but land allocation was also used by the colonial administration as a means of supplementing local civil servant salaries.

38 It was also suggested that people avoided settling in the lowlands as a means of evading the Portuguese colonial head tax.

39 One official from the Land and Property Department suggested that few people obtained title to land during the Portuguese period, mainly owing to lack of resources, lack of access to information or because they saw no practical need to obtain title. He believed that those who did obtain title to land were able to do so because the colonial authorities favoured them.

40 Two of the larger land owners in Maliana known to have obtained title during this time did so for the use of land for cattle grazing (*aforamento com motivo da criaçao do animais*).

described how people fled the Indonesian troops and intensive bombing campaigns seeking refuge in the mountains on the slopes of Loelako Mountain or towards Bobonaro sub-district and Atsabe in Ermera district. Once the Indonesian troops had gained control of the area a number of sites such as the townships of Bobonaro and Maliana became 'holding centres' for the 'surrendering' civilian population. It was not until the early 1980s that the Indonesian authorities permitted the civilian population to leave these heavily guarded areas.

In the case of Uat, some but not all families were resettled to the 'new' town of Maliana. The process of resettlement was coordinated by the local East Timorese leadership in collaboration with the Indonesian military and civilian authorities. Informants recall how each family was allocated 20m × 20m plots of land on which to build their houses and house gardens. Some people claim they were resettled close to land that their family had farmed during the Portuguese period. But others suggest that there was little or no negotiation with local land-holding groups or customary authorities. New settlements had to be established along main roads, close to military posts or administrative centres. As a result, people tended to be resettled close to members of their own community in hamlet or village clusters and populations that had once formed part of dispersed upland communities essentially became members of close-knit neighbourhoods of the rapidly expanding town of Maliana.

From the early 1980s, the Indonesian authorities also began 'developing' Maliana town. As in other regional towns such as Ainaro, the authorities initially simply appropriated land without any attempt to identify previous owners and with little, if any, compensation. The present-day administration buildings, government housing schemes, schools, police and army barracks, and the hospital were all built during the Indonesian period. The town also experienced an influx of Indonesian settlers including civil servants, teachers, military, police, transmigrants and owners of small businesses. Most informants believe that the arrival of outsiders created a demand for land where this had previously not existed and people's attitudes towards land began to change. Land was no longer valued simply for its productivity but as an asset that could be transferred and transacted.

Increasingly, the state became the main reference point in relation to land and property in the lowlands. By the mid to late 1980s anyone wishing to build a house had to get planning approval and pay a house tax. Those who wished to obtain a title for their land and property, including agricultural land, could (for a fee) apply to the Lands Department (known in Indonesian as Kantor Agraria) to survey their land and issue a title.[41] Some informants from Uat claim to have obtained titles for land and property through this process. Others suggested that during the Indonesian period titles were often issued without investigating the

41 Informants from the current Directorate of Land and Property (*Direcção Terras e Propiedades*, DTP) have stated that despite a number of 'national projects' implemented to register land titles many people chose not to take part in order to avoid paying tax on their land or property.

history of the land or prior claims based on occupancy and use. Some believed that those in positions of authority, or individuals favoured by the Indonesian authorities, were able to take advantage of this oversight to grab large areas of land for themselves or political allies. DTP staff stated that there was a standard procedure for issuing titles for land and property during the Indonesian period. When a person approached the Lands Office to survey their land/property for the purposes of obtaining a title, the authorities were obliged to place a notice at the *suku* office that stipulated that any counter-claims had to be made within a certain period of time. However, reportedly this process was seldom transparent or fair – people could easily be intimidated from coming forward during the allocated time to make a counter-claim. Some informants from Maliana town suggested that, although these procedures may have existed in theory, in practice most people were either uninformed or unaware of their right to submit counter-claims.

Informants from Uat who were civil servants during the Indonesian period were offered public service housing (PERUMNAS) in one of two areas in Maliana town – near the airstrip in Ritabou village or in the neighbourhood of Ramos Kore. They claim that under the terms of such leases they were able to purchase the house outright over a period of seven years. One informant who returned to his property following the displacement in 1999 was concerned that the state might not recognize his rights to this property after independence. In particular, he questioned whether or not the state would recognize the rights of those who were yet to make final payments to purchase the property outright and what the status of individuals and families who occupied properties after 1999 might be.

In the violent aftermath of the UN-organized popular consultation in 1999, thousands of Maliana residents were forcibly displaced on trucks to camps in Indonesian West Timor. Those who were not taken by pro-integration militia, working in collaboration with the Indonesian military, sought refuge in surrounding mountains. The vast majority of refugees began returning from camps across the border or their mountain refuges once news of the arrival of INTERFET (International Forces for East Timor) had been announced. During the early weeks of spontaneous returns people sought shelter wherever they could. This included empty public buildings or private dwellings that had not been totally destroyed during the militia post-ballot rampage. Later, once local leaders who had formed part of the clandestine movement were able to reconnect, international agencies such as UNHCR were on the ground, and the UN Transitional Administration was in place, a more orderly system was implemented to facilitate return to places of origin. However, the violence and displacement of 1999 reawakened past land conflicts and created new tensions as some individuals and groups took advantage of the situation to either repossess land allegedly lost as a result of dispossession during the Portuguese and Indonesian periods, or reoccupy land and property that had been previously occupied by their political rivals.

A minority of informants from Uat acknowledged that they were currently living on land or property that was formerly occupied by someone else. In most of these cases informants sought to explain their current situation by suggesting that the owners had fled to West Timor in 1999 and were unlikely to return, or that they were directly related to the rightful owners. In some cases informants justified their actions in political terms by suggesting that the former owner was a member of the pro-integration militia or ex-Indonesian military, or that the former occupant had originally stolen/occupied land on which the property was built from his or her family.

Since independence, some informants from Uat claim to have purchased land and/or property in the lowlands directly from individuals claiming prior ownership. While in many cases this has been done in good faith, informants suggested that following the displacement of 1999 some individuals had taken advantage of the situation, claiming ownership to property that they had already sold outright to Indonesian civil servants or East Timorese who were unlikely to return.

Few informants interviewed held any form of documentation in the form of official land titles or transaction records regarding the status of their land and property. It was common for informants to claim to have negotiated access to land 'according to custom' (Tetun: *tuir adat, tuir kultura*), whether through marriage, through the exchange of certain goods and services with local land-holding groups, or through long-term occupancy and use.[42] In cases of long-term occupancy and use informants regularly referred to investments made in land or property such as the planting of specific trees or crops and the building of permanent housing.

According to the hamlet head of Uat, who lives in the lowlands, any members of the upland community of Uat currently seeking to transfer to the lowlands would most likely have to arrange access to land through share-cropping or rent agreements with current land owners. In general these arrangements are made directly between private individuals and do not appear to have to be mediated through customary authorities or the local community leadership. However, the hamlet head also suggested that parties to any form of land or property transaction might organize a meeting with neighbours and key figures in the community where traditional offerings of betel nut, palm wine and tobacco might be exchanged between parties and those present would act as witnesses to the transaction.

While in the upland settlement of Uat attachments to land continue to be governed by principles and practices that draw on ancestral histories and patterns of settlement and cultivation, for the lowland population of Uat the impact of Portuguese colonial and Indonesian occupational policies of resettlement and land development have brought about a transformation in patterns of land relations. The gradual take-up and utilization of blocks and cultivated fields in the growing township of Maliana and its hinterland has seen a shift in the basis of claims away from customary principles of mythic origins and precedence, to highly individualized assertions of ownership derived from occupation or physical possession in some cases but by no means in all sanctioned by the regulatory authority of the state. This process of transition highlights the limits of recognizing custom as the default legal basis

42 It is commonly claimed that any documentation was lost or burnt during the post-ballot violence and displacement or in some cases no documents were issued either in Portuguese or Indonesian times.

for land entitlements in rural districts, where histories of colonial and neo-colonial administration, combined with patterns of population mobility and changes in cultivation techniques, have created claims based on possession (and dispossession) rather than grant from customary authority.

## Conclusion

In this exploration of the political and historical context of land relations in Maliana sub-district, processes of continuity and change have significantly altered perceptions and practices associated with land attachment. In some areas, most notably those that have been least affected by colonial processes of improvement, contemporary practice continues to be strongly guided by traditional appeals to locally emplaced political authorities and patterns of land entitlement drawn from ancestral precedence. Land attachments for these communities are anchored in the oral histories of founder ancestors and the networks of kinship and alliance that inform the social basis for claims to land. These principles and appeals are evident in claims and assertions of land ownership throughout the area, exemplified by the mountain community of Saburai, which offers a striking example of the resilience of customary conventions and the continuing relevance of ritually sanctioned decision making that works to bind members of Saburai within a moral community.

Elsewhere, and particularly in the lowlands of Maliana and the Nunura plain, the intrusion of Portuguese and later Indonesian development agendas overruled or marginalized the role of customary authority and introduced competing avenues for securing access to land and formalizing a commoditized land ownership. This was secured by relocating highland communities on to the lowlands and coercively encouraging the opening up of previously uncultivated savannah lands for irrigated agriculture and seasonal cropping. For the people of Uat this has led to a settlement division into upland and lowland residential communities with continuing interaction and membership of lowland settlers with their origin settlements in the mountains.

Competing forms of authority and the highly modified land tenure arrangements that have been produced over half a century of engagement with regulatory state systems have also created a degree of uncertainty and the potential for disputes and land conflicts to emerge over contested claims to the new lands secured at the urging of government. In Chapter 10 we examine the long-standing conflict between Uat and Meganutu householders over a subdivision of rice paddy land in the lowlands that could not be resolved through mediation channels. The numerous failed attempts to secure a solution only highlight the limits of customary authority in these circumstances where there are no longer more encompassing levels of customary authority through which to appeal. In the past, inter-group or inter-village conflict could easily lead to violence and physical reprisals, and, as village communities continue to wait for law and administrative clarity from state regulated institutions, land conflicts remain a source of resentment and ill-feeling between rival groups.

**References**

CAVR 2005. Chega! Report of the Commission for Reception, Truth and Reconciliation of Timor Leste. Dili: CAVR.

Census 2010. Census of Population and Housing. Dili: Direcção Nacional de Estatística and United National Population Fund.

Clamagirand (-Renard), B. 1980. The Social Organization of the Ema of Timor, in J.J. Fox (ed.), *The Flow of Life: Essays on Eastern Indonesia*. Cambridge, MA: Harvard University Press, pp. 134–51.

Forman, S. 1980. Descent, Alliance and Exchange Ideology among the Makassae of East Timor, in J.J. Fox (ed.), *The Flow of Life: Essays on Eastern Indonesia*. Cambridge, MA: Harvard University Press, pp. 152–77.

Fox, J.J. 2002. Drawing from the Past to Prepare for the Future: Responding to the Challenges of Food Security in East Timor, in H.d. Costa, C. Piggin, C.J. d. Cruz and J.J. Fox (eds), *Agriculture: New Directions for a New Nation East Timor (Timor Leste)*. Dili, East Timor: ACIAR.

Fox, J.J. 1995. Installing the 'Outsider' Inside: The Exploration of an Epistemic Austronesian Cultural Theme and its Social Significance. Paper to the First Conference of the European Association for Southeast Asian Studies: Local Transformation and Common Heritage in Southeast Asia, 29 June to 1 July 1995.

McWilliam, A.R. 2008. Customary Governance in Timor Leste, in D. Mearns. (ed.), *Democratic Governance in Timor Leste: Reconciling the Local and the National*. Darwin: Charles Darwin University Press, pp. 143–59.

Oxfam 2004. *Overview of the Rice Sector in Timor Leste*. Oxfam.

Sherlock, K. 1983. East Timor: Liurais and Chefes de suco; indigenous authorities in 1952 – Timor Leste: liurais e chefes de suco; as autoridades indigenas no ano de 1952. Darwin: Kevin Sherlock.

Traube, E.G. 1986. *Cosmology and Social Life: Ritual Exchange among the Mambai of East Timor*. Chicago: University of Chicago Press.

# Chapter 9
# Possession, Custom and Conflict around the Town of Ainaro

This chapter provides a case study from the rural town of Ainaro located in Ainaro sub-district 110 kilometres southwest of Dili. While previous chapters have focused on the relative resilience of customary communities in East Timor, and the capacity of customary frameworks to manage tensions over land arising from historical patterns of displacement and resettlement in rural areas, this chapter considers the impact of Portuguese and Indonesian era policies and practices on land tenures within a predominantly peri-urban setting. It highlights, in particular, the complexity of claims based on competing interpretations of possessory legitimacy and authority. This complexity is relevant to the potential application of the draft 2012 land law, including its rule of long-term possession, which we consider further in Chapter 11.

The chapter begins with some background to Ainaro sub-district. This is followed by an overview of customary relations and the nature of customary land tenures among the southern Mambae of Ainaro sub-district. The chapter then focuses on Ainaro town and its hinterland. It describes the impact of Portuguese policies aimed at extending territorial control and improving agricultural productivity as well as the destructive effects of displacement and resettlement during the Indonesian occupation on customary relationships with land. It illustrates the various categories of competing land claimants in contemporary East Timor, including current occupiers and Portuguese and Indonesian titleholders, as well as the role played by the state. Finally, it considers the way in which emerging issues of individuation, commodification and titling of rights have complicated these competing categories of claim.

## Locating Ainaro

The rural town of Ainaro is located within the administrative boundaries of the village (*suku*) of Ainaro, which is situated in Ainaro sub-district, in the district of Ainaro (see Map 9.1).

Ainaro sub-district represents the south-eastern limits of a Mambae speaking territory that spans across the central highlands of Timor Leste from Dili into the districts of Ermera, Aileu, Same and Ainaro. The sub-district comprises seven villages. The vast majority of the population of the villages of Ainaro, Suro Kraik, Soro, and Manutasi speak a southern variant of Mambae (Hull 2003), while the people of Cassa and Mau-Nunu are predominantly Bunak-speakers. In some of the upland communities of Mau-Ulu village a dialect of Kemak is also spoken.

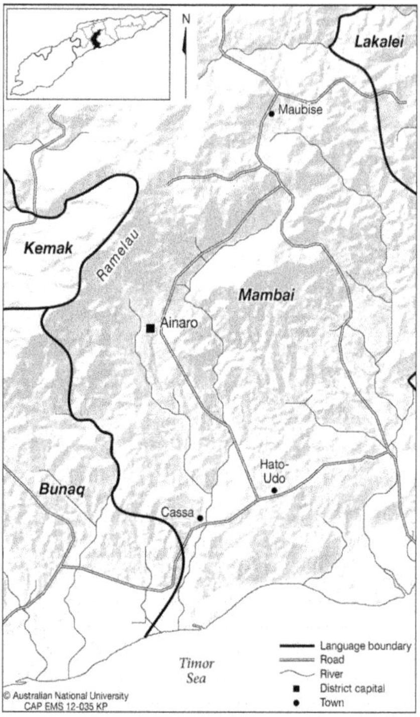


**Map 9.1 The Mambai language group in Ainaro district**
*Source*: ANU Cartography 2012

**Table 9.1 Population figures for Ainaro sub-district**

| Village | Male | Female | Total |
|---|---|---|---|
| Ainaro | 3,640 | 3,297 | 6,937 |
| Suro-Kraik | 580 | 508 | 1,088 |
| Soro | 931 | 930 | 1,861 |
| Manutasi | 902 | 802 | 1,704 |
| Cassa | 1,267 | 1,228 | 2,495 |
| Mau-Ulo | 246 | 224 | 470 |
| Mau-Nuno | 517 | 486 | 1,003 |
| **Total** | **8,083** | **7,575** | **15,558** |

*Source*: Census 2010

Throughout the sub-district households are engaged in the swidden cultivation of staple foodstuffs such as maize, cassava, sweet potatoes and beans. In the upland areas to the north of the sub-district, elevated terrain and relative humidity provide optimal conditions for coffee cultivation, while to the south the flood plains of the Sarai and Mau Mali rivers are used for rice cultivation. Coconut production was a significant crop during the Portuguese colonial period.

In order to understand the complexity of current claims to land within Ainaro town and the political sensitivities related to access to land and natural resources within Ainaro sub-district, some historical background is required. Ainaro sub-district represents the heart of the former kingdom of Suro-Ainaro. According to local histories, customary authority within the kingdom of Suro-Ainaro was constructed on two complementary pillars. On the one hand, kinship relations and 'internal' affairs of the community relating to the moral and social order were known as the *nam meta ni* (affairs of the night). On the other hand, political jurisdictions and the management of 'external' relations with 'outsiders', such as the state, formed part of the everyday affairs of the world, the *nam ada ni* (affairs of the day) (Corte-Real 2000). Historically, issues relating to land and natural resources have engaged both these areas of customary authority. Access to land and natural resources was, and continues largely to be, embedded in kinship relations and inseparable from local understandings of what constitutes social and moral order. However, issues regarding the territorial boundaries of broader political jurisdictions involve more complex networks of exchange and alliance.

According to local historians, by the beginning of the twentieth century the kingdom of Suro-Ainaro was divided into four territories, corresponding to the present-day villages of Soro, Nunumogue, Mau-Ulo, Ainaro and Manutasi, each under the jurisdiction of paired ruling houses or *um dato*.[1] These four pairs of houses were described in kinship terms as *an-hine pat, an-mane pat* (four daughters, four sons) and fell under the overall jurisdiction of the *liurai* (king/noble) houses of *Pucoli-Sarin, Dar Ha' and Ai-Tua*, known collectively as *In nor Am* (mother and father), based in what is now the village of Suro Kraik (Corte-Real 2007). The villages of Cassa/Maununu and Hatu-Udo, which now form part of Ainaro sub-district, did not fall within the traditional jurisdiction of Suro-Ainaro. However, relations between these groups and Suro-Ainaro were expressed in terms of sibling kinship whereby Suro-Ainaro *Nai-Mane* (male kingdom) was 'brother' to Cassa and Hatu-Udo, both *Nai-Hine* (female kingdoms) (Corte-Real 2007).

On the surface, the language of kinship served to legitimize local political hierarchies and to establish conditions of reciprocity between the various political entities that made up the kingdom of Suro-Ainaro and its neighbours. However, the history of Ainaro sub-district, and the former kingdom of Suro-Ainaro, has been marked by ongoing power struggles and shifting alliances between various groups. In 1907, the Portuguese military post (*posto*) of Ainaro was established

1 The houses of Bissimau and Dacicoli ruled over a territory corresponding to the village of Soro, Lequiteti and Dadia over Nunumogue, Aloko and Mausuru over Mau-Ulo and the houses of Laubei and Mauteni governed the people of the present-day village of Ainaro and Manutasi (Corte-Real 2007).

on the site of present-day Ainaro town.[2] This event marked the establishment of a long-term alliance between the Mambae-speaking rulers of Suro-Ainaro and the Portuguese colonial authorities. In the context of the Wars of Pacification, the kingdom of Suro-Ainaro fought alongside the Portuguese against the 'rebel' kingdoms of Manufahi and their allies in the southern kingdom of Kamenasa (Pélissier 1996). And, later during the Second World War, the king of Suro-Ainaro, Dom Aleixo Corte-Real, was most famously captured and killed 'in the defence of Portugal' by the Japanese occupying forces. In reward for their loyalty to Portugal the rulers of Suro-Ainaro were able to extend their authority over a vast territory that included the *postos* of Maubisse, Hatu-Builico, Ainaro, Hata-Udo, Turiscai, parts of Zumalai and briefly also incorporated Alas and Same (Sherlock 1983).

Undoubtedly, local rivalries and contested positions of authority pre-date the establishment of the Portuguese military post in 1907 (see Rawski 2002). However, these enmities were exacerbated by colonial interventions during the Portuguese colonial period and reinforced throughout the Indonesian occupation. For example, the Indonesian authorities took advantage of the lingering resentment felt by those forced to submit to the authority of the rulers of Suro-Ainaro. Some of the founding members of the pro-integration party APODETI and key members of the local pro-Indonesian local militia Mahidi were recruited amongst those who lost land and power as a consequence of fighting against the Portuguese during the Manufahi wars or allying themselves with the Japanese during the Second World War.[3] Present-day episodes of communal violence and tensions over access to land and natural resources must be placed within this wider historical and political context.

## Customary Relations and Claims to Land

*Um nor Ap Hat nor Rae* – House and hearth (fire), Rock and Land.
Ancient Mambae saying:

> Without a home you won't belong,without a flame you cannot see and if there is no solid foundation you are nobody.Respect the land, because it gave you life and within that land should be your last resting place![4]

2 *Posto* denotes a Portuguese-era administrative centre.

3 Associacão Popular Democratica Timorense (Timorese Popular Democratic Association), APODETI was founded on the 27th May 1974. The first Indonesian-era governor of East Timor, Arnaldo dos Reis Araujo, a founder member of APODETI was from Manutasi. Established in 1998, Mati Hidup dengan Indonesia (Life or Death with Indonesia), MAHIDI was based in Cassa.

4 Thanks to ACR for quotation.

### Customary Relations

Among the southern-Mambae communities of Ainaro sub-district, rights to access land and natural resources are embedded in customary relations between lineage-based groups centred on sacred houses called *um lisa.*[5] The term *um lisa* is used to describe both the physical structure of the sacred house and its members. In 2007, the village head of Ainaro town compiled a list of all the *um lisa* of Ainaro sub-district. A total of 251 *um lisa* were identified, 148 of which were from predominantly southern-Mambae-speaking areas. Many of the original sacred house structures were destroyed during the course of the Indonesian invasion and occupation, or fell into disrepair as a result of population displacement and resettlement. However, since independence there has been a clear trend towards rebuilding these houses. In 2007, of the 251 houses, 25 were in good condition, 5 were almost complete and 147 were in the planning stages of being rebuilt.[6] The widespread rebuilding of sacred houses in Ainaro sub-district is consistent with the revival of custom since the end of the Indonesian occupation in other parts of East Timor.

Membership of an *um lisa* usually consists of agnatically related male kinsmen, their in-married spouses and children. However, there are exceptions. In some cases a person may be incorporated into a particular *um lisa* because they have been chosen by members of a community of related houses to perform a specific ritual or political role historically associated with that house. In other cases membership may be determined by the status of (generational) marriage prestations between *um lisa*. The exchange of gifts, known as *barlake* in Tetun, as part of marriage negotiations is still common practice in Ainaro sub-district. At different stages during the course of marriage negotiations, members of the husband's family (*hin-hat*) will provide the wife's family (*um-man*) with money, buffalo and gold discs and receive traditional cloth, pigs and rice in exchange. In some cases only upon completion of this bridal exchange will the wife and any children usually become full members of the husband's house.

An *um lisa* is typically divided into a number of 'branch' houses. These subsidiary houses represent individual sibling lineages stemming from a single common ancestral house also known as an *um tu*. Lineage houses are either referred to as elder (*kaka*) or younger (*ali*) houses based on their relative proximity to their common ancestral house. Overall moral and ritual authority for the members of houses constituting an *um lisa* usually lies in the oldest male kinsmen of the *um tu*. The most important of these are referred to as the *mai ta bali* (keeper of the house), whose role is to safeguard the sacred objects of the group; and the *gase'e ubu*

5 The word *um* means house and the word *lisa* can be translated as 'culture' or 'cult'; it is used to refer to the particular cultural practices to which members of an *um lisa* adhere. In some cases *lisa* has been translated as customary law but its application is much broader.

6 No data was available for the remaining houses.

(keeper of the words),[7] whose role is to be the spokesperson for the *um lisa* group and also to pass judgement or arbitrate in traditional conflict resolution processes.

Membership of an *um lisa* entails a number of entitlements but also a set of obligations. These entitlements and obligations constitute a moral code broadly described as *lisa*. Obligations range from dietary restrictions to the use of family names or providing goods and services associated with ceremonial exchange. Entitlements include spiritual protection, the opportunity to draw on reciprocal obligations in time of need, and access to ancestral lands and specific natural resources. Adherence to one's *lisa* is essential to full participation in the social and ritual life of the broader community. Failure to do so may result in personal illness or loss and the imposition of a fine or sanctions by elders of the *um lisa* group. It is still commonly felt that until reparations, such as the payment of a fine or the performance of an appropriate ritual, are made an individual (and in some cases the immediate family) remains at risk of further misfortune and may be excluded from certain activities and rituals. This phenomenon of widespread belief in spiritualized sanctions for transgressions of custom is present in all our field sites.

*Um lisa* are exogamous and therefore must seek marriage with members of other groups. *Um lisa* related by marriage are classified as 'wife-givers' (*um-man*) and 'wife-takers' (*hin-hat*) in relation to one another. Traditionally, marriage alliances between houses were negotiated settlements involving the exchange of goods and services. Over time, preferential 'paths' of alliance have developed between certain *um lisa*, reinforcing bonds of interdependence aimed at maintaining lineage authority and collectivity. For example, throughout Ainaro sub-district it is still common practice for men to marry their mother's brother's daughters. For the southern Mambae, this form of cross-cousin marriage is called *kai ana, nai ana* and is believed to reproduce the 'ideal' relationship of their founding ancestors or in ritual language *do oe hati* ('to follow in the footsteps of the ancestors') (Corte-Real 2007).

Socially, wife-giver houses have a higher status than wife-taker houses on the basis that wife-giver groups are vital for the continuation of a wife-taker lineage. Although younger generations – many of whom have moved to larger towns or Dili in search of education or employment – are challenging these traditional marriage practices, for those who remain in more rural settings the pressure to conform is strong as family livelihoods are intimately bound to these enduring networks of alliance and exchange.

In the past, groups of *um lisa* were often ordered around various 'origin' settlements. Located on elevated ground called a *ria* or *lau*, most of these sites

7 Multiple terms, often mixed with Tetun vocabulary, are used. The keeper of the house or elder who sits in the house is sometimes described as *bei lulik* (sacred ancestor), or *tata bei* (grandfather ancestor) in reference to his position as oldest living descendant of the founder ancestor. The spokesperson or the keeper of the word is sometimes referred to as *tat gas*. Often the person holding this office has the power to arbitrate or resolve conflict *des* (or *Tes*) *ter* – traditional justice system.

are now abandoned in a physical sense, but still have cultural power as sources of collective identity and affiliation. According to local narratives, among a group of houses sharing an origin settlement there was usually a pair of houses whose ancestors were considered to be the founders of that community.[8] Representing respectively female and male and referred to as *in nor am* (mother and father), these houses originally laid claim to overall ritual and political authority over the group. Narratives of origin and settlement link these houses to specific sites as hilltops, springs, rocks or caves. While these links serve to reinforce the emplaced nature of ritual authority and the privileged relationship between founder *um lisa* and the land, defining the distinct territories that fell under the jurisdiction of these houses is not an easy task. Territorial boundaries are notoriously fuzzy: they are shaped by histories of war and alliance, migration and displacement but also by the influence and imposition of administrative boundaries such as village and hamlet. As discussed in Chapter 11, the fuzziness of group boundaries in Ainaro sub-district is significant for the legal determination of community property and community protection zones under the draft land law of East Timor.

Local narratives describe how over time the founder houses gradually devolved political power to certain subsidiary or 'in-marrying' houses. Retreating into a purely ritual role, the elders of these founder houses are often described as those who 'sit and look after the house' or 'sit and look after the rock and tree'. Today their principal role is to manage the relationship between people, the land (which is the source of life) and the cosmos. In the process of devolving political power, the founder houses are said to have designated various roles and functions to the remaining houses. Historically, such distinctions were made manifest during communal rituals or ceremonies where members of each house performed specific functions, and ceremonial wine, food and betel nuts were distributed according to a prescribed order. Other ranks and titles were bestowed on various houses, as discrete communities of houses sharing an origin village were incorporated into broader networks of alliance and exchange that formed the basis of the 'kingdoms' that emerged during the slow course of the Portuguese colonization (Forman 1978). The intricate webs of ritual and political authority in Ainaro, as in other rural districts of East Timor, illustrate the mechanisms through which collective order was maintained in contexts of political change and population growth.

The collective identity of groups of *um lisa* sharing a settlement of origin was originally maintained through periodic participation in communal ceremonies and rituals. Although the vast majority of origin settlements have now been abandoned, a number of informants stated that house members do continue to reconvene at these sites to take part in specific communal rituals and in particular those related to the agricultural cycle. For example, houses from the hamlet of Nugufu assemble yearly

8 Narratives of origin vary greatly across Ainaro sub-district. While some trace their ancestors to the land itself, others relate to 'root' houses in the central highlands and recount narratives of arrival and settlement sometimes involving the displacement or alliance with original inhabitants.

at the sacred site of *Hat Mau Bis* to partake in a harvest ceremony of thanksgiving to the sun and the earth for their bounty. In Hatumera, related houses convene at the altar of the founder house of Mailako, or at the sacred tree of *Gou' Pu* to pray for a successful planting season. However, other informants suggested that there has been a marked decline in the level of participation in these ceremonies.

Some informants traced the decline in participation to the Portuguese era. One informant claimed that the Portuguese introduced a tax (or fine) on the slaughter of animals, which undermined the element of commensality central to many communal rituals and ceremonies. Another suggested that, with the introduction of Catholicism, local missionaries and new converts discouraged participation in what they perceived to be 'pagan' or idolatrous rituals. Most informants said that displacement and restrictions on movement and large gatherings during the Indonesian occupation reduced the possibilities for communal ceremonies. However, a minority suggested that, rather than experiencing a decline, certain customs remained strong during Indonesian times since many Indonesian soldiers and immigrants came from areas in Indonesia with a strong sense of *adat* or custom. In general, informants felt that during this time, rather than abandon certain rituals, people turned to their own *um lisa* and conducted smaller, family rituals. Others clarified that, whilst participation in *um lisa* level activities such as *lia mate* (mortuary rites) or *lia moris* (life-cycle rites) remained strong, fewer people were likely to partake in larger communal rituals, which represented a significant burden especially to poorer households.

According to community elders and ritual specialists interviewed for this study, reduced participation in communal ritual over time has meant that today few people fully understand the meanings and histories at the heart of ceremonies aimed at reinforcing the sense of community between *um lisa,* and interdependence with the land. One informant believed that individualism and the influence of outside cultures and trends brought about by globalization are undermining the sense of community. He feared that most young people think about themselves or their immediate family rather than the broader, more traditional community of *um lisa.* Changing attitudes and changing practices in relation to ritual also reflect changes in attitudes and practices regarding the relationship between people and the land. As people have moved or been displaced farther from their ancestral lands, many have also abandoned the cultural practices associated with the land that serve to reinforce these bonds of interdependence and collective action.

### *Customary Claims to Land*

*Um lisa* members claim rights to portions of a common landed inheritance. Typically, *um lisa* land comprises land farmed and settled by a named pair of founder ancestors and any land subsequently acquired by their descendants. Although *um lisa* elders stated that it is the responsibility of each generation to safeguard the integrity of the legacy of their ancestors, a number acknowledged that today the ancestral lands of various *um lisa* are not 'common property' as such, and that individual members of subsidiary houses often have heritable rights to specific parcels of land passed on from father to son. Despite this process of fragmentation into individually held parcels of land, a residual notion of what constitutes 'communal' or 'ancestral' land remains insofar as *um lisa* elders continue to be called upon to resolve land disputes between house members and/or members of other houses and, in some cases, may be consulted with regard to transactions of land considered to form part of the ancestral legacy.

Across Ainaro sub-district, informants described how any disputes, including land disputes, between *um lisa* members had to be managed within customary *um lisa* social hierarchies. More difficult or complex disputes also involve reference to village government authority. The starting point for any conflict resolution is the headman (*mone tu*) of a particular branch or *um lisa* lineage, who is able to *tesi lia* (Tetun: 'cut the words' or arbitrate). If the dispute is not resolved at this level then it should be brought to the attention of the elders of the *um lisa* (usually male heads of household and the *gase'e ubu* (Tetun: *lia nain*, spokesperson/keeper of the word). If no resolution is found within the *um lisa* then a dispute might be taken to the hamlet head. In these cases, it is common for the hamlet head to reconvene with the *um lisa* elders to try to find a solution. Where the hamlet head is unable to resolve the problem then the dispute will be taken to the village head who often calls on the village *lia nain* (village elder member of village council). If the dispute involves people from two or more *um lisa* then representatives from both groups are involved in mediation and arbitration. Many informants stated that it was problematic for members of *um lisa* related by kin or marriage to take their disputes or problems to the village head or to the local sub-district authorities. They suggested that this would then require a process of 'reconciliation' between the houses to restore the balance of reciprocal relations. All informants stated that in the case of any dispute involving violence such cases had to be referred directly to the police.

### *Access to Land through Marriage Agreements*

One of the most common ways of gaining access to another *um lisa*'s land was (and continues to be) through marriage. Historically, the granting of access to land and natural resources for in-marrying males was used as a means of establishing a political alliance with another *um lisa* group, in particular where the in-marrying group posed an external threat to a founder house or group of houses. It also seems to have been a means of securing labour required for the slashing, clearing and burning of new swidden fields.

Generally, rights to land conferred through marriage do not involve the transferral of outright 'ownership' to in-marrying males and their associated *um lisa* but do grant extensive rights to control access to this land and harvest produce. In some limited cases where long-established reciprocal relations through marriage exist between *um lisa*, members of the in-marrying *um lisa* are considered to have authority over all matters concerning the management of land granted by their wife-givers. However, where the sale of land is contemplated, issues of the overall authority of the original wife-giver *um lisa* over the land come into play. In some cases, the children of in-marrying males also have rights to inherit this land from their grandfather through the female line. However, these claims appear to be weak as informants stated that it was often the case that male relatives on the mother's side (and sometimes even the father's side) contest these claims. They also clarified that, in some cases, members of one *um lisa* might negotiate access to another *um lisa*'s land, regardless of whether there was a history of marriage alliance between the two groups. In these cases usufruct rights might be granted in exchange for some offering or part of the harvest (Tetun: *rai te'en*).

### *Contested Interpretations of Possession: The Commodification of Customary Land*

Rights to land embedded in these customary relations have been progressively challenged by the policies and practices of successive colonial powers, which has led to the differentiation and commodification of land. Differing notions of possessory entitlements among informants reflect their own particular experiences of colonial policies and practices and highlight the difficulty of reconciling claims to land based on multiple sources of authority and legitimacy. For example, informants asserting ancestral rights to land argue that the founder ancestors allocated all land to the constituent houses of Ainaro and therefore that no land remains 'unclaimed' or 'abandoned'. They back up their claims with reference to ancestral histories of settlement and particular geographical markers or features.[9] Echoing ancestral histories of first possession, individuals and groups recruited into work groups during the Portuguese colonial era, and responsible for 'opening' up previously unfarmed tracts of land, argue that this previously unclaimed land was rightfully theirs. In some cases narratives of historically negotiated access to land with local land-holding groups serve to back up these claims. Informants who were forcibly displaced and relocated to Ainaro town during the Indonesian occupation emphasize the strength of long-term occupancy and use of land, and in some cases refer (incorrectly) to Indonesian land law regarding an alleged right to claim ownership of land after a five-year occupancy period.[10]

9 It is difficult to judge whether such insistence on the pre-allocated nature of all land is a reaction to the fear of future loss of land or a reaction to historical acts of dispossession For example, under Portuguese colonial law of 1901 all land proved not to be held by Portuguese title was deemed to belong to the state. A map of Portuguese Timor was produced dividing land held by loyal *liurai* and land 'without a master'. The latter was vested in the Portuguese state and therefore could be the subject of land title. Later, in 1910 the governor of Timor issued a decree enabling him to make grants of up to 2,500 hectares of 'unoccupied' land – to establish native tenure the occupier had to have built or cultivated at least half the area.

10 As with other civil law systems, Indonesian law allows for a right of prescription after 20 years occupation: see further Fitzpatrick 1997.

The following case study from Ainaro town aims to examine the development of these differing notions of possessory entitlements. It describes the impact of colonial policies and practices on forms of land tenure embedded in customary relations and illustrates the various categories of competing land claimants in contemporary East Timor, including current occupiers and Portuguese and Indonesian titleholders, as well as the role played by the state. This urban/peri-urban example includes a more prominent role for the state, under its various guises in East Timor, particularly as the infrastructure needs of urban development have led to land acquisition under legal powers of eminent domain. As in Lautem, but more notably because of its urban context, increased demand for land in Ainaro has promoted individualization of property claims, while also promoting chronic uncertainty and conflict where overlapping claims have interacted with multiple reference points for property legitimacy and authority. The case study also highlights the way in which some claims to alienable ownership under the draft 2012 land law of East Timor, on the basis of long-term possession, will be inconsistent with long-standing customary limits to entitlement based on histories of in-marriage, in-migration and forced resettlement.

## Case Study:
## Ainaro Town

The rural town of Ainaro is the administrative capital of Ainaro district and Ainaro sub-district. It is located within the administrative boundaries of the village (*suku*) of Ainaro. The village of Ainaro is composed of seven hamlets. Of these Hatumera, Lugatu and Teliga are considered to be 'mountain' (*foho*) or rural hamlets, while Ainaro, Sabago, Builco and Nugufu constitute the bulk of Ainaro town.[11]

Ainaro town was almost completely destroyed in 1999 by pro-autonomy militia and elements of the Indonesian military. Practically all public buildings including the district hospital were destroyed; the Catholic mission school, Canossian residence and almost 80 per cent of all private dwellings were also burnt and looted. Many of the inhabitants of Ainaro town fled or were forcibly displaced to West Timor; others sought shelter in the surrounding hills and mountains. While the majority of East Timorese former residents of Ainaro have now returned, or resettled in the capital Dili, some remain in West Timor or elsewhere in Indonesia and many non-East Timorese former residents, including Indonesian civil servants and business people, have not returned and are not expected toreturn.

Although the rehabilitation and reconstruction of basic infrastructure in Ainaro town has been slow, a number of public services now are available. There are two public primary schools, a public pre-secondary and secondary school, an out-patient health clinic, a hospital, and a police station. In 2007, the town water

11 To clarify the various administrative units known as 'Ainaro': Ainaro hamlet falls within Ainaro village, which is situated in Ainaro sub-district, in the district of Ainaro.

supply and electricity were also rehabilitated. The town market and abattoir is in the process of being refurbished and housing for the local police is also being built. The district and sub-district administration continue to occupy buildings rehabilitated during the UN Transitional Administration.

While a number of local residents are employed as public servants, the majority are engaged in various forms of subsistence farming. Households farm a variety of crops including maize, beans, potatoes and root crops in swidden gardens on land surrounding Ainaro town. Permanent and seasonal fruits and other market vegetables are often grown in house plots or uncultivated areas of land in and around Ainaro town. A number of households have access to rice fields to the south of the town, near the neighbouring village of Cassa, or to the east near Manutasi. Many households also cultivate coffee in small plantations in upland areas. It is common for households to keep pigs and chickens; only a limited number graze cattle in upland pastures.

There are two markets in Ainaro town. The first is located close to the old town centre and was originally built during the Portuguese period. The second, larger market is temporarily located in the 'new' town close to the Indonesian-era district administrator's office, which is currently being rebuilt. Saturday is the main market day in Ainaro and people travel from surrounding villages, sub-districts and districts to buy and sell their produce. There are also a number of shops in town selling a wide variety of manufactured goods. Many of these shops are owned and run by Chinese-Indonesian or Chinese-Timorese.

The size and composition of Ainaro town has changed considerably over time. Today, Ainaro village has a population of 6,937 people, the majority of whom live in Ainaro town (Census 2010). This accounts for approximately 45 per cent of the total sub-district population. The population of Ainaro town rose rapidly in the aftermath of the Indonesian invasion as communities were displaced from remote areas and resettled closer to military installations and administrative centres such as Ainaro town. Since independence, the rate of return to remote areas has been relatively slow with larger numbers of people continuing to migrate from rural areas to urban areas. While a small proportion of the current population includes persons displaced from Dili in the aftermath of the political violence in 2006, the most common reasons for moving to urban areas since independence are access to education and employment opportunities (Census 2010).

Demographic changes have led to changing attitudes and practices associated with access to land and natural resources. Since the Portuguese first established a permanent presence in Ainaro town, customary beliefs and practices relating to the land and land use have come under stress. Over time, Ainaro town residents have developed a more commodified view of land leading to the differentiation of land into smaller household-based holdings. The principles of land access based on *um lisa* ancestral attachments and relations between *um lisa* groups have been challenged by notions of rights to land based on long-term occupancy as well as Portuguese and Indonesian land law. Since independence, multiple and competing claims to land in and around Ainaro town have emerged between individuals, and between individuals and the state. Claims are based on ancestral attachments, long-term occupancy and local understandings of entitlements carried over from Portuguese and Indonesian land law.

*The Portuguese Period:*
*Compulsory Labour and Land Differentiation*

According to local informants, prior to the arrival of the Portuguese, there were few settlements on the plain of Orluli between the Mau Mali and Sarai Rivers where the town of Ainaro is now located. Most of the land was uncultivated or swamp land and bamboo forest. In 1907, on the recommendation of the rulers of Suro-Ainaro, the Portuguese established a military post close to the bamboo forests near the Mau Mali river (Corte-Real 2007). Later in the 1930s, the Catholic Church founded a large church and established a mission school in the town. For most of the Portuguese period, Ainaro Vila (Portuguese: town) consisted of a few dusty streets, inhabited mainly by colonial troops, civil servants, Chinese traders and local East Timorese notables, *assimilado* families mainly from the *liurai*, or ruling families of Sur-Ainaro.[12]

The land on which the Portuguese established the *posto* of Ainaro was considered to form part of the territories under the jurisdiction of *Laubei* and *Mauteni*, the ruling *um lisa* of the hamlet of Ainaro-Sabago Leophat.[13] Within the social hierarchy of customary governance, described above, the *dato* (rulers) of *Laubei* and *Mauteni* were politically subordinate to the rulers of Suro-Ainaro based in Suru-Kraik. The arrival of the Portuguese marked the rise in importance of the noble houses of Suro-Ainaro. And, as Ainaro town grew, members of these families moved to the plain of Orluli occupying land for residential and agricultural use.

At the time of the arrival of the Portuguese, the majority of the population of Ainaro-Sabago Leophat was engaged in shifting cultivation and lived in dispersed highland settlements. The current head of Ainaro hamlet claimed that the majority of the *um lisa* of Ainaro-Sabago Leophat were originally located in the mountains near Ai Mer Lau and Foho Lema and later they settled closer to the current location of Ainaro town at a hill called Sabago Lau.[14] Settlements were generally composed

12 *Assimilado* was a Portuguese colonial category of citizen that existed until the 1960s. It referred to individuals considered by the colonial authorities to have met certain formal standards indicating that they had successfully absorbed (assimilated) the Portuguese language and culture. Informants stated that restrictions were placed on who could enter the town and that for the most part non-Portuguese or non-assimilados were not permitted to enter except on market days or for the head tax count.

13 Today Ainaro and Sabago are considered to be two separate hamlets.

14 In 2007, the village head of Ainaro identified a total of nine *um lisa tu* (principal *um lisa*) in the hamlets of Ainaro and Sabago. Of these many are considered to have their 'roots' in areas such as Atsabe in Ermera or other locations close to Mount Ramelau. Sabago Lau was abandoned after the Japanese occupation during the Second World War.

of four or five related households, located close to the fields they were cultivating. Although a group of related households, usually brothers or first cousins from the same *um lisa* and their spouses and children, might live at the same location for a number of years these settlements were not considered permanent. *Um lisa* members who might live apart for most of the year would reconvene at their *um tu* for important rituals during the course of the agricultural year.

Many informants argued that prior to the arrival of the Portuguese there was no impediment to farming. That is to say that the nature of shifting cultivation was such that groups of related households cooperatively farmed as much land as they had the strength and resources to manage. Plots were seldom contiguous and could be dispersed over vast areas. Originally, people simply abandoned land that no longer yielded good harvests and moved on to more fertile land. Later, people began to leave permanent markers, by laying rocks or planting certain species of tree, on land that they let fallow as 'proof' of a prior occupancy. Many informants also stressed the fact that their 'ancestors' did not understand the economic value of the land but rather that land formed part of the cycle of life and the reciprocal relations that existed between the living and the hidden world of the ancestors. The process of 'opening' previously unused land by clearing, burning and cultivating involved various stages of ritual and prayer to 'ask permission' or attenuate the anger of the spirits who might inhabit the land or guard its resources. The memory of these acts and the precise location of farmed land was then transmitted from one generation to the next thus forming part a legacy of specific *um lisa* lineage lands. This account of the development of customary authority and possessory rule complexity, as resource management moved beyond simple acts of possession of abundant land, is consistent with our theoretical account of rule complexity and second party property enforcement mechanisms in Chapter 3.

The establishment of the Portuguese *posto* in 1907 signalled the beginning of gradual changes in the relationship between people and the land as the population of the kingdom of Suro-Ainaro (including the people of Ainaro-Sabago Leophat) became incorporated into the colonial state. Initially, the Portuguese authorities and the Catholic Church appear to have, at least nominally, acknowledged the authority of the customary rulers. According to local histories, the Portuguese consulted the *liurai* of Suro-Ainaro, *Na'i Kau* and *Na'i Koso*, as to where they should establish their military post. Later in the 1930s, when the Catholic missionaries based in Ainaro town sought land on which to build a larger church and expand the mission, they consulted with the local *chefe povasaun* who called the elders of Ainaro-Sabago Leophat together to discuss which land, and how much, could be given to the Church.[15] However, after the Second World War, the colonial authorities began

15 The history of the granting of Ainaro Church land was written up in 2003 by the current hamlet head of Sabago in response to a dispute over Church land. The document was viewed by the author and discussed with the parish priest.

to exercise more control over the territory, affecting the way in which communities gained access to land and changing settlement patterns and farming practices.[16]

As part of a general drive to make the colony more productive, or at least self-sufficient, the Portuguese authorities enacted a number of 'development' policies during the post-war period (Clarence-Smith 1992). In Ainaro sub-district, in general, 'slash and burn' practices associated with shifting cultivation and burning out of season were severely punished and large areas of land were terraced and used for rice cultivation. It was during this period that informants recalled that 'origin' villages, such as Sabago Lau, were abandoned as the Portuguese authorities encouraged (or ordered) people to live in larger, more accessible settlements. This policy appears to have been aimed at facilitating the collection of head tax and organizing labour. All members of the community were expected to farm a quantity of rice land. The hamlet head of Ainaro called this 'bitter work' (Tetun: *servisu moruk*). Access to land was not determined by *um lisa* membership or agreements between *um lisa* with ancestral attachments to the land. Under Portuguese colonial law any land that was unused or uncultivated was deemed to belong to the state (Fitzpatrick 2002: 35–40).

The colonial authorities identified suitable arable land and the village and hamlet heads were expected to organize labour to work on these fields. Today, the signs of terracing are still visible, in particular to the west of the Sarai River in the hamlets of Hatumera and Nugufu. Local residents stated that this land was exposed to seasonal high winds that made farming difficult and often destroyed crops. Later these fields were abandoned when the Indonesian authorities diverted the water from the river used for irrigation towards the town supply. Another area of rice fields is located south of Ainaro town, on the flood plains near the confluence of the Mau Mall and Sarai Rivers, on land bordering with the neighbouring village of Cassa. Informants from Ainaro village and the hamlets of Ainaro, Sabago and Builico, in particular, claimed that their families farmed this land for generations. However, they also acknowledged that this is not their ancestral land but that their 'ancestors' or 'grandfathers' originally negotiated access with local groups – either through *um lisa* marriage relations or as part of an agreement between local ruling houses. Informants from Cassa, on the other hand, suggested that the Portuguese colonial authorities had encouraged people from Ainaro to 'occupy' this land in retaliation for the alliance of the ruler of Cassa with the Manufahi rebels during the Wars of Pacification and later with the Japanese during the Second World

16 The people of Ainaro sub-district experienced considerable social upheaval and displacement during the Second World War. Japanese and later Australian troops occupied Ainaro town. Some local leaders resentful of Portuguese favouritism towards the Mambae rulers from Suru Kraik chose to ally themselves with the Japanese. Later these leaders, including the *chefe povasaun* of Sabago, were declared traitors – some were imprisoned, exiled to Atauro or dispossessed.

War.[17] Competing histories of land use and political affiliation have thus led to overlapping customary and individual claims to land, in particular, in the southern plains in areas such as Diru Kede, Fau Lata and Fatu Naru.

Some areas of land closer to Ainaro Vila were appropriated for 'communal gardens' (Tetun: *to'os komunal*). The local population was expected to contribute time and labour to cultivate this land. It was common for this work to be done on a rotational basis by work groups from each *povasaun* under the leadership of their *chefe povasaun*. Persons unable to afford the head tax might be expected to contribute up to four months' labour. Unlike the produce from larger rice fields, the harvest from these gardens did not benefit the community but was given to local troops, members of the colonial administration and in some cases local *liurai* and village heads.[18] Today, some of these former communal gardens are the subject of multiple claims by the state, customary groups, former hamlet heads and individuals who took part in the work groups. These claims include competing references to sources of property legitimacy, including state grant, possession and input of labour, and agreement with customary authority.

One unresolved case involves an area of land called Gur Ulu in the neighbourhood of Mau Lore. This case illustrates the contestation of possessory entitlements in the context of state land acquisition. Prior to the Indonesian invasion this land had formed part of a communal garden and during the Indonesian occupation a police station and barracks were built on the site. In 2003, a complaint was made to the local district, sub-district administration and the district Directorate of Land and Property regarding plans to build a new police barracks on the site. The claimant argued that the land had belonged to his grandfather, a former *chefe povasaun,* and had been passed on to his son who farmed the land immediately prior to the Indonesian invasion. The claimant argued that his grandfather had gained entitlement to this land (Portuguese: *aforado*) by building a fence around the perimeter. The current hamlet head of Sabago intervened in the case by stating that the land in question fell under the jurisdiction of the *um lisa* of Ainaro-Sabago Leophat. However, he also recognized that this land had been appropriated by the state during Portuguese times and therefore, according to the law, continued to be state land. In 2006, a case was taken to court but was rejected by the judge, who stated that the claimant had no argument and that the land belonged to the state. However, supporters of the claimant continue to sabotage any attempts to redevelop the land. At the time of the fieldwork, the land where the shell of the

17 See Pélissier 1991. Raimea, Ria and Leo Lelo were declared 'domain land' following the defeat of the Manufahi rebels. Later this land was destined to be transformed into plantation land called 'Republica'.

18 One local informant claimed that a 1958 'requerimento' stated that all men over 18 had to do compulsory work. As an ordenanza or auxiliar one was then exempt from the head tax. Anecdotal evidence suggests that the obligation of labour on these communal fields created considerable resentment.

former police station and barracks now stands was being used by local residents to farm maize and other vegetables.

The Portuguese drive for increased productivity also had a significant impact on farming practices. Although farming of swidden gardens on a rotational basis continued to be dominant practice, more and more land was being used for perennial crops. From the 1930s onwards the intensification of rice farming and the introduction of cash crops such as coffee and coconut facilitated the visible differentiation of land parcels. In the rice fields, ditches, walls and irrigation channels between plots all served to demarcate areas of land being farmed by individual families (or allocated to individual heads of household by the village head). Rice fields are usually considered to be the individual legacy of those responsible for having first cleared the land and built the irrigation channels to feed the rice fields.

Coffee was first introduced to Ainaro sub-district during the inter-war years when seedlings were brought from the large plantations in Fatubesi (Ermera district) and distributed to the population through village and hamlet heads. Informants described how areas of land traditionally used as swidden gardens were gradually transformed into coffee plantations. Individuals would stake claim to previously uncultivated or abandoned land that was part of their *um lisa* ancestral legacy by planting coffee shade trees such as *casurina* surrounded by a perimeter hedge. Then, once the shade trees were tall enough, they would plant coffee seedlings. A number of informants stated that during the Portuguese period coffee production remained relatively low. It was not until the Indonesian period that seedlings became more widely available and people began to feel the economic benefits of coffee cultivation directly.[19]

Claims to land, in particular to land in Ainaro town, made by former (or relatives of former) village and hamlet heads and other local potentates dating from the Portuguese period are not uncommon.[20] Clarence-Smith (1992) has suggested that, at least until the 1920s, some village heads and prominent local authorities had the right to corvée labour to cultivate their specially demarcated land or to tend their animals.[21] However, in the case of Ainaro, it appears that few claimants ever officially obtained Portuguese title to this land. For example, recently there was a dispute over the ownership of an area of land called Rusgoa located close to the village office (*sede suku*) of Ainaro. A Church group seeking land on which to build its premises negotiated the purchase of a plot of land in

19 Previously, coffee trade was monopolized and prices were fixed by the SAPT, Sociedade Agricola Patria e Trabalho.

20 Informants claimed that the customary rulers of the former kingdom of Suru-Ainaro were allocated plots of land in and around Ainaro Vila by the colonial authorities in recognition of their 'loyalty'. However, a number of claims to land are also based on histories of negotiated access to land through marriage or some other form of agreement.

21 Clarence-Smith argues that Governor Duarte put an end to local chiefs' rights to land allocation in the 1920s but confirmed this land as their private property.

Rusgoa from two persons claiming to be the rightful owners. Once the transaction had been made, the hamlet head of Sabago intervened to contest the sale arguing that the land belonged to members of the *um lisa* of Ainaro-Sabago Leophat. The dispute was taken to the sub-district administration, the Directorate of Land and Property and the village head of Ainaro to be resolved. According to the village head of Ainaro, the sale of the land had not necessarily been made in bad faith. He claimed that the land had been used during the Portuguese period as a communal garden but that once the soil had been exhausted it had been 'given' to the father of one of the persons claiming ownership because he was 'close' to the Portuguese colonial authorities.

Informants from the Directorate of Land and Property were only able to identify three Portuguese land-title owners in the whole sub-district of Ainaro. Two were members of ruling families of Suro Kraik and Cassa; one was a former civil servant from Cabo Verde. In general, it was felt that only those close to the colonial authorities, business people or foreigners (Portuguese nationals) were able to obtain title for land. Colonial law was such that in order to obtain an *alvara indigena* (a Portuguese title of customary land ownership) the occupier had to prove that at least half the land had been cultivated or lived on. The nature of swidden agriculture and customary notions of ancestral claims to land and natural resources did not fit this production-based model of rights (Fitzpatrick 2002). Many of those who did obtain title often did so by fencing off an area of land to pasture livestock. Exclusionary policies, lack of resources and a lack of access to information all contributed to the low number of titles issued during the Portuguese period. Based on informants' responses, it is unlikely that the majority of the population of Ainaro were aware of the details of Portuguese property law.

Although most people continued to perceive land to be abundant and land allocation and transfers were largely managed within customary frameworks embedded in *um lisa* relations, Portuguese colonial politics and policies effectively began to undermine these processes. In some cases the colonial authorities used land allocation as a means of rewarding their political allies or punishing their foes. Work groups were directed to occupy and farm areas of land that fell within the customary jurisdiction of other groups, those bypassing customary mechanisms for gaining access to land involving negotiations and alliances between *um lisa* groups. Changing farming techniques and the introduction of cash crops led to the differentiation of land into individual or family holdings that were no longer considered to form part of a broader *um lisa* communal property. During the late Portuguese period, communal ancestral attachments to land bound to particular histories of arrival and settlement began to be gradually superseded by individual claims to differentiated plots of land based on labour and occupancy. The impact of changing attitudes and practices towards land became increasingly apparent with the introduction of an explicitly commodified view of land during the Indonesian occupation.

## The Indonesian Period: Displacement, Resettlement and Relocation

Claims to land based on changing attitudes and practices towards the land introduced during the late Portuguese colonial period were further complicated during the Indonesian invasion and occupation. Customary tenures were challenged by patterns of mass displacement followed by restrictions on movement and resettlement programmes that led to new forms of land occupancy and use. Furthermore, the appropriation of land by the state for the development of local infrastructure and the introduction of Indonesian land law severely undermined the capacity of customary structures to retain authority over the land.

At the time of the Indonesian invasion in late 1975, the population of Ainaro district had already experienced considerable displacement. Bitter fighting between supporters of the the opposed political parties, UDT and Fretilin, during the country's brief internal armed conflict had forced many people to flee their homes. News of the invasion led to further displacement. Some families from Ainaro with friends and relations in Dili were able to escape the region entirely. Within Ainaro district, most people initially fled to the mountains. However, by the time Indonesian troops reached the area in February 1976, many had already returned to their own settlements. During the course of 1976 and 1977, the security situation deteriorated once again as a result of continued attacks on Indonesian troops by the armed resistance. Indonesian reprisals targeted the civilian population, prompting more displacement as people sought refuge in numbers closer to the population centres such as Ainaro town or fled to the mountains to join the resistance.

Between 1977 and 1979, resistance strongholds, or *bases de apoio* as they were called, began to fall and the civilian population started to 'surrender' from the mountains. Ainaro town became a 'transit' or 'concentration' centre for displaced persons from Ainaro and surrounding districts and sub-districts. Other significant sites were Fatuk Maria in Manutasi, Cassa, Suru Kraik and Soro. Conditions in these concentration centres were extremely difficult. In Ainaro town, informants described how people built makeshift shelters on any available land around the old town centre. Food was scarce and people were not permitted to go far to plant crops or tend to their gardens.

It was not until 1982–83, that the Indonesian military authorities began to allow the civilian population to return to their places of origin. Although the majority of those who had been displaced to Ainaro town were able to return to their village of origin, they were seldom permitted to return to pre-invasion settlements but were 'resettled' along main roads or clustered around village offices (*sede suku*/*kantor desa*). A number of communities were not permitted to return to their village of origin but were relocated to neighbouring villages. For example, the populations of Mau-Nunu and Mau-Ulo were relocated to Cassa and Ainaro town respectively. Their village territory, located to the west of the Sarai River, was classified as an area of continued armed insurgency and was strictly out of bounds for most of the Indonesian period. Although access to agricultural land in these areas was later eased, remote settlements in the highlands between Ainaro, Bobonaro and Ermera remained off limits until the mid 1990s.

The size and population of Ainaro town expanded considerably during the Indonesian occupation. Today, the town has spread beyond the ancestral lands of the *um lisa* of Ainaro-Sabago Leophat to include territory under the jurisdiction of Nugufu and Builico. Many people from the more remote localities of Ainaro village, such as Hatumera, Lugatu and Teliga, were directed to resettle closer to Ainaro town on the Orluli plain. And the people of Builico were resettled on land in Ai Melilo and Seu Lau. The population of the neighbouring village of Mau-Ulo was relocated 'en masse' to two 'new' settlements on the road from Ainaro town to Cassa. Later, as the Indonesian authorities extended their control over the territory and developed local infrastructure, Ainaro town also grew to accommodate 'new settlers' including Indonesian and East Timorese civil servants, military and police personnel, traders and business people.

In general, return to places of origin or relocation to 'new' settlements was organized by the Indonesian military in collaboration with newly designated *kepala desa* and *kepala kampung* (formerly, village head and hamlet head). Recollections of the process of return or resettlement vary. Most informants claimed that they were directed to move to 'new' settlements with their village head and hamlet head. In some cases the land on which they were resettled fell under the overall jurisdiction of their own hamlet (*povasaun/kampung*) and they were still able to access their ancestral lands for cultivation or settlement. Others were directed to resettle on land to which *um lisa* from a different hamlet or village laid claim. In many cases, owing to restrictions on movement imposed by the Indonesian authorities, people were unable to access land they had farmed during the Portuguese period as part of hamlet and village work groups.

A number of informants described how the local authorities allocated each household a plot of land on which to build their house and farm a small garden. However, some stated that the process was less organized and that they negotiated access to land directly through *um lisa* relations, and others claimed that they eventually purchased land from local land 'owners' or the Church. For example, one informant described how, during the Indonesian occupation, he had built his house on land belonging to the *um lisa* of Um Cab Lia Nai. At the time he said he wanted to build his house on his own *um lisa* (Hatilo-Baboe) land but the Indonesians directed people to build their houses near the main roads. He gave the people of Um Cab Lia Nai traditional cloth and some money in exchange for the land and, to make sure the community was aware of the transaction, he invited his neighbours and representatives from the *um lisa* of Sabago hamlet to take part or witness the building of his house.

In general, 'new' settlements in and around Ainaro town were located on land that was previously 'unused', 'abandoned', or had been used for rice cultivation and communal gardens. Those obliged to resettle on land that was not their own stated that, at the time, they did not seek permission (nor did their community leaders) from the customary *um lisa* landowners. Many argued that the social and political situation was such that people settled and farmed wherever they could in order to survive. Others suggested that because the land was previously unused or unclaimed there was no one to ask. In some cases, informants justified their claims to land based on long-term occupancy by stressing that, at the time, nobody approached them to make their prior claims known. Today, informants who claim that their ancestral lands were occupied argue that under the circumstances there was little they could do to stop the military or civilian authorities from relocating people on to their land. In cases where access to land was negotiated through *um lisa* relations – based on kinship or marriage – the original land-owning groups claim that this was done on the understanding that access was granted on a temporary basis. These patterns of conflict-caused displacement, and its effect on claims to land, reflect the experience in other parts of rural East Timor.

*The Indonesian Period:*
*Resettlement from Neighbouring Villages to Ainaro Town*

Despite these challenges, the resettlement of people from hamlets under the jurisdiction of Ainaro village was not as problematic as the relocation of 'outsiders' from neighbouring villages such as Mau-Ulu to Ainaro town. The people of Mau-Ulu held in 'transit' centres in Ainaro town and Cassa were not permitted to return to their village lands but were relocated to an area of uncultivated land along the main road out of Ainaro town towards Builico and Cassa. According to local informants from Mau-Ulu, the Indonesian authorities initially allocated plots and distributed building materials to approximately 30 households. Once the first group had begun to establish themselves on this land, more followed and the 'new' villages of Mau-Ulu I and Mau-Ulu II were established.

In the mid 1990s, the security situation improved and the Indonesian authorities allowed some access to land in Mau-Ulu village. However, settlement west of the Sarai River continued to be restricted to an area surrounding the village offices in Uko Rema. Despite increased access to their own ancestral lands during the 1990s most of the residents of Mau-Ulu I and Mau-Ulu II have lived in their 'new' villages for over 30 years. During this time they have built their homes, planted trees and gardens and raised their children on this land. Despite living within the boundaries of Ainaro village, in Ainaro town, the population of Mau-Ulu has remained under the jurisdiction of their own village head and hamlet heads, and retains social distinctions based on customary *um lisa* social hierarchies.

Since independence few families from Mau-Ulu have chosen to return permanently to their pre-invasion settlements. There is little incentive to return to areas where there are few public services, poor access roads and little, if any, development. Some of those who have returned more permanently claim that they did not want to remain in Mau Ulu I and II where they had to either buy food or ask permission to farm other people's land. One upland community in Dagamesa has rebuilt the local primary school to encourage people to return. However, a common choice among people from Mau-Ulu now seems to be to re-establish temporary dwellings on ancestral lands while maintaining a residence in the 'new' settlements of Mau-Ulu I and Mau-Ulu II in order for their children to attend secondary school, to access health services or because they have jobs in the local administration.

Today, there is increasing pressure on the residents of Mau-Ulu I and II to either return to their original village lands or submit to the local authority of the village head of Ainaro. The call to submit to local authority is directly linked to claims that the people of Mau-Ulu are occupying the ancestral lands of groups from Sabago and Builico without consent. Some individuals and groups from Ainaro argue that people from Mau-Ulu should return to their own village lands and pay compensation to the customary landowners for lost rents during the period of the Indonesian occupation. The people from Mau-Ulu, on the other hand, state that they will not return to their village lands unless they receive compensation for the investments they have made in the land – fruit trees and houses – and would be forced to leave behind. Others from Mau-Ulu argue (incorrectly) that, according to Indonesian land and property law, the land is lawfully theirs as they have occupied the land for more than five consecutive years.

The village head of Ainaro stated that the current situation has created a lot of resentment among certain groups within Ainaro and Mau-Ulu villages, which has occasionally flared up into violent episodes. He felt that what is required is some form of administrative clarification whereby residents of Mau-Ulu with evidence of ownership or legal documentation (including land titles but not only) should be allowed to retain their land and property, while others, who he believes have been occupying land and property illegally since 1999, should be resettled to their own village lands. The village head of Mau-Ulu also deferred to the state to clarify the status of Mau-Ulu residents in Ainaro but was more guarded in his response, suggesting that people would be more willing to return to their own ancestral lands if there were better roads and services. There will be significant tensions and perhaps conflict if the state's response takes the form of the draft 2012 land law, namely to grant alienable ownership rights on the basis of possession since 31 December 1998. We discuss this prospect further in Chapter 11.

## State Intervention and the Development of a Local Land Market

In the 1980s and 1990s, the Indonesian military and civilian authorities undertook large-scale building and infrastructure projects in Ainaro town. Military barracks, the district and sub-district (*kabupaten* and *kecamatan*) administrative offices, schools, a hospital, electricity and water works, public housing for civil servants and teachers, and the town's roads were all built during this period. The development of Ainaro town as a regional administrative centre also attracted a considerable number of 'new' settlers, mainly Indonesian and East Timorese civil servants, health workers, military and police personnel as well as traders and business people. Although some civil servants, including the military, police and teachers, were provided with public housing, others had to rent, buy or lease land and property locally.

Staff from the Directorate of Land and Property (DTP) argued that, in the late 1980s, the introduction of an (albeit limited) system of monetary compensation for land acquired by the state for public development and the demand for land from 'new' settlers had a major impact on local understanding of the value of land, particularly in terms of the individuation of rights to parcels of land. Individuals started to claim ownership to parcels of land that had previously formed part of the legacy of a whole *um lisa* group. In some cases this led to conflict between family members over land that had been cultivated and abandoned by earlier generations. In other cases, land that had been made freely available for long-term use to *um lisa* relations (whether wife-givers or wife-takers) was reclaimed by the 'original' owners. In a number of cases that have come to light post-independence, land abandoned by those who fled the area or the country in 1975–76 was occupied by others and sometimes sold or 'leased' to third parties. While those holding land under long-term 'leases' may fall within the category of 'mere occupier', under the draft 2012 land law, other claimants will rely on possession since 31 December 1998 in order to support claims to alienable ownership.

### *Compensation and the Status of State Land*

DTP staff claimed that most of the land appropriated by the Indonesian authorities for the development of public infrastructure in Ainaro was either uncultivated land or land that had been used as 'communal gardens' during the Portuguese period. This land, they argued, was Portuguese state land that subsequently became Indonesian state land. However, they also acknowledged that some land occupied by the Indonesian authorities had been previously cultivated or used by private individuals or the Church.

DTP staff described three distinct periods in the development and implementation of Indonesian land administration in Timor Leste. During the first 'emergency' period, between 1976 and 1981, the Indonesian military were in complete control. Land was appropriated in order to establish strategic military posts and develop basic communications infrastructure. Land was simply occupied and used – no compensation was paid and there was no attempt to identify local landowners. During the second 'consolidation' period, between 1982 and 1989, the Indonesian authorities began establishing a civilian administration, including the equivalent to the Directorate for Land and Property (Indonesian: *Badan Pertanahan Nasional,* commonly referred to in Timor Leste as *Agraria*). Authorities continued to appropriate land 'by force' (or by fear of threat of force). However, in some cases a nominal level of compensation was given to those who could prove previous long-term occupancy or ownership. During this period, the authorities also went about informing the public about the role and function of the land administration and Indonesian land law and some people were also issued certificates and titles for their land and property. During the third 'stabilization' period, between 1990 and 1999, there were many more East Timorese civil servants working in the land administration. The administration began to apply compensation rates, based on Indonesian national standards for land appropriated by the state for public works.

Many informants from Ainaro felt that land acquired by the state for public development was taken without due process or adequate compensation. Some also suggested that East Timorese close to the Indonesian authorities took advantage of the system to acquire land privately and disenfranchise or punish their political rivals. However, others stated that within the constraints of the system some compensation could and was obtained. In some cases people were successful in asserting their claims to landownership, and in one case at least were able to stop further loss of their land. In 1982, the Indonesian authorities built a primary school on land located in Kareta Fatin. Family X claimed that their paternal grandfather had farmed this land prior to 1946. However, at the time the Indonesians appropriated the land they were living in Dili. In 1994, when they heard that the authorities planned to build another school on the same premises, they approached the village head of Ainaro to complain about the arbitrary occupation of their land. At the time, the village head authorized the family to seek redress with the state and with a private individual who had also occupied part of the land. Although the private individual refused to cooperate, arguing that he had obtained title for the land, the local district administrator (*bupati*) halted the construction of any further school buildings on the land.

### *The Issue of Land Titles during the Indonesian Period*

During the Indonesian occupation, the authorities implemented a number of national 'projects' aimed at issuing certificates or titles for land and property. Under Indonesian land law, three types of land title could be obtained: permanent ownership rights (*Hak Milik*); temporary usufruct rights (*Hak Pakai*), usually renewable after a period of 5 years; or long-term building rights (*Hak Guna Bangunan*), usually renewable after 25 years.

Local perceptions of these projects and the titling process in general were that they were affected by corruption. Informants either felt that individuals took advantage of the system to obtain official title to land that they had occupied following the Indonesian invasion, or that those involved in the titling 'projects' benefited from grafting funds from the state. However, according to DTP staff in Ainaro, few land parcels or properties surveyed in the course of these projects were ever actually issued any form of documentation, as many people were not able to pay the administration fees involved or were unwilling to pay taxes on land and property. DTP staff also stated that many of those who did obtain title were Indonesian citizens who left in 1999 and have not returned (see also de Sousa 2005, Elderton 2002).[22] Under

22 This assessment was also made by former head of the Directorate of Land and Property (De Sousa 2005). Figures suggest that the majority of titles issued were for land or property either in Dili, where half the population were non-East Timorese in the 1990s, or transmigration areas in Covalima, Bobonaro and Liquisa (Elderton 2002).

the draft 2012 land law, land subject to ownership titles held by foreign citizens, including Indonesian citizens, falls within the private domain of the state (art. 8).

*The Development of a Land Market*

Despite the fact that few certificates or titles to land and property were actually issued during the Indonesian occupation, a land market appears to have flourished in Ainaro during this period. In particular the demand came from Indonesian and East Timorese civil servants posted to Ainaro town. As with the formal land titling system, questions of corruption and illegitimacy surround many of the transactions that occurred during this period.

Under Indonesian law, land and property transactions had to be prepared and witnessed by a public notary (PPAT). Given that few people had titles for their land or property, the verification process appears to have relied heavily on a system of 'self-certification' or the presentation of 'declaration letters' (*Surat Keterangan Pernyataan Hak Tanah*) containing a description of the land or property to be transacted and confirmation of the identity of the 'owner' by local authorities, usually the village head (*kepala desa*) or the sub-district administrator (*camat*).

DTP staff felt that this system was open to abuse and that often declaration letters were signed in the knowledge that the person claiming ownership was not the real owner, or signed in good faith but without local knowledge or confirmation from third parties. In Ainaro, DTP staff felt that only Indonesian citizens and East Timorese who had access to information ever registered land transactions, or sought to obtain a declaration letter. Furthermore, they suggested that most land sales were to, or between, Indonesian citizens and 'outsiders', as local people tended to negotiate access to land through more informal agreements or traditional *um lisa* structures.

Today, a number of people who are known to have sold their land to Indonesians during the occupation are claiming that they never sold the land outright. They claim they either 'leased' or 'rented' the land to the Indonesian occupants, or that they permitted the occupant to build a house or other structure on their land but never transferred ownership of the land itself. In some cases they claim that the Indonesian occupant built a house on the land 'in lieu' of rent and consequently that the house and land still belong to the original owner. The verification of claims is hampered by the fact that where documentation might have existed to prove or disprove claims most of this was lost during the course of the post-referendum violence in 1999.

The relocation of communities to Ainaro town, the appropriation of land for public development and the influx of 'new' settlers during the Indonesian occupation all contributed to undermine customary claims and processes for access to land. Although some groups were displaced or relocated within or close to their ancestral lands, often their ability to maintain authority and entitlements to land was curtailed by fear or the lack of means or influence to seek redress.

In the context of military occupation it is inevitable that questions of abuse of power and illegitimacy surround the implementation of policies and practices relating to land, property and natural resources. The development and application of a system of land administration during this period was at best incomplete, at worst corrupt and inequitable. Even where transactions were conducted in good faith, the contested legitimacy of state institutions has left the holders of rights open to competing claims based on historical acts of dispossession.

## The Post-independence Environment

Between 4 and 23 September 1999, Mahidi pro-Indonesia militia based in Manutasi and Cassa attacked villages throughout Ainaro sub-district, burning and looting houses and public buildings. It is estimated that some 13,000 persons from Ainaro district were forcibly displaced to West Timor during this period by pro-Indonesia militia with the logistical support of the Indonesian military and police (CAVR 2005). Those who escaped forcible displacement to West Timor fled to the mountains towards the districts of Bobonaro and Ermera. Ainaro town was among the most affected areas by the wave of militia violence that followed the announcement of the UN-sponsored ballot results in which the East Timorese people voted overwhelmingly in favour of independence. Almost all public buildings in Ainaro were burnt down and looted as the militia and Indonesian military and police left the territory. It is estimated that in Ainaro town almost 80 per cent of private dwellings were also burnt and looted.

Those who fled to the mountains began to return to Ainaro as early as late September. Most returned to find their houses destroyed and many recall having sought temporary shelter in any buildings that still had walls and perhaps roofing. Most informants acknowledged that during this period both public buildings and private houses were occupied. However, once material and humanitarian assistance was made available most returned to their own dwellings, or at least the site of their former dwellings. Despite this narrative of orderly return to land and property the illegal occupation of property in and around Ainaro town, including state, private and Church property, continues to be an issue.

Some of the occupations that took place during this period were politically motivated or the result of long-standing historical rivalries. The Ainaro district police commissioner stated that this was particularly the case with disputes concerning productive land and in particular coffee plantations. He suggested that the main difficulty in resolving these disputes lay in the fact that many involved political rivalries dating back to the period of political party formation (1974–75) or earlier. What emerges is a cyclical history of possession and dispossession where competing notions of legitimacy come into play. Individuals and groups forced to flee at the time of the Indonesian occupation claim that their land was occupied by their political rivals. And those who farmed the land during this period claim that they were the victims of earlier acts of dispossession following the Second

World War. In some cases no prior claims to landownership exist but land has been occupied by those seeking redress or revenge for past injustices or, in some cases, by those who simply feel a sense of entitlement to land that they perceive to be just reward for having fought on the winning side.

The following example concerns conflict over a coffee plantation that is intertwined with allegations of collaboration with the Indonesian occupiers. It illustrates the way in which claims to possession can move beyond questions of physical occupation to notions of underlying social legitimacy. It also illustrates a relatively innovative dispute-management approach involving election of a hamlet head from the neighbouring hamlet.

### *Tensions over Coffee Plantations in Manutasi*

Since 2000, there have been sporadic violent clashes over coffee plantations between people from the hamlets of Hatumedaudo and Raebuitudo in the village of Manutasi. The hamlet of Hatumedaudo became a Mahidi militia stronghold during 1998 and 1999. Many former residents of this hamlet have not returned to Timor Leste since the mass forced displacement of the population in September 1999. Local informants believe this is because many members of the community joined the militia or were related to former militia members. The hamlet of Raebuitudo, on the other hand, is historically linked to the pro-independence movement.

According to local informants, in 2000 a group of former pro-independence supporters from Raebuitudo began occupying and harvesting coffee plantations belonging to people from Hatumedaudo, who had been involved with pro-autonomy groups or the Mahidi militia, as 'payback' for the violence and terror they inflicted on the population in 1999. The occupation led to violent confrontation between those who had occupied the land and family members of the plantation owners.

Despite existing bonds of kinship and marriage between the *um lisa* of the groups involved, local informants stated that when the clashes got violent and 'blood was spilt' the elders were not 'brave' enough to deal with the matter 'internally' within the sphere of *um lisa* relations so the matter was taken to the police. As is common with many cases involving conflict over land or property, the police dealt primarily with the issue of assault while the underlying dispute over the coffee plantations was left in the hands of the local community.

This dispute over access to coffee plantations continues to be the subject of internal community negotiations. One of the ways in which the community Manutasi village has chosen to negotiate the sensitive political rivalries behind the dispute is by electing a hamlet head of Hatamedaudo from one of the senior *um lisa* of the neighbouring hamlet of Bahatilau. The hamlet head of Hatumedaudo explains this anomaly, suggesting that he was chosen as hamlet head because so few people from Hatumedaudo had returned from West Timor and that as the *gas' ubun* (spokesperson) of one of the three main *um lisa* of the village of Manutasi, which was also traditionally one of the *dato* or 'ruling' houses of Hatumedaudo, he can legitimately perform this task. It appears that through this arrangement the different house-based groups of Manutasi have been able to keep the peace within their village. The arrangement provides a further example of accommodation of customary authority and village government mechanisms, through the election of a customary elder as hamlet head, and the potential for this approach to play an influential conflict-management role. We discuss local approaches to land dispute management further in the following chapter.

## Dealing with Land Claims at the Local Level

Local authorities, including the village head of Ainaro, the sub-district administrator, district administrator and DTP staff all suggested that within Ainaro village and Ainaro town there was ongoing tension between individuals and groups claiming ancestral or customary rights to land, those who had been resettled or relocated during the Indonesian occupation, and former residents of Ainaro who had fled abroad in 1975, been displaced to neighbouring villages, sub-districts or districts, or had moved to Dili for education and/or work during the Indonesian occupation.

Senior DTP staff in Ainaro felt that the resurgence of claims to ancestral land had been harnessed by 'modern' claims to individualized rights to land. One staff member stated that, given the increased value and commodification of land during the Indonesian period, today many children and grandchildren of an older generation involved in shifting cultivation were making claims to land that had long been abandoned by their direct family or even *um lisa* members. While in the past this land would have formed part of the *um lisa* legacy and would have been available to any members of the *um lisa* who wished to farm it (unless it was being used by someone else), today individuals and families argue that it is their own property inherited directly from their father or grandfather.

Some of the population, which had been resettled or relocated within or to Ainaro village and Ainaro town during the Indonesian occupation, have chosen to return to their pre-1975 villages of origin or pre-invasion settlements. However, for many there is little incentive to return to areas where there are no services and poor roads. As with the case of people from Mau-Ulo described above, many families have established dual residence in Ainaro town and areas of origin. Individuals, families and groups who were displaced at the time of the Indonesian invasion and later resettled or relocated in Ainaro village or Ainaro town seldom had the opportunity to ascertain whether the land they had occupied was previously used or farmed. During the Indonesian occupation only a limited number of people were able to obtain legal title to land and property. Today, many of those who have chosen to remain in Ainaro village or Ainaro town base their claims to land and property on long-term occupancy and use.

Former residents of Ainaro, or family members of those who were forced to flee or left Ainaro during the course of the Indonesian invasion and occupation, are making claims to land that they were forced to leave or abandon. These claimants include individuals or families with ancestral ties to the land or rights to land gained through customary agreements and relations, as well as former local authorities, *liurai* and village heads. According to local DTP staff, not all these claims to land are well founded. They believe that a number of claimants sold their land prior to leaving Ainaro or during the Indonesian occupation. Returning individuals and family members often have little physical proof of ownership such as legal titles or transaction documents and rely on the testimonies of local authorities and in some cases former civil servants or functionaries from the Portuguese and Indonesian period.

At a national level, the promulgation of Law 1/2003 on the Juridical Regime of Real Estate established a process for registering private claims to land. However, the vast majority of claims to private rights lodged through this process are from foreign nationals (72 per cent). It is possible that the low number of East Timorese national claims lodged (26 per cent) reflects the general undisputed nature of claims to land and property but also the limitations of the land claims and disputes registration process (de Sousa 2005).[23] According to DTP staff in Ainaro only 59 claims were lodged for land and property in Ainaro district. According to their mandate DTP is also able to provide mediation services to individuals and groups involved in land disputes. Between 2000 and 2006, a total of 36 cases were presented to the local DTP for Ainaro district. Of these only six cases were successfully resolved. One case was referred to the courts and 27 remained 'pending'. According to the Ainaro DTP mediation officer, DTP has not been formally approached to provide mediation for the majority of 'pending' cases. We discuss mediation by the Land and Property Directorate further in the following chapter.

Given the reality of ongoing transactions and recent cases of disputed land sales or leases to outsiders (see example above on Rusgoa), in the absence of government initiatives or the availability or presence of local notaries, the current village head of Ainaro has tried to put into place a system for documenting transactions. Although he is aware that the vast majority of transactions go unrecorded and he believes that most are probably undertaken in good faith, the village head suggested that some system of verification and registration is required to ensure that there are no instances involving the 're-sale' of land or the sale of disputed land, or land belonging to someone else. According to the village head, if anybody approaches him to issue documents or declarations regarding the sale of land he will not sign anything until he has verified the veracity of claims – by visiting the land or property in question and seeking advice from neighbours and local elders. Any documents regarding land and property ownership are signed by the village head, hamlet head and at least two witnesses (usually persons with adjoining plots or neighbours). Copies of the documents are given to the interested parties but not necessarily (or seldom) to the DTP or the sub-district administration.

In the case of Ainaro village, and in particular Ainaro town, it is clear that in the absence of national legislation or institutions capable of dealing with private land and property claims and transactions, and in the face of the considerable challenges

23 This process was mainly Dili based with little impact in rural areas. See de Sousa (2005) for more information on the breakdown of claims.

faced by under-resourced decentralized institutions such as DTP, local communities continue to rely on 'customary' structures or innovative local initiatives in order to manage land conflict and provide some sense of tenure security.

## Conclusion

Ainaro district reflects the complexity of competing constructions of possession and possessory authority found across the districts of East Timor. While the majority of the population continue to turn to customary structures in the first instance as a means of managing land and natural resource relations, the influence of customary authority has been increasingly challenged by the intrusion of other forms of authority and legitimacy, including in particular the state. Portuguese and Indonesian era policies and practices have transformed the relationship between people and land in Ainaro. Processes of individuation, commodification and titling of rights to land enacted during the Portuguese colonial period and the Indonesian occupation have given rise to various categories of competing land claimant. In the context of historical acts of dispossession and displacement, these possessory claims became entangled with competing sources of authority and legitimacy and contributed to chronic land conflict, as periodic regime change revived disputes based on narratives of grievance and histories of past cultivation and occupation. The case of Ainaro town, in particular, highlights the complex nature of current land claims in peri-urban and urban areas of East Timor. This intricate web of competing possessory claims, and contested interpretations of possessory entitlement, is far removed from Demsetzian predictions of evolving property rights, under the influence of rising resource values, and illustrates the challenges of developing secure and certain property rights in independent East Timor.

## References

CAVR 2005. Chega! Report of the Commission for Reception, Truth and Reconciliation of Timor Leste. Dili: CAVR.

Census 2010. Census of Population and Housing. Dili: Direcção Nacional de Estatística and United National Population Fund.

Clarence-Smith, W.G. 1992. Planters and Small Holders in Portuguese Timor in the Nineteenth and Twentieth Centuries. *Indonesia Circle*, 57: 15–30.

Corte-Real, B. 2007. *Em Comemoracao do Centenario da Vila de Suro-Ainaro*. Ainaro.

Corte-Real, B. 2000. Social Order and Linguistic Symmetry: The Case of Mambai, Suru-Ainaro. *Studies in Languages and Cultures of East Timor*, 31–56, 31–57.

de Sousa, P. 2005. East Timor, Land Management: A Long Way To Go, But We Have Started. Paper to Expert Group Meeting on Secure Land Tenure: New Legal Frameworks and Tools in Asia & Pacific, 8–9 December 2005.

Elderton, C. 2002. East Timor: Land Issues and Independence. Paper to Transforming Land Conflict, 10–12 April 2002.

Fitzpatrick, D. 2002. *Land Claims in East Timor*. Canberra: Asia Pacific Press.

Forman, S. 1978. East Timor: Exchange and Political Hierarchy at the Time of the European Discoveries, in K. Hutterer (ed.), *Economic Exchange and Social Interaction in Southeast Asia: Perspectives from Prehistory, History, and Ethnography*. Ann Arbor, MI: University of Michigan, p. 318.

Hull, G. 2003. *Southern Mambai*. East Timor Language Profiles No. 5. Dili: Instituto Nacional de Linguistica, Universidade Nacional Timor Lorosa'e.

Pélissier, R. 1996. *Timor en guerre: le crocodile et les Portugais, 1847–1913*. Orgeval.

Rawski, F. 2002. Truth-Seeking and Local Histories in East Timor. *Asia-Pacific Journal on Human Rights and the Law*, 1: 77–96.

# Chapter 10
# Possession and Dispossession: Mediating and Managing Complex Land Conflicts

In this chapter we build on the foregoing case studies to analyze further the interaction between possessory claims and social order in East Timor. We discuss three examples of complex land conflicts: on the Uato Lari coastal lands of Viqueque, the floodplains of Ainaro, and the upland Nunura plains of Maliana. These disputes illustrate a number of core themes of this book: that complex land conflicts are based on competing references to possessory legitimacy and authority; that these conflicts are embedded in historical links between forced population movements and regime change; that there is a relationship between social order and configurations of interpretive complexity and simplicity in legal rules of possession; and that chronic property uncertainty may be the inevitable price of interpretively complex rules designed to avoid violent conflict in a weak state environment. The disputes provide a further insight into trade-offs involving rule complexity and simplicity in fragile post-conflict environments. On the one hand, bright-line rules of property have the potential to cause further outbreaks of conflict if they disenfranchise groups with ready access to means of violence. On the other hand, rule complexity that provide legal alternatives to violence may contribute to the chronic nature of property uncertainty when the courts have little capacity to apply complex rules to complex cases, or deliver authoritative determinations that are enforceable by the state.

We focus on cases of intractable land conflict not because they are necessarily pathological symptoms of social disorder, but because they illustrate important issues of institutional complexity in East Timor. While our case descriptions include attempts at mediation by the Land and Property Directorate, we do not limit our analysis to prospective application of the draft land law, even though a number of disputants display a willingness to take matters to court. The process of social reordering in the new post-conflict state involves a complex range of narratives deployed in the absence of law. Indeed, much of what we describe involves strategic production of legitimacy and authority in circumstances of 'waiting for law' in East Timor. This phenomenon illustrates a paradox of land law development in East Timor: some disputants will not engage in mediation because they are waiting for law, and yet of itself the new law is unlikely to provide authoritative resolution of complex land conflicts. Indeed, as our analysis of property rules and state-formation suggests (see Chapter 5), the incentives associated with the proposed new land law of East Timor are likely to favour a focus by the government on grant of leases over state land, and a degree of paralysis or delay in the implementation of private property rules.

Our fieldwork chapters have identified two basic types of complex land conflict in East Timor. The first involves the status of relocated groups in areas that are acknowledged as subject to the landed authority of origin group elders. Relocated groups tend not to contest origin group authority, but do often assert heritable rights to land on the basis of long-term occupation. The most obvious solution to the resulting land tensions lies in traditional mechanisms for incorporating relocated groups into customary order, through marriage and agreement, rather than the attempt by the draft 2012 land law to base alienable rights of ownership on long-term possession in customary districts. This will require responses to the suppression of traditional mechanisms for in-migrant incorporation by colonial government policies that established people-based systems of village government. The second type of complex conflict involves contested claims of possession and dispossession in lowland areas cleared and cultivated under colonial resettlement programmes. Residents of these areas may acknowledge the ritualized land stewardship of origin group elders, but their claims to land are based on historical acts of possession by recent forebears, in association with village government figures, and are separated from relationships with customary group hierarchy. This chapter focuses on the second type of case because, generally speaking, claims by relocated groups in areas of acknowledged customary authority are yet to cause violent conflict, and have not been the subject of attempts at mediation by officials of the Land and Property Directorate. In the following chapter we analyze the potential application of the draft 2012 land law to both types of cases.

Attempts at mediation by the Land and Property Directorate represent the first tentative steps by the East Timorese state to manage land conflicts in rural districts. In theory, mediation acts as a facilitating device to reduce the transaction costs that prevent agreements among disputants, particularly in terms of establishing mechanisms for exchange of information and development of trust. The transaction costs of complex land cases in East Timor are large, not only because of grievances over possession and dispossession, but also because of the large numbers and high stakes involved, especially given the circumstances of poverty and the importance of land to livelihoods. In simpler cases, involving small numbers and a degree of repeat interactions among claimants, the Land and Property Directorate has had some success with its mediation programme. Yet it has been less successful in the complex cases described in this chapter, which is not surprising in high transaction cost contexts, as mediation cannot reduce either the numbers or the stakes involved. While we discuss attempts at mediation as a potential alternative to bright-line rules of property, particularly in terms of managing the potential for violence, in the long run some type of enforceable legal rule will be necessary to allow the possibility of authoritative resolution of disputes. The challenge for weak states is that historical circumstances of war, displacement and regime change – creating competing claims of possession and dispossession – militate against development of a broad social consensus on simple rules such as respect for possession, or remedies for dispossession (see Chapter 1). And while the state may adopt a rule of adverse possession to harness the 'violence advantage' of current possessors, who are costly to evict, it must be careful to avoid non-context specific allocations that cause violent counter-reactions by dispossessed groups in some districts.

## Land Conflicts and Customary Dispute Resolution in East Timor

The legacy of colonial and neo-colonial interventions in East Timor includes multilayered constructions of possession and possessory authority to land and its resources in East Timor. As we have seen, the consequences of this disruptive legacy give rise to complex patterns of land conflict, and overlapping claims to authority over land. In most cases land disputes are highly localized and involve relatively small numbers of protagonists in situations of close familiarity and common residence. They often involve issues of inheritance or access among parties engaged in repeat forms of interaction, and their resolution is similarly one that is sought within the close confines of local authorities and shared cultural conventions of dispute resolution. Babo Soares (2004) has described one such cultural mechanism for dispute resolution known as *Nahe Biti,* a Tetun language phrase, translated as 'unfolding the woven mat'. The phrase is a metaphor for engaging in negotiated settlements or agreements between groups ranging from meeting traditional exchange obligations to the reconciliation of differences, including those over land entitlements. The idea of protagonists gathering together on the large woven mat (*biti bo'ot*), publically negotiating a mutually agreeable solution and sealing it with commensality or binding oath, represents a shared and familiar cultural institution among the diverse language communities of East Timor.

Third-party surveys identify preferences among Timorese for localized forms of dispute resolution procedures in local contexts (Timor-Leste Land Law Program 2004). For example, a national survey undertaken by the Asia Foundation (2004), which explored attitudes towards law and justice, found an overwhelming preference (81 per cent) for community leaders to take primary responsibility for law and order including land issues involving local community members (Asia Foundation 2004: 39). A similar survey in 2008 reported an even higher result – 89 per cent – for the same question (Asia Foundation 2008: 16). Unfortunately, the survey did not distinguish customary and village governance: it defined community leaders to include elected heads of settlement (*chefe aldeia*/hamlet head, *chefe suco/ village head*) and the customary elders and ritual leaders (*lian na'in, katuas*) of the local ritual community. The great majority of respondents felt that 'customary arrangements', as defined, reflected both the local values of their communities and provided a familiar and effective avenue for seeking redress for local grievances, in particular those involving divorce, theft and land disputes (Asia Foundation 2004: 56). Customary arrangements extend to other cultural institutions such as the *tara bandu* prohibitions that are widely enacted in rural East Timor to invoke behavioural and moral injunctions against transgressive behaviour. These prohibitions are also subject to fines and community-based sanctions (see also Meitzner Yoder 2005).

Our fieldwork chapters describe a relatively graduated and hierarchical process of *de facto* land dispute resolution in East Timor, through family, lineage and village government structures, which is consistent with other studies of dispute management in East Timor (Timor Leste Land Law Program 2004, Myat Thu 2008). As a general proposition, it seems that when a dispute occurs between members of the same family or extended family, the dispute will be dealt with in the first instance by calling upon family elders. If a meeting occurs at extended family level, then the head of the house, community elders and any person whose traditional task is to monitor land use might be involved. If the dispute cannot be resolved at this level, or the parties involved are not members of the same community, the dispute is taken directly to the hamlet head, or to the village head if the problem persists.[1] The hamlet or village head often calls upon customary authorities to attend meetings at the hamlet and village level. In general, it is only after the failure of dispute mediation or resolution at village level that there is any potential for a case to be taken to the sub-district authorities, which may or may not then request assistance of the Directorate of Land and Property.

Our case studies do not identify the degree of pluralism in dispute resolution arrangements noted by a number of studies of post-colonial Africa and Indonesia. These studies identify patterns of 'legal forum shopping', where disputants assert property claims through authority and legitimization systems outside of law, such as households, clan groups, religious systems, local government, village courts, non-governmental organizations, human rights commissions and parliaments (Berry 1993, 1997, Shipton 1994). Our case studies provide numerous examples of competing references to sources of claims legitimacy, including affiliation with customary authority, acts of possession with permission by village or hamlet heads, the grant of a hoe or other farming implement through Portuguese agricultural programmes, or rights derived through sales or other forms of transactional agreement. While these plural sources of claims legitimacy indicate a certain degree and type of negotiability in property arrangements, we do not find widespread patterns of disgruntled disputants attempting to 'shop' their claims to other sources of public authority. We attribute this relative absence of legal forum shopping practices to the relative absence of the state in rural districts, and the relatively high degree of accommodation between village government and customary authority structures described in Chapter 2. In this chapter we also note the preference of Land and Property Directorate officials to include village and community leaders in the mediation process. However, our finding of relatively cooperative and accommodative local dispute management structures does not deny the potential for legal forum shopping practices to increase as the new government seeks to extend its reach into rural districts. We discuss this possibility further in the following chapter.

---

1 Conflicts involving parties from different *aldeias* or *suco* will involve local authorities from both communities.

## Mediation and the Land and Property Directorate

In 2000 the UN Transitional Administration introduced a system of mediation by land and property officials to manage land disputes in East Timor. Law No 1 2003 on the Juridical Regime of Real Estate confirms the authority of the Land and Property Directorate to mediate land disputes. The following mediation procedures are set out in the Land and Property Directorate guidelines:

1. An individual claimant or a group of complainants goes to the national Land and Property Directorate or the district Land and Property Directorate office and requests mediation. A dispute may also be referred to the directorate by a village head (*chefe de suco*) if the parties have agreed to submit the case to the directorate.
2. The other parties to the dispute are informed of the claim. Mediation will proceed only when all the parties to the dispute voluntarily accept the mediation, and where there has been no previous legal or administrative resolution to a dispute regarding the same land. Mediation will not occur if the land that is the subject of the dispute is the property of the state, if one of the parties is an officer of government, or if the subject matter of the dispute is considered a crime.
3. The parties to the dispute agree to a Land and Property Directorate mediator or panel of mediators.
4. A Land and Property Directorate mediator visits the disputed land and gathers information about the history of ownership from local informants such as the village head, neighbours and other informed and credible witnesses.
5. The Land and Property Directorate mediator invites the claimant and the current occupant to separate meetings to hear each side of the dispute. Evidence presented during mediation may include public and private documents, witnesses and physical proof such as borders, trees, buildings and plantations.
6. The Land and Property Directorate mediator may then meet with the claimant and the current occupant together to attempt to find a solution that is acceptable to both parties. This may occur on up to three occasions. A draft law on mediation also allows for a further stage – mediation by a Mediation Panel of Appeal.
7. During the meetings the mediator may facilitate interim agreements relating to land use and commitments not to engage in violence pending resolution of the conflict. The mediator will also suggest a variety of ways in which the dispute may be resolved, including selling, leasing, dividing or swapping the land.
8. The matter will be resolved if a solution is found that is agreeable to both parties. If the parties fail to reach agreement after three joint meetings, the dispute is referred to the courts.

9. If a settlement is reached, a report is produced and signed by the parties to the dispute and the members of the panel. The settlement is registered with the Land and Property Directorate.
10. A reconciliation ceremony may occur if the parties resolve to do so and meet their responsibilities and costs incurred in doing so.

The Land and Property Directorate has had some degree of success in mediating a number of rural land conflicts. According to its records, of the 972 disputes brought to the Land and Property Directorate to January 2006, 314 were resolved through mediation.

**Table 10.1 Land and property directorate mediation**

| District | Documents | Disputes | | | |
|---|---|---|---|---|---|
| | | Resolved | Tribunal | In process | Total |
| Oecussi | 64 | 34 | 3 | 27 | 64 |
| Aileu | 40 | 22 | 2 | 16 | 40 |
| Ainaro | – | – | – | – | – |
| Bobonaro | 22 | 9 | 3 | 10 | 22 |
| Baucau | – | – | – | – | – |
| Covalima | 22 | 2 | 1 | 19 | 22 |
| Dili | 337 | 64 | 23 | 250 | 337 |
| Ermera | 18 | 12 | 3 | 3 | 18 |
| Liquica | 136 | 68 | 23 | 45 | 136 |
| Lautem | 29 | 14 | 4 | 11 | 29 |
| Manatuto | 7 | 1 | 3 | 3 | 7 |
| Manufahi | 13 | 6 | – | 7 | 13 |
| Viqueque | 57 | 8 | – | 49 | 57 |
| **Total** | **749** | **240** | **65** | **440** | **749** |

*Source*: LAND AND PROPERTY DIRECTORATE 2006

These figures correspond to the period from May 2002 to June 2007. In 2006 mediation services were minimal owing to the politico-military crisis. According to the head of Land Disputes and Mediation at the National Land and Property Directorate office, the reason no cases were brought for resolution/mediation in Baucau and Ainaro districts was that people in these districts preferred to use community-based mechanisms. However, Land and Property Directorate officials in Ainaro informed us that 36 cases were presented for mediation between 2000 and 2006, of which 6 cases were successfully resolved. The following sections take a closer look at Land and Property Directorate mediation in 3 districts: Ainaro, Maliana and Viqueque.

## Mediating Land Conflicts in Ainaro

As discussed in Chapter 9, a number of district government informants in Ainaro were sceptical of land dispute mediation by the Land and Property Directorate. They noted a lack of information on Land and Property Directorate services, and a degree of distrust of central government involvement in complex land conflicts. There is also a chronic lack of resourcing of district Land and Property Directorate offices, with 3 staff and 1 motorcycle to cover a district with a population of 52,400. These problems affect the willingness of disputants to have matters referred to Land and Property Directorate mediation, and the potential for cooperative action among land management agencies above the village level, including sub-district and district administrators, the police and the Land and Property Directorate itself.

In Chapter 9 we discussed complex cases in Ainaro arising from Portuguese and Indonesian era land practices that transformed the relationship between people and land. The following descriptions of attempted land dispute mediation in Ainaro draw attention to the difficulties of dealing with group-based claims to land that are tied to processes of territorialization of village government authority beginning during the Portuguese colonial period and continuing throughout the Indonesian occupation. The first case involves a dispute between the villages of Cassa and Mau-Nuno regarding land in the hamlet of Civil, Cassa Village, in the sub-district also known as Ainaro. There is a long history of political rivalry and violent conflict between these two communities pre-dating the establishment of the first military post in the area by the Portuguese colonial authorities (see Rawski 2002). Although the people of Cassa and Mau-Nuno are both predominantly Bunak-speaking and originally fell under the jurisdiction of a single *liurai* (petty-king/ruler) based in Cassa Tutun (Cassa Mountain), simmering tensions between these communities have periodically manifested themselves in outbursts of violence.[2] Locally, the land dispute in Civil is understood as forming part of this much longer history of conflict between the two communities. Attempts to mediate or resolve the conflict have been complicated by the involvement of a range of social actors and not only the immediate interested parties.

The Cassa group claim that, following the Second World War, land belonging to their ancestors was taken over by people from Mau-Nuno. They claim that the land in question was seized by force from the five resident families when Senhor A became chief of village of Mau-Nuno.[3] The Cassa families contend that they did not oppose the appropriation because of the political power of Senhor

2 According to informants from Cassa and Mau-Nuno, it was sometime immediately prior to the Second World War that 'Greater Cassa' was divided into two separate *sucos*.

3 Psuedonyms have been used for individuals involved in land dispute cases.

A.[4] They claimed that, geographically, the land was located within the territory of Cassa village and not that of Mau-Nuno. The Cassa group provided evidence of historical acts of possession – large foundation stones that they claimed were remnants of houses built there by their ancestors many years previously. For their part, the Mau-Nuno group claimed that the disputed land was an unoccupied rainforest when Senhor A became the chief of village in 1949. He and his brothers had cleared and cultivated the land. As evidence of these acts of possession, the Mau-Nuno group pointed to the few coconut trees growing on the land. In 1950, Senhor A and his brothers also dug a traditional irrigation system to change the land from a dry farm into a paddy field, and their descendants pointed to traces in the landscape to support their claim. As in other cases of land conflict, therefore, this case rests on contested historical narratives of possession. It also indicates that land disputes are often embedded in larger, frequently dialectic disputes between opposing interests. Such disputes require a close examination of local understandings of the conflict and an awareness of how these relate to broader historical processes involving relations of power.

On 13 December 2004, the two disputing groups converged on the land with traditional weapons including knives, machetes, and so-called 'Ambon' arrows. Reportedly, a police contingent then arrived to defuse the situation and seize the weapons. On 29 December 2004, a mediation team, consisting of the sub-district administrator of Ainaro, the village heads from Cassa and Mau-Nuno and staff from the Land and Property Directorate, invited the parties to the sub-district administration office for mediation talks. The mediation team recommended that the parties either find a way to utilize the disputed land together or agree to divide the land into two portions. According to the mediation case file, the Mau-Nuno party accepted the suggested alternatives and was willing to compromise, but the Cassa group refused them both, broke off negotiations and elected to take the case to court. In the interim the mediation team suggested that all activities on the disputed land be stopped while the parties waited for the court process.

Land and Property Directorate staff reported that the people of Mau-Nuno and Cassa were willing to solve the problem through the mediation process and share the use of the land, but owing to the advocacy of one man, Senhor B, who was a civil servant in Dili, the people of Cassa sought to pursue the land dispute before a civil court. Responding to the suggestion that the parties cease all activity on the land until the court process was heard, Senhor B wrote a letter to the Land and Property Directorate stating that if he received any report of people going hungry in the area he would ensure that the mediation team itself was prosecuted. The mediation team noted in their report that they felt Senhor B had missed the point and that stopping farming activities on the disputed land would prevent the likelihood of violence. In the absence of land law, there is yet to be a court hearing on the matter.

---

4 The *liurai* of Cassa had supported the Japanese occupying forces based in the Ainaro region during the Second World War. On the re-establishment of Portuguese colonial rule the *liurai* of Cassa was in a position of political weakness.

A second and related case involving the villages of Cassa and Builico highlights another long-standing dispute arising from the territorialization of village government structures under the Portuguese. This dispute concerns an 843 square metre portion of land used for irrigated rice in Dirukede. Based on information collected from the Builico group, the disputed land in question had been cleared by the people of Builico prior to the Japanese occupation during the Second World War. At that time, the prospective land was part of the territory of Raimea village. The Liurai of Raimea village, Malbiduk, was related to the people from Builico and so he let them cultivate the land for rice production in 1941. The Builico people dug an irrigation canal for this purpose. The Builico group also argued that they had physical evidence of their claim including coconut and mango trees growing on the disputed field. The Cassa group countered that from 1979 to 1999 they had occupied and farmed the disputed land, although they were unable to provide any evidence of their occupation in the form of plantation crops or settlement markers. In any event they noted that the land was geographically within Cassa village and formally within their administrative jurisdiction. The case was reported to the Land and Property Directorate district office by Senhor C, the nephew of one of the men who had excavated the irrigation canal, who asked the Land and Property Directorate to help mediate the case. On 17 January 2003 the Land and Property Directorate visited the disputed land with a view to hearing the competing claims, but the Cassa group failed to appear and, consequently, no resolution was achieved as both parties asserted their rights over the disputed land and refused to conciliate.

## Mediating Land Conflicts in Maliana

This section describes attempts at mediating a number of land disputes in Maliana. The first regards a relatively simple land dispute, involving two related individuals who agreed to divide the land in a mediated settlement. The second illustrates the accommodation of customary authority by Land and Property Directorate mediators, who returned the case for resolution by customary elders on the basis that there had been a traditional agreement (*juramento*) between the parties. The third is a complex conflict involving large numbers of claimants, and various accusations of collaboration with foreign occupiers. While this matter was not resolved through mediation, it does illustrate the successful use of interim 'no violence' agreements by Land and Property Directorate mediators.

The first case concerns a dispute between two claimants – Mateus and Abilio[5] – over the ownership of an irrigated rice field of little more than 2 hectares. The case demonstrates the manner in which 'ordinary' disputes over family ownership of land can become tangled in allegations about support for or opposition to the Indonesian occupation. According to Mateus, his father had farmed 4 hectares of rice field before and after the Indonesian invasion in 1975. Mateus claimed

5 Psuedonyms have been used for individuals involved in land dispute cases.

that Abilio began using the land under dispute in 1981 under a share-cropping agreement with Mateus's father. Abilio disputed this history and alleged that his father had owned and farmed the disputed plot of land until he gave it to the Catholic Mission for safekeeping after he was exiled by the Indonesian invasion. According to Abilio, his family returned to Maliana in 1997 and began farming the land again. When Mateus tried to claim the land in 1997, Abilio accused him of wanting to use it to feed the pro-independence resistance. Abilio was forced to flee the land once more in 1999 and returned later that year, recommencing farming in 2000. In his written deposition to the Land and Property Directorate, Abilio stated that after the Indonesians left in 1999 Mateus's father told Abilio to leave the land. At the time, Mateus's father was accompanied by Luis. The suggestion in Abilio's written deposition was that Luis was a member of the armed resistance and his accompanying Mateus's father was a veiled threat.

The dispute escalated in January 2001, when Mateus came to the rice fields with numerous members of his family and allegedly threatened Abilio, accusing him of having been an Indonesian collaborator and suggesting that the harvest from the rice field would be used to feed the pro-independence Falintil soldiers who had returned from Aileu. Abilio then made a complaint to the Land and Property Directorate office in Maliana, the police and the local village heads on 21 February 2001. A meeting was held the next day between the parties to the conflict, the police and community elders. One village head suggested to Abilio that he agree to share the land with Mateus, but Abilio refused. Abilio and Mateus ultimately agreed that neither party would farm the land while they took their case to the Land and Property Directorate. It seems that nothing further occurred until 2003. Mateus filed a complaint at the Land and Property Directorate on 18 February 2003. Abilio wrote to the head of the Land and Property Directorate on 2 March 2003 outlining his arguments. Both letters were copied to the sub-district administrator and the local village heads.

The Land and Property Directorate subsequently invited both parties to a meeting where the mediator asked each of them questions separately. The mediator told the parties that there were a number of options available to them. For example, one could keep all the land; both could share the land; or one could relinquish his claim to the land. The mediator advised the parties that if they could not reach an agreement through mediation, they should take their case to court. Both parties demonstrated a reluctance to take the case to court and argued that it was the other party's responsibility to do so. In interviews for this case study, Mateus stated that he wished to resolve the problem through mediation because he and Abilio were from the same hamlet and were related through marriage, and should therefore try to resolve the case so that neither family lost out completely. He also wanted to avoid 'locking' the land in a dispute and ultimately having it 'taken back' by the state.

The parties ultimately agreed to divide the land. On 4 March 2003 an agreement letter was co-signed by the parties to the dispute, the head of the Maliana Land and Property Directorate office, the sub-district administrator and four witnesses. It provided that the disputed land should be divided in two, with Abilio keeping the east side of the field and Mateus keeping the west side of the field. The division of the field was calculated according to the amount of rice produced, and it was agreed that, since Abilio had invested more in maintaining the terracing, and so on (*kabubu*), he should retain slightly more land than Mateus. The letter included an acknowledgement that the agreement was reached together and that no person had forced or threatened the parties to make the agreement.

After signing the agreement at the Land and Property Directorate office, both parties went to the field to establish the border with the sub-district administrator, the head of the district Land and Property Directorate and the village head. The border was established by sight and marked using stakes and rope. It was decided that Mateus would make the mound/terracing along this agreed border. While the case appears to be an example of successful dispute resolution by the Land and Property Directorate, it is notable that the agreement was reached in the context of the displacement of one of the parties, Abilio, who may have had few options other than to agree to the division of the land. The case highlights the 'home court' advantage of a current possessor, particularly in a weak state environment where decisions to evict may be met with violent acts of resistance.

*Return to Customary Authority:*
*Tapo/Memo and Odomau villages*

This case concerns a dispute over the border of a rice field of approximately 60 hectares between two villages: Tapo/Memo and Odomau. It provides an example where the Land and Property Directorate did not allow legal forum shopping in relation to a dispute purportedly resolved in 1974. The people from Tapo/Memo claim that in 1968–69 their community was involved in digging an irrigation channel to the disputed land and that in 1970 they started planting rice on the land. The people of Odomau argue that the land is theirs, they have been farming it since the end of the Japanese occupation and they were responsible for digging the irrigation channels to the disputed land. The dispute over the land appears to have first emerged in 1974, at which time the district administrator ordered the village heads of Tapo/Memo and Odomau to resolve the problem. The people of Odomau claim that the village heads resolved the dispute at this time by agreeing to a border with witnesses from leading families of each village.

The dispute came to the attention of the Land and Property Directorate in December 2002 when the district police responded to a fight between groups of farmers from each village. Police officers took four farmers from Tapo/Memo who had been involved in the dispute to the Land and Property Directorate office in Maliana. Forty farmers from Odomau also went to the Land and Property Directorate office and told staff there that when they went to their fields they found that a group of farmers from Tapo/Memo were working 'their' land. For their part, Tapo/Memo villagers alleged that the 1974 agreement was tainted by the two village heads' subsequent support for the Indonesian occupation.

An official complaint was made by a representative from Tapo/Memo who claimed that people from Odomau were 'occupying' Tapo/Memo land. The mediator told the groups to return in one week, and in the interim he talked to elders from both communities to learn more about the history of the rice fields. It became apparent that there were a number of people who had witnessed the establishment of the village boundary, including customary elders from the origin group lineage. As a result the Land and Property Directorate decided to 'hand back' the case to customary authorities. In the interim, the directorate facilitated an agreement between the parties that provided the Odomau group could continue to farm the land, and would accept pursuit of the case through legal channels by the people of Tapo/Memo. The agreement also included a no violence commitment. The form of agreement is significant in that, even though Land and Property Directorate officials reverted the case to customary authorities, on the basis of the agreement reached in 1974, they also countenanced the possibility of a claim through a court of law. Ideally, a court would enforce an agreement reached in the absence of fraud, misrepresentation or duress; and, in that event the post-conflict state would increase its legitimacy by co-opting the authority of a local customary determination. Conversely, however, there would be scope for legal forum shopping, and implicit competition between customary and state processes, should the court rule in favour of the Tapo/Memo claims.

## Conflict and Contestation on the Nunura Plain in Maliana

The third Maliana mediation case involves a complex case on the Nunura plain. As the population of Maliana district grew, people from the hilltop settlement of Uat settled on the Nunura plain just south of Maliana town (see Chapter 8). While some narratives describe the grant of rights to Nunura land by local origin groups – the houses of Achu and Achu Plaza – it was common for informants from Maliana town, including Uat, to suggest that in the past (pre-Indonesian times) most of the land on the Nunura plain was 'free' or 'wild', and people were able to farm where they pleased, according to their own resources. Within this general narrative of first possession in circumstances of land abundance there are a number of subsidiary bases for claims. Some informants from Uat link their claims to land on the Nunura plain to colonial 'development' programmes implemented during the post-war period. Others claim to have negotiated access to land more recently, 'according to custom' (Tetun: *tuir adat, tuir kultura*), either through marriage, the exchange of certain goods and services with local land-holding groups, or long-term occupancy and use.[6] This category of claimant illustrates the emergence of 'customary' justifications for land entitlements even in areas first claimed and cultivated under colonial programmes.

6 Informants claimed that, in the case of fallow fields, they maintained occupancy by planting markers of ownership such as teak trees around the perimeter, or a particular type of shrub that is later used as mulch when the field is cleared for farming.

Others again claim to have purchased land or property outright – either from the state or private individuals – during the Indonesian period, or since independence. The strategic decisions of claimants to refer to different sources of legitimacy for their claims supports a theoretical proposition set out in Chapter 3: that as resource values rise rules of first possession may not only take on complexity, in an attempt to manage in-migration, but may compete with emergent institutional alternatives for property legitimacy such as state grant or adverse possession. In the absence of a state capable of enforcing a single rule of entitlement, there is an increased likelihood not of Demsetzian transition to better-defined rights under the influence of rising resource values, but of chronic property uncertainty and latent land tensions because there is no authoritative determination of entitlements, and displaced groups agitate for political change in order to change the net pay-offs of resort to violence.

Currently, a number of people from Uat are involved in an ongoing land dispute with other groups from the village of Ritabou. The land dispute concerns approximately 42 hectares of rice paddy fields located in Ai-Kiar in Maliana sub-district. According to the village head of Ritabou (2005–09), the conflict involves 32 people from the hamlet of Uat, who claim that their land is being occupied by a smaller group of 11 people from the hamlet of Meganutu. People from Uat situate this land conflict within a much longer and broader history of inter-group conflict involving highly localized political rivalries, the effects of Portuguese colonial policy and political disenfranchisement during the Indonesian occupation. It serves as an excellent example of the complexities involved in disentangling land conflicts from their broader social, economic and political context in East Timor.

According to informants from the village of Ritabou, during Portuguese times the village comprised four hamlets: Uat, Ritabou, Dai Tete and Meganutu.[7] In the late 1950s and early 1960s, the population of these hamlets was organized into work groups by their village head and hamlet head to work on schemes initiated by the colonial authorities to 'develop' the Nunura plain for agriculture.[8] Some informants claimed that the local authorities negotiated access to land directly with local land-holding groups on behalf of the community. Others claim that the vast majority of the land in and around present-day Maliana town was, during the post-Second World War period, uncultivated or forested land that had never been used or had long been abandoned. Consequently, the local authorities simply identified an area of land and allocated plots to the members of the work groups.

In the case of Ai-Kiar, informants claim that the work groups involved in first clearing this area of land came from the hamlets of Uat, Meganutu and Dai Tete. They had to work hard to clear the land, which they described as thick Eucalypt

7 The original settlement of the people of Meganutu was located on the steep slopes of Loe Lako Mountain.

8 Although this presumably occurred under the auspices of the Colonial Agricultural Department, few informants describe working on these fields in terms of taking part in a state initiative. Most informants referred exclusively to the role played by their village head and hamlet head in 'opening up' the land.

forest (Tetun: *ai bubur laran*). Those involved in the clearing of the land considered this forest to be *rai lulik* (Tetun: sacred land) because it was old forest that had not yet been farmed. To add to the 'sacred' and therefore 'untamed' nature of the forest and land, informants from Uat claim that one person died in the process of clearing the forest for failing to adhere to certain taboos regarding natural resources.[9] Informants from Uat stated that more families from Meganutu came from the uplands to farm and they negotiated with the people of Uat to 'open' a larger tract of land to the south of the original plot. Groups from Uat, Meganutu and Dai Tete continued to farm this land up until the early 1970s.

The Carnation Revolution in Portugal during April 1974 generated a great deal of excitement and anxiety in Portuguese Timor. Not long after 25 April 1974, embryonic political parties started to form in the colony.[10] Political participation during this time was largely the privilege of elite groups – sons and daughters of *liurai*, plantation owners, educated *mestizos*. In Maliana sub-district, as elsewhere in Timor Leste, the vast majority of informants described having made choices about party membership or affiliation based on highly localized patterns of allegiance rather than party policies (CAVR 2005).[11]

The choices made by key figures within the community were based on pre-existing allegiances and rivalries. There is a long history of animosity between the houses of Uat and the house of origin of the *liurai* of Ritabou.[12] By the 1970s, this rivalry manifested itself as an ongoing dispute over who had the authority to rule over the village of Ritabou. Elders from Uat state that the Portuguese gave the title of *liurai* (king) and a *bandeira* (flag) as a sign of office to the *txu'uman* (headman) of the house of Bau Ubun – one of the original ten houses of *Sapulu Nera* (Uat) and the ancestral house of the former *liurai* of Ritabou. However, they later granted

9 Informants claim one man died for failing to adhere to the prohibition on eating river shrimps. Although informants did not explicitly associate the death of one member of the community with the process of 'taming' the land, they implied that this death was a 'blood sacrifice' of sorts to the 'keepers of the forest', the shades or spirits that originally inhabited the area Ai-Kiar. In reference to histories of migration of the people of Uat described above, one informant claimed that representatives of the houses of Duas Mali and Lua Laben performed the necessary rituals to 'tame' the spirits of the land.

10 UDT, União Democratica Timorense, founded on 11 May 1974, ASDT (renamed itself Fretilin in September 1974) Associação Social Democrata Timorense, 20 May 1974, Apodeti, Associação Popular Democrática Timorense, 27 May and Kota, Klibur Oan Timor Aswain on 20 November 1974.

11 See also page 25, Chapter 3, CAVR 2005.

12 Although it is not clear whether this happened before or after the granting of the flag to the house of Bili Ubun, elders from the house of Manephat described how the house of Bau Ubun (the *liurai's uma fukun*) was 'expelled' from Uat for persistently breaching the moral code. Eventually, the people of Bau Ubun, who had been captured and held ransom by a neighbouring village, were 'freed' by representatives of one of the houses of Usi, who paid their ransom (one large *belak* or gold plate) and gave them some land on which to settle. This land was called *Rita Bou* meaning 'silkwood grove').

another symbol of office to representatives of the house of Bili Ubun.[13] Informants from Uat believe that, by granting this flag, the Portuguese authorities bestowed on the house of Bili Ubun the role of village head.[14] The advent of political parties gave the main parties of this dispute an opportunity to consolidate constituencies. The majority of the people of Uat and part of Dai Tete followed the political choice of their village head and joined Fretilin (Frente Revolucionária de Timor Leste Independente), while many of the people of Meganutu chose to support UDT (União Democratica Timorense), the political party of the former *liurai* of Ritabou.

Regular work on the fields at Ai-Kiar was disrupted by the Indonesian invasion in late 1975. When describing the displacement caused by the invasion many informants from Maliana sub-district made the distinction between those who fled to West Timor and those who fled to the mountains. Often the implication was that those who had joined UDT or Apodeti fled to the west, while those who supported Fretilin fled to the mountains. Informants from Uat claim that they fled from their upland and lowland settlements to Loelako Mountain or towards Bobonaro and Atsabe. They also claim that on their return to Maliana they found that the fields in Ai-Kiar had been occupied.

The original work group from Uat to work on the fields in Ai-Kiar included the village head and his sons. Relatives of this original group claim that after the Indonesian invasion their political rival, the *liurai* of Ritabou, ordered families from Meganutu to occupy these fields. Following the invasion, the *liurai* of Ritabou allied himself with the Indonesian authorities, together with other local UDT representatives, such as João Tavares.[15] Informants from Uat claim that the *liurai* of Ritabou took this opportunity to effectively 'banish' (*desterra*) the hamlet of Uat, placing it under the jurisdiction of an upland village Malilait, Bobonaro sub-district. Although they were not physically removed or forced to resettle in their upland village, some people from Uat felt that the actions taken by the *liurai* effectively disenfranchised their community who no longer had a say in the local government of Ritabou village. Not all land in the lowlands, previously farmed by members of the community of Uat, was occupied. It was mainly those who were politically active, the village head and his close relatives, who were affected.

13 This flag – which bears the modern Portuguese standard – remains in possession of the community of Uat and is kept with the *sacra* of the house of Manephat, who are considered to be the 'deputies' of the house of Bili Ubun.

14 During the 'monarchia' (pre-Republic) the Portuguese authorities bestowed military ranks on petty-kings and local 'big men'. It was not until the early 1900s that the colonial authorities gradually imposed a uniform system of administration based on the Tetun model of *suco* (see Traube 1986: 100), It is possible that the Portuguese authorities wittingly or unwittingly exacerbated existing rivalries between houses and clans as a means of bringing the population under colonial control.

15 Formerly a member of UDT, João Tavares was appointed as *Bupati* (district administrator) by the Indonesian authorities. He established the notorious *Halilintar* militia in the mid 1970s responsible for killings at the Maliana Police Station 8 September 1999. For more information see: http://www.villagechief.com/mot/cons92z%20-%20Joao%20 Tavares.htm, or Tanter, Ball and Van Klinken 2006.

Tensions between the family of the former village head and those who were accused of occupying their land came to a head in 1987. During this year, the Indonesian administration began implementing a national project (PRONAS) to register title to land. When the authorities were called to Ai-Kiar to survey plots located between the boundaries of land that had been originally farmed by people from Meganutu and Dai Tete, representatives from the former village head's family intervened to stop the surveyors. Informants from Uat claim that one of the parties occupying the land made threats to the previous occupants from Uat to the effect that while Indonesia was in power they would continue to farm the land. Despite these threats a small group from Uat continued to farm land in the lowlands. The implicit threat of violence in 1987 illustrates the risks of attempts to clarify rights, in this type of conflict-affected environment, through bright-line land titling programmes.

In 1992, the son of the former *chefe suco* (village head during Portuguese times) was 'elected' *kepala desa* (Indonesian title for village head) in spite of the fact that the people from his original hamlet, Uat, were not able to vote because they had been placed administratively under a different village. According to relatives of the *kepala desa*, he tried to negotiate with the head of Malilait village, the sub-district and district authorities to try to restore relations between the people of Uat and the *liurai* of Ritabou. He prepared a petition letter to the district administrator asking for Uat to be restored to Ritabou, acknowledging the authority of the *liurai* and the village head (*kepala desa*) in their respective roles and reiterating the ties that bound the communities together as members of the broader *uma fukun boot* (large ancestral house) of Leo Sibe.[16] However the land dispute in Ai-Kiar was not resolved, notwithstanding the systematic attempt to co-opt sources of property legitimacy.

Since 1999, the hamlet of Uat has been reincorporated into the village of Ritabou and the first village head to be elected post-independence (2005–09) was from the houses of Duas Mali and Manephat of Uat. As early as October 2000, members of Uat community attempted to make some reconciliatory moves towards the people who were occupying their land. According to informants from Uat, they wanted to try to resolve the problem according to customary relations of *maun-alin* (siblings and agnates) and *uma mane, mane foun* (affinal relations). The readiness of the people of Uat to participate in informal dispute resolution appears to be motivated in part by their belief that they would not receive a fair trial through the courts because of the real or perceived influence that the *liurai* of Ritabou, with whom the Meganutu group are close, might have over a formal process through the courts.[17]

16 Petition letter sighted by the author, including list of signatures and declaration of readiness to pay the administrative fee required to transfer Uat back under the jurisdiction of Ritabou. The petition also included a more contentious request to change the name of the *suco* from Ritabou to Uat.

17 The suggestion was that the *liurai* would intervene in the process through family connections or by virtue of having contacts with 'more educated' Dili-based civil servants and lawyers.

This dispute was officially taken to the Land and Property Directorate in January 2002. A memorandum of understanding between the parties to the conflict was signed on 11 January 2002. Under the memorandum the parties agreed to participate in mediation and agreed that while this process was underway neither party would farm the land under dispute.

The Land and Property Directorate organized a number of meetings between January 2002 and July 2003 in an effort to mediate between the two parties. The mediators included the village head of Ritabou and the local sub-district administrator. However, the people from Uat were not satisfied with the process and wanted more mediators to be involved, including the local church and human rights organizations. It appears that the people from Uat did not want to discuss the land issue in isolation from other issues of disenfranchisement that occurred during the Indonesian period.

An agreement was signed on 7 March 2003 by representatives of the Uat and the Ritabou groups, and the local village head. The agreement provided that the parties to the dispute:

- survey the land at Ai-Kiar so that a map could be created for mediation purposes;
- not engage in violence during the survey process; and
- send a representative from each group to a mediation meeting of the Land and Property Directorate together with the village head, sub-village head and the sub-district administrator.

A group of mediators and staff from the national Land and Property Directorate office came to interview individuals involved in the conflict in April 2003. The National Chief of Mediation sent a letter to the head of the Maliana Land and Property Directorate on 23 July 2003 advising that the National Director of the Land and Property Directorate had directed that the case be resolved through the courts. According to the letter, this direction had been made owing to the failure of mediation on 18 July 2003. The case represents an unsuccessful attempt at mediation, which is not surprising given the large numbers, heterogeneous sources of property legitimacy, and group grievances over alleged collaboration with foreign occupiers. Nevertheless, it is notable for its use of an interim no violence agreement.

No violence agreements were emphasized in the mediation training Land and Property Directorate officials received in 2005. Typically, they include acknowledgement that the parties to the conflict have entered voluntarily into the agreement, commitment not to engage in violence while the case is going through mediation, and to continue the agreement if the case goes to court, and some arrangement concerning the disputed land (for example, agreement that neither party can farm in the interim, agreement to rotate use, or agreement that one party can farm the land). No violence agreements are usually documented and witnessed by local authorities, such as the village heads, the sub-district administrator and the Land and Property Directorate.

## Chronic Possessory Conflict on the Coastal Plains of Viqueque

Our final example of attempts at land conflict mediation concerns a well-publicized series of land disputes on the Uato Lari coastal plains of Viqueque that involves claims of possession and dispossession resulting from the development of coastal land for agriculture under colonial supervision. The notoriety of these land disputes lies in the politically charged context in which the development of the coastal plain originally took place and the way in which these disputes have subsequently been worked into local narratives of grievance and memories of inter- and intra-community conflict (see Gunter 2007: 8). This case illustrates once again the difficulties of extrapolating complex land conflicts from the socio-political dimension of disputes between opposing interests and their relation to historical processes involving relations of power.

The land disputes in question mainly concern areas of valuable irrigated rice paddy close to Darabai, the current seat of Uato-Lari sub-district administration;[18] land that traditionally falls within the claimed domain of the customary rulers of Vessoru-Uaitame.[19] The land disputes involve an estimated 30 to 50 individual cases relating to specific rice paddies each with separate histories and particular circumstances.[20] Collectively these cases have come to represent shifting power relations between predominantly Makassae-speaking villages of Makadiki and Matahoe and the majority Naueti population of Vessoru/Uaitame, Afaloicai and Babulo, which is linked to respective historical alliances with Fretilin (Frente Revolucionária de Timor Leste Independente) and with Apodeti (the pro-Indonesian, Associação Popular Democratica Timorense). However, these cases are not consistently divided along ethnic and political lines, nor is the actual composition of the village populations involved as homogeneous as this analysis might suggest. The risk of over-simplistic

18 Most reported disputes are from areas such as *Ofo-oan, Narekisi, Gaelaran, Aitara-oan* and *Fahidebun*. It should be noted that over time other land disputes have arisen in the area between individuals and within families over issues such as inheritance, marriage exchange agreements, unrecorded sale and purchase transactions as well as disagreements over share-cropping or tenancy arrangements. By and large these disputes have been settled locally between the interested parties. Furthermore, not all land on the coastal plain is contested, nor is farming entirely constrained by various types of dispute. Agricultural productivity in the area is held back by a number of factors including – lack of infrastructure, lack of markets, poor or low seed quality and distribution, availability of labour and the availability of resources such as buffalo or mechanization to prepare fields for cultivation and harvesting.

19 'Lords of the land' from the village of Babulo claim that their ancestors originally delegated stewardship of the sacred springs of *bee matan saketo* and *been matan lobuto* to the rulers of Vessoru-Uaitame and also ceded an area of land between the rivers of *bee lia* and *bee saketo* – corresponding to land around Darabai – in exchange for the role they played in establishing the peace between the people of Babulo and Builo (see Chapter 4).

20 Source: case files viewed by the author from the Land and Property Directorate and the Justice and Peace Commission of the Catholic Church based in Uato-Lari.

analysis is that it serves not only to obscure the root causes of the conflict but also obstructs any meaningful attempts to mediate between the individuals and groups involved in the underlying land disputes.

In very general terms, most of the land disputes have their roots in the way the Portuguese colonial administration ordered the development of the Uato Lari coastal plain for rice cultivation and the real or perceived use of the rice fields as a tool by the Portuguese colonial authorities to 'punish' their enemies and by the Indonesian authorities to 'reward' their allies.

According to the testimonies of local informants and case files collected by the Directorate for Land and Property and the local Justice and Peace Committee of the Catholic Church, the customary rulers of Vessoru-Uaitame allocated areas of land on the Uato Lari plain to different groups through traditional kinship and marriage arrangements, some as early as 1865, others after the 1950s. These customary arrangements were interrupted by the implementation of colonial programmes aimed at clearing the coastal plain for rice cultivation. Again, therefore, the disputes illustrate the intractability of conflicts over possession and dispossession in circumstances of foreign occupation and periodic regime change.

Beginning in the mid to late 1930s and gathering pace in the 1950s, the Portuguese colonial authorities instructed heads of the upland villages, including Afaloicai, Uaitame and Babulo, to organize people to clear land for rice cultivation on the coastal plain. The land was cleared and planted for irrigated rice cultivation. Working with hamlet heads, the village headmen mapped and divided the land among those who took part in the clearing and cultivation efforts. While the people of Vessoru-Uaitame and Afaloicai were mainly involved in clearing land west of the Bee Bui River, the people of Babulo worked east of the river and on land surrounding the coastal lagoon of Bee Saen.[21]

It was during this period that some village and hamlet heads began to grow in prominence and in some cases were able to accumulate considerable areas of land. Local informants claim that certain village heads and *liurai* were able to requisition free labour from *asuliar* (auxiliaries) and *ema reinu* (people of the suku) or *atan* (slaves) to 'open' up large tracts of previously heavily forested or swamp land on the coastal plain and claim these as their own.

Those who occupied the rice fields developed under village government supervision appear to have acknowledged the overarching ritual and spiritual authority of the customary rulers of Vessoru-Uaitame over this land. However, the acknowledgement of customary land stewardship did not necessarily extend to recognition of authority over the use or generational transfer of land. In fact, the rice fields are claimed on the basis of heritable individual rights, notwithstanding that these rights were never translated into documentary rights of statutory ownership. In this sense, therefore, there has been a transition from collective to private property arrangements under the influence of rising resource values. The

21 This land was part of the domain of the Darlari lords of the land of Babulo. Some rice fields close to Bee Saen were also cultivated by people from Afaloicai.

mechanism of transition was individuated claims based on possession and input of labour, under the aegis of colonial village government authority.

In 1959, a number of elites from Afaloicai, Vessoru-Uaitame, and to a lesser degree from Babulo, were implicated in what became known as the 'Rebellion of '59' against Portuguese colonial rule (see Gunter 2007 and Chamberlain 2009 for in-depth analysis of the rebellion).[22] In the aftermath of the rebellion not only the elites but also the general population suffered. The Portuguese authorities resorted to the use of pro-Portuguese Timorese militia known as *arraiais* from areas such as Ossu, Venilale, Baguia, Viqueque and Lospalos to 'quell' the rebellion.[23] The *arraiais* swept through the area burning, looting, raping and killing. A number of elites, including the *liurai* of Afaloicai, were shot in the Bee Bui River while others were imprisoned in Angola.[24] People from Afaloicai and Vessoru-Uaitame who had settled on the coast and worked on the rice fields were forced to flee to their upland settlements close to the Matebian mountain range.[25]

Between 1960 and 1962, the Portuguese authorities through the administrator of Uato Lari sub-district established work groups of *volontarios* (volunteers) from the villages of Matahoe and Makadiki (mainly Makassae speakers originally settled in the upland areas between Ossu and the Matebian mountain range) to work on the vacant rice fields. Allegedly, these work groups included members of the *arraiais* who had been mobilized to subdue the rebellion in 1959 and had not otherwise received any payment from the colonial authorities (JPC 2000). The new possessors undertook repair of damaged infrastructure and a further round of clearing and planting land.[26] As with the people from Afaloicai, Vessoru-Uaitame and Babulo, the members of the new work teams received no documentary proof of title from the colonial administration.

In 1972, a group from Afaloicai village lodged a claim with the Uato Lari sub-district administrator for the return of some land to Afaloicai village members. This

22 The rebellion was centred in Viqueque district and included a number of village heads with kinship ties to a senior customary leader affiliated with the Japanese during the Second World War. It has been suggested by Gunter that viewed from a local perspective the rebellion was an expression of localized power struggles and motivated by the grievances of local elites who had been punished by the colonial authorities for having allied themselves with the Japanese during the Second World War rather than an organized ideological resistance to colonial rule.

23 The word *arraiais* has its roots in medieval Portuguese and was associated with 'royal' encampment during war. In the context of Timor Leste, it was used to describe a group mobilized to attack another group, something like a war party or punitive column (Gunter 2008: 55, Pélissier 1996).

24 Gunter 2007:, 34; *see* also Cases 10, 13 and, 16 of Land and Property Directorate Uato Lari mediation records held on file with the authors.

25 See case notes: Cases 1, 6, 9, 10, 11, 12, 13, 14, 15, 17, 20, 21 and 25 of Land and Property Directorate Uato Lari mediation records.

26 See case notes: Cases 1, 2, 6, 7, 9, 10, 11, 12, 14, 16, 18, 20, 21, 23, 24 and 25 of Land and Property Directorate Uato Lari mediation records.

claim was granted.[27] The remainder of the land seized after the 1959 rebellion was left in the possession of the *volontario* work groups and their descendants, who continued to improve the irrigation and infrastructure of the rice fields. In 1980, during the period of Indonesian occupation, the dispossessed people of Afaloicai and Vessoru-Uaitame made another claim to local government. By this time a number of local leaders from Afaloicai had prominent roles in the Indonesian administration (Gunter 2007).[28] This appeal resulted in a gathering of hamlet and village heads in Uaitame village who decided that some land should be returned to the pre-1959 possessors.[29] Other land was returned by order of the Indonesian-appointed sub-district head of Uato Lari and, in one case, by an Indonesian court.[30] According to some former members of the *volontario* work groups, some of the land subject to restitution orders included areas first cleared and cultivated by their forebears after 1962.[31] Some Afaloicai claimants also allege that certain areas land were never returned, notwithstanding acts of first clearing and cultivation before 1958.[32]

In early 2000, following the violence and displacement that occurred in the aftermath of the UN-organized popular consultation on 30 August 1999, a number of descendants of the *volontario* work groups took advantage of the Indonesian withdrawal to claim or take possession of the Uato Lari land held by their forebears from 1962 to 1980. Some of the land was vacant as a result of the 1999 displacements;[33] other areas of land were seized by force.[34] Those reoccupying the land alleged collaboration of certain groups from Afaloicai, Vessoru-Uaitame and Babulo with the Indonesian occupiers, while associating themselves with the pro-independence Timorese resistance movement (Gunter 2007). The dispossessed from Afaloicai, Vessoru and Babulo did not engage in large-scale confrontations to recover their land as many believed that regime change would favour the re-

27 The group was led by Antonio 'Metan' Costa Soares, one of the main protagonists of the '59 rebellion who had by this time returned from exile and imprisonment in Angola – see Case 1 of Land and Property Directorate Uato Lari mediation records.

28 The Afaloicai claim was based not on legal rights and remedies to recover possession, but on the basis that, as security in the area is now maintained by the Indonesian military, there was no longer a need for the pro-Portuguese militia to occupy the land.

29 See case notes: Cases 1 and 7 of Land and Property Directorate Uato Lari mediation records. The meeting was convened by the sub-district head Mr Eugenio da Costa Soares in Uaitame village and involved four village heads, one hamlet head, two community leaders and one customary leader. The village heads were also all customary leaders. Six rice fields were returned to their previous owners.

30 See case notes: Cases 2, 3, 6, 17 and 25 of Land and Property Directorate Uato Lari mediation records.

31 See case notes: Cases 4 and 7 of Land and Property Directorate Uato Lari mediation records.

32 See case notes: Case 18 and 23 of Land and Property Directorate Uato Lari mediation records.

33 See case notes: Cases 1, 3, 11, 16 and 24.

34 See case notes: Cases 2, 10, 12, 13, 14, 15, 19, 20 and 21.

occupiers. However, there was a great deal of social tension and some outbreaks of violence between members of the two groups.[35]

In June 2000 a team from the UN Transitional Administration in East Timor (UNTAET) was invited to participate in a series of 'community dialogues' organized by the Justice and Peace Commission of Uato-Lari Parish, together with the Investigation and Consultation Commission established by the CNRT (Conselho Nacional de Resistêcia Timorense) and the Dili-based human rights organization Yayasan-Hak. The dialogues aimed at resolving the ongoing land disputes in a peaceful manner. Local participants agreed in principle to systematically document individual land disputes and engage in a mediation process or refer cases to the courts. Based on training from Canadian experts, the dialogue organizers focused on obtaining interim agreements that the disputants would not engage in violence while the disputes awaited local mediation or hearings before the courts (JPC 2000). While this limited approach achieved a degree of success in terms of forestalling further violence, it did not lead to mediated agreements in any of the cases.

Since 2000, there has been little progress resolving the disputes.[36] According to members of the local Justice and Peace Commission, of the 36 cases they documented and handed over to the Directorate for Land and Property during this period, only 4 cases have been resolved through mediation and 1 case has been taken to court but is yet to be heard.[37] In 2004, a number of disputants approached the Commission for Reception, Truth and Reconciliation (known by its Portuguese acronym CAVR) to intervene in the case and arrange for a community reconciliation meeting. However, the CAVR had no authority to mediate or arbitrate land conflicts. During field work conducted in the area in 2006–07, it was apparent that those involved in these land disputes had chosen to 'wait for the law' rather than engaging in any new 'dialogues' or 'mediation' attempts. The political tensions that underpin the land disputes continue to simmer below the surface and there is a risk that any future application of legal rules to the area will reignite the conflict there.[38]

---

35 Buffalo thefts, acts of intimidation and attacks on property in Uato-Lari sub-district became a major source of concern not only for the local community but also for the Timorese national leadership and the United Nations Transitional Administration (UNTAET).

36 According to case files held by the Land and Property Directorate there were high expectations that UNTAET would be able to 'resolve' the land disputes. However, in late 2000, a decision was made by the East Timorese Transitional Administration (ETTA – developed under UNTAET as part of the process of Timorization of the Transitional Administration) that no decisions would be made regarding land and property issues until after official independence in 2002.

37 Under Law No 1 of 2003, the Land and Property Directorate has jurisdiction over disputes relating to land and property.

38 Outbursts of violence have continued, most notably during the presidential campaign of 2007 when scores of families were displaced and over 200 houses burnt down, and again most recently during the 2012 presidential campaign.

## Conclusion

Surveys suggest that traditional dispute resolution mechanisms in East Timor are regarded as cheaper, faster, fairer, more accessible, easier to understand, subject to less corruption, and more likely to promote reconciliation than the courts (Timor Leste Land Law Program 2004).[39] While there is an obvious need for state recognition of traditional justice, traditional mechanisms are performing well without state assistance in the vast majority of land disputes involving small numbers and related parties. Far more significant problems of dispute resolution concern more complex forms of conflict, involving groups of claimants or individuals from different ethno-linguistic groups, with competing narratives of possession and dispossession overlaid by accusations of collaboration with colonial or neo-colonial forces. Notwithstanding the widespread use and effectiveness of local dispute resolution procedures in East Timor, there are evident limits to the capacity of local authorities and customary institutions to deal with complex land disputes that have arisen as a result of changing government regimes or policies of land development or population displacement and relocation. These conflicts require involvement by the state, not only through mediation but also in terms of law.

Our case studies suggest that land dispute mediation by the Land and Property Directorate can play an important dispute management role but is limited by issues of capacity, jurisdiction and legitimacy. Land and Property Directorate mediation has had some success with simpler cases and with interim no violence agreements. Mediation offers the potential to 'fill the gap' between local mechanisms for resolving disputes and legal rules applied by the courts. Mediation can incorporate traditional institutions and reconciliation ceremonies if the parties agree, and allow referral to the courts of disputes that cannot be resolved by mediation. Yet, the authority of the Land and Property Directorate to mediate disputes does not apply to disputes over state land or to disputes where the state is otherwise a party. Moreover, in the current circumstances of East Timor, involving mediation without a law on private ownership of land, there are perverse incentives for disputants to 'wait for law' rather than attempt voluntary agreement. Clearly there is a need for some type of legal rule to supplement mediation and provide the possibility of authoritative resolution of land conflict. The question is the design of the legal rule and its potential effect on complex land conflicts.

At the end of the next chapter we discuss broad choices between interpretive complexity and simplicity in the formation of property rules relating to land disputes after armed conflicts. On the one hand, there are arguments for fuzzy rules that avoid 'winner take all' solutions, in circumstances of potential violence, and allows flexible regulatory space for local negotiations (Gillespie 2010).

39 Timor-Leste Land Law Program. 2004. Report on Research Findings and Policy Recommendations for a Legal Framework for Land Dispute Mediation. Dili. February 2004, pp. 48, 49, 52. Available online at: http://www.jsmp.minihub.org/Traditional%20Justice/Reports/LLP_Mediation%20Report/LLPMediationReportEnglish.pdf [accessed 24 June 2007].

This type of regulatory approach provides for weak state circumstances, which inhibit the scope for coercive enforcement of legal determinations, and allows more regulatory space for co-option of non-state sources of property authority. On the other hand, there are arguments favouring a relatively simple rule of possession in weak state circumstances, as it avoids the need for forced evictions, which challenge state capacity and potentially provoke violent conflict, while also building on the 'home-court' advantage of current possessors. This 'home-court' advantage derives from the defensive benefits of occupation, the territorial incentives to protect possession, and the costs of eviction. We conclude that the appropriate rule in post-conflict cases of contested possession involves context-specific assessment of the relative capacity for violence of the claimants, and the prospects for peaceable resolution through flexible accommodation of overlapping claims. In either case this chapter suggests a role for mediation, particularly in relation to simpler forms of land conflict.

## References

Asia Foundation 2008. Law and Justice in Timor–Leste: A Survey of Citizen Awareness and Attitudes Regarding Law and Justice in East Timor.

Asia Foundation 2004. Land and Justice in East Timor: A Survey of Citizen Awareness and Attitudes Regarding Law and Justice in East Timor.

Babo-Soares, D. 2004. Nahe Biti: The Philosophy and Process of Grassroots Reconciliation (and Justice) in East Timor. *Asia Pacific Journal of Anthropology*, 5: 15.

Berry, S. 1997. Tomatoes, Land and Hearsay: Property and History in Asante in the Time of Structural Adjustment. *World Development*, 25(8), 1225–41.

Berry, S. 1993. *No Condition is Permanent: The Social Dynamics of Agrarian Change in Sub-Saharan Africa*. Wisconsin: University of Wisconsin Press.

CAVR 2005. Chega! Report of the Commission for Reception, Truth and Reconciliation of Timor Leste. Dili: CAVR.

Chamberlain, E. 2009. The 1959 Rebellion in East Timor: Unresolved Tensions and an Unwritten History, in M. Leach, N. Canas Mendes, A.B. da Silva, A. da Costa Ximenes and B. Boughton (eds), *Understanding Timor-Leste: A Research Conference*. Dili: Swinburne Press.

Da Silva, A.B. 2004. Potential of Education for Conflict Transformation and Identity Reconstruction in the Cultural Context of Uato-Lari and Uato-Carbau Paper to Instituto Católico Para Formação de Professores, Baucau, 20 September 2004.

Fitzpatrick, D. 2008. Mediating Land Conflict in East Timor, in *Making Land Work: Reconciling Customary Land and Development in the South Pacific*. Vol. II. AusAID, pp. 175–98.

Gillespie, J. 2011. Exploring the Limits of the Judicialization of Urban Land Disputes in Vietnam. *Law & Society Review*, 45(2), 241–75.

Gunter, J. 2007. Communal Conflict in Viqueque and the 'Charged' History of '59. *Asia Pacific Journal of Anthropology*, 8: 27–41.

JPC, Justice and Peace Commission (Uato-Lari Parish) 2000. Report on Uato-Lari Land Dispute Dialogue 12–17 June 2000. Uato–Lari.

Meitzner Yoder, L.S. 2005. Custom, Codification, Collaboration: Integrating the Legacies of Land and Forest Authorities in Oecusse Enclave, East Timor. PhD Thesis: Yale University.

Myat Thu, P. 2008. Land Forgotten: Effects of Indonesian Re-Settlement on Rural Livelihoods in East Timor, in D. Mearns (ed.), *Democratic Governance in Timor Leste: Reconciling the Local and the National*. Darwin: Charles Darwin University Press, pp. 143–59.

Nixon, R. and Urresta, E. 2004. Report of Research Findings and Policy Recommendations for a Legal Framework for Land Dispute Mediation. ARD East Timor Land Law Program. Dili, February 2004.

Shipton, P. 1994. Land and Culture in Tropical Africa: Soils, Symbols, and the Metaphysics of the Mundane. *Annual Review of Anthropology*, 23: 348.

Tanter, R., Ball, D. and Van Klinken, G. 2006. *Masters of Terror: Indonesia's Military and Violence in East Timor*. New York: Rowman and Littlefield.

Timor-Leste Land Law Program 2004. Report on Research Findings and Policy Recommendations for a Legal Framework for Land Dispute Mediation. Dili.

Traube, E.G. 1986. *Cosmology and Social Life: Ritual Exchange among the Mambai of East Timor*. Chicago. University of Chicago Press.

# Chapter 11
# Implementing the Land Law: Possession, Protection and Community Property

This final chapter considers the potential application of the draft 2012 land law to rural districts in East Timor. It is a predictive exercise, based on our case studies, that highlights a further aspect of rule complexity and simplicity in conflict-affected environments, namely the possibility that all types of legal rule – simple or complex – take on a degree of interpretive complexity as they traverse a variety of administrative, communicative and cognitive settings (Baldwin 1990, Braithwaite 2002, Merry 1988: 879–80). In the previous chapter we highlighted the potential for legal rules to provoke violent conflicts when they deny the property claims of powerful groups in circumstances of state weakness. In this chapter we suggest a further possibility: that new rules in new state contexts will be implemented in an incomplete and indeterminate fashion as a result of divergences in epistemological understandings of law, and a process of competition for public authority relating to law. The analysis further illustrates our argument that property systems affected by armed conflict may develop path-dependent forms of institutional complexity, as a result of contested events of possession and dispossession, and unresolved tension between customary systems and the state.

In Chapter 1 we noted that the draft 2012 land law allows for long-term individual possessors of land in customary districts to claim statutory rights of ownership. The draft law also establishes new legal categories of community property and community protection zones. In this chapter we consider these legal constructions of possession, protection and community property in the context of their potential application to rural districts. Our argument suggests that legal rules will develop interpretive complexity where there is little or no epistemic consensus on core terms such as possession, community and property. As our case studies illustrate, customary relationships with land in East Timor are entwined with localized understandings of social and spiritual order. While there are deep-seated principles of possession, they involve overlapping notions of actual possession and ancestral first possession that are embedded in mythical narratives of origin, exchange and precedence. There are also notions of community and community property but these too are rich with contextualized structures of hierarchy, exclusion and authority. Inevitably, therefore, there will be interpretive complexity as customary principles, including localized notions of possession and community, are translated into legal constructs interpreted and enforced by agents of the state. This accrual of interpretive complexity is related to, but conceptually distinct from, the interpretive content of the rules themselves (that is whether they are bright-line or fuzzy in nature).

Our discussion of simple rules and complex interpretation draws on two heuristic strands of recent socio-legal scholarship: notions of epistemic distance and autopoietic systems (Gillespie 2008, 2011, Luhmann 2004, Teubner 1988, 1992, 1998), and concepts of negotiability and plural authority in property relations (Berry 1993; Juul and Lund 2002; Lund 2010). Gunther Teubner (1998: 15–25) sets out an influential view of legal transfers as a communicative process that involves distinct 'autopoietic' systems, which interpret legal information in accordance with internal processes for the production of meaning (see also Luhmann 2004). New law is more likely to achieve its intended effects where there are structural linkages, and a degree of mutual intelligibility, between the epistemic frameworks of law and the target social sub-system (Gillespie 2008, 2011; Teubner 1992, 1998). Yet, at least in relation to property rights in land, the interpretation of new law does not only involve system linkages and recursive processing of meaning within a system, as complex interpretation of simple law may also emerge where plural sub-systems act as sources of authority for the assertion of property claims. Property and authority have mutually constitutive elements, meaning that simple laws may take on complexity when competing property claimants adopt strategies of affiliation with competing sources of property authority (von Benda-Beckmann 1993: 127–30; Berry 1993, 1997; Bourdieu 1990; de Sardan 1999; Lund 2002; Moore 1986, 1998). In these circumstances, the interpretation of new land law not only takes place within a target sub-system, but it also involves the conscious manipulation of meaning across systems, as competing property claimants 'shop' their claims across multiple arena for property legitimation (Bruce 1998; Fitzpatrick 2006: 1015; Lavigne-Delville 2000: 108; Toulmin and Quan 2000: 219, Platteau 1996: 41–6; Toulmin et al. 2002: 13).

## Autopoietic Systems: A Framework for Analyzing Interpretive Complexity?

The systems theory notion of autopoiesis provides a potential framework for analysing complex interpretation of information across diverse social settings (Luhmann 1995). Autopoiesis describes a self-organized or self-regenerating system that receives external information but adapts that information according to its own self-referential processes of communication. The internal processes of the system are devoted to self-regeneration rather than production of something external to the system. The autopoietic system retains its distinct method of self-organisation, while interacting with other systems through a process of 'structural coupling' (Luhmann 2004: 1). Niklas Luhmann (2004) and Gunther Teubner (1988, 1993) argue that law constitutes an autopoietic system as its processes are self-referential: it produces laws that have a 'legal' quality because they satisfy internal processes of recognition.

Moreover, law interacts with other social systems – the economy, industry, even groups of resource users – through structural coupling mechanisms that involve the 'mutual misreading' of information according to the self-organisation imperatives of each system (Teubner 1992: 1456).

Autopoietic social systems have distinct epistemic frameworks and preferences that shape the interpretation of legal information (Gillespie 2008: 685–86). Paterson and Teubner (1998: 455–61) provide an example from regulation of the offshore oil industry in the United Kingdom. Their analysis of new safety regulations identifies three relevant autopoietic systems: lawmakers, industry regulators, and the industry itself. Lawmakers aimed to minimize the difference between an unregulated industry, involving a number of safety accidents, and a desired outcome of improving occupational safety. The industry regulators had a similar safety objective, but could not adopt the standard strategy of prescriptive regulation backed by sanctions as there was insufficient information on emerging technologies and hazards. Their strategy involved broad guidelines and lines of communication with the industry. For their part, the industry had a different systemic preference based on profit rather than safety. This preference could not simply be displaced by tougher enforcement or more detailed regulation, as it was 'deep-seated and internally coherent' (Paterson and Teubner 1998: 462).

John Gillespie (2011) utilizes related systems theory concepts in his analysis of land law in Vietnam. His fieldwork identifies four systems that regulate access to urban land in Vietnam: Central Party policymakers, land management technocrats, judicial communities and self-organized urban communities. These communities differ in terms of their core norms and cognitive assumptions (Gillespie 2011: 247 57). Generally speaking, while policymakers and officials advocate strict adherence to formal legal rules, judges and local residents desire socially relevant outcomes, which include the possibility of multiple interests in an area of land (Gillespie 2011: 253). These co-existing interests may be unlawful according to the binary legal/illegal coding of formal law, but are valid according to the self-organized traditions of the 'informal' residential system. Based on a survey of Court cases in Hanoi, Gillespie (2011: 257–67) finds that judges are unable to provide lasting resolution of many urban disputes through application of formal law, because the results are inconsistent with the internal logic of the residential system. As a result, judges often either transfer the case to bureaucratic agencies for resolution, or seek to apply fuzzy notions of 'reason and sentiment'. Gillespie notes (2011: 252, 266–67) that this latter approach – the judicial incorporation of ex post discretionary standards into bright-line legal rules of property – is subject to political and professional limits. A key insight of his analysis is that increases in the bright-line nature of rules, through increased ex ante delineation of entitlements, may act in a perverse way to reduce the capacity of Courts to resolve complex urban land disputes, because rule formalism further limits the application of situational standards to meet local expectations (Gillespie 2011: 271–72).

Autopoietic theory emphasises the recursive production of meaning within self-organized epistemic systems. In relation to land law, lawmakers have a systemic preference for the projection or territorialization of state authority. They 'see like a state' and interpret complex social relations with land through a legal lens of abstraction and objectification, as rights enforceable in autonomous terms, without the necessity of reference to cultural context or non-state systems of authority (Scott 1998; see also Banner 2002). Land law maps the landscape through inherent processes of misreading, omission and distortion, because it has its own linguistic, institutional and cognitive processes for the production of meaning (Blomley 2003; Santos 1987: 281; Teubner 1992: 1452–53). In James Scott's terms, the intent of the state is to reduce the 'chaotic, disorderly, constantly changing social reality ... to something more closely resembling the administrative grid of its observations' (Scott 1998: 82). At the same time, the target of land law – groups of resource users – may include separate self-organized local systems for resource governance, with preferences for managing competition and appropriation that contradict legal preferences for extension of state authority or reductions in information costs for outsiders. A self-organized local system of resource users may interpret information in a different matter from the legal system, not only in terms of distinct linguistic and cognitive frameworks for the understanding of property, but as a result of core distinctions between the 'legal/illegal' code of law and the self-reproducing code of the resource governance system (see, for example Benda-Beckmann von, F. et al. 2006).

Our case studies of East Timor illustrate differences in the generation of meaning – in relation to concepts of space, territory, authority and possession – between the 'legal' and customary systems of East Timor. They highlight incompatibility between the self-reproducing code of customary systems (origin/non-origin) and the draft legal rule that long-term possession is the basis for ownership. In addition, there is little by way of structural coupling between the systems of custom and law in East Timor, as the new state has very little presence in rural districts. Yet epistemic distance and weak structural linkages are not the only variables favouring complex interpretation of simple legal rules in East Timor. The *in rem* nature of property is important because it establishes incentives for individuals to assert meaning – the significance of their claims – across multiple systems for property legitimation. The production of meaning across systems provides the basis for the assertion of rights 'against the world'. Teubner (1992: 1454–5) characterizes the negotiation of meaning across systems as a form of 'mutual misreading' of information by self-organized systems, which develops because of differences in the production of meaning within each system. We suggest that this argument overly reifies systems as interpretive actors in their own right, and under-plays individual acts of strategic negotiation across multiple systems for rights legitimation. Gillespie's study of Vietnamese land law provides an example: not only did members of the informal residential community bring claims to court, but the judges also selectively drew on norms and beliefs from outside the legislative system to achieve their situational ends (Gillespie 2010: 447; see also Santos 1977).

Postcolonial land studies highlight the extent to which individuals assert property claims through legitimization systems outside of law, including households, clan groups, religious systems, local government, village courts, non-governmental organizations, human rights commissions and parliaments (Berry 1993: 14, 1997, Shipton 1994). In sub-Saharan Africa, in particular, a number of studies highlight endemic processes of negotiation and adjustment in which authority plurality is exploited to achieve the situational ends of property claimants (Berry 1993, 1997, Moore 1978: 50, Lund 2002, 2008). The cross-system negotiation of property claims is encouraged in circumstances where the state lacks the legitimacy or authority to enforce property claims in accordance with law, and property claimants have the opportunity to negotiate across diverse sources of legitimacy and authority, including contested landscapes of custom, group identity and status (Peters 2002: 46, Shipton 1994: 348, Lund 2002, Berry 1997: 1228). A multiplicity of sources of authority can contribute to 'legal forum shopping', which undermines authoritative settlement of claims (Fitzpatrick 2006), and 'shopping forums' where sources of authority – state and non-state – compete for interpretive and adjudicatory influence over contested claims (K. von Benda-Beckmann 1981). In pluralist circumstances of this kind, the meaning of land law is not only formulated within social sub-systems, or stipulated by authoritative state institutions, but is negotiated and contested simultaneously across multiple socio-legal spaces for property ordering.

Christian Lund (2008: 17–22) provides a useful example from Ghana of authority plurality and cross-system interpretation of property claims. In 1901 the British colonial administration assumed formal control over the northern territories of Ghana. As in other colonies, the British introduced a system of indirect rule, which provided a mechanism for organising local political structures in order to simplify administration and collect revenue (Chanock 1991: 64). The colonial administration delegated authority over land administration to tribal chiefs even though spiritualised authority or stewardship of the land resided in local 'earth priests'. The chiefs then consolidated their authority through the manipulation and invention of 'customary law' – itself a colonial construct – and through their legal powers over the endorsement of land leases. Yet the earth priests also asserted their authority outside 'custom', through participation in the political structures of the colonial and postcolonial state. In 1979, a constitutional change that divested the state of ownership of northern lands, led to further contestation between chiefs and earth priests across a range of domains, including legal claims to restoration of land ownership, local tax collection, and decentralisation and the creation of districts. Lund (2008: 23) concludes that successive socio-political changes in Ghana have created opportunities for the periodic re-opening and re-negotiation of property settlements, both at the national and local levels.

## The Potential Implementation of the 2012 Draft Land Law in Rural Districts

The 2012 draft land law establishes a rule of possession as a basis for ownership in rural districts of East Timor (see Chapters 1, 5). To analyse the potential effect of the draft law we distinguish two broad areas of land relations in rural districts. These areas are not subject to clear boundaries, as the true position is not a binary division but more a spectrum with overlapping elements. Nevertheless, the typological distinction is useful to assess the prospects for indeterminate implementation of the draft law. The first area involves districts of acknowledged customary domain. Resource users predominately obtain rights through membership of, agreement or intermarriage with lineages descended from a mythologized source of origin. The second area involves districts first cleared for settlement by work groups organized under colonial agricultural programmes. Resource users predominately derive rights through historical acts of cultivation and construction, accompanied at times by the grant of agricultural implements from sources of colonial authority. While land users in areas cleared or cultivated under colonial supervision may acknowledge the underlying land stewardship of nearby origin groups, or even attempt to mythologize their forebears' acts of first possession as productive of customary legitimacy, the key land allocation and conflict-management actors tend to be hamlet and village heads rather than origin group elders. Hamlet and village heads may consult with origin elders, particularly where they are family or marriage relations, but nevertheless retain a primary role in local questions of land management.

In areas of acknowledged customary domain we argue that any attempt to apply a legal rule of long-term possession may be productive of violent conflict or negotiated indeterminacy, both as a result of competing epistemic understandings of possession as a basis for entitlement, and the potential for possessory claims to undermine long-standing systems of customary authority. In customary systems the relevant acts of possession enumerated by the draft 2012 land law – construction, settlement, cultivation – only have significance for property entitlements in a context of social status and affiliation. There is no customary rule or norm that length of time in possession alone gives rise to property entitlements, as the possessory significance of acts of clearing, cultivation and residence is negotiated with reference to customary order. Whether or not possessory acts lead to property entitlements depends on issues such as affiliation with an origin group, participation in rituals, respect for customary prohibitions, and acknowledgement of the land stewardship of the *rai na'in* or its local equivalents. Moreover, not only do local understandings of possession and property differ substantially from legal definitions, at least among members of origin groups, but there is an inherent potential for legal rules of possession to challenge customary systems of land authority, particularly by supporting the claims of displaced groups that have not been incorporated into customary systems of order. The potential application of the possessory rule to areas of customary domain thus involves a combination of epistemic distance and authority plurality.

In areas first cleared and settled under colonial supervision, where rights to land were not allocated through customary mechanisms, a legal rule of long-term possession is preferable to its primary legal alternatives, which include restitution of pre-independence rights to land or nationalization followed by state processes of land grant or option. Our qualified preference for a legal rule of possession applies to rural townships such as Los Palos in Lautem and Ainaro town in Ainaro, and areas of irrigated rice cultivation such as the plains of Uato Lari in Viqueque or Nunura in Maliana. In areas first cleared under colonial supervision, it seems more likely that a legal rule of possession will apply according to its legislative intent, with less indeterminacy or interpretive contestation than in areas of customary domain, because there is greater epistemic consensus on the meaning of possessory acts and less competition among customary and state-based systems of property enforcement. However, we also argue that a possessory rule in areas first cleared or settled under colonial supervision should be based on fuzzy rather than bright-line formulations of possessory entitlements, in order to allow space for situational processes of adjustment that minimize the possibility of violent conflict. As discussed in Chapter 10, this preference for fuzzy formulations of possessory entitlements has particular relevance to areas of chronic possessory conflicts such as in Uato Lari or Nunura, where attempts to apply a bright-line possessory rule may lead to outbreaks of violence between current possessors and historical possessors with long-standing claims of dispossession. Fuzzy formulations of possessory entitlements include the discretion not to apply a rule of possession where the state has limited property enforcement capacity, and dispossessed claimants retain access to means of group violence.

## Possessory Claims in Areas of Customary Domain

In areas of acknowledged customary domain, members of lineages that trace direct descent from a mythical founder or source of origin have the strongest claims to possessory entitlements to land. In the following discussion we assume descent-reckoning through the paternal line (while noting that there are matrilineal groups in East Timor, including most notably the Bunak and Tetun-speaking communities on the southern coast). For members of founding lineages or houses, the notion that permitted forms of long-term household possession may give rise to heritable rights of control is not necessarily controversial, at least in areas other than sacred sites and designated sites of communal access. Even land left fallow is often subject to long-standing household claim, with other households seeking agreement or permission to farm or use that area of land. These heritable rights of control may not necessarily mean unqualified rights to exclude, as other group members may have access rights for activities such as grazing livestock during fallow periods. Nevertheless, there are traditional understandings of household control that, subject to overarching acknowledgement of customary authority, have a degree of consistency with legal concepts of possessory entitlement. Where traditional understandings are not consistent with legal concepts, however, is in relation to the sale or transfer of land to group outsiders. We discuss the contentious question of alienation of customary land further below.

In an area of customary domain, members of in-migrant lineages or houses will have different degrees and types of possessory entitlement than members of founding lineages or houses. Our case studies identify a number of agreement-based mechanisms for in-migrants to gain possession of customary land. In general terms, in-migrant lineages with long-standing wife-giver/wife-taker ties to a founding lineage have heritable *in rem* entitlements to cultivate and use defined areas of land, which are often obtained pursuant to bride-price agreements between the two family groups. In a small number of cases the claims of children of in-marrying males may be contested by maternal relatives from the founding lineage, depending on the social status of the in-migrant house and the degree of competition to land. Additionally, as a separate mechanism from marriage agreements, in-migrants may access land through traditional agreement with a founding house, in which case a form of use right is agreed in exchange for some offering or part of the harvest (Tetun: *rai te'en*). From the perspective of founding houses or lineages, this type of arrangement does not give rise to indefinite rights of control, with the status of the in-migrant group often subject to descriptions such as 'friends and acquaintances' or even 'passengers'. These traditional mechanisms for managing in-migration are critical to avoiding land conflicts after forced population displacement. Yet in legal terms, as we have seen, under article 10 (3) these secondary or subordinate rights may give rise to ownership even though rent is paid to a customary claimant.

Historically, the grant of access to land to in-marrying males was used as a means to establish a political alliance with another group, particularly when the in-marrying group posed a threat or offered support against a neighbouring enemy. The incorporation of in-migrant males also secured labour for new areas of swidden cultivation. As discussed in Chapter 2, at times the in-migrant group had sufficient size or power to warrant transfer of forms of political authority, through the metaphor of the 'stranger king'. These powerful allied lineages had obligations to 'defend the borders' of the customary domain, which included carriage of relations with external actors such as the colonial state. Under the colonial system of indirect rule, some in-migrant lineages and their representatives – designated as *liurai* and *dato* – became major land-holders in their own right, either as a result of direct grant of land by Portuguese authorities, or through their role in organizing work groups to clear land, or because of opportunities created by their incorporation into colonial systems of village and sub-district authority. To the extent that *liurai* or *dato* claim 'under customary domain', they may not meet the possessory criteria of the draft land law, where the land is farmed by others under contract or lease, and under article 10 (3) those farming the land since 1998 may claim ownership in their own right.

*Forced Relocation during the Indonesian Occupation*

There is a further category of in-migrant in areas of customary domain: those who occupied land during the war-torn years of the Indonesian occupation without contemporaneous agreement with local origin groups. As also discussed in Chapter 2, there was involuntary displacement of almost all East Timorese during active periods of military conflict in Indonesian times. Some informants recounted a relatively organized process of relocation, to separate local sources of support and sustenance from the guerrilla resistance, with Indonesian military officials collaborating with hamlet and village heads to allocate each household a plot of land on which to build their house and farm a small garden. Others stated that the process was less organized and that they settled and farmed wherever they could in order to survive, without seeking permission from village government or local origin group elders. As a number of our case studies illustrate, many of these new settlements remain *in situ*, with their inhabitants reluctant to return to pre-displacement land and housing because the new locations are close to roads and services. Some of these cases involve land tensions that are likely to be exacerbated by attempts to claim ownership on the basis of possession alone under the draft law.

Some East Timorese were displaced to land within their own hamlet or village territory, and retained access to their ancestral land for cultivation and other activities. Their claims of possessory entitlement are less likely to be contested because of family connections to the area. Contested cases are more likely to arise where East Timorese were relocated to land in a different hamlet or village, often in an area claimed by a different origin group. Our case studies indicate that these types of claim are subject to a range of local legitimation strategies, which will have various degrees of potential either to produce or avoid crystallized forms of land conflict. Some relocatees acknowledge customary authority through participation in ceremonies, payment of money or other items to origin group elders, or even entry into marriage alliances with an origin lineage. As noted, in this last possibility we see signs of a peacebuilding mechanism, worthy of support from law, that builds on the resilient processes of customary incorporation of outsiders discussed in Chapter 2. Other relocatees claim they purchased the land after their relocation from local land 'owners'. Others again claim entitlements on the basis of a relatively widespread (and erroneous) belief that five years' possession gave rise to ownership rights under Indonesian law. It is likely that these claimants will also refer to the rule of possession in the draft land law, once awareness of the law filters to remote areas. In this last case, in particular, any attempt at coercive state enforcement of relocatee claims of ownership has the potential to crystallize land tensions into open conflict.

The right to alienate land to outsiders provides a further source of potential land conflict arising from application of the new law in customary districts. In 2004, the US-based technical advisory firm, Associates for Rural Development (now known as ARD Inc) conducted a survey on attitudes toward property rights, as part of a

USAID-funded project on developing a new land law. According to the report issued by Associates for Rural Development, 'a sound majority of respondents believe private property ownership to be associated with the right to sell, transfer and freely administrate property'. This conclusion may be accurate in peri-urban areas, and areas first cleared under Portuguese or Indonesian supervision. It is not applicable in areas of ancestral customary domain. On the basis of extensive qualitative fieldwork in remote parts of Lautem, Viqueque, Maliana and Ainaro, we conclude that there are strong social restrictions, if not prohibitions, on alienation to outsiders in areas of acknowledged customary domain. While most informants stated that they 'owned' land inherited from their father or another family member, and stated that they would eventually pass this land on to their children, it is clear that this type of statement did not extend to acknowledgement of rights to sell or transfer land to community outsiders. In response to specific follow-up questions on rights of sale, some informants responded that it was unlikely outsiders or even other community members would want to buy a plot of land, as there were substantial areas of land not in use. Other informants stated that agreements could be made for outsiders to use land, but that there could be no sale of land to non-group members.

### *Epistemic Distance and Authority Plurality in Customary Districts*

Our case studies describe complex systems of social ordering in East Timor, which include resource governance mechanisms based on a nested set of private and common property arrangements. The mosaic of property-like arrangements among the customary systems of East Timor are not specified through precise written agreements but through a broad principle of social organization, namely proximity of descent from a mythical source of ancestral origin. In the absence of specific agreements enforced by a coercive third party, the ordering principle of ancestral origin acts as a focal point that provides a pathway for agreement over resources, and an alternative to costly conflicts over land (see Chapter 3). In a fundamental sense, East Timor's customary systems are engaged in autopoetic self-reproduction because the ordering principle of origin provides the primary basis for the avoidance and management of conflict, in historical circumstances of population growth, exogamous marriage, and settlement movements.

The self-organizing processes of East Timor's customary systems are predicated on shared acceptance of the ordering principle of origin, as the sole or primary basis for resolving resource competition. The principle of possessory entitlement set out in the draft land law of East Timor will threaten the self-reproducing origin/non-origin code of customary systems because it allows subsidiary households, including groups relocated during the Indonesian military occupation, to claim alienable rights to land outside customary mechanisms, while also establishing the state as the default titleholder to lands not subject to lawfully recognized acts of possession (see Chapter 5). Systems theory provides a partial framework for analyzing the likely result – interpretive complexity notwithstanding rule simplicity – as the rule of possession is not only incompatible, in an epistemic sense, with customary conceptions of possessory entitlement, it undermines the origin/non-origin code of customary society. This threat to the self-organizing processes of customary systems creates autopoetic imperatives to adapt and alter the meaning of a rule of possession. At the same time, the draft law would establish incentives for strategic assertion of entitlements on the basis of possession, even by affiliates of customary groups, which would not only trigger adaptive responses by the customary system but also assertions of the meaning and significance of possession through non-customary systems for the legitimation and enforcement of property.

## Possessory Claims in Areas Cleared or Settled under Colonial Supervision

In areas first cleared or settled under colonial supervision, we have noted a greater degree of individuation and commodification of claims to land than in established customary districts. Many of these areas involve irrigated or 'flooded' rice cultivation that was encouraged by Portuguese authorities to create marketable agricultural surpluses. Initial participation in clearing land and constructing irrigation channels, through work groups organized by hamlet and village heads, led to allocation of individual plots for housing and cultivation. Most informants stated that these plots were subject to heritable rights of control and exclusion, and could even be leased or sold to residents of other hamlets of villages. In many areas these transactions are documented, with the local village head acting as a witness to the agreement. However, a number of land-holders also acknowledged the traditional claims of a local origin group to ritualized stewardship of land, and participated in ceremonies organized by the group to celebrate harvests and the like. Some even sought customary elder permission for transactions involving their land. Even in areas first cleared or settled under colonial supervision, therefore, there are still property legitimation strategies involving reference to different sources of customary as well as village government authority. This residual reference to custom suggest that a legal rule of possession may still lead to legal forum shopping, involving competing references to state and customary sources of property legitimation, even in areas first cleared under colonial supervision. In these circumstances, a flexible discretion not to apply the rule of possession will form part of a 'do no harm' approach based on a baseline default of respect for custom.

Notwithstanding the continuing relevance of customary authority, as an underlying principle of land stewardship, local social practices in areas of irrigated rice cultivation, and other areas first cleared or settled under colonial supervision, are broadly consistent with a legal rule that alienable rights of ownership may arise from long-term acts of household possession. In terms of epistemic understanding of possession, and its significance for property, there is not a great deal of distance between farmers working irrigated rice fields and state actors charged with interpreting a draft land law. But that is most emphatically not to say that there will be no complexity, negotiability or potential for conflict in the application of a rule of possession. For example, as with areas of customary domain, there are plots of land claimed by a local *liuirai* or *dato*, either directly on the basis of ownership, or as an area available for communal farming under *liuirai* or *dato* supervision. Where they involve tenant or contract farming these cases will raise questions of 'mere occupancy' and legal possession. Even more productive of difficulty will be those areas with chronic possessory conflicts, including those examples set out in Chapter 10, which raise the possibility that strict application of the possessory rule induces violent counter-reactions from historical possessors with long-standing dispossessory grievances.

Rural townships such as Maliana and Ainaro provide a further illustration of an area where long-term household possession is consistent with the grant of alienable ownership. These townships increased substantially in size and population during the period of Indonesian rule, as a result of economic migration and forced relocation of households to centres of Indonesian military control. In the early 1980s, the Indonesian civil administration assumed responsibility from the military for services and infrastructure development in rural townships. As in Indonesia itself, prior to the fall of President Suharto in 1997, the administration utilized laws on land acquisition for development that often involve the payment of little or no compensation to land-holders. Where compensation was offered, land-holders often claimed that substantial amounts were diverted to corrupt officials before actual payments were received. Grievances over Indonesian land acquisition continue to affect public infrastructure, and in some cases residential settlements, in East Timor. An influx of Indonesian settlers, and their exodus in 1999, also contributed to the development of markets in rights to land. In rural townships and surrounding areas there are large numbers of people living on land whose claims are contested, either on the basis of unjust land acquisition or because of competing titles issued under the Indonesian administration, or as a result of clouded chains of title arising from a series of unregistered transactions. We note a number of these cases in our case studies from Ainaro (see Chapter 9). These cases are amenable to resolution by a rule of adverse possession, as they involve urban and peri-urban areas where the state has a greater degree of property enforcement capacity.

## Conclusion: Property Rules in a Post-conflict State

Our analysis has identified two broad alternatives for the legal regulation of land systems after armed conflicts: interpretively simple bright-line rules that reduce the costs of identifying, measuring and enforcing rights to property, and interpretively complex 'fuzzy' rules that provide greater flexibility for social and political ordering. This distinction relates to the interpretive content of rules as they are formulated, rather than their interpretation in the process of implementation (as described above). Bright-line rules of property have considerable advantages in post-conflict environments. Their relative simplicity reduces the scope for variable or incomplete application, particularly in circumstances involving shortfalls in state capacity. They provide incentives for economic reconstruction through crystalline allocation and delineation of endowments, and reduction of the information costs for a broad class of potential investors (Smith 2003, 1108–13). They also reduce the potential for land-grabbing or official corruption by limiting the interpretive discretion of rent-seeking agents (Buchanan 1980: 3, 8–11, Rose 1985: 91). Interpretively complex rules, on the other hand, may be important to resolve the problem of violence itself. Fuzzy rules avoid ex ante 'winner-take-all' solutions that may provoke violence by disgruntled groups of claimants. They provide greater regulatory space for local officials to take into account notions of situational justice (Gillespie 2010). They allow more scope for formation of property understanding around common points of epistemic reference, in plural customary environments, and potentially more scope for recognizing customary sources of property enforcement authority. They also provide flexibility for interest group bargaining to stabilize a state in circumstances of violence. In particular, while bright-line property allocations may increase resource values for members of the governing elite, fuzzy rules of allocation allow readjustment of property rights in response to shifts in power among the elite (North et al. 2009: 77–8).

Although we are sceptical of bright-line property rule solutions in conflict-affected environments, we do not suggest that fuzzy rules necessarily provide a normative template for the design of laws on conflict-affected customary land systems after armed conflicts. There is an all-too-easy transition from state stabilization, involving flexible or interpretable rules of private property, to endemic state corruption that includes land-grabbing by well-connected elites. The capacity to readjust property rights, so as to maintain balances of power among the elite, can also act as an instrument of dispossession that creates conditions for long-term insecurity and grievance. While there may be correlations between state stabilization, and the development of fuzzy rules of property after armed conflicts, the result may not necessarily be conducive either to equity or to property security for the general populace. This suggests that the focus of normative enquiry should not so much be on all-or-nothing choices between bright-line and fuzzy property rules, but on the ease and nature of transition from stabilizing fuzzy rules to bright-line rules that protect property from state appropriation. The nature of rules to channel and constrain state action, in particular, will be important aspects of new laws on land after armed conflicts.

A key aspect of our analysis is that responses to post-conflict problems involving customary land systems should draw on long-standing examples of local resilience, as illustrated by principles of origin in East Timor. We argue that resilient customary systems provide the best institutional option for managing costly races relating to resources after armed conflicts, at least in 'frontier' areas where the state is unable to enforce legal claims in a coercive manner. We highlight, in particular, the role of traditional agreements for incorporating in-migrants into customary order, as important mechanisms for managing the legacies of forced displacement. However, we do not suggest that customary focal points for social ordering, such as principles of origin, can readily translate into bright-line legal frameworks on land. In rural districts, we argue for a default rule of custom that creates legal space for resilient local processes of in-migrant accommodation, and maintains a shared norm or focal point for cooperative bargaining over rights to land. A default rule of custom replaces a default rule of state ownership of land, and places the onus on the state to prove state title to land. Our rationale for a default rule of custom not only includes its focal point role in managing post-displacement racing for private rights to resources, but also the need to protect against the likelihood of land grabbing by state interests, once a state stabilizes after armed conflict.[1]

Under a default rule of custom there is no baseline need to define which groups hold what land, or for legal intrusion into areas governed by customary authority. The allocation of rights and boundaries to land is left for determination by customary authority according to customary principles. There may not even be a need for the state to establish and enforce the external boundaries of customary land authority. As we have noted in relation to East Timor, individual plots of land may be relatively well defined in customary areas of East Timor, but the boundaries and nature of customary are a social rather than a territorial concept. The territorial boundaries of a customary domain extend and recede according to socio-political circumstances, with a spectrum of claims of authority from allocative control to generalized responsibility for cosmological order. Moreover, even within an acknowledged area of customary domain, there is negotiated, contested and 'fuzzy' devolution of land authority among constituent or allied lineages of an origin group.

A simple default rule of custom allows the possibility that customary leaders will use their authority to expel displaced 'outsiders' living on customary lands. In East Timor, as we have seen, this possibility creates a substantial risk of violent conflict in customary areas where there are large numbers of displaced residents from Portuguese or Indonesian times. As an interim measure, East Timor could adopt a default rule of custom relating to land while also providing a prohibition on evictions in rural districts. For example, in South African the Interim Protection of Informal Land Rights Act 1996 establishes a baseline rule that no person may be deprived of any informal rights to land without his or her consent (s. 2). However, in the longer run there will need to be solutions to potential conflicts between displaced groups and customary systems of land authority other than interim protections of informal rights to land. These solutions need to take into account the possibility that the application of new legal rules will exacerbate rather than resolve costly post-conflict racing for rights to land (see Chapter 10).

We have argued that a rule of long-term possession may be productive of conflict in areas of customary domain, but may be a better option than other

1 We agree with Braithwaite et al. (2010) that peacebuilding requires early attention to separation of powers, including the recognition of customary systems of authority, in order to prevent 'networks of resistance' developing into 'networks of tyranny'.

alternatives for allocating rights to land in areas first cleared and settled under colonial supervision. We also noted the absence of clear boundaries between land under customary domain, and land first cleared and settled under colonial supervision. We do not recommend delineation of areas of customary land, in a territorial sense, and application of different sets of rules – one based on custom and the other on possession – to distinct geographical areas of jurisdiction. While this type of pluralist arrangement is common in the South Pacific, in our view it is not appropriate to East Timor given the degree of displacement of people on to customary lands over a long span of colonial and neo-colonial rule. In circumstances such as East Timor, the imperative for a new property system in a new nation-state to form around common points of epistemic reference suggests a default rule of custom, familiar to rural landholders, with flexible carve-outs for a rule of possession in areas first cleared and settled outside customary mechanisms. In other words, we suggest a nested set of institutions: a default rule of custom that includes an interim prohibition on evictions, legal onus on the state to prove state title to land, and a rule of long-term possession applied on a discretionary basis by a decentralized system of land administration. The rule of possession would include distinctions between actual and legal possession, for all areas, which will allow recognition of traditional agreements between relocated groups and customary land-holders.

We propose these normative recommendations because land policy is important after armed conflicts. Yet we are not confident that a post-conflict state such as East Timor is open to normative persuasion. In Chapter 5 we argued that rules emerging from post-conflict processes of elite formation may not lend themselves to the development of social consensus on property, which is essential for a property system to avoid costly reliance on coercive enforcement of property claims. The East Timor example illustrates the potential for chronic property uncertainty in post-conflict environments as legislative configurations of complexity and simplicity respond to a stabilizing elite, and imperatives to avoid state-destabilization, without reflecting or securing the consensus required for a cooperative property order. Merrill and Smith (2007: 185 –2) suggest that the social consensus required for a cooperative property system is more likely to coalesce around simple rules, such as deference to possession or respect for the first to possess. The East Timor example illustrates the challenges of property rule simplicity in a post-conflict environment, as deference to possession creates conflict with prior possessors, and respect for prior possession requires costly investigations into title and forced evictions by a capable state. Moreover, a simple rule to standardize custom will create conflict or chronic uncertainty where the post-conflict state lacks the capacity to enforce legal claims to customary land, and competing customary and state-backed claimants have similar capacities to engage in violent assertions of their claim. Hence we conclude with the rather pessimistic prediction that in East Timor the political economy of post-conflict property rule formation will stabilize the state but fail to create institutional simplicity or broad-based security for private property rights in land.

**References**

Baldwin, R. 1990. Why Rules Don't Work. *The Modern Law Review*, 53(3).

Banner, S. 2002. Transitions Between Property Regimes. *J. Legal Stud.*, 31: S359.

Braithwaite, J., Dinnen, S., Allen, M., Braithwaite, V. and Charlesworth, H. 2010. *Pillars and Shadows: Statebuilding as Peacebuilding in Solomon Islands*. ANU E-Press.

Berry, S. 1997. Tomatoes, Land and Hearsay: Property and History in Asante in the Time of Structural Adjustment. *World Development*, 25(8), 1225–41.

Berry, S. 1993. *No Condition is Permanent: The Social Dynamics of Agrarian Change in Sub-Saharan Africa*. Wisconsin: University of Wisconsin Press.

Blomley, N. 2003. Law, Property and the Geography of Violence: The Frontier, the Survey, and the Grid. *Annals of the Association of American Geographers*, 93(1), 121.

Bourdieu, P. 1990. *The Logic of Practice*. [trans. Richard Nice.] Cambridge: Polity.

Bowles, S. 2004. *Microeconomics: Behavior, Institutions, and Evolution*. New York: Russell Sage; Princeton: Princeton University Press.

de Sardan, O. 1999. A Moral Economy of Corruption in Africa? *Journal of Modern African Studies*, 37(1), 25–52.

Ellickson, R.C. 1991. *Order Without Law: How Neighbors Settle Disputes*. Cambridge, MA: Harvard University Press.

Fitzpatrick, D. 2006. Evolution and Chaos in Property Systems: The Third World Tragedy of Contested Access. *Yale Law Journal*, 115: 996–1048.

Fitzpatrick, D. and Barnes, S. 2010. The Relative Resilience of Property: First Possession and Order without Law in East Timor. *Law and Society Review*, 44(2).

Gillespie, J. 2011. Exploring the Limits of the Judicialization of Urban Land Disputes in Vietnam. *Law & Society Review*, 45(2), 241–75.

Gillespie, J. 2008. Towards a Discursive Analysis of Legal Transfers into Developing East Asia. *New York University Journal of Law and Politics*, 40: 657.

Habermas, J. 1996. *Between Facts and Norms: Contributions to a Discourse Theory of Law and Democracy*. Cambridge: Polity Press.

Heller, M.A. 1997. The Tragedy of the Anticommons: Property in the Transition from Marx to Markets. *Harvard Law Review*, 111: 621.

Juul, K. and Lund, C. 2002. *Negotiating Property in Africa*. Portsmouth: Heinemann.

Lavigne-Delville, P. 2000. Harmonizing Formal Law and Customary Land Rights in French-Speaking West Africa, in C. Toulmin and J. Quan (eds), *Evolving Land Rights, Policy and Tenure in Africa*. London: Wiley and Mbaya, p. 97.

Luhmann, N. 1985. *A Sociological Theory of Law*. [trans. E. King; (ed.) M. Albrow.] London: Routledge.

Luhmann, N. 1995. *Social Systems*. [trans. J. Bednarz, Jr. with D. Baecker.] Stanford, CA: Stanford University Press.

Luhmann, N. 2004. *Law as a Social System*. [trans. K.A. Ziegert.] Oxford: Oxford University Press.

Lund, C. 2010. Recategorizing 'Public' and 'Private' Property in Ghana, in T. Sikor and C. Lund (eds), *The Politics of Possession: Property, Authority and Access to Natural Resources*. Oxford: Wiley-Blackwell.

Merrill, T. and Smith, H. 2007. The Morality of Property. *Wm. & Mary L. Rev.*, 48: 1849.

Moore, S.F. 1998. Changing African Land Tenure: Reflections on the Incapacities of the State. *European Journal of Development Research*, 10(2), 33.

Moore, S.F. 1986. *Social Facts and Fabrications: 'Customary' Law on Kilimanjaro 1880–1980*. Cambridge: Cambridge University Press.

Moore, S.F. 1978. *Law as Process: An Anthropological Approach*. London; Boston: Routledge.

Paterson, J. and Teubner, G. 1998. Changing Maps: Empirical Legal Autopoiesis. *Social & Legal Studies*, 7: 451.

Rose, C. 1986. The Comedy of the Commons: Custom, Commerce, and Inherently Public Property. *University of Chicago Law Review*, 53: 711.

Santos, B. de Sousa 1987. Law: A Map of Misreading; Toward a Postmodern Conception of Law. *Journal of Law and Society*, 14: 279.

Santos, B. de Sousa. 1977. The Law of the Oppressed: The Construction and Reproduction of Legality in Pasagarda. *Law & Society Review*, 12: 5.

Shipton, P. 1994. Land and Culture in Tropical Africa: Soils, Symbols, and the Metaphysics of the Mundane. *Annual Review of Anthropology*, 23: 348.

Teubner, G. 1984. Autopoiesis in Law and Society: A Rejoinder to Blankenburg. *Law & Society Review*, 18: 291.

Teubner, G. 1992. The Two Faces of Janus: Rethinking Legal Pluralism. *Cardozo Law Review*, 13: 1443.

Teubner, G. 1998. Legal Irritants: Good Faith in British Law or How Unifying Law Ends Up in New Divergences. *Modern Law Review*, 61: 11, 15.

Teubner, G. 1988. Introduction to Autopoietic Law, in G. Teubner (ed.), *Autopoietic Law: A New Approach to Law and Society*. Walter de Gruyter, p. 1.

Teubner, G. 1993. *Law as an Autopoietic System*. [trans. A. Bankowska and R. Adler.] London: Blackwell Publishers.

Von Benda-Beckmann, F., Von Benda-Beckmann, K. and Wiber, M. 2006. The Properties of Property, in F. von Benda-Beckmann, K. von Benda-Beckmann and M.G. Wiber (eds), *Changing Properties of Property*. New York: Berghahn Books, pp. 1–39.

Von Benda-Beckmann, K. 1981. Forum Shopping and Shopping Forums: Dispute Processing in a Minangkabau Village in North Sumatra. *Journal of Legal Pluralism*, 19: 117.

# Index

For Product Safety Concerns and Information please contact our EU representative GPSR@taylorandfrancis.com
Taylor & Francis Verlag GmbH, Kaufingerstraße 24, 80331 München, Germany

www.ingramcontent.com/pod-product-compliance
Ingram Content Group UK Ltd.
Pitfield, Milton Keynes, MK11 3LW, UK
UKHW022013180926
475701UK00003B/350
* 9 7 8 1 1 3 8 2 5 7 0 2 3 *